CW00684192

# ADAPTATION, CANONISATION AND IDEOL ......... LITERATURE

# NEVER-ENDING STORIES

## ADAPTATION, CANONISATION AND IDEOLOGY IN CHILDREN'S LITERATURE

Sylvie Geerts and Sara Van den Bossche (eds.)

© Academia Press
Eekhout 2
9000 Gent
T. (+32) (0)9 233 80 88        F. (+32) (0)9 233 14 09
info@academiapress.be          www.academiapress.be

The publications of Academia Press are distributed by:

UPNE, Lebanon, New Hampshire, USA (www.upne.com)

Sylvie Geerts and Sara Van den Bossche (eds.)
*Never-ending Stories – Adaptation, Canonisation and Ideology in Children's Literature*
Gent, Academia Press, 2014, 254 pp.

Lay-out: proxessmaes.be

Cover: Studio Eyal & Myrthe

ISBN 978 90 382 2254 7
D/2014/4804/32
U 2156

*No part of this publication may be reproduced in print, by photocopy, microfilm or any other means, without the prior written permission of the publisher.*

# Contents

# Preface

## Sylvie Geerts & Sara Van den Bossche

'Adaptation both appears to require and to perpetuate the existence of a canon,
although it may in turn contribute to its ongoing reformulation and expansion.'
(Sanders 2006: 8)

In *Adaptation and Appropriation*, Julie Sanders observes that adaptation is inextricably intertwined with canon formation. Within the domain of children's literature research, adaptation studies and canonisation studies are traditionally separate fields of study, despite the observable connection. Bridging the gap between those two separate fields was one of the main aims behind the symposium 'Adaptation of Canonical Texts in Children's Literature', which was held at Ghent University in January 2011 and which forms the basis for this collection of essays. The growing amount of academic work on the subject published since 2011 (Kümmerling Meibauer & Surmatz 2011; Lefebvre 2013; Müller 2013; Paruolo 2011)[1] bears witness to the increasing interest for the cross-pollination of the fields of adaptation and canonisation studies. The aim of this volume is to bring together recent scholarly work in which the link between canonisation and adaptation is addressed explicitly. We build upon the premise that adaptation processes play a role in canonisation processes and vice versa. The canonical status of a text may prompt adaptation processes, while adaptations have the potential to perpetuate the status of the work.

As will become evident throughout the book, a wide range of possible methodological approaches can be adopted to tackle the topic at hand. Nevertheless, there is a deliberate choice underlying all of the contributions, namely to dissociate adaptation from a source-text-oriented view, in which *an* adaptation is considered to be 'an autonomous work', 'a *product*', as Linda Hutcheon clarifies (2006: xiv; emphasis added). However, one can also look upon 'adaptation' not merely as a *product* but rather as a '*process* of creation and reception', emphasising the 'deliberate, announced, and extended revisitation of prior works' involved in that very process (ibid.). Following Linda Hutcheon, we therefore chose to investigate the way in which stories are reworked to function in a new literary and social context as well as the products which are the result of such processes.

Applying such a broad view of adaptation allows us to tackle a variety of transformative adaptation processes drawing upon existing texts, including translations, abridgments, retellings, and transmediations. As the subtitle of this volume suggests, we approach adaptation processes from an ideology-critical point of view and take into account the specific nature of the field of children's literature. In addition, the cases reflect all three of the categories of texts identified by Emer O'Sullivan as common sources for 'children's literary classics': 'works from adult literature'; 'traditional narratives often originating in oral stories' and books written specifically for children (2005: 132). Moreover, the volume contains contributions discussing canonised text from South-African through European and American to Persian culture. This strong international spread neatly illustrates the rich variety of the subject.

Finally, we would like to take the opportunity to thank all participants in the Never-ending Stories conference and contributors to the volume. Special thanks go to our publisher, Pieter Borghart, for his advice and guidance throughout the peer review procedure, and to Kristoffel Demoen and Sylvia Warnecke for their helpful comments to the introduction. Moreover, we are greatly indebted to John Stephens for sharing his expertise during the entire process of compiling this book and writing the introduction. His unremitting support has been of invaluable importance to our project.

## Notes

1.   Kümmerling-Meibauer, B. & A. Surmatz. 2011. *Beyond Pippi Longstocking. Intermedial and International Aspects of Astrid Lindgren's Works*. New York/London: Routledge; Lefebvre, B. (ed.) 2013. *Textual Transformations in Children's Literature. Adaptations, Translations, Reconsiderations*. New York/London: Routledge; Müller, A. (ed.) 2013. *Adapting Canonical Texts in Children's Literature*. London: Bloomsbury; Paruolo, E. (ed.) 2011. *Brave New Worlds. Old and New Classics of Children's Literatures*. Brussels/New York: Peter Lang.

# Never-ending Stories

## How Canonical Works Live on in Children's Literature

### Sylvie Geerts & Sara Van den Bossche

Never-ending Stories. The title of this volume (and chapter) refers to *Die unendliche Geschichte* [The Never-ending Story] by German author Michael Ende. The book was first published in 1979 and soon became one of the most widely acclaimed works of children's literature. It was translated into 36 languages and adapted numerous times. The film adaptation directed by Wolfgang Petersen in 1984 was hugely successful. Furthermore, a considerable number of computer games, musicals, plays and operas have been based on this story. All this has literally turned *Die unendliche Geschichte*, which deals with the eternal connection between reality and fantasy, into a never-ending story. Michael Ende's children's novel is just one of many examples of stories which in a similar way, by means of adaptation, continue being reshaped and therefore live on. Our title encapsulates this process of adaptation in which both the contents and the form of existing stories are adjusted to the assumed needs of a new audience and changed social and cultural conventions.

This observation, that stories are adapted to correspond with a new context, points to the ideological implications of the process. In fact, all storytelling is inevitably informed by ideology. John Stephens was the first to extensively describe and discuss the way in which ideology is pervasive in discourses of children's literature (*Language and Ideology in Children's Fiction*, 1992).[1] He revisited these matters in *Retelling Stories, Framing Culture* (1998), which he co-wrote with Robyn McCallum. This study was ground-breaking in that it was the first attempt at drafting an overarching theory of literary adaptations within children's literature. The concepts and ideas outlined in this book proved to be seminal and have come to be widely used when retellings in children's literature are discussed.

Here Stephens and McCallum further develop the observation that adjustment to the receiving context is central to the process of retelling. In outlining their point of departure, they shift attention to a culture's implicit ideologies:

> any particular retelling may purport to transmit elements of a culture's
> formative traditions and even its sustaining beliefs and assumptions, but what
> it always discloses is some aspect of the attitudes and ideologies pertaining at
> the cultural moment in which that retelling is produced. (Stephens &
> McCallum 1998: ix)

The two authors also pinpoint the transmission of the norms and values of the existing narrative as one core motivation for adaptation. Traditional narratives are seen as a society's cultural heritage. The process of retelling these stories, however, is inevitably influenced by the 'attitudes and ideologies' which characterise the new context. These ideologies are not fixed but rather ever-evolving. Stephens and McCallum term these ideological undercurrents 'metaethics'. *Retelling Stories, Framing Culture* meticulously maps out the evolution of the (specifically Western) metaethics influencing adaptations within children's literature until the late 1990s.

However, the field of children's literature has undergone significant changes since the mid-1990s, not in the least as regards its relationship with the broader context within which it functions. The preconditions of the field itself, too, have evolved. For instance, new ideas regarding the child as a reader have emerged. The recent rise of crossover texts bears testimony to many of these changes. As Rachel Falconer argues, the crossover novel reflects the 'hybridisation of child and adult cultures from the mid-nineties to the early years of the new millennium' (2009: 7).

Several of the contributions to this volume focus on *recent* adaptations. In doing so, those chapters mirror the latest developments in the field along with their influence on research into adaptations of canonical texts. The contributions in this book, however, cover adaptations from a broad range of periods and places. Because all the examples belong to the field of children's literature, they display characteristic features of the field. One of our main aims is to stress both diversity and evolution in the process of adaptation within children's literature. Moreover, we wish to highlight the correlation between adaptation and canonisation which is widely recognised but has not yet been studied in detail.[2] We do not refer to a canon as some tangible artefact of conscious canon formation,[3] nor is it our goal to define what different factors are involved in processes of canonisation.[4] Nevertheless, we do wish to clarify that in line with Deborah Stevenson we conceive of a canonical work as invoking a 'broad awareness of [that very work] as indispensable' (1997: 112).

Building upon the basic assumption that adaptation is an ideologically informed process, we distinguish between three fundamental aspects of adaptation: socio-political, socio-cultural and transmedial.[5] This distinction underlies the three-part structure in both this introductory chapter and the entire volume. The contributions will illustrate both the sameness and difference of these aspects of adaptation within children's literature and how they have evolved over time and across regions.

## Socio-Political Aspects of Adaptation

A common feature of the wide range of objects our study addresses is described in Katharine Jones' characterisation of children's literature as 'literature written almost entirely by adults that assumes various conceptions of the child, childhood, and the childlike, with child readers being the target of the book' (2006: 305). Jones' description of the asymmetrical relationship between the originators and the putative audience of children's literature points at another vital aspect of writing for children. Her careful mentioning of 'conceptions of the child' and children as target readers, neatly illustrates the ambivalent relationship children's literature, and for that matter its criticism, maintains with its readers. The crux lies in the gap between the child as a textual construct and as an actual reader. Against this backdrop, we can identify some preoccupations central to the practice of creating texts for young readers. Because writing for children is informed by an impetus to introduce readers into the society and culture in which they grow up and are expected to function, children's literature appears to be concerned mainly with social, political and ethical issues:

> Children's fiction belongs firmly within the domain of cultural practices which exist for the purpose of socializing their target audience. Childhood is seen as the crucial formative period in the life of a human being, the time for basic education about the nature of the world, how to live in it, how to relate to other people, what to believe, what and how to think – in general, the intention is to make the world intelligible. (Stephens 1992: 8)

In her study on *Power, Voice and Subjectivity in Children's Literature*, Maria Nikolajeva defines the socialising aspect in terms of power relations:

> nowhere else are power structures as visible as in children's literature, the refined instrument used for centuries to educate, socialize and oppress a particular social group. In this respect, children's literature is a unique art and communication form, deliberately created by those in power for the powerless. (Nikolajeva 2010: 8)

Through the alignment of educating, socialising and oppressing, Nikolajeva, who firmly denounces adult power over children, appears to suggest that the socialising function of children's literature frequently results in adults' oppressing children, that is to say, their imposing particular rules and patterns of behaviour on children. Furthermore, her portrayal of children as powerless and 'a particular social group' seems to deny them individuality and – more importantly – agency. Clémentine Beauvais, who takes Nikolajeva's point further, redefines the concept of 'power' in children's literature. She attributes children with 'might' and adults with 'authority' and relates the power structures to the concept of time:

> Children are *mighty*, because their specific form of 'power' is dependent on the existence of a future for them in which to act. They are consequently diametrically opposed to authority, though they are evolving towards it. What one loses in might one gains in authority. This is because the essential variable is time, and the values which societies have taught us to see as associated to time – experience and expertise, primarily. (Beauvais 2013: 82; emphasis in original)

We subscribe to Beauvais' more refined distinction, which aligns well with Robyn McCallum's assumption that children possess agentic potential, 'a capacity for conscious and deliberate thought and action' (as quoted in Stephens 2013: 3). Along with John Stephens and Robyn McCallum we assume that texts direct readers' construction of meaning. Every text, understood as a way of explaining the world, guides readers' responses towards a particular position. Through its representational strategies, the text takes up a certain position towards social practices, as is described in *New World Orders in Contemporary Children's Literature*:

> children's literature is marked by a pervasive commitment to social practice, and particularly to representing or interrogating those social practices deemed worthy of preservation, cultivation, or augmentation, and those deemed to be in need of reconceiving or discarding. (Bradford, et al. 2008: 2)

The rewriting of canonical texts can illustrate the double-edged commitment to social practice Bradford et al. describe, as retellings can simultaneously express a preoccupation with the preservation of a traditional text and a need for revising the very tradition it adheres to. The latter can emanate from an incommensurability between the ideologies inherent in the pre-text and the ideologies in the new context.[6] In short, any text – including adaptations – has the potential to offer several possible subject positions, all of which adopt their own specific stance with respect to the pre-text. The individual child reader, then, can either accept or resist the ideologies inherent in *any* particular text.

Adaptations in children's literature can very overtly be deployed in order to transmit such ideological positions. John Stephens draws on the distinction between implicit and explicit ideology, first introduced by Peter Hollindale, and indicates that such obvious instances 'disclos[e] the writer's social, political or moral beliefs' (Stephens 1992: 9). In a recent article on the subject of ideology in children's literature, Stephens and McCallum point out that a text's ideological position may be 'topicalised', which means that it 'may appear as an overt or explicit element in the text, expressing the writer's social, political, or moral beliefs' (2011: 361). Such books overtly promote certain subject positions for the readers to align themselves with. Ultimately, they can be seen as outspoken attempts at socialising the child reader.

The examples discussed in the first three chapters of this book are all to a different extent examples of explicit ideology, as their producers appear to be very much aware of the desired effect of their adaptations. The contributions by Sanna Lehtonen, Mohsen Hanif and Tahereh Rezaie as well as by Sylvia Warnecke all deal with adaptations with a clear political agenda and as such demonstrate how ideology operates on an explicit level. It is no coincidence that in all of these cases the texts used for the purpose of spreading strong ideological messages are canonical. The authority of the pre-texts lends authority to the contents the authors of these particular retellings aim to convey.

In her chapter, Sanna Lehtonen points out how Finnish author Lahja Valakivi transformed Edgar Rice Burrough's famous *Tarzan* novels to fit the context of postcolonial Finland during World War II. Lehtonen scrutinises how the novel is used as a form of nation building whereby the Finnish identity – represented by the protagonist Tarsa – is strongly and overtly opposed to the identity of the former Russian colonisers. At the same time, however, it also mirrors social differences within Finnish society itself. Similarly, Mohsen Hanif and Tahereh Rezaie demonstrate how the tenth-century classical Persian narrative *Shahnameh* has been used for nationalist purposes throughout Persian history.

A diachronic analysis of the treatment of the story shows how adaptation strategies were applied under the influence of the ruling authorities in Iran. By means of selection, omission or transformation, the retellings serve to either perpetuate or oppose the socio-cultural implications of the original *Shahnameh* narratives. In such a manner, the analysis by Hanif and Rezaie may serve as an illustration of the opposing forces at work in processes of adapting canonical stories. Another example of how a cultural-political agenda can try to direct the treatment of canonical narratives is given by Sylvia Warnecke. She describes a publishing programme in the German Democratic Republic in which myths, sagas and epics were retold for children. The programme was designed to produce retellings in conformity with socialist ideology and to establish a canon of esteemed cultural heritage. Her contribution outlines how the convictions of the most prolific contributor, Franz Fühmann, moved from assent to dissent with the ideological doctrine in the process of adapting the Prometheus myth.

However different the temporary and geographical contexts addressed in these chapters may be, all three cases clearly illustrate children's literature's engagement with social, political and ethical issues. Canonical texts, such as *Tarzan*, *Shahnahmeh* and the myth of Prometheus, can actively and overtly be employed to convey outspoken ideological messages. Within the framework of the new socio-political context the purpose and effect of such adaptations strongly deviate from those of their pre-texts. As such, these chapters bring to the fore oppositional forces at work in adaptations of canonical texts in children's literature.

## Socio-Cultural Aspects of Adaptation

We use the phrase 'socio-cultural aspects of adaptation' to capture the possible effects of adaptations, as seen from a literary sociological perspective. More specifically, we refer to the ways in which they can influence processes of canonisation. 'Canonical', then, is being employed here as a label for texts which are endorsed by a certain culture, to the extent that they have become 'requisite for *understanding* a part of literature' (Stevenson 1997: 113; emphasis added) and belong to its broader frame of reference. It is thus understood that what constitutes 'canonical' is variable and dependent on the cultural and social preferences of the age.

Within this framework as well, ideology comes to the fore, more specifically when one takes into account the canonical work's orientation towards the prevailing ideological convictions at that point in time. Roughly speaking, canonisation processes are informed by two different kinds of impetus: top-down and bottom-up. In processes guided from above, a literary work becomes canonised because it expresses and confirms the ideology of the dominant majority. However, a book can also gain acclaim from the bottom upwards, by a dynamic force emanating from questioning and subverting that very ideology. These two canonising currents need not necessarily work against each other. Rather, canonisation quite often is the result of an interplay between academic and critical acclaim and wide popularity. As Carey Kaplan and Ellen Cronan Rose contend, canonisation processes are determined by 'the oscillation between the needs and desires of the common reader and the ideological interests of a cultural/academic elite' (1990: 14). Thus, a canonical text embodies a certain duality. On the one hand, it epitomises the Romantic ideal of a unique and innovative piece of art, a quality which grants it esteem and creates an artistic standard for the following generations to live up to. On the other hand, it is by no means hampered by the boundaries of these dominant circles and succeeds in making a broader cultural impact, appealing to the common reader. This is precisely where adaptations come into play, as they make the canonical work readily available to larger audiences.

Regardless of the forces at work in the canonisation of the pre-texts, once the latter have acquired canonical status, they are presented as belonging to the 'heritage' of their culture of origin. As a result, the retold texts are not only 'requisite for understanding a part of *literature*' (Stevenson 1997: 113; emphasis added), but also for understanding the broader *culture* they stem from. Hence, acquiring knowledge of the texts is a seminal part of the process of acculturation. Child readers, in particular, are introduced to canonical texts through education.[7] Moreover, the literary practice of adapting a canonical text for an audience of children equally plays an important role in the process of initiating a child into a culture. Another result of the fact that canonical works are so strongly embedded in their specific cultural and social context is that the ideological messages can remain tacit.[8] Such implicit transmission of ideology works on an unconscious level as it ties in with values which are generally accepted, unquestioned and even presupposed as being universal. The impact of this kind of transfer is commonly known to be more effective than the explicit transmission of ideology.

As a culturally accepted narrative, a canonical pre-text is usually considered as prestigious. A commonly held belief is that through being adapted, it leaves its ivory tower. This view mirrors the general negative attitude towards adaptations which, by and large, are accorded low status in comparison with their sources. This highlights that the Romantic ideal of originality is still a dominant aesthetic standard. Both Linda Hutcheon and Julie Sanders, who address the phenomenon of adaptation from a broad theoretical point of view – in *A Theory of Adaptation* (2006) and in *Adaptation and Appropriation* (2006) respectively – point at this determining feature of adaptation. Riita Oittinen makes a similar observation in her influential study *Translating for Children*:

> As long as there has been literature, there have been adaptations. Yet very often adaptation is seen as a negative phenomenon: compared to its original, the adaptation is of little value; it is secondary, a nonoriginal. (Oittinen 2000: 76)

Linda Hutcheon equally highlights how the low status of the adaptations themselves stands in marked contradiction to their high popularity and rightly uses this as an argument against fidelity criticism (Hutcheon 2013 [2006]: 2-6).

From this point of view, adaptations do not undermine the status of the pre-text but rather perpetuate the work's standing, thus maintaining its canonicity. Without all of the transformations, which keep the work available, it would no longer be read and therefore 'die out'. In *Turning the Page. Children's Literature in Performance and the Media*, in which the relation between children's literature and other media is investigated, Fiona M. Collins and Jeremy Ridgman find the following:

> One of the traditionally recognised functions of adaptation and transposition, of course, has been to bring classic texts to life for a new audience within a particular historical context. It could be argued that such adapations keep the book in print and read by different generations and thereby contribute to the status of the book as a 'classic'. (Collins & Ridgman 2006: 11)

The sheer amount of adaptations and remediations bears witness to the pre-text's canonical status: 'surely the number of times a book has been adapted for stage, screen or radio will convince us that this is a work of art which is part of our cultural baggage' (ibid.: 11-12). The impact of adaptations actually goes beyond mere affirmation, they add not only to cultural transfer but also to the further canonisation of their pre-text (Stevenson 1997: 120). We consider translation as a form of adaptation which widens the distribution of a pre-text. Both Vanessa Joosen and Lien Fret address this type of dissemination in their chapters in this volume. Joosen argues that the adjustments in the English translation of the Grimm brothers' *Kinder- und Hausmärchen* can be shown to have contributed to its canonisation. Adaptation as a translational strategy determined by the translator's ideological assumptions and conceptions of childhood is the central point of Lien Fret's contribution. She analyses the various ways in which Dutch translators from the eighteenth century onwards have shaped the figure of the godmother in Perrault's 'Cinderella'. Besides the Brothers Grimm and Charles Perrault, Hans Christian Andersen is also considered an authority within the field of fairy tales, whose works are frequently adapted. In many cases, the film adaptations by the Disney Studios have come to replace the pre-text as the version commonly referred to. In his chapter, Jan Van Coillie looks into the 'Disneyfication' of Andersen's 'The Little Mermaid' from a narratological point of view. Finally, Bettina Kümmerling-Meibauer discusses the fairy tale 'The Nutcracker and the Mouse King' by E.T.A. Hoffmann in a case study illustrating (de)canonisation processes of the pre-text itself as well as of German children's literature as a whole.

When we combine the insights which we elaborated on above, we can conclude – rather paradoxically – that adaptations suffer from low status but nevertheless can enhance processes of canonisation. Linda Hutcheon endorses this observation:

> An adaptation is not vampiric: it does not draw the life-blood from its source and leave it dying or dead, nor is it paler than the adapted work. It may, on the contrary, keep that prior work alive, giving it an afterlife that it would never have had otherwise. (Hutcheon 2013 [2006]: 176)

As such, adaptations contribute to the conservation of cultural memory. In their introduction to a special issue of *European Journal of English Studies*, Astrid Erll and Ann Rigney argue that one of the roles literature can play in the production of cultural memory is that of 'an object of remembrance':

> Because literary works typically circulate at later points in time, they provide an important bridge between generations. In other words, recollecting texts composed or written in earlier periods is an integral part of cultural remembrance. Many of the traditional discussions about canon-formation within literary studies can indeed be revisited as exemplifying the ways in which societies squabble over which foundational texts deserve commemoration or not. Of more direct concern to us here, however, is the way in which literature establishes a 'memory of its own' in the form of intertextual relations that give new cultural life to old texts. A significant part of literary production consists of the rewriting of canonical texts, and, more generally, of earlier cultural narratives such as folk tales and myth. (Erll & Rigney 2006: 112-113)

Moreover, adaptations highlight essential traits of human society as a whole. We are made aware of those defining characteristics through adaptations, not just in 'texts' in their entirety but also in the form of recurring archetypes, patterns or scripts.[9]

## Transmedial Aspects of Adaptation

Erll and Rigney's mention of adaptations of folk tales and myths hints at another concept, namely that of transmediality, which is inherent in (albeit not essential to) the process of adaptation. In fact, the writing down of oral 'earlier cultural narratives' constitutes the very beginning of all literature and, therefore, in preserving these texts, establishing cultural memory. Transmediality is, in other words, as old as adaptation itself and a precondition for canonisation: oral stories can be passed on orally but need to be written down in order to become canonised. See the contribution of Franci Greyling, this volume, in which she illustrates how oral stories in South Africa were handed down, first by means of written versions and in a next stage even through other transmedial adaptations. These practices of adaptation inevitably alter the nature of the oral story and at the same time secure its position in the canon.

Adaptation itself is also altered by ongoing societal developments and their implications for reader roles. Among the most significant of such developments are the rise of new media and technologies, as Piret Viires indicates in her research on 'Literature in Cyberspace': 'Modern society has advanced into an information or communication society, and this change has necessitated the reconceptualisation of progress in the cultural sphere' (2005: 153). This evolving socio-cultural context gives way to the development of new forms of literature influenced by technology and cyberspace, 'synthesising different means of expression' (ibid.) and characterised by multilinearity, hyperlinking, and interactivity, among other things (ibid.: 154). The latter suggests that the more digitalised society becomes, and the more people communicate, the more a reader is expected to find his or her own way in the broadening pool of information.

The expanded concept of literature inevitably affects practices of adaptation in the field of children's literature. As a result, a surge in free and innovative modes of adaptation can be observed. As regards adaptations of canonical texts, this is expressed in a preference for combining different plots from various traditions. Also, traditional and popular genres are often mingled. This point is elaborated in the contribution of John Stephens and Sylvie Geerts to this volume. A similar kind of metaphor occurred, very significantly, in the title of an article by Cristina Bacchilega and John Rieder. In 'Mixing it up' they discuss 'the generic complexity or hybridization' of 'recent, popular, big-budget films that feature fairy tale elements as a major part of their appeal but do not rely on a single fairy tale plot' (Bacchilega & Rieder 2010: 26). They argue for picturing 'the fairy tale genre today as a web whose hypertextual links do not refer back to one authority or central tradition' (ibid.: 25).[10] The attitudes towards traditional genres such as fairy tales seem to mirror the overall effect of digitalisation on society. Bacchilega and Rieder further argue that such generic hybridity results in 'a multiplicity of position takings' and, in such a manner, gives way to 'complex alignments and alliances' (ibid.). The argumentation of Stephens and Geerts, this volume, develops along the same lines. They demonstrate that other traditional genres, such as myths, are treated similarly and that the outcome of such adaptations is ambivalent or even disruptive. We can therefore argue that the metaphor of the web can be applied to describe the current practice of adaptation in children's literature as a whole. Adaptations in which genres blend envisage new, more active roles for children as readers of canonical narratives. This idea of an active role for the reader is treated by both Joe Sanders and John Patrick Pazdziora, this volume. Sanders describes how the literary technique of dramatic irony requires the reader to actively make connections between an adaptation and its pre-text. Pazdziora explores how in online journals the contemporary reader of fairy tales can become an author of adaptations in his or her own right.

The current prevalence of looser forms of adaptation not only manifests itself on a formal level, but also has significant consequences for the subject positions of readers of traditional narratives. In choosing how to treat the pre-text, the author of an adaptation suggests that the readers take up a certain position towards that pre-text. Whereas adaptations formerly were used primarily to perpetuate the incontestable status of the adapted work, in this age of information the canonical pre-text no longer appears to be sacrosanct. An ever-increasing number of adaptations seem to be distancing themselves from their very pre-texts. Any adaptation can be defined in terms of its relationship with its pre-text, by analogy with the pre-text's stance towards the ideology prevailing at the time of its production, as described above. If we consider the number of possible relationships as a continuum, we can try to describe what position a particular adaptation occupies. As Erll and Rigney point out, there can be two approaches to the pre-text, that 'of pious commemoration (or re-citation as it were) or of critical contestation' (2006: 113). We consider these to be the extremes of a sliding scale, ranging from transmission on the one end to challenge on the other. From this perspective, transmission can be seen as prompting readers to align with the ideology invested in the pre-text. It is indicative of a culture-affirming impulse and fosters the further dissemination of the dominant ideology. Challenge, conversely, incites readers to question the values the pre-text is based on.[11]

The challenging approach to adaptation ties in with a view on children's literature as 'radical', that is, as 'an important vehicle for ideas that challenge the status quo', in Julia

L. Mickenberg and Philip Nel's words (2011: 445). Kimberly Reynolds, too, theorised the radical, 'transformative' power of children's books. Her description of radical children's literature as 'encouraging readers to approach ideas, issues, and objects from new perspectives and so prepare the way for change' can easily be applied to challenging adaptations (Reynolds 2007: 1). They, too, have the potential to 'contribut[e] to the social and aesthetic transformation of culture' (ibid.).

We conclude our introductory remarks with a brief discussion of two Flemish books which in different ways offer challenging approaches to adaptation by interpreting traditional stories from the perspective of contemporary social concerns. One such example is Bart Moeyaert's *Het Paradijs* ([Paradise], 2010), an adaptation which relates to its pre-text in an ambivalent way. This book is the established Flemish author's retelling of the creation narrative and deals with the perceived duality between nature and culture. The main question underpinning Moeyaert's narration seems to be whether or not man should interfere with his environment.

In a sense, *Paradise* plays on the pre-text's fame, thus affirming it. The setting is, of course, invoked by the very title of the book and by the opening phrase '*In the beginning we were never alone*' (Moeyaert 2010: 5; emphasis added).[12] Moreover, Moeyaert relies on the well-known components of the narrative he draws on: a man and a woman, unnamed, naked, all alone in a natural, forest-like setting. The narrator merely hints at the fall of man but refrains from tackling the question of guilt. Initially, the man and the woman seem to be happy, but as the story unfolds, a sense of friction between the two of them arises. They seem to be in disagreement as to how to deal with their natural environment. The male narrator indicates that it is their responsibility to maintain and regulate the land they were given: 'We had gotten four rivers and a piece of woodland. [...] The wood needed to be cleaned up and kept clean. [...] I looked ahead. I told the woman: "We got here not a day too early" (ibid.: 7).[13]

By contrast, the idea of meddling with nature and restricting its expansion makes the woman utterly unhappy. At first sight, the woman's attitude towards nature seems to bear out the traditional dichotomy between man as representing culture and woman as embodying nurture. We can link this fundamental strand in the plot with early ecofeminist ideas, as described by Alice Curry as centering on

> a physiological connection between women and nature arising out of female reproductive processes (the menstrual cycle, birthing, nursing) and a woman's consequent propensity towards care, nourishment and nurturance. These 'female' qualities are perceived to invest women with a spiritual and embodied understanding of nature unshared by men. (Curry 2013: 3)

An additional conviction shared by early ecofeminists is that 'male-domination' is a biological phenomenon (ibid.: 2). Also in *Paradise*, male predominance is presented as self-evident. Firstly, the entire story is related from the point of view of the man, who serves as a first-person autodiegetic narrator. Secondly, the woman is portrayed as weaker than the man. Not only is she physically less strong ('The woman was tired more often than I was' Moeyaert 2010: 17),[14] she is also depicted as mentally weaker and prone to depression: 'She was not well. She rolled her eyes at whatever I said to her. She leant more often than she stood.' (ibid.: 25)[15]

As Curry points out, ecofeminism strives to 'revalue, rather than deny, the woman-nature connection as a caring and transformative response to environmental crisis' (Curry 2013: 2). In a similar way, *Paradise* actually contests some of its seemingly reactionary undercurrents, as it can be said to frame the relation between women and nature in a resistant way. As the man notices that the woman becomes all the more miserable as nothing changes, he decides to give in and deal with matters her way. The end of the story depicts the man and the woman letting nature take its course. The woman flourishes again and even takes over the active role:

> I went and laid down next to the woman in the mud and asked how she was doing.
> She was doing well.
> Provocatively, she rolled me over, to my side and then to my belly. Around and around and around it went. [...]
> Then we had some food. We drew a table-cloth for the chicken and put on some clothes. (Moeyaert 2010: 35)[16]

In addition, Moeyaert subtly undercuts traditional Catholic beliefs. He does so by not mentioning God in his story at all, thus overthrowing Him as the creator of all life. Moreover, he overtly critiques creationism, by tying in with the Darwinistic notion of survival of the fittest:

> Many of the things that hadn't been around for a long time, disappeared straight away. *They hadn't been made properly.* The fragile animals broke first. The small ones, the frail ones. Animals which were too thin curled up because of the drought. (ibid.: 15; emphasis added)[17]

In his interpretation of the creation narrative Moeyaert shows that controlling and limiting nature is detrimental, also for humanity, thus allowing for an ecocritical reading of his adaptation. In doing so, he raises awareness in his readers and offers the possible subject positions of ecologically competent children,[18] opening up the opportunity for generating commitment and 'green ideas' (Lehtimäki 2013: 122). All in all, with this initially seemingly affirming retelling of the creation narrative, Moeyaert does go against the grain of Catholic ideology as conveyed by the Bible.

The possibility that a retelling can deconstruct culturally situated metanarratives inherent in or associated with canonical narratives is demonstrated by *Soepletters* ([Soup Letters], 2011) by Mieke Versyp. The reader follows the protagonist of the book, an immigrant boy who is looking for his younger sister. Hence, the general outline is that of a quest or even detective story. In the course of the story, the realistic setting of a Turkish neighbourhood in a Flemish city is gradually interspersed with fantastic elements – a swimming pool turned into a sea, a cave with a one-eyed giant, a ship named 't.i.t.A.n.i.C' (Versyp 2011:

19) and some sirens. These references draw on canonical stories, such as the Odyssey, and stories which belong to a more popular cultural memory, such as the Titanic catastrophe. The realistic setting of the Ghent-Turkish neighbourhood is in itself a defamiliarisation of the typical Flemish image of the city and is further defamiliarised by the fantastic elements.

Finally the boy finds his sister at a Flemish-Turkish candy store and releases her with a password which is a combination of Flemish and Turkish names for candy ('Babelut en Bubbelgum, Zure Bol en Nonnenbil, Baklava en Lokum...'; ibid.: 56). The first four are all names for candy recognisable for the Flemish reader whereas the Turkish boy only knows the last two, 'Baklava' and 'Lokum'. Thus, the solution to the quest involves a mixture of languages and culture. However, as the immigrant boy is the protagonist, the reader is likely to align with his perspective, which in this case entails alienating the well-known and identifying with foreign elements. Hence, we could argue that the process of acculturation, which is central to the practice of retelling canonised narratives, is deconstructed in this story. A commonly held belief is that stories like the Odyssey belong to 'our (i.e. the Western) cultural heritage'. This process of appropriation of canonical stories is strongly subverted in *Soup Letters*. Firstly, the familiar elements are defamiliarised for the reader, through encouraging him or her to align with the foreign protagonist. Secondly, canonical narratives are deployed to reinforce this effect of alienation. Usually, they subscribe to the predominant Western metanarrative. In this case, conversely, they are embedded in a multicultural setting, thus subverting that very metanarrative. Therefore, *Soup Letters* neatly illustrates the 'radical' potential of adaptations.

We can conclude that contemporary adaptations propose ambivalent positions for child readers of canonical narratives. To a certain extent, iconoclastic adaptations question not only the metaethics underlying their pre-texts, but also the metaethics of culture as a whole.

## Bibliography

Bacchilega, C. & J. Rieder. 2010. 'Mixing It Up: Generic Complexity and Gender Ideology in Early Twenty-first Century Fairy Tale Films', in: P. Greenhill & S.E. Matrix (eds), *Fairy Tale Films. Visions of Ambiguity*. Logan, Utah: Utah State University Press, 23-41.

Beauvais, C. 2013. 'The Problem of "Power": Metacritical Implications of Aetonormativity for Children's literature Research', in: *Children's Literature in Education* 44: 74-86.

Bradford, C., K. Mallan, J. Stephens & R. McCallum (eds). 2008. *New World Orders in Contemporary Children's Literature. Utopian Transformations*. Houndmills/Basingstoke/Hampshire/New York: Palgrave Macmillan.

Collins, F.M. & J. Ridgman (eds). 2006. *Turning the Page. Children's Literature in Performance and the Media*. Bern: Peter Lang.

Curry, A. 2013. *Environmental Crisis in Young Adult Fiction. A Poetics of Earth*. Houndmills/Basingstoke/Hampshire/New York: Palgrave Macmillan.

Dixon, B. 1977a. *Catching Them Young 1. Sex, Race and Class in Children's Fiction*. London: Pluto Press.

Dixon, B. 1977b. *Catching Them Young 2. Political Ideas in Children's Fiction.* London: Pluto Press.

Erll, A. & A. Rigney. 2006. 'Literature and the Production of Cultural Memory: Introduction', in: *European Journal of English Studies* 10.2: 111-115.

Falconer, R. 2009. *The Crossover Novel. Contemporary Children's Fiction and Its Adult Readership.* New York: Routledge.

Gallagher, S.V. 2001. 'Contingencies and Intersections: The Formation of Pedagogical Canons', in: *Pedagogy* 1.1: 53-67.

Guillory, J. 1993. *Cultural Capital. The Problem of Literary Canon Formation.* Chicago/London: The University of Chicago Press.

Hutcheon, L. 2013 [2006]. *A Theory of Adaptation.* New York/London: Routledge.

Hutcheon, L. 2009. 'In Praise of Adaptation', in: Maybin J. & N.J. Watson (eds), *Children's Literature: Approaches and Territories.* Houndmills/Basingstoke/Hampshire/New York: Palgrave Macmillan, 333-338.

Jones, K. 2006. 'Getting Rid of Children's Literature', in: *The Lion and the Unicorn* 30.3: 287-315.

Kaplan, C. & E. Cronan Rose. 1990. *The Canon and the Common Reader.* Knoxville: University of Tennessee Press.

Kümmerling-Meibauer, B. 2003. *Kinderliteratur, Kanonbildung und Literarische Wertung.* Stuttgart/Weimar: J.B. Metzler.

Lehtimäki, M. 2013. 'Natural Environments in Narrative Contexts: Cross-Pollinating Ecocriticism and Narrative theory', in: *StoryWorlds* 5: 119-141.

McCallum, R. & J. Stephens. 2011. 'Ideology and Children's Books', in: S. Wolf, K. Coats, P. Enisco & C. Jenkins (eds), *Handbook of Research in Children's and Young Adult Literature.* New York: Routledge, 359-371.

Mickenberg, J.L., & P. Nel. 2011. 'Radical Children's Literature Now!', in: *Children's Literature Association Quarterly* 36.4: 445-473.

Moeyaert, B. 2010. *Het Paradijs.* Amsterdam/Antwerp: Em. Querido's Uitgeverij B.V.

Nikolajeva, M. 2010. *Power, Voice and Subjectivity in Children's Literature.* New York: Routledge.

Rajewsky, I.O. 2005. 'Intermediality, Intertextuality, and Remediation: A Literary Perspective on Intermediality', in: *History and Theory of the Arts, Literature and Technologies* 6: 43-64.

Reynolds, K. 2007. *Radical Children's Literature. Future Visions and Aesthetic Transformations in Juvenile Fiction.* Houndmills/Basingstoke/Hampshire/New York: Palgrave Macmillan.

Sanders, J. 2006. *Adaptation and Appropriation.* London/New York: Routledge.

Soetaert, R. 1994. 'Wat heet klassiek? Over jeugd en traditie', in: *Leesgoed* 21.5: 137-139.

Stephens, J. 1992. *Language and Ideology in Children's Fiction.* London/New York: Longman.

Stephens, J. 2013. *Subjectivity in Asian Children's Literature and Film. Global Theories and Implications.* New York: Routledge.

Stephens, J. & R. McCallum. 1998. *Retelling Stories, Framing Culture. Traditional Story and Metanarratives in Children's Literature.* New York/London: Garland.

Stevenson, D. 1997. 'Sentiment and Significance: The Impossibility of Recovery in the Children's Literature Canon or, The Drowning of "The Water Babies"', in: *The Lion and the Unicorn* 21.1: 112-130.

Ullström, M. 2012. 'Vargen kommer! Bilder av varg i svensk barn- och ungdomslitteratur', in: S. Kärrholm & P. Tenngart (eds), *Barnlitteraturens värden och värderingar*, Lund: Studentlitteratur, 147-164.

Versyp, M. 2011. *Soepletters.* Tielt: Lannoo.

Viires, P. 2005. 'Literature in Cyberspace', in: *Folklore* 29: 153-174.

## Notes

1.  His work was preceded by Peter Hollindale's article 'Ideology and the Children's Book' in *Signal* 55 (1988): 3-22. Bob Dixon was one of the first to draw attention to the specific nature of the ideological assumptions which children's books are invested with was probably in *Catching Them Young 1. Sex, Race and Class in Children's Fiction* (Dixon: 1977a) and *Catching Them Young 2. Political Ideas in Children's Fiction* (Dixon: 1977b). See also McCallum & Stephens 2011.

2.  See for instance Sanders 2006: 8. Compare Linda Hutcheon's contention that well-known stories often are being adapted 'not only because they are familiar, but also because they should be familiar' (2009: 334; emphasis in original).

3.  Compare John Guillory's description of the canon as 'an imaginary totality of works' (1993: 30; emphasis in original).

4.  For elaborate discussions of canonisation processes, see for instance Kümmerling-Meibauer 2003; Soetaert 1994 or Gallagher 2001.

5.  The term 'transmedial' is used here to describe two different aspects. First, the phenomenon which usually is termed '*inter*medial', or 'a crossing of borders between media' (Rajewsky 2005: 46). In addition, we also wish to encapsulate '*trans*medial' in the sense of 'the appearance of a certain motif, aesthetic, or discourse across a variety of different media' (ibid.).

6.  We use the term 'pre-text' as it was coined by John Stephens and Robyn McCallum in *Retelling Stories, Framing Culture*, viz. as a fairly neutral alternative for 'source text' (1998: 4).

7.  See also Gallagher 2001.

8.  For a more elaborate argumentation on this subject, see Stephens & McCallum 1998: 6.

9.  Compare Irina O. Rajewsky's concept of 'transmedial' as a label for 'a certain motif, aesthetic, or discourse [which appears] across a variety of different media' (Rajewsky 2005: 46).

10. Thus, the recent trends in dealing with fairy tales seem to contradict the authority of for instance Perrault's or the Grimms' established versions, as they are discussed in Joosen's and Fret's chapters, this volume.

11. It should be noted that neither extreme ever occurs in a pure form. Full transmission of meaning is impossible as the author always is grounded in his or her own cultural assumptions, while even the most challenging adaptation implies a certain confirmation of the status of that story simply by selecting it.

12. In het begin waren we nooit alleen.

13. We hadden vier rivieren en een stuk bebost land gekregen. [...] Het bos moest schoongemaakt en schoongehouden worden. [...] Ik zei tegen de vrouw: 'We komen hier geen dag te vroeg.'

14. De vrouw was vaker moe dan ik.

15. Het ging niet goed met haar. Ze draaide met haar ogen als ik ook maar iets tegen haar zei. Ze leunde meer dan ze stond.

16. Ik ging naast de vrouw in de modder liggen en vroeg of het ging.
    Het ging goed. [...]
    Om me te plagen rolde ze me op mijn zij en daarna op mijn buik. Het ging om en om en om.
    [...]
    Daarna gingen we eten. We legden een tafelkleedje voor het kippetje en zelf trokken we ook iets aan.

17. Veel dingen die er nog niet lang waren, verdwenen meteen weer. Die waren niet goed gemaakt. De breekbare beestjes gingen het eerst kapot. De fijne, de frêle. Diertjes die te dun waren, krulden van de droogte op.

18. See Ullström 2012: 162.

# PART 1

# SOCIO-POLITICAL ASPECTS OF ADAPTATION

# Tarzan of the Apes – the Bearman Tarsa

## Discourses of National Identity and Colonialism in a Finnish Adaptation of an American Classic

### Sanna Lehtonen

At first glance, a tropical jungle in a Belgian colony in Africa at the turn of the twentieth century and a coniferous forest in eastern Finland in the 1940s might not have much in common in terms of the scenery, weather conditions, inhabitants or history. Yet, in fictional depictions, each setting has inspired authors to introduce a peculiar hero, a man raised by animals – Tarzan of the apes in Africa and the bearman Tarsa in Finland. Anyone who has ever read any of Edgar Rice Burroughs' *Tarzan* books or seen any of the film or television adaptations will immediately recognise the following depiction as yet another version of the story of the fierce forest god, the leader of the apes:

> The lonely wanderer was then already twenty steps further away and did not even glance back. But he jumped on a high hummock, spread his arms, smacked his hands together, repeated it, threw his head back, and the clear autumnal morning air was split by a shuddering, long whistle that froze the blood in the veins of everyone who heard it. […] (Valakivi 1940a: 6)[1]

> Tarsa rose to his full height – and was truly like a bear, the king of the forest, the honey paw, indeed! He raised his sno… sorry, his face towards the way he was going to head, smacked his birch bark handshoes together, whistled quietly, growled as if muttering some kind of a departing spell and then jumped over a bog hole. But what on earth?! He did not fall on his feet, but, like an animal, first on his front paws, followed by his back limbs! And so he went, – lolloping on all fours from one tussock to another, slightly slouching like a real bear. Four limbs must have been swifter and steadier on the quaking bog! (ibid.: 23)[2]

By introducing a strong, lonely, animal-like man yelling and banging his chest or, here, whistling and smacking his hands together in the middle of a forest, may seem a blatant pastiche of the original work by Burroughs. The name of the hero that has undergone only minimal phonetic adaptation from English into Finnish (Tarzan – Tarsa) also serves as a clear reference to the original works. Yet, in the adaptation, the image of a man going on all fours wearing the traditional Finnish birch bark shoes both on his feet and hands, as well as the narrator's chatty discourse create a humorous tone distinct from the original books – the character of Tarsa is not merely an imitation of Tarzan but parodies him. The extracts are from a Finnish adaptation of Tarzan, *Tarsa Karhumies* ([The Bearman Tarsa],

1940a) by Lahja Valakivi. While the above extracts might suggest that Valakivi's aim has mainly been to produce a parody of Tarzan, his text serves other functions as well.

Burroughs' *Tarzan of the Apes* (2010 [1914])[3] and its sequels are world-famous crossover classics of popular literature. While originally aimed at adults, the novels as well as the film adaptations soon became favourites among child audiences also. When the first *Tarzan* novel was translated into Finnish in 1921, it was marketed as a boys' adventure story and the novel and its sequels have remained popular throughout the decades, evidenced by the number of reprints and newly translated editions in the 1970s and the 1990s. The Finnish adaptation of Tarzan discussed here, Valakivi's four-book series featuring the bearman Tarsa, was published in 1940-1941. By that time the first twelve Tarzan novels (1914-1928) had been translated into Finnish at a very fast publishing rate due to their popularity (Havaste 1997: 315-316). The translations were published by Karisto, which also published the *Tarsa* novels. While Valakivi and his publisher were, without doubt, motivated to adapt the *Tarzan* books because of their vast popularity in Finland at the time, the adaptations include traces of other motivating factors. In terms of terminology, the Tarsa novels are adaptations in the sense of rewriting or retelling original works. In Linda Hutcheon's terms, an adaptation involves 'repetition without replication' or 'an announced and extensive transposition of a particular work or works' that does not necessarily involve remediation (2006: 7-8). Moreover, the Tarsa novels are what Hutcheon refers to as transculturated adaptations where 'almost always, there is an accompanying shift in the political valence from the adapted text to the 'transculturated' adaptation' (ibid.: 145). Of course, changes in the ideological aspects of the narrative occur in retellings in general when there is a spatial and/or temporal distance between the original text and the adaptation, as pointed out by John Stephens and Robyn McCallum (1998: ix) and Geerts and Van den Bossche in the introduction to this volume.

In the *Tarsa* novels, the source text is transformed to suit the Northern environment as well as the Finnish wartime politics of the early 1940s. As Paula Havaste notes in her study of Tarzan, the *Tarsa* books include plot elements and characters that directly copy the original texts (1997: 274-275). Nevertheless, Tarsa, the recontextualised hero, is significantly different from his model. In research on Burroughs' novels, the hero, Tarzan, a representative of a colonial power in Africa, is usually interpreted as the epitome of white male superiority and imperialism.[4] John Newsinger, for instance, states that the first novel, *Tarzan of the Apes*, is 'the story par excellence of the whiteman's conquest of African savagery, of the primeval forest and its savage denizens' (1986: 62). While Tarsa – also known as Colonel Calamity – is a king and conqueror of the wilderness, his relationship to the inhabitants of the country, that is, to his own people, is significantly different from the white Tarzan's relationship to the black people. In the adaptations Tarsa becomes a representative of the postcolonial Finland who fights the former colonisers, the Russians; moreover, the exotic jungle becomes the recognisable northern forest that Finnish readers are familiar with. Like Tarzan, Tarsa has the intelligent mind of an upper-class civilised human combined with the primordial instincts and the strength of a wild animal. While the *Tarsa* novels parody the portrayal of the apeman in Burroughs' novels to a certain extent, they also associate the hero with nationalist discourses of Finnishness in a more serious tone. In this article, I will examine the discourses of national identity and colonialism in the *Tarsa* novels in a postcolonial cultural studies framework (Hall 1992; Bhabha 2004).

My aim is not to study the similarities and differences between the originals and the adaptations in detail, partly because the adaptations are not based on any single *Tarzan* novel but on several books and possibly also the films. While some comparisons are made, I will discuss why the *Tarsa* books were published between the wars and what was added to the Finnish version of the story of a man raised by animals. My focus is thus on the adaptations in their sociohistorical context. While the novels do not belong to the canon of Finnish children's literature, they are examples of ways in which the boys' adventure story functioned not only as entertainment but also as a form of nation building during the Second World War. The *Tarsa* novels are typical war-time adventure stories: while the colonialist hero of Burroughs' books here becomes a representative of a postcolonial nation, the conventional discourses of nationality, ethnicity, race and colonialism are appropriated in relation to Finnishness. Yet the Finnishness in the books is less unified than might be expected.

## Discourses of Nationality

National identity and nation building are, as Stuart Hall and Homi Bhabha argue, discursive or narrative constructions. National and cultural identities are created and maintained through the use of various images, symbols and stories in the process of what Bhabha terms the 'narrating or writing the nation' (2004: 209), the product of which is, in Benedict Anderson's terms, an 'imagined community' (2006: 6), the nation as an imagined political community consisting of a unified, homogenous group of people. Although national identity is heterogeneous rather than unified, it is, as Hall writes, represented as unified in the 'common sense views of national belonging or identity' (1992: 293) that only exist 'through the exercise of different forms of cultural power' (ibid.: 297). While forms of cultural power occur in various institutions and practices from government, jurisdiction and national media to local, small-scale bodies such as village associations or families, children's literature has close connections to two sites of cultural power: the educational system and the publishing industry. The *Tarsa* novels never appeared on the recommended reading lists in school curricula since they were popular fiction and thus not considered quality literature. Yet, a similar discourse of Finnishness and nation building that circulated in the texts promoted by the educational system was also circulating more widely in all kinds of children's literature published at the time. Both the publishing industry and the educational system played a central role in promoting a nationalist discourse of Finnishness in fictional and non-fictional texts for young audiences. In terms of this discourse, I find Bhabha's notion of the 'pedagogical discourse' of national identity particularly apt here (2004: 209).

Bhabha writes that the pedagogical discourse of national identity is based on the nation's past history and strives for unity, although it is challenged by the performative aspect of nationality (ibid.: 209) – that is, the heterogeneous ways in which actual people who are members of the nation perform their cultural identities, depending on whether they belong to the majority or to various social or ethnic minorities. This heterogeneity is problematic in regard to the pedagogical discourse of unified national identity, since, as Bhabha suggests, although national identity is constructed in relation to 'the Other of the Outside' (ibid.: 212) – other nations and foreign cultures – the performative aspect of national identity challenges the pedagogical or master discourse of national identity because it reveals the Others who are inside. To cite Bhabha, '[t]he problem is not simply the "selfhood" of the nation as opposed to the otherness of other nations. We are confronted with the nation split within itself, articulating the heterogeneity of its population' (ibid.: 212). While the pedagogical discourse of national identity attempts to erase this split by offering a view of a unified nation and people, the split cannot be overcome because in actuality a living society is characterised by heterogeneity and difference, not sameness. Bhabha's concept of pedagogical discourse is revealing here, since during the late nineteenth and early twentieth centuries the dominant discourse of Finnishness was created by the political and cultural elite to increase the sense of national identity among Finns. This discourse is indeed 'pedagogical' in the sense that it was promoted in literature as well as in schools to ensure that the elite's idea of Finnishness was spread among the population, including children from various social and regional backgrounds. In this discourse Finnishness is constructed both in relation to the Others of the outside as well as the Others of the inside. I will discuss these groups in greater detail below in regard to the *Tarsa* novels.

While Bhabha discusses the heterogeneity of identities and discourses as the performative aspect of national identity in modern society, this heterogeneity is also reflected in literary texts as heteroglossia (Bakhtin 1981): different socio-cultural discourses are represented through various characters. The *Tarsa* novels are heteroglot in the sense that they introduce the voices of characters from several different social and ethnic groups. Yet this is not a sign of equality between the characters or the groups that they represent; in the construction of Finnishness in the novels characters are positioned as exemplary/ideal or as Others.

In terms of nation building and colonialism, Finland is obviously not a postcolonial nation in the same sense as any of the former colonies in Africa, as portrayed in the *Tarzan* books. Yet, as Mikko Lehtonen and Olli Löytty point out in their discussion of Finland and colonialism, Finland remained for about 700 years under Swedish rule and then, since 1809, for just over a hundred years under Russian rule (2007: 107-109). The whole question of national or ethnic Finnish identity was not introduced until the Russian period in the nineteenth century. While this was partly due to nationalist ideologies spreading to Finland from elsewhere in Europe, the emphasis on Finnish identity also suited the colonising power, Russia. The emphasis on the Finnish language and Finnish traditions was seen to decrease the political and cultural power of the Swedish-speaking Finns and thus weaken the ties to the earlier coloniser, Sweden. At the turn of the twentieth century, however, Russia changed its attitude out of fear that Finland might aim for independence. In discourses of Finnishness, the history of Finland as a former colony is repeated again and again.

The creation of Finnishness began in the nineteenth century among politically and culturally elite groups: as elsewhere in Europe, folk poetry, stories and songs were collected and appropriated by artists, writers and composers to construct a national identity based on folk traditions and the Finnish language (see Sevänen 1994: 42). The most notable example of this is the Finnish epic *The Kalevala*, collected and partly composed by Elias Lönnrot. The nationalist ideas were also present in the writing of nineteenth-century children's authors, including Zachris Topelius who emphasised patriotism, religion and the importance of (Finnish) nature in his works. As with other European nations, in the Finnish discourse national identity overlaps with ethnic Finnishness. A curious feature of the project of creating and (re)inventing Finnishness and Finnish culture in the nineteenth and early twentieth century was that a significant part of the cultural elite at the time consisted of Swede-Finns, such as Topelius, who spoke Swedish as their first language. Thus, Swede-Finns were not, in the nineteenth century, considered a distinct group of Others against which Finnishness was defined. However, later, during the first decades of the twentieth century, fierce debates about linguistic rights and the legal status of Finnish and Swedish in Finland occurred and racial theories were adapted to differentiate between Swede-Finns and Finns (see Kortti 2009). The other linguistic and ethnic minorities in Finland, the Sámi, the Romani and Russians, came more clearly to represent the ethnic Others in relation to which Finnishness was defined. This shows in the *Tarsa* books that introduce Sámi and Russian characters, and even mention the Romani people, while Swede-Finns are completely absent. Despite these specific features, the pedagogical discourse of Finnishness resembled the discourses of national identity in other European countries and was a result of conscious attempts to create a national identity for the country that indeed aimed for and soon gained independence.

## Building the Nation in Postcolonial Finland

Conscious nation building continued to be important during the first decades of Finland's independence, particularly because there was a need to create a sense of national unity after the civil war between 1917 and 1918 that occurred right after the newly emerged Bolshevist Russia had granted Finland independence (see Sevänen 1994: 98). In short, the civil war was between 'the reds', a group that aimed at a socialist revolution in Finland, were aided by the Soviet Union and included working-class people and communist intelligentsia in the urban areas, and 'the whites', who consisted of upper and middle-class people, obtained aid from Germany, and were supported in rural areas. The whites won, Finland remained independent and, as regards politics and arts, the nationalist-bourgeois discourses became dominant – Finland after the civil war has often been described as 'White Finland'. In regard to the *Tarsa* books, it is worth mentioning that the author, Lahja Valakivi (earlier Lahja Johannes Aalto) was a lieutenant colonel in the Finnish army. He had received part of his military training in Germany between 1915-1917 in the Prussian Jaeger Battalion 27, which was illegal at that time since Finland had no army of its own and was still a part of Russia. Most of the soldiers, including Valakivi, trained in Germany and joined the whites during the civil war. Valakivi also served in the Finnish army in World War II (*Suomen jääkärien elämäkerrasto* 1975). His military background might provide some explanations for the patriotic and nationalist views presented in the *Tarsa* novels, yet one should also bear in mind that similar views circulated widely in Finnish society at that time and were not restricted to military personnel.

In his study of the social regulation of literary production and mediation in Finland between 1918 and 1939, Erkki Sevänen suggests that after the Civil War 'the bourgeoisie and the ideological elite developed a nationally integrative value and meaning system. Bourgeois social relations, state independence, the agrarian spirit, Christian virtues, anti-communism and military preparedness were the ingredients in this value and meaning system' (1994: 509). The patriotic and nationalist 'white' discourses were promoted and the 'red' – that is, communist or working-class – discourses were censored in politics, literature and schools, in part to avoid new disintegration along class and ideological lines. Children's literature published in the 1920s and 1930s was aimed at a middle-class audience and Finnish national identity was a central theme. Important values included patriotism, love of nature, religion, Protestant work ethic and diligence, but while they aimed to increase national self-confidence, the books were often openly racist, particularly towards Russian, Romani and Sámi people (Hakala 2003: 74-76).

National unity was seemingly reached when in 1939 a war broke out between Finland and the Soviet Union. According to the nearly mythological accounts of this so-called Winter War, Finnish people forgot their mutual disagreements and came together to fight a common enemy, the Soviet Union, that was amazingly defeated by tiny Finland – defeated in the sense that Finland remained independent even though some territories were lost in the war. If most Finnish literature before the Second World War reflected nationalist and patriotic ideas of one people in a unified nation, the Finnish nation and fatherland became 'religious-romantic holy concepts' in the Winter War (Lassila 1998: 9) and the phrase 'the spirit of the Winter War' was then coined as a signifier for the national unity gained during the war. The so-called Continuation War between 1941 and 1944 was a different story. Finland allied with Germany – partly because Finland was willing to enter into a war of compensation – and was again at war with the Soviet Union. The Continuation War was not a great success, nor did it develop into such a national myth as the Winter War. After the war, Finland remained independent but ceded several territories, including the Karelian regions, paid substantial reparations and had to agree to several other terms specified in the peace treaty and by the Allied Control Commission – including the censorship of literature hostile to the Soviet Union (Ekholm 2000:19). The *Tarsa* books were among the banned books for rather obvious reasons – the representation of nationality and ethnicity in the books may certainly be considered hostile to their Eastern neighbour.

## The Bearman Tarsa: The Ideal, Heroic Finnishness

In 1940, during the Interim Peace, when the first *Tarsa* novel was published, the patriotic and nationalist discourses of Finnishness were perhaps at their height. Valakivi's *Tarsa* novels – *Tarsa Karhumies* (1940a), *Tarsa Hyrsylän mutkassa* ([Tarsa in Hyrsylä],

1940b), *Tarsan kuudes kolonna* ([Tarsa's Sixth Column], 1941a) and *Tarsa ja pakoluolan salaisuus* ([Tarsa and the Secret of the Refugee Cave], 1941b) – were published during the Interim Peace and the early stages of the Continuation War. The books form a chronological continuum, and given that the last novel ends rather abruptly further sequels might have been planned. The books were produced at a fast rate and include some inconsistencies in the plot-lines. The events in the novels take place right before, during and after the Winter War, between November 1939 and March 1940. However, even though the novels include some historical dates, they also depart from the known history: the novels involve accounts of wars against the Eastern enemy that did not occur in the real world, describe Tarsa defending areas that were actually lost in the Winter War, and, like the *Tarzan* stories, also introduce a lost civilisation, when Tarsa and his companions find the secret palace of the queen of the Lappish (Sámi) people, Louhi XXVII, in a mountain situated in the Kola Peninsula.[5]

Unlike Tarzan, Tarsa is not born and raised by animals in a foreign country, but by bears in his home country. Moreover, unlike Tarzan, who miraculously learns how to read on his own, Tarsa is guided by an old witch, Musta Leena [Black Leena], who lives in the middle of the forest – Tarsa thus learns human language from a pagan Finnish woman. Like Tarzan, Tarsa later finds out that he is actually of noble birth: he is the son of the master of the Harmaja estate, a small fortress in Eastern Finland; the name of the estate (*harmaja/harmaa* [grey]) refers to the name of Lord Greystoke in the original books. As suggested above, at some points Tarsa clearly parodies Tarzan and in several instances his actions serve as a source of mirth. Among other things, Tarsa wrestles with an aeroplane in the air, rides a whale, and uses a bear – his step-brother Körri, to be specific – as a launching pad for a field gun. The poor bear is also made fun of in a passage focalised through Körri where he finds a bottle of vodka, drinks it and enjoys his intoxicated state (Valakivi 1940b: 182). This is not to mention the lengthy descriptions of Tarsa's morning exercises – consisting of beating himself with a pine stub, pole vaulting, and other rather peculiar acrobatics performed in the pine trees through which Tarsa moves as easily as a 'villiorava' [wild squirrel] (ibid.: 46). In these scenes the double voiced discourse of parody is most obvious: on the one hand, the muscular, active hero is admired as in the original *Tarzan* books but, on the other hand, the trials and tribulations of Tarsa and his bear friends are clearly exaggerated in order to obtain a humorous effect.

Yet, Tarsa is also a hero and, despite being the product of an adaptation, suits the Finnish environment rather well. A solitary man who feels awkward in a civilised environment and prefers roaming in the forests and wrestling with wild animals is, as Havaste points out, a rather familiar image in Finnish discourses of masculinity (1997: 273-274). Heroes that killed and wrestled with bears had occurred in earlier stories and texts – the bear was, after all, a sacred animal in the Finnish mythology. Famous examples of this kind of male hero include Topelius's tale about Matti Kitunen, a famous killer of bears whose story was included in a collection titled *Maamme Kirja* ([The Book of our Country], 1876: 196-200), which was read in Finnish schools for decades. Another well-known example is the following extract from a famous poem 'Metsämiehen laulu' [The Song of a Woodsman] from *Kanervala* (1866), a collection of poems by Finland's national author Aleksis Kivi.

When compared to an extract from Valakivi's novel, it can be seen that both reflect a similar mindscape of a man who escapes the (human) world into the woods:

> I want to be a son of the forest,
> A champion of the solemn woods
> In the heaths of Tapiola [the kingdom of the forest god, Tapio; S.L.]
> I will wrestle with bears
> And let the world be forgotten
> ('Metsämiehen laulu', Kivi 1866: 56)[6]

> The further into the woods Tarsa came, walking along the river towards the dam, the lighter and more relaxed his mind became, he felt more and more like home. He was always at ease in the woods, whereas among people he felt a constant, disturbing stress and never got used to it. (Valakivi 1941a: 93)[7]

As a stereotypical Finnish man, Tarsa is more at ease alone in the woods than socialising with people. When angry or distressed, Tarsa escapes to the woods to thump some trees (Valakivi 1941b: 11) and thus deals with his emotions by exhausting himself physically. Obviously, a male hero in the wilderness was not an exclusively Finnish idea during that time – at the beginning of the twentieth century, Finnish boys' adventure stories were modelled after British and American examples and were thus often situated in the wilderness and emphasised survival skills, bravery, and self-control (Huhtala 2003: 44-45). Helvi Hakala suggests that the aim of these 'pedagogical robinsonades' was to teach survival skills to urban readers: the boys in the stories grow up into men who survive in the wilderness and fight the beasts (ibid.: 81). Tarsa has these skills, although it is made clear that the skills alone do not make him a hero. It is his willingness to use his strength and skills to defend his home country that has earned him his high social status despite his strange habits, such as eating raw meat and turnips with honey. His uncivilised habits are peculiar but acceptable, since apart from bravery and perseverance – as reflected in bear wrestling, in the desire to wander in the wilderness and in the willingness to defend one's country – a central feature of Tarsa is that he is not spoiled by urban culture. The wilderness is not only a setting for adventures: for all sympathetic characters in the novels, the forest is a holy place. The beauty of the Finnish forests is described at several points and the familiarity of the scenery is emphasised by describing Finnish fauna and flora. This use of a familiar setting is in sharp contrast to the description of the wild, exotic and foreign jungle of the *Tarzan* books. In the *Tarsa* books, it is expected that readers share the respect and affection for the forests of their home country – a crucial aspect of Finnishness is the Finnish forest, not the modern city.

Although these images of heroic or ideal Finnishness are masculine – as Tarzan, Tarsa reflects a particular discourse of ideal masculinity where sheer physical force is combined with a civilised mind – women can strive for the same. The ideal Finnish women here are not passive, fainting heroines. Active, healthy, brave women are appreciated; a female character that would be as completely passive as Jane in *Tarzan of the Apes* does not occur here. The fearless women include Tarsa's sister Tuila who is a skilful pilot, as well as the Karelian girl Siema Vägöinen, who escapes from Russians and wanders through the wilderness to get across the border to Finland. The counterpart of Jane, Tarsa's fiancé Varja Manttali, is an actress, which indicates her middle-class, urban identity. However, the narrator provides readers with information that ensures that Varja cannot be seen as a stereotypical urban lady. It is explained that even though she now lives in Helsinki, she is originally from Karelia and has healthy looks due to all the physical training in her youth – among other things, 'few maidens who had reached adulthood could tell that they had taken part in such real hunting trips in the great forests as she had' (Valakivi 1940b: 18).[8] When kidnapped, she is capable of saving herself and finding her way through the woods. At points the narrator also explicitly comments on gender stereotypes, as when Professor Levä suspects that women are not interested in history but the narrator explains that this was 'an old man's prejudiced and mistaken judgement' (Valakivi 1941b: 34).[9] Yet, the female gender is not quite as capable as the male. When Tarsa and his two companions begin to plan a dangerous trip to the Koli Peninsula to search for Tarsa's long-lost mother, Tarsa commands Tuila to stay at home (ibid.: 91-92), and women in general are excluded from the main action throughout the novels – which is, of course, typical of boys' adventure stories. Those Finnish heroes whose actions are not restricted in any way thus remain males. Furthermore, the matriarchal society led by the Lappish queen Louhi is portrayed as unnatural and a Finnish man who has spent a long time there announces that he has 'turned a bit strange here in the hag house' (ibid.: 226).[10] As in the *Tarzan* books, a matriarchal society is clearly a foreign, potentially dangerous phenomenon.

However, not everyone is included among the group of admirable Finnish heroes or heroes' assistants, nor is Finnishness only about forests and bravery. The novels include both the Others of the outside and the Others of the inside in relation to whom the heroic Finnish identity is constructed.

## The Others of the Outside: Enemies, Foreigners and Kindred Nations

As regards the Others of the outside, it comes as no surprise that the portrayals of the Eastern neighbour, or enemy, are less than flattering. The derogatory term for Russians, *ryssä*, is in use, as well as the term *vainolainen* [persecutor] that is used only for the eastern enemies in the novels. All the news that originates on the non-Finnish side of the border is Soviet propaganda, while honesty is the property of Finns. It is also suggested that Russians are always the attackers, whereas Finns are, in fact, peaceful. The narrator claims that 'the reasons [for the war] could not be comprehended by human reason on this side of the border' (Valakivi 1940b: 52)[11] and later on suggests that peacefulness might be an inherent quality of Finns, since 'our tribe never had a god of war' (Valakivi 1941b: 24).[12] This view of Finns as a civilised, rational, peaceful people is further emphasised in a scene where the description of the Fenni people in the Roman historian Tacitus' *Germania* (98) is proven false: a document miraculously found in an ancient refugee cave reveals that Tacitus described the Fenni as barbarians because he had fallen in love with the wife of Tarsa's forefather and thus had a feud with a Finnish man (ibid.: 74-75).

Russians are mainly represented as stupid, ugly and unnecessarily cruel. A few exceptions are certain exceptionally good-looking and clever individuals – the baroness Irina de

Marédiable and the spy Pavel Lutshki, 'paholainen miehenhahmossa' [a devil disguised as a man] (Valakivi 1941a: 154) – who are, despite these more positive qualities, described as inherently evil. What is more, they stink, hence the word 'lemunahat' [stinkskins] (Valakivi 1940b: 240) that Tarsa and his bear friends use of Russians. Even the wolves that come across the Soviet border stink. In terms of rather crude animal imagery, the brave Finnish bears help Tarsa to defend the border, whereas Russians are associated with the despised wolves, as in the following example:

> When he uttered the first words, his peculiar mouth was revealed: two strong, protruding incisors flashed into view and, between them, nothing; he had lost all his upper front teeth in some incident, which gave a special tone to his speech that sounded helplessly soft in contrast to the hard words. [...] his eyebrows were so close to each other that they seemed to form one continuous furry line over his nose when he wrinkled his forehead. And, what is more, when he got angry, his protruding ears seemed to be pulled back, not to mention the piercing look in his peppery eyes. Sigor Nagoinov's face at least was the mirror of his soul. (Valakivi 1941a: 29)[13]

The lack of intelligence of Russians is reflected in their superstitions. At one point Tarsa suggests that '[t]he enemy that is on a low developmental level should be hit on its tender spot, that is, ignorance and superstition' (ibid.: 166).[14] The subsequent events demonstrate that Russians can indeed be frightened by simple tricks that involve no magic at all. It is worth noting that superstition here is a sign of weakness, whereas in sections where belief in supernatural or magic events is associated with Tarsa himself or the Finnish people, it has a more ambivalent status. Tarsa, for instance, does not mind his foster mother Musta Leena saying healing spells when she is treating him – while Tarsa thinks that the spells are only 'old rhymes' he also admits that 'Musta Leena had often been a skilful healer' (Valakivi 1940b: 40).[15] I will return to Musta Leena's spells below.

Importantly, Russians are clearly set apart from other ethnic groups living in the northern parts of the Soviet Union – the communist country is not presented as unified at all. Instead, it is suggested that unity can and should occur among those groups that are ethnically related. Thus, the imagined Finnishness relies strongly on ideas about race and origins and emphasises the ties between Finnish people and the supposedly related ethnic groups living in the Northern parts of Russia. The assumption at that time was that since the languages are related, the people must be genetically related as well; an assumption that has later been contested in linguistic and genetic research.[16] The discourse about the kindred nations was most apparent in the ideas of a Greater Finland that were popular in Finland in the 1930s, although never supported by most Finns (Lehtonen and Löytty 2007: 107). In the pan-Finnicist visions, the Greater Finland would have included at least the whole of Karelia but potentially also other areas in Russia where the kindred nations live (Sevänen 1994: 118). In the *Tarsa* novels, it is suggested that the Finno-Ugric ethnic groups should join their forces to beat the common enemy, as expressed explicitly by Morda, a Komi soldier, who helps a Finnish boy to escape Russians. Morda first explains that they are both originally of the same tribe and thus of the same blood and then states that they should join forces:

> But we, your people and mine, have been humiliated too greatly and for too long by the foreign oppressor. We have been beaten to the ground, they have tried to kill our consciousness of ourselves. Only a few, the strongest ones, have survived, and only a few, the utmost strongest ones, have the courage to show resistance against injustice and oppression – as you have just done … and I did once. (Valakivi 1941a: 122-123)[17]

In their essay about Finland and colonialism, Lehtonen and Löytty write that the stories about Finland's independence and national awakening are postcolonial in the sense that they emphasise the freedom from the oppressor (2007: 109). This emphasis can also be seen here. Yet, the discourse about resistance and self-defence is combined with the nationalist, pan-Finnicist views where Finns and related nations are, in fact, superior to their neighbours. At one point, Tarsa's father, who has served as an officer in the Soviet army but is secretly building a resistance army, explains that 'our peoples' – that is, the kindred nations – 'have throughout the ages shown tendencies towards culture and organised civilisation that might have reached a very high level were there not the destructive neighbours' (Valakivi 1941a: 225).[18] Here we have an imaginary account of a great Finnish history that might have been realised if Finns had been left in peace by the colonising powers.

However, it is not only the Russians who are depicted in negative terms. Apart from the kindred nations, all the foreigners and ethnic groups that occur in the books are somehow suspicious, even though they would be among friends and helpers of Tarsa. For instance, the foreign magicians who help Tarsa and speak Turkish prove to be cowards because they flee when the fighting really bursts out. Typically, one of them, Mustranovus, who is a dark-skinned, curly-haired man, is described as an animated and chatty person whose talkativeness is not restricted by his 'vaillinainen kielitaitokaan' [insufficient language skills] (ibid.: 92) – this trait is juxtaposed with Tarsa's levelheaded style. According to the common stereotype or ideal – depending on one's point of view – the silent, sensible Finn speaks only as much as is necessary.

Apart from these Others of the outside, the ethnic minorities living in Finland, the Romani and the Sámi, are also portrayed as different from the honest Finns. They are similar to those living outside Finnish borders since they have either come here from elsewhere (Romani) or live in the far north (Sámi). The Romani, or *mustalaiset* ([gypsies], the (now) derogatory term is used in the novels) are mentioned once in passing by referring to the stereotype according to which gypsies frequent horse markets where they behave in a loud and intrusive manner (Valakivi 1940a: 37). The Lappish (Sámi) people in the north are characterised through their 'racial features', including 'high cheekbones' and 'short bowlegs' (Valakivi 1941b: 188)[19] and depicted as friendly, although strange, partly because of their pagan beliefs. They are also represented as suspicious because their folktales involve heroes who rely on their cunning, not on their bravery – cunning being suspicious because it is associated with dishonesty.

Furthermore, there are certain characters who are Finnish but are portrayed as outsiders since they collaborate with the enemy and thus betray their nation. These characters are also represented as stupid and dishonest, or, in the case of Kurt Sateus, a young urban middle-class Finnish man who works for the Russians, intelligent but dishonest and both mentally and physically weak. His fault is his urban background – since he has learned to walk in a city and only leaves it in a car, he goes insane when left alone in the woods. His urban identity is also evident in 'his [language] skills and his interest in foreigners [that] had partly led him to keep suspicious company' (Valakivi 1940b: 91);[20] that is, in his cosmopolitan lifestyle that seems to lead to non-patriotic behaviour. These Others who are both inside and outside do not really disturb the pedagogical discourse of Finnishness since they are associated with the Eastern enemy; yet, there are also those Others of the inside whose position in regard to the ideal Finnishness is more problematic.

## The Others of the Inside: Modern City-Dwellers and the 'Folk'

Apart from the traitors who are liminal characters because they are, in a sense, on both sides of the border, the Others of the inside include the urban, educated people, the working class people, and the witch, Musta Leena – the two latter groups seem to form what is referred to as *kansa*, the 'folk'.[21]

The urban, educated, middle-class characters are mocked throughout the novels because of their lack of survival skills – yet, if they are honest, brave, willing to defend their country and love nature, they are represented as sympathetic. The two middle-class characters, Professor Levä and Leo Karo, a detective writer, who join Tarsa on his search for his mother, cannot survive in the wilderness without Tarsa's help. At one point Levä notes that men like Tarsa were more common in the past, representing a culture different from the urban culture to which Levä and Karo have been 'uhrattu' [sacrificed] (Valakivi 1941b: 112). The absent-minded Levä is willing to learn about the wilderness, however, and at a different point the narrator explains that Leo Karo, even though from Helsinki, is not just 'asfalttikulttuurin tuote' [a product of the asphalt culture] (Valakivi 1940b: 159) but has also spent time in healthy outdoor activities. Valakivi here employs the term 'asphalt culture' which was introduced by the German sociologist Werner Sombart at the beginning of the twentieth century to criticise the processes of modernisation and urbanisation that produced people who lacked a real relationship to nature and formed 'an artificial species' (Sombart cited in Frisby 2001: 164). Thus, even though the sympathetic urban characters in the *Tarsa* books do not represent ideal rural Finnishness, they do appreciate the values associated with it and at several points criticise themselves for their education that is of no help in the wilderness. This sets them clearly apart from Kurt Sateus who is put forward as a prime example of a man destroyed by the urban, cosmopolitan culture. The indication seems to be that even modern, urban Finns should keep in good physical condition and have a close relationship to nature. As the reference to Sombart suggests, however, this was not a particularly Finnish concern but rather one expressed by critics of modern urbanisation all over the Western world; as Löytty points out, similar concerns are central in the original *Tarzan* books where Tarzan moves between (urban) civilisation and wild nature (1997: 71).

The working-class characters here represent the rural working class. Although there are passages that describe the life of the middle-class characters in cities, there is no mention at all of the urban working class. This may be seen as another sign of the nationalist-bourgeois discourse where the urban working class was associated with red ideologies and thus excluded from ideal Finnishness. Moreover, the rural workers represented the healthy, agrarian spirit. The rural workers in the *Tarsa* novels are represented as brave and hard-working but simple, and most of them are veterans of war living with their families on Tarsa's estate as servants. Social class is indicated through characters' speech: all the main characters use standard Finnish whereas some – if not all – of the rural working-class people speak in different dialects and are addressed informally by nicknames. The simple working-class people pick their noses, do not quite know how to behave in a civilised way, and respect their leaders. Tarsa is self-evidently accepted as the master of the Harmaja estate. Also Professor Levä is respected when he gives orders to the servants: 'The folk listened and obeyed as is their habit' (Valakivi 1941b: 28).[22] Because of the last quality the rural working class can, however, be included in the category of Finnishness, as long as it knows its place in the social hierarchy. It is clearly suggested that these people are not really capable of acting without a strong, informed leader. This patronising attitude towards the working-class people might be compared to the relationship between Tarzan and his subjects – both apes and savages – in the original texts. Here the hierarchical relationship is based on class and was present in the nationalist-bourgeois discourse of Finnishness where it was assumed that the working-class people are not naturally hard-working or brave but can develop these qualities under the guidance of the educated elite (Rantanen 1994: 20).

There is one character, however, that seems to disrupt the dominant, or pedagogical, discourse of Finnishness in the novels. This is the character of the witch, Musta Leena, who is associated with a culture that has, according to the narrator in the novels, almost disappeared from Finland: '[Musta Leena's shack] represents such "culture" that will never rise in these parts of the world again. And its owner represents the power that is (almost) doomed to disappear with its practitioners' (Valakivi 1940b: 5-6).[23] Previously the narrator has suggested that the ancient shack with its inhabitant could be placed in an outdoor museum in Helsinki – a supposedly humorous hint that Musta Leena indeed represents a dead or dying culture, the past of Finnishness. As her name, *Musta* [black], as well as the name of her dwelling place, *Hiidenvuori* [devil's mountain], indicate, she is associated with the earlier pagan beliefs reflected in folk traditions. While she is portrayed as a stereotypical, not specifically Finnish fairy tale witch – a crooked nose, a scarf, a cackling laugh, and an owl and a snake as companions – all her spells derive from Finnish folklore. The novels include several spells that follow the so-called Kalevala measure (that is, a trochaic tetrameter) and at points exact quotations from *The Kalevala* are included to illustrate the long relationship between Finns and nature, as in the instance where Tarsa cites the poem about the birth of the bear to Körri:

> Short of feet, with crooked ankles,
> Wide of mouth and broad of forehead,
> Short his nose, his fur-robe velvet.[24]

The idea of including references to *The Kalevala* in the *Tarsa* books was not necessarily Valakivi's, since in the first Finnish translations of *Tarzan of the Apes* some of the names of nature spirits had been replaced with Finnish equivalents from *The Kalevala* (see Havaste 1997: 269). While the references to *The Kalevala* are an obvious means to introduce Finnishness into the books – particularly in passages where Tarsa cites old poems or is compared to Väinämöinen, the heroic old sage in *The Kalevala* – in relation to Musta Leena they also reveal the contradictory attitudes towards folk traditions.

The traditions that were appropriated by artists and writers and thus turned from a belief system into a myth here seem to hold their power. The magic elements disrupt the construction of modern, Christian Finnishness. Tarsa is suspicious of Musta Leena's magic, but the events in the books actually suggest that many of her spells are effective. While religion usually plays a central role in the (quality) children's literature of the time, here Christianity is only mentioned in passing a few times. The pagan beliefs have a more significant role: Musta Leena's spells manage to draw people to her hut and the old nature spirits lead and help those who wander in the woods.

> It was a miracle that the young, now extremely exhausted Uuro Vägöinen had managed to escape death – perhaps Hongatar, the protector of the cattle, had sent her agile daughters, sinipiikanens [small wood spirits; S.L.], to shepherd the lost wanderer – with his last strength he was climbing up the south-eastern slope of the Devil's Mountain. (Valakivi 1941a: 200)[25]

At several points, however, realistic explanations are offered for the seemingly supernatural events and it is indicated that it is only the (simple) 'folk' who believe in magic and supernatural creatures. Musta Leena is clearly a representative of the folk that is the source of traditions – be it spells or stories of the spirits of the forest – and it seems inevitable to the narrator that the sources of these traditions are a disappearing culture. Musta Leena does not belong to the category of modern, Christian Finnishness and must thus eventually be excluded. Poems and myths can be incorporated, spells and pagan beliefs cannot. However, folklore is treated with a proper respect – after all, the pedagogical discourse of Finnishness needs to be built on a past that sets it apart from other nations and ethnic groups. Ironically, as elsewhere, the result of creating modern nationality means both appreciating and denying the past traditions and practices of the 'folk' who form the foundation of the nation but are excluded from the venues where the story of a nation is created. As Hall writes, '[n]ational identity is also often symbolically grounded on the idea of a pure, original people or 'folk'. But, in the realities of national development, it is rarely this primordial folk who persist or exercise power' (1992: 295). The uneasy relationship between the educated classes and the folk has been a central challenge to a unified notion of Finnishness throughout Finland's independence and continues to be so (see Lehtonen and Löytty 2007: 116). The heterogeneity of people, made manifest in the performativity of national identity, will always challenge the pedagogical discourse of national identity.

The solution to this dilemma in the *Tarsa* novels is the solution of the nationalist-bourgeois, white discourse that emphasises bourgeois social relations and patriotism: as long as people know their place and are willing to defend their country against the outer threat, everything will be in order in the Finnish nation. In fact, patriotism seems to be more important than nationalism, since while the nation falls into several groups of people with their own cultural identities, the decision to serve and defend one's country can function as a common denominator. In the end, what unifies the different Finns in the novels is not their actual or imagined sameness but a common enemy. Indeed, it is explicitly stated in several instances that Tarsa's 'perintötehtävä' [inherited mission] (Valakivi 1940b: 83) is to defend his home against the eastern persecutors and it is implied that every brave Finn is to help him in his mission, which reflects the ideas associated with the phrase 'the spirit of the Winter War'. This emphasis on patriotism rather than nationalism is understandable in the context of war, but, as seen above, nationalism, even pan-Finnicism, has a significant role in the books and while patriotism may constitute a choice, national identity is based on race.

The appeal of the character of Tarsa himself lies in his status as a liminal figure who seems to be able to combine the contradictory features in the pedagogical discourse of 'Finnishness'. Due to his inheritance and social status he clearly belongs to the elite world, yet he also has the knowledge of the forests and the old spells as well as the uncivilised manners shared with the rural people, the 'folk'. However, while Tarsa moves between these worlds fairly easily, most of the other characters have fixed positions in the social hierarchy. Thus, as a whole, the *Tarsa* books clearly belong to the mainstream strand of Finnish children's literature at the time that, as Hakala (2003: 74-76) and Päivi Heikkilä-Halttunen (2003: 167) maintain, emphasised middle-class values, patriotism and the importance of being Finnish.

It is easy to see why an adaptation of Tarzan appealed to Finns (as did the original books). Tarzan is not only similar to earlier Finnish forest-roaming male heroes, but is also an answer to the anxieties about modernisation and urbanisation, present in the national-bourgeois discourses of Finnishness. The pedagogical discourse of Finnishness shares such anxieties with many other discourses of national identity in the Western world at the beginning of the twentieth century. It was therefore easy to accommodate a hero from a culture that shares similar concerns. However, in the context of war, where national unity was essential, turning Tarzan into a specifically *Finnish* bearman Tarsa seems a logical choice, particularly since this transformation could be achieved by rather few changes to the hero in the original books. Add Finnish blood, patriotism, bears, northern forests, a few habits of the Finnish 'folk' and references to *The Kalevala* and the representative of a colonial power is turned into a hero of a small, postcolonial nation. The heroic Finnishness that Tarsa represents is not, however, the Finnishness shared by all Finns but is effectively constituted in opposition to the Others of the inside, people of different classes, values and belief systems.

## Conclusion: Censorship and Revival of Nationalist Discourses

As several other wartime books, the *Tarsa* novels were partly forgotten because they were removed from several libraries after the war as anti-Soviet propaganda (Ekholm 2000). In his study of forbidden books, Kai Ekholm explains that censorship after the war concerned both bookshops and public libraries.[26] However, as regards libraries, the censorship was not systematic. While bookshops were required to withdraw a specific list of titles, libraries were given only general instructions to censor books that were considered hostile to the Soviet Union – individual librarians were responsible for choosing the titles that were withdrawn and thus the selection was varied. According to Ekholm's listing of the most commonly censored books, the *Tarsa* books were removed from the shelves in several libraries, although not nearly all (2000: 213-219).

Instead of the exact numbers, however, it is more interesting that, in terms of their reception, the *Tarsa* novels were considered hostile by Soviet representatives as well as Finnish librarians. Already in 1940, during the Interim Peace, the first *Tarsa* novel had specifically attracted the attention of no one less than Vyacheslav Molotov, the Soviet People's Commissar for Foreign Affairs, who had criticised certain books – including the *Tarsa* novel – as books whipping up hatred against their neighbour (Ekholm 2000: 15-16; 86). The original cover of *The Bearman Tarsa*, portraying a fierce-looking Soviet soldier, was changed during the same year, although I do not know whether this happened before or after Molotov's comments. The cover for the second book in the series, *Tarsa in Hyrsylä*, was also changed: in the original one Tarsa stands among a pile of dead Russians, whereas in the second one he shakes hands with a bear. Despite these changes, the books were withdrawn from the shelves and locked away in many libraries – after all, the changes only concerned the covers, not the contents.[27]

The stacks holding the forbidden books remained closed until 1958. While some of the censored books had been reprinted even before censorship ended, the *Tarsa* novels were not reprinted until the end of the 1990s, when the books were republished as large-print editions by Seaflower, a small publishing house that also republished a number of other works of popular fiction from the 1940s. In all the libraries that I have checked, the novels are now firmly categorised as adult literature and the new editions are no longer termed boys' adventure stories. The assumed audience now seems to be elderly generations who want to refresh their childhood memories. Reasons for recategorisation may include the fact that the language is outdated – although thus at points particularly amusing – and that most Finnish children now live in an urban environment and might have difficulties relating to the stories. The most important reason, however, is that the literary institution is no longer similar to the nationalist-bourgeois establishment of the first decades of the twentieth century, and, as the publishing trends and critical reception show, ideas promoted now include, among other things, anti-racist discourses.

Since these novels are no longer promoted as popular reading for boys, it might be easy to ignore the rather simplified notions of national identity present in the *Tarsa* novels and assume that we have moved beyond essentialist assumptions. However, the republished *Tarsa* books might have a wider appeal than merely to the elderly generations. At a time when the nationalist party, *The Finns* (earlier *True Finns*), has gained 19% of the vote in the parliamentary elections in April 2011, thus becoming the third largest party in Finland, the nationalist discourses about unified Finnishness and racist discourses about suspicious, dangerous or criminal immigrants/Others seem to be ubiquitous again. Indeed, recent children's fiction might be one of the few places where these discourses are *not* present. The emphasis on a simple, semi-rural or close-to-nature Finnish way of life, manual labour, anti-intellectualism, anti-communism and prejudiced views of other ethnic groups are some of the common features of the Finnishness in the *Tarsa* books as well as in the present, 'true Finnish' discourses of national identity. There are some significant differences, of course. For instance, The Finns have a stronger emphasis on Christian values (as a reaction to the assumed values of Muslim immigrants) and the anti-intellectual strand is significantly clearer than in the *Tarsa* books: instead of making fun of the 'folk', in the current discourses the simple, uneducated common (wo)man, blessed with a healthy dose of common sense, is the 'true' Finn who is defined against the immigrant groups (the Others of the outside) as well as against the urban, liberal, educated Finns (the Others of the inside). In the discourse of the supporters of True Finns, the 'folk' is now changing Finnish politics and must be consulted; in contrast, in other venues this 'folk' is mocked because of its uncivilised manners and lack of education. Thus, the main dilemma of Finnishness, the difference between the educated elite and the common folk, remains.

Moreover, a common feature of the current discourses of nationality and the *Tarsa* books is also that the simplified assumptions about nationality are presented as honest, true, common-sense and, to a certain extent, innocent, for surely there is nothing wrong with national pride, since we are, after all, part of a young, postcolonial nation. Yet, while these assumptions may reflect honest reactions to recent social, political and cultural developments in Finland, they are certainly not innocent or inconsequential. Whereas the racism of the *Tarsa* novels might be understood in relation to the historical context and explained away as a thing of the past, it is less easy to explain away the racism when similar discourses of nationality surface in the present. Listening to the present discourses of national identity and nationalism convinces me that it is necessary to revisit the discourses of the past to understand what is occurring in the present; importantly, the past texts and discourses demonstrate that there has never been a unified, homogenous Finnish nation that we could now return to by closing our borders. Research on past adaptations can be particularly revealing when examining socio-cultural or political discourse, because comparisons between the original text and the adaptation can make the discourses and politics of the context of the adaptation more apparent – as when Tarzan of the apes is transformed into the bearman Tarsa and transported from the African jungle to Finland to defend the Russian border.

# Bibliography

Anderson, B. 2006 [1991]. *Imagined Communities: Reflections on the origins and the spread of nationalism*. Second edition. London: Verso.

Bakhtin, M.M. 1981. *The Dialogic Imagination*. Austin: University of Texas Press.

Berglund, J. 1999. 'White, right, white, rite: literacy, imperialism, race, and cannibalism in Edgar Rice Burroughs' *Tarzan of the Apes*', in: *Studies in American Fiction* 27.1: 53-76.

Bhabha, H.K. 2004 [1994]. 'DissemiNation: time, narrative and the margins of the modern nation', in: H.K. Bhabha, *The Location of Culture*. London: Routledge, 199-244.

Burroughs, E.R. 2010 [1914]. *Tarzan of the Apes*. Oxford: Oxford University Press.

Ekholm, K. 2000. *Kielletyt kirjat 1944-1946. Yleisten kirjastojen kirjapoistot vuosina 1944-46*. Jyväskylä: Things to Come.

Frisby, D. 2001. *Cityscapes of modernity: critical explorations*. Cambridge: Polity Press.

Hakala, H. 2003. '1920- ja 1930-luvun nuortenromaani: pyryharakoita ja sankaripoikia', in: L. Huhtala, K. Grünn, I. Loivamaa & M. Laukka (eds), *Pieni suuri maailma. Suomalaisen lasten- ja nuortenkirjallisuuden historia*. Helsinki: Tammi, 74-85.

Hall, S. 1992. 'The question of cultural identity', in: S. Hall, D. Held & T. McGrew (eds), *Modernity and Its Futures*. Cambridge: Polity Press, 273-325.

Havaste, P. 1997. *Tarzan ja valkoisen miehen arvoitus: tutkimus maskuliinisestä identiteetistä Edgar Rice Burroughsin Tarzan-sarjassa*. Helsinki: Like.

Häkkinen, J. 2009. 'Kantauralin ajoitus ja paikannus: perustelut puntarissa', in: *Suomalais-Ugrilaisen Seuran Aikakauskirja* 92: 9-56.

Heikkilä-Halttunen, P. 2003. '1940- ja 1950-luvun klassikot', in: L. Huhtala, K. Grünn, I. Loivamaa & M. Laukka (eds), *Pieni suuri maailma. Suomalaisen lasten- ja nuortenkirjallisuuden historia*. Helsinki: Tammi, 166-176.

Huhtala, L. 2003. 'Kasvun aika', in: L. Huhtala, K. Grünn, I. Loivamaa & M. Laukka (eds), *Pieni suuri maailma. Suomalaisen lasten- ja nuortenkirjallisuuden historia*. Helsinki: Tammi, 38-46.

Hutcheon, L. 2006. *A Theory of Adaptation*. New York: Routledge.

Kivi, A. 1866. *Kanervala*. Helsinki: The author, in: Finnish Literature Society: <http://www.finlit.fi/kivi/index.php?pagename=teokset-nimio&set=2369> Accessed 30 May 2011.

Kortti, J. 2009. '*Ylioppilaslehti* and the University's Language Struggle in the 1920s and 1930s', in: *Kasvatus & Aika* 3.4: 7-23.

Lassila, P. 1998. 'Rauhan kriisi ja kirjallisuuden murros välirauhan jälkeen', in: A. Viikari (ed.), *40-luku: kirjoituksia 1940-luvun kirjallisuudesta ja kulttuurista*. Helsinki: Finnish Literature Society, 9-16.

Lehtonen, M. & O. Löytty. 2007. 'Suomiko toista maata?', in J. Kuortti, M. Lehtonen & O. Löytty (eds), *Kolonialismin jäljet: keskustat, periferiat ja Suomi*. Helsinki: Gaudeamus, 105-118.

Lönnrot, E. 1888. *The Kalevala*. Translated from Finnish by J. M. Crawford, in: Project Gutenberg: <http://www.gutenberg.org/cache/epub/5186/pg5186.html> Accessed 10 January 2011.

Löytty, O. 1997. *Valkoinen pimeys. Afrikka kolonialistisessa kirjallisuudessa*. Jyväskylä: The Research Centre for Contemporary Culture.

Newsinger, J. 1986. 'Lord Greystoke and the Darkest Africa: the politics of the Tarzan stories', in: *Race & Class* 28.2: 59-71.

Rantanen, P. 1994. 'Hevosenkaltainen kansa – suomalaisuus topeliaanisessa diskurssissa', in: M. Kylmänen (ed.), *Me ja muut: kulttuuri, identiteetti, toiseus*. Tampere: Vastapaino.

Salmela, E., T. Lappalainen, I. Fransson, P. M. Andersen, K. Dahlman-Wright, A. Fiebig, P. Sistonen, M-L Savontaus, S. Schreiber, J. Kere & P. Lahermo. 2008. 'Genome-Wide Analysis of Single Nucleotide Polymorphisms Uncovers Population Structure in Northern Europe', in: *PLoS ONE* 3.10: <http://www.plosone.org/article/info%3Adoi%2F10.1371%2Fjournal.pone.0003519> Accessed 5 October 2011.

Sevänen, E. 1994. *Vapauden rajat. Kirjallisuuden tuotannon ja välityksen yhteiskunnallinen sääntely Suomessa vuosina 1918-1939.* Helsinki: Finnish Literature Society.

*Suomen jääkärien elämäkerrasto* 1975. Sotatieteen laitoksen julkaisuja IV. Vaasa: Jääkäriliitto.

Stephens, J. & R. McCallum, 1998. *Retelling Stories, Framing Culture: Traditional Story and Metanarratives in Children's Literature.* New York: Routledge.

Topelius, Z. 1866. *Maamme Kirja.* Helsinki: G. W. Edlund. Translated from Swedish by J. Bäckwall, in: Doria: <http://www.doria.fi/handle/10024/69393> Accessed 31 May 2011.

Valakivi, L. 1940a. *Tarsa Karhumies.* Hämeenlinna: Karisto.

Valakivi, L. 1940b. *Tarsa Hyrsylän mutkassa.* Hämeenlinna: Karisto.

Valakivi, L. 1941a. *Tarsan kuudes kolonna.* Hämeenlinna: Karisto.

Valakivi, L. 1941b. *Tarsa ja pakoluolan salaisuus.* Hämeenlinna: Karisto.

## Notes

1.  'Yksinäinen vaeltaja oli silloin jo parikymmentä askelta kauempana eikä vilkaissutkaan taaksensa. Mutta hän hypähti korkealle mättäälle, levitti käsivartensa, mäiskäytti sitten kämmenet vastatusten, toisti saman uudelleen, kohotti päänsä takakenoon, ja syysseesteisen aamuilman halkaisi selkäpiitä karmaiseva, pitkä vihellys, hyytäen veret suonissa niiltä, jotka sen kuulivat. [...]' Unless otherwise indicated, all the translations from Finnish to English are mine. I have tried to keep the amount of adaptation to minimum. The translations are fairly rough and mostly follow the punctuation of the original Finnish text.

2.  Tarsa kohoutui täyteen komeuteensa – ja olipa kuin olikin ilmetty kontio, metsänkuningas, mesikämmen, todellakin! Hän kohotti kuo... anteeksi, kasvonsa lähtösuuntaan, löi kerran kämmenvirsujaan vastatusten, vihelsi hiljaa, murisi kuin jonkin lähtöloitsun ja sitten loikkasi suonsilmäkkeen yli. Mutta mitä merkillistä?! Hän ei pudonnutkaan loikkauksesta jaloilleen, vaan kuten eläin etusien varaan ensin ja sitten takaraajat perästäpäin! Ja niin hän jatkoi, – lönkytti nelin kontin mättäältä toiselle, hieman löntystäen kuten karhu ainakin. Kai neljän raajan vauhti oli kantavampi hyllyvällä nevalla!

3.  *Tarzan of the Apes* was first published in 1912 in the pulp-magazine *The All Story.*

4.  See Berglund 1999, Havaste 1997, Löytty 1997, Newsinger 1986.

5.  *Louhi* is the name of the powerful Northern sorceress in *The Kalevala.*

6.  Metsänpoika tahdon olla // Sankar' jylhän kuusiston // Tapiolan vainiolla // Karhun kanssa painii lyön // Ja mailma Unholaan jääköön.

7.  Mitä syvemmälle korven sisään Tarsa tuli, yhdysväylän vartta patolaitteelle astellessaan, sitä keveämmäksi ja vapautuneemmaksi kävi hänen mielensä, olo yhä kodikkaammaksi. Metsässä hänen oli aina hyvä olla, kun sen sijaan ihmisten ilmoilla tuntui alituinen rasittava pingoitus, johon ei ottanut tottuakseen.

8.  harva täysi-ikäiseksi kehittynyt neitonen saattoi kertoa ottaneensa osaa sellaisiin todellisiin metsästysretkiin suurilla saloilla kuin hän.

9.  vanhan miehen ennakkoluuloinen ja väärä tuomio.

10. tainnut tulla vähin tämmöiseksi omituiseksi täällä akkatalossa.

11. vaikkei niiden [sodan oireiden] syytä ja aihetta rajan tällä puolen voitukaan ihmisjärjellä käsittää.

12. heimollamme ei koskaan ollut sodanjumalaa.

13. Kohta ensimmäisillä sanoilla paljastui hänen suunsa erikoisuus: näkyviin välähti kaksi vahvaa, ulkonevaa yläleuan kulmahammasta, mutta niiden välillä ammotti tyhjää; jossakin yhteydessä hän oli menettänyt kaikki yläleuan etuhampaat, mikä antoi oman vivahduksensa puheelle, joka väkisinkin kuulosti ponnettoman pehmoiselta sisältöön verrattuna. [...] kulmakarvat niin likekkäisiksi, että ne otsan rypistyessä näyttivät muodostavan kuin yhden pörröisen viivan nenän yläpuolelle. Ja vielä lisäksi muuten ulkonevat korvalehdetkin suuttuessa ikäänkuin menivät luimuun, puhumattakaan pippurinkirpeiden silmien tehokkaasta ilmeestä. Sidor Nagoinovin kasvot ainakin olivat sielun peili.

14. [a]lhaisella kehitystasolla olevaa vihollista on iskettävä sen heikkoon kohtaan, joka on tietämättömyys ja taikausko

15. vanhoja loruja [...] taitava parantelija on Musta Leena monasti ollut

16. As studies on language history and variation suggest, the geographical distribution of languages is not inherently tied to certain groups of people and their migration; languages can be adopted by foreign groups, for instance, due to trade, intergroup marriages, or warfare, to the extent that the original language of a group is completely replaced by the new foreign language. For example, as Jaakko Häkkinen (2009) maintains, the history and origins of Uralic languages (the larger group to which Finno-Ugric languages belong) are still fairly obscure: while researchers agree that the origin of these languages can be located somewhere in the area of present Russia, the questions of when and how some of these languages arrived/were adopted by people in the Baltic and Finnish regions is still a matter of dispute. When it comes to genetic relatedness, recent studies have shown that Finns themselves are not genetically a homogenous nation but that, for instance, differences between eastern and western Finns are larger than those between the British and the German (see Salmela et al. 2008). While recent studies offer no final answers to the origins of Finns and their language, they certainly suggest that the earlier assumptions about a tight connection between a language, people and nation is rather problematic.

17. Mutta meitä, sinun kansaasi ja minun, on nöyryytetty liian kovin ja liian kauan vieraan ikeen alla. Meitä on piesty lamaan, meiltä on koetettu tappaa tietoisuus omasta itsestämme. Vain aniharvat, vahvimmat ovat kestäneet sen, ja vain jotkut, kaikkein vahvimmat, uskaltavat nousta vastarintaan vääryyttä ja sortoa vastaan – niinkuin äsken sinä ... ja kerran minäkin.

18. meikäläiskansoilla on kautta aikojen ilmennyt taipumusta kulttuuriin ja järjestäytyneisiin oloihin, jotka olisivat ehkä korkealla ilman tuhoamisvimmaisia naapureita

19. ulkonevine poskikulmineen, lyhyine länkäsäärineen ja muine rotumerkkeineen

20. osittain juuri tuo [kieli]taito ja muukalaisharrastus olivat vieneet hänet epäilyttävään seuraan.

21. The Finnish word *kansa* can refer either to 'folk' or 'people' or 'nation'. In this context it is clear that *kansa* is not used of the Finnish population as a whole but precisely of the rural working class people, the source of old beliefs and folklore.

22. Kansa kuuli ja totteli, niinkuin kansan tapa on

23. [Mustan Leenan tönö] edustaa sellaista 'kulttuuria', jota näille maille ei enää ikinä nouse. Samoin kuin sen asukaskin sitä mahtia, joka on (melkein) tuomittu menemään maan rakoon mahtajain mukana.

24. lyhytjalka, lysmä polvi // tasakärsä talleroinen // päälevyt, nenä nykerä // karva kaunis röyhetyinen'(Lönnrot 1888, Rune XLVI; the Finnish version cited in Valakivi 1940b: 197).

25. Kuin ihmeen kaupalla oli nuori, nyt äärimmilleen nääntynyt Uuro Vägöinen onnistunut välttelemään syöverit – ehkä oli Hongatar, karjan kaitsijatar, lähettänyt ketteriä paimentyttäriään, sinipiikasia, eksyneelle oppaaksi – ja viimeisin voimin oli hän nousemassa Hiidenvuoren kaakkoisrinnettä.

26. According to Ekholm, about 300 titles were withdrawn from bookshops and about 1,700 titles from public libraries (2000: 19).

27. The back cover of *Tarsa ja pakoluolan salaisuus* includes the following note in regard to *Tarsa's Sixth Column*: 'Ilmestyminen toistaiseksi ehkäisty.' [Publication prevented for the moment] This may be yet another sign of censorship.

# Adapting the Rebel

## Reading *Shahnameh* in Tehran

### Tahereh Rezaei & Mohsen Hanif

## An Overview of Children's Literature in Iran

Serious literature for children began to flourish in Iran in the late nineteenth century. Although some works were composed sporadically in the mid-nineteenth century, the beginnings of children's literature in Iran can be dated from 1893, with the publication of *Ketab-e-Ahmad* [Ahmed's Book] by Mirza Abdurrahim Talbof (1834-1911), in which children were addressed specifically. The slow but steady development of this literature continued until Rasul Parvizi (1919-1977) revolutionised children's literature with his collection of short stories under the title *Shalvarhaye Vasledar* [Patched Pants] in 1957, in which he narrated the tales from a child's viewpoint. Children's literature became of significant importance when it was co-opted for the purposes of education and maintenance of the existing ideologies. Late in the rule of Reza Pahlavi, the Shah of Iran (1925-1941), a literary renaissance occurred through which the mindset of many authors shifted to consider children. Children's literature reached its acme in the 1960s and 1970s during Mohammad Reza Shaha's rule (1941-1979), and novelists like Ali Ashraf Darvishian (1941-), Samad Behrangi (1939-1967), Mansur Yaghuti (1948-) and, most prominently, Hushang Moradi Kermani (1944-) wrote prolifically and exclusively for children. What distinguishes these writers and offers a basis on which to classify their works, is their thematic approach. Early writers of children's stories adopted the point of view of an adult, featuring protagonists who nostalgically recounted their memories of a distant past when they were young. Gradually writers developed styles and forms influenced by children's discourse and language. Hushang Moradi Kermani is the most well-known writer who writes solely from a child's perspective (Taslimi 2009: 170). Hence, children could finally recognise their voice in literature.

Some contemporary critics such as Zohreh Parirokh, Mostafa Rahmandust and Sorur Katbi agree that children's literature lapsed into a state of inertia after the Iranian Revolution in 1979. Yet there are a few authors, such as Ja'far Ibrahimi and Mohamad-Reza Shams, who maintain that after the Revolution children's literature started to emerge quickly and successfully. However, almost all of these authors and critics addressed the same topics and themes (Anonymous 2008). The writings for children were – with a few exceptions – dominated by an adult voice and dealt with political issues. The influence of the Iranian Revolution and the Iran-Iraq war (1980-1988) was evident throughout the late 1980s. Even before the Revolution the stories were mostly symbolic enactments of suppressed political desires put in the language of children in order to avoid persecution.

Samad Behrangi (1939-1967) was among the few writers who wrote for children just before the Revolution. However, his works, like those of his contemporaries who suffered the pain of deprivation, were affected by socialist ideals that had seeped into a society deeply in turmoil. Therefore, in his works children are represented as small-scale adults. This shortcoming continued after the Revolution and persisted through the Iran-Iraq war with such vigor that any concern for children paled into insignificance in the aftermath of the 1979 Iranian Revolution. In this period a large number of realist works were authored which focused merely on the content and the moral message of the stories. Writers carried the burden of educating the Post-Revolution generation. Thus, their works were heavy with ideology. Harsh realism stripped children's literature of any fantasy and imaginative resonances. Male adults and objective first person narrators were the norm. All writings had to adopt a realist, biographical stance. It was not until the 1990s that children's literature was revitalised and came into contact with experiences of love and emotion. Even when children started to become of central importance in the writings of this period and fantasy finally found its way into their literature, realism remained a respected tradition.

When Mohammad Reza Pahlavi was ruling, Iranian children's literature had established itself and some organisations, such as *The Institute of Intellectual Education of Children and Teenagers* and *The Institute of Children's Books*, were working to systematically promote the educational standards and shape the malleable minds of children. The open political atmosphere of the first seven years of Mohammad Reza Pahlavi's rule had encouraged many socialists and Islamists to churn out pamphlets, booklets, short stories, and plays. To counter these movements, the ruling party promoted myths of pre-Islamic Persia in schoolbooks, propagated racist nationalism on public radio and celebrated kingship by implying that the Pahlavids descended from the Great Cyrus, king of Persia (558?-529 B.C.) and were the founders of the Persian empire. Two of such books addressing the subject of Zoroastrian mythology, an ancient Persian religion, also received awards as the best books of the year. The first one was *Jamshid Shah* by Mehrdad Bahar in 1975, and the second book was *Afsane-y Baran* [The Myth of Rain in Persia] by Mahdokht Kashkuli in 1976; both of these works were written for children. *The Institute of Children's Books* was seemingly trying to give ideological schooling to children to prepare them for the further absorption of the pre-Islamic Zoroastrian culture (Didar 1988: 62). Yet, how far such Nativist approaches to culture were successful is disputable.

In the heat of nationalism, the practice of adapting and summarising Abu al-Qasim Firdausi's *Shahnameh* [The Book of the Kings] became widespread. The aestheticism of this period required 'audacious heroes' who would protect the country and its glory (Azhand 1985: 27). In these adaptations, central roles were attributed to the ruling power and the aristocrats, and gallantry and valour, as well as picaresque narratives, were rampant. Meanwhile, the works created for children have always been in line with the ideas about children as the 'Men of Future' (the word 'men' is used advisedly) (Hasheminasab 1992: 43). Thus, *Shahnameh* was adapted to educate and mostly to enculturate children with the favoured ideology of the age.

## *Shahnameh* and its Legacy

The first international congress on Abu al-Qasim Firdausi (940?-1020?), the supreme Persian epic poet, was held in 1934 in Mashhad. It was considered to be the most scholarly and important congress on Firdausi ever held in Iran. In the same year and for the first time, many schools and streets were named after Firdausi. The second commemorational and scholarly congress on Firdausi was not held until about forty years later, in 1973, and a few years after that, in 1976, the Week of Firdausi became part of the national calendar. This epic poet's popularity rose to its peak when UNESCO announced 1990 as the year of Firdausi (Rastegar Fasaie 2002: 330). A much-revered figure, Firdausi has been a controversial character, too. His popularity owes a great deal to his protean masterpiece, *Shahnameh*, completed in 1010 A.D, comprising 60,000 rhyming couplets. In order to fully realise the significance of this work and acknowledge its status in Persian literature and culture, we should take into account the history and milieu of its composition.

When the Army of Islam conquered Persia in the seventh century A.D., many Persians gradually forsook Zoroastrianism and embraced Islam. After the invasion of the Arabs, Persian Poetry lapsed into a deadening silence for at least two centuries, until it reappeared during the reign of the Samanids (875-1005), the third most prominent Islamic dynasty. However, in the tenth century the Qaznavids overpowered the Samanids and occupied a vast area of their territory. Abu al-Qasim Firdausi emerged in the tumultuous late tenth and early eleventh centuries in the lands under the rule of the Qaznavids. This was a time of religious controversies aggravated because of the dominance of the Sunni Qaznavids over a great part of the Persian Plateau, whose inhabitants were mostly Shiite. At this time, in addition to conflicts with competing religions such as Manichaeism, Zoroastrianism, Judaism, Christianity, and so on, different Islamic branches were also in conflict with each other. The Turkish Qaznavids were Sunni and not friendly with the Shiites, who constituted a large number of the Muslim Persians. With the dominance of the Turks, the situation became hostile, especially for the Shiite Persians. Before the reign of the Turks, the government had adopted a neutral position in religious matters, but the Qaznavids chose the path of interference, exacerbating religious enmities (Safa 1999: 217-229).

Firdausi embarked on composing his magnum opus at the age of thirty-five and did not complete it until he was seventy. *Shahnameh*, unlike what its title – 'The Book of Kings'– might imply, does not praise kings or kingship, but takes a strong stance against the ruling power in general and insidiously censures the Turks in particular – whose original territory in *Shahnameh* is named Turan, that is the Eastern and North-Eastern part of Persia (Safa 1999: 458-521). Sultan Mahmood Qaznavi accepted patronage over Firdausi and assured him a coin of gold for each couplet when the work was accomplished. However, when Firdausi returned to his court and asked the king to fulfil his promise, the Sultan, displeased by the content of *Shahnameh*, did not welcome the poet warmly. The Sultan was only willing to pay silver and not gold coins for each couplet, a decision which profoundly enraged Firdausi and made him leave the court without accepting anything in return for his toil (Safa 1999: 482).

The geographical boundary designated in *Shahnameh* encompasses a vast territory from China to Rome. This terrain is divided into three parts: Salm, Turan and Iran. The latter is the region whose superiority over Salm and Turan is repeatedly boasted about. Furthermore, in this work three phases of Pahlavani, mythological and historical periods can roughly be specified. Among the three phases, the tales of the Pahlavani period have played the most significant role in preserving the name of *Shahnameh* and Firdausi in the Persian literary canon. The mythological period begins with Kiyumarth, the first king of the world, and ends with the reign of Fereydun. After Fereydun's death, the world is divided among his three sons, Iraj, Salm and Tur. The Pahlavani era commences with the death of Iraj at the hands of his brothers after animosity builds up among the three lands. This age comes to an end with the death of Rustam, the most renowned Pahlavan in *Shahnameh*, caused by his half-brother Shoqad. The third period begins after the decline of the Pahlavani system and discourse. At this narrative juncture, a historical order dominates Firdausi's poem. In this epoch, Bahman – whose portrayal in *Shahnameh* is very close to the real historical figure, Ardishir Derazdast – begins his rule over Iran.

What makes *Shahnameh* enchanting for its audience is primarily the representation of the Pahlavans and their valour (Sorrami 2004: 835). 'Pahlavan' in the Persian language and culture denotes a person who is brave, powerful, and morally decent. Although the word has close affinities with the concepts of 'hero' and 'cavalier' in Western culture, its application in *Shahnameh* has a more unique resonance. Men do not become Pahlavans but are born so, and the title is then passed from father to son. They not only have strong physiques and towering intellects, but also enjoy a distinguished and privileged status in society. People seek shelter with the Pahlavans in adverse conditions. However, they rebuke the Pahlavans when they sacrifice an ethical objective for a more vital goal. When, for instance, Rustam took the life of Sohrab, his own son, in a battle between the Iranians and the Turanis to avert the enemy threat from his country, people reproached him.

In *Shahnameh* and most notably in the Pahlavani part of it, Firdausi surreptitiously shows how power was not exerted by the kings on the Pahlavans but vice versa. As Firdausi indicates, kings and many other higher-class families did not desire that the conduct and manners of the aristocrats and courtly figures be inculcated in the minds of their children but that their children receive education from the Pahlavans. To this end, they chose a prominent Pahlavan to raise their sons. The deep influence of the Pahlavani ethics on royal dynasties inaugurated the age of Pahlavani in *Shahnameh*, which succeeds the mythological period. Fereydun, the last mythological king of Iran, makes Sam, Rustam's grandfather, responsible for the education of Iraj's grandson, Manuchehr, who establishes Iran. Siyavosh, the son of Kavous, another mythological king of Iran, and Bahman, the son of Isfandiar, are sent to Rustam to be brought up under his supervision – and not in the royal court. Moreover, although Tahmineh, the princess of Samangan, knows that she can be Rustam's wife only for one night, she chooses Rustam to be the father of her child rather than a blue-blooded man. Her promise to Rustam not to marry anybody after him also indicates how influential and dominating Pahlavani ethics were over court members.

The Pahlavans are in many aspects superior to the regal dynasties; nonetheless they never succeed to the throne in *Shahnameh*. To be a king, it was believed, *Farr-e-Izadi* was needed – a heavenly endowment and a spiritual quality which presumably brought divine glory and grandeur to the person who received it (Yahaghi 2007: 608). Sam, Rustam's grandfather, had both the power and the consensus of the people, which allowed him to ascend the throne, but refused to put on the crown for he believed that a rightful king should have *Farr-e-Izadi*. Firdausi, moreover, implies the supremacy of the Pahlavans and their tradition over the ruling class when he shows that the only character who survives is not the invulnerable Isfandiar or any other king, but Zal, Rustam's father. Although Rustam finally dies at the hand of his half-brother, Shoqad, and Sohrab is killed by his own father Rustam, Zal, who is the father and the originator of the Pahlavani world in *Shahnameh*, remains alive to the end of the work.

Sohrab, who is a young and ambitious man, naively assumes that his physical power and his upbringing as a Pahlavan qualify him to rule not only his land but also the world. He, ironically, could be regarded as the most covetous character in *Shahnameh* (Sorrami 2004: 826). Even Kavus, who some believe to be the greediest creature depicted in *Shahnameh*, never nurtured the idea of subduing the whole world. However, Sohrab, a fifteen-year-old teenager, dreams about defeating Kavus and replacing him with his father, Rustam. Yet ironically, he is tragically and unknowingly killed by his own father. In addition, Isfandiar, both a prince and a Pahlavan, desires to succeed his father as soon as possible but his greed draws him to his death in Zabulistan, now a region on the eastern border of Iran. These potentialities in Firdausi's masterpiece to question the ruling class and, at the same time, keep the throne and kingship in an aura of holiness, make the text extremely ambivalent.

Rustam, the greatest Pahlavan and hero in *Shahnameh*, lived all his life freely in Zabulistan; only in dire situations did he come to help the Iranian people, kings, and princes. Throughout his life Rustam's battles were for glory and against ignominy, especially in the story of 'Rustam and Isfandiar' in which Rustam – representing independence and freedom – fights with all his heart and soul to ward off evil; yet to accomplish his mission he needs to fight off his internal conflict with greed and fanaticism, too. His battles, on two levels of external political grounds and internal private sphere, provide the work with an adaptable reading potential. *Shahnameh* has always been revived at times of intense national feelings, and following the weakening of a sense of nationalism, the role of its central figure, Rustam, has been downplayed in literature (Yahaghi 2007: 395).

## Ideology and the Adaptation of *Shahnameh* for Children

Before they were written down, almost all of the sixty-two tales recounted in *Shahnameh* widely circulated among the common people as oral folktales and mythologies. Myth is rooted in the collective consciousness of a people; thus, it can play a central part in directing the general world view of a nation. Mythology is the heritage of the masses that is constantly being transfigured in line with social and political changes. The transformation of myths depends fundamentally upon their functionality and occurs as a result of a process in which myth accommodates itself to an era's cultural constructs. When this process is intentionally manipulated to give a certain direction to its changes, myth becomes a means of enforcing ideology. Often religious and political powers helped by the intelligentsia manipulate myths to contain them in their ideological framework. In fact, in periods when nationalism has been crucial to the ideological construct of a nation, myths have been represented in a way to convey nationalistic sentiments (Vahed-doust 2002: 88). The factors that decide their transfiguration are socio-political transitions, religious contexts and the influence mythic tales receive from those of other countries which lead to the hybridisation of different thoughts and cultures of various historical periods (ibid.: 92). Thus, in some eras, some specific parts of *Shahnameh* were highlighted and others were mostly disregarded.

The adaptation of *Shahnameh* in Iran began in 1933, when Abulhossein Sepanta cinematised *Firdausi* (Mahdavi). The film was presented privately for the authorities who subsequently placed it under a ban. Reza Shah, the king of Iran at the time, seemingly did not approve of some parts of the film. To re-film the movie, the director, Abulhossein Sepanta, had to make some changes to the cast. Most importantly, he had to change the actor playing Sultan Mahmood Qaznavi because he apparently looked too much like Reza Shah. Before the 1979 Revolution in Iran, three other successful cinematic adaptations of *Shahnameh* were produced, the most popular one of which was *Siavosh dar takht-e Jamshid* [Siavosh in Persepolis], which was a new experiment in form. Even though the critics gave it no commendation, it aroused the audience's ovation when it was staged in Paris Cinematheque (Mahdavi 2006). Since then there have been a lot of theatrical stagings and cinematisations of stories from *Shahnameh*. Most of the early adaptations and rewritings begin where Firdausi has begun his narrative and end where he has finished. Alterations go no further than to turn the sophisticated verse into simplified prose. In some instances, the author would not even go to any trouble at all and draw the same old-fashioned unfamiliar words into the 'adaptation'. Adapters often fail to discover a modern role for mythic figures and events. For instance *Chehel Sarbaz* ([Forty Soldiers], 2007) directed by Nourizade staged Rustam with an overemphasis on his physical features, namely a long forked beard and a stout body in armour. This adaptation failed to create any aura of glory or greatness for Rustam and was instead ridiculed by the audience.

About thirty stage and film adaptations based on Firdausi's masterwork were produced during Reza Pahlavi's reign (1925-1941), but this number amounts to more than sixty in the period coeval with Mohammad Reza Shah's rule (1941-1979). The rise in the number of adaptations in the second period was mostly due to the booming economy, which could support the production of more films. The 1960s and to a lesser extent the 1970s are mostly considered the Golden Age of Film production in Iran. From 1946 to 2005, *in toto*, at least 150 adaptations were made based on *Shahnameh*, only four of which are serious and worthy. This is important when one realises that after the Revolution, especially towards the end of the Iraq-Iran war, there was a noticeable decline in the number of adaptations of *Shahnameh* (Hanif 2005: 141).

During Reza Shah and Mohammad Reza Shah's rules, one third of the entire bulk of stage and puppet-show adaptations of *Shahnameh* were based on the story of 'Rustam and Sohrab', the most famous tale recounted in *Shahnameh* (ibid.:196-203). The fervour of nationalism, concomitant with the rule of Reza Shah and then Mohammad Reza Shah, gave impetus to the productions that set the Iranian Rustam against the threat of a Turani enemy, Sohrab. This preference for the story of 'Rustam and Sohrab' was reverted to after the Revolution. During Mohammad Reza Shah's reign only one tenth of the adapted stories were retellings of 'Zahak', the story of a cruel king who usurped the throne and started a rule of fear, but in Post-Revolution Iran about one third of the adaptations were based on this story (ibid.). Zahak had two giant terrifying serpents growing on his shoulders, where Satan had kissed him. To prevent being eaten by the serpents himself, he sacrificed two young men every day and fed their brains to the serpents. After years of living in terror and pain, Kaveh, a blacksmith, revolted against Zahak and overthrew him. In Post-Revolution Iran, Zahak came to symbolise the kingly and cruel rule of the previous regime, the Pahlavids. Furthermore, the story showed how a man from the lower classes can revolt and overthrow a dictatorship. Moreover, in Post-Revolution Iran 'Siyavosh and Sudabeh' – the story of the doomed love of Sudabeh for her virtuous stepson Siyavosh – has been as often reworked as 'Rustam and Sohrab'. The story of Sudabeh has been highlighted because of the message it imparted to the audience. Sudabeh, King Kavouse's young wife, who is in love with her stepson Siyavosh, asks him for his love, but Siyavosh, who represents chastity and purity, refuses. Fearful of her secret being revealed to her husband, she accuses Siyavosh of sexual advances. To determine the sinner, King Kavous asks them to pass through a great fire. Siyavosh accepts the challenge and survives the fire and in this way Sudabeh is revealed to be the sinner. Hence, Siyavosh becomes the personification of true morality after the Revolution. *Potiphar's wife + Joseph.*

Since one of the primary functions of *Shahnameh* has been to unite people on national grounds (Hasheminasab 1992: 72), before the Revolution and especially during the rise of nationalism, the story of 'Rustam and Sohrab' was emphasised. This story in effect depicts the confrontation between Turan and Persia. On the other hand, the story of 'Siyavosh and Sudabeh', which is almost bereft of nationalistic thematic features, is marginalised. In the former story, Sohrab's father, Rustam, is from Persia and his mother, Tahmineh, from Turan. Sohrab, however, has been brought up by his Turani mother and has never met his father. Unaware of each other's identity, Sohrab, who was then the most powerful Turani warrior, challenges his father, Rustam, the most revered and recognised Persian warrior. Sohrab intends to subdue the greatest Persian hero and thereupon conquer the Persian Empire. The struggle between the warriors is almost physical and not until Rustam fatally wounds his son do they recognise each other. In Pre-Revolution adaptations, however, the focus is on Rustam, who represents Persian dignity. Rustam deems his son's death to be God's will in order to protect Persia. This portrayal insinuates that in Pre-Revolution adaptations, national sentiments pushed kinship and blood relations into the background.

Nevertheless, Post-Revolution Iran views 'Rustam and Sohrab' from a new vantage point, and even in recent years new light has been shed upon *Shahnameh*. Instead of stressing the physical struggle between Rustam and Sohrab, who represented national alterities in Reza Shah and Mohammad Reza Shah's period, moral issues and internal conflicts are underlined. For instance, recent adaptations imply that it is Sohrab's arrogance which will not allow him to introduce himself to Rustam. Moreover, Rustam's reluctance to inquire into the other warrior's identity suggests that he is almost assured of Sohrab's identity before the battle; but Rustam is too proud, and not too nationalist, to disclose his identity to a fifteen-year-old warrior (Hanif 2005: 145).

Although this point has recently been widely acknowledged, it still finds little expression in children's literature. Additionally, the Post-Revolution adaptations are generally dependent on the emotional functions of these stories. For instance, in the case of 'Rustam and Sohrab', the adaptations attempt to downplay Sohrab's Turani lineage and, by referring to him as a martyr, shed an aura of religiosity over his murder by his father. Therefore, by remaining silent on the issue of Sohrab's identity, the contemporary adaptations of 'Rustam and Sohrab' insinuate that he also is a Persian and thus only a rival but not an enemy.

Both before and after the Revolution, overemphasis on educating children directed the adaptation process towards ideological ends. However, emphasis was placed not so much on the creative quality of the works as on loyalty to historical facts and the preservation of original plots. That is, selections and omissions were mostly applied at the level of story rather than foregrounding or minimising a particular thematic perspective. Moreover, although the *Institute for the Intellectual Education of Children* and *The Institute of Children's Books* were not formally closed down after the Revolution, the ruling system was not so very much interested in their indirect pedagogical methods. Instead, the clergy, in mosques and religious gatherings, radio and TV programs, etc. were held responsible for propagating the ideologies of the ruling class without any notable reference to inherited national mythologies. Therefore, for at least a decade after the Revolution, until the end of Iraq-Iran war in 1988, there was no remarkable adaptation of a mythically-based work. Thus, for some time, adaptations of *Shahnameh* were less popular. In recent years, however, a remarkable rise in the number of adaptations from *Shahnameh* has been reported. About 40% of all adaptations based on *Shahnameh* were produced between 1990 and 2000 – and the number is steadily rising – all of which fall into two categories: in the first category loyalty to the history represented in *Shahnameh* and preserving its originality are central. Morvarid Taghi Beyg wrote a twelve-volume series of books for children in which she tried to be as loyal as possible to Firdausi's account. The other trend attracted figures like Manouchehr Karimzadeh and Mostafa Rahmandust. They argue that there have not been enough innovative adaptations based on *Shahnameh* for children. They hold that creative adaptation of *Shahnameh* should be given priority. Among the proponents of this idea is also Manuchehr Akbarloo who believes that the tragic endings of many stories in *Shahnameh* need revision and should be superseded by more genial denouements in the contemporary adaptations for children (Akbarloo 2009).

Since *Shahnameh* occupies a sacred status in the Persian literary canon, adapters do not venture into sharply manipulated adaptations, but often try to remain loyal to the general narrative line and even to the language of the work. Thus, lack of innovation in adaptations results in the production of tedious and uninspiring works. Manuchehr Akbarloo wisely suggests a reconsideration and representation of lower and marginal characters with whom the modern audience feels more sympathetic. He also believes adaptation of a tragic episode from *Shahnameh* does not necessitate a tragic adaptation, especially for children who seek joy and entertainment in what they watch or read (ibid.: 20).

However, it is noteworthy that adaptations have become qualitatively more creative from the 1990s onwards. A successful and recent adaptation of *Shahnameh* was brought to the stage in 2010. The puppet show, under the title *Ghesehaye to va man va Rustam va Shahnameh* [The Stories of You and Me and Rustam and Shahnameh], was directed by Maryam Mo'etaref (2010). In this work, different episodes from *Shahnameh* are combined into a coherent narrative. In her adaptation of 'Rustam and Sohrab', Mo'etaref dulls the story's tragic edge. For instance, the death scene of Sohrab is very short, unlike in many productions that try to elaborate this scene and add to the feelings of pain and suffering of the characters in a melodramatic outburst of passion, regardless of the age group of the targeted audience. Mo'etaref also makes room for a secondary character in the story to share the limelight. Rakhsh, Rustam's horse, draws more attention to itself than the heroic Rustam. Rakhsh also provides much of the humour and joy of the show. In the same work 'Zahak' – the story of the eponymous cruel usurper of kingship mentioned previously – also appears, but in a humorous light. Zahak is depicted as a funny and clumsy character and the snakes on his shoulders are just two strings of balls. The play proved successful with child audiences, who were allowed to enjoy it and be entertained, rather than be preached at and educated.

Another recent adaptation of *Shahnameh* is *Haft Khan-e Omid* [Seven Labours of Omid] by Mahmud Teimuri (2011) which played on an episode from *Shahnameh* entitled 'Seven Labours of Rustam'. In this play, the contemporary life of a boy whose name is Omid is linked to the life of Rustam. A child thus replaces the stout and manly figure of the hero and creates childish humour in his actions. Rustam's horse, Rakhsh, is also a central character in this adaptation, with other figures such as the lion and the dragon being accentuated. The message of the work is very far from a faithful adaptation of *Shahnameh*: that darkness is not frightening. Although not a very successful production in terms of acting, the proliferation of a similar outlook toward adaptations of *Shahnameh* shows that recent adaptations are distancing themselves from a didactic framing of the works and are trying to be more entertaining. These productions are normally not sponsored by the government.

The Post-Revolution policy with regard to *Shahnameh* or any canonical text is primarily based on yoking them to religious and ideological principles. From among the practical instances of this manipulation is the foundation of the first *Shahnameh and Children Community* in Mashhad – a religious city in Eastern Iran – which tries to keep at bay the 'cultural assault' of the new generation. This Community endeavours to stand out against cultural colonisation by attracting children to Persian mythic heritage. While amusing the younger generation, it also tries to inject Islamic norms and values into these stories. These values have considerable overlap with the epic genre at large. Its epic tradition of courage, gallantry and valour, for instance, are comparable to the bravery and martyrdom of Islamic discourse. For instance, in *Chehel Sarbaz* ([Forty Soldiers], 2007), a serial movie broadcast on Iran's national TV channel in 2005, the director made an attempt to yoke mythological incidents to contemporary issues such as the conflict between Iran and the United States. This interconnection, however, led to the awkward confrontation of Iranian mythic figures with modern American soldiers.

In response to adaptations sponsored by the ruling class, a number of resisting adaptations have been produced since the Iranian Revolution. By hybridising dramatic features, they rely on either nationalist and political or non-religious yet ethical *leitmotifs*. For instance, a computer game, *Invincibility*, was produced in 2008, which aimed at regenerating the supernatural and fantastic aspects of stories in *Shahnameh*. In addition, a cartoon, 'Izhdahak', was distributed in 2011, which creatively interfuses thematic elements and plots in *Shahnameh* with elements of science fiction stories; most noticeably, *War of the Worlds*. In addition, Asadullah Sha'bani published a voluminous book for children under the title *Dastanhaye Shirin Shahnameh* [Sweet Tales from Firdausi's Shahnameh] in 2010. This work recounts a selected number of stories taken from *Shahnameh* in ordinary and straightforward language. The important point about this author and others with a similar approach is that, like Firdausi in *Shahnameh*, they seek to avoid Arabic words as much as possible in their narratives, in order to develop resistance to the governing trend in lexicography, which tends to Arabicise the Persian language. In fact, one of the central goals pursued by Firdausi in *Shahnameh* was to defy the ever-increasing penetration of non-Persian words into Persian.[1] The dominant Islamist ideologies and nationalist elites have long been engaged in controversies over linguistic issues. The Post Revolution ruling class has been advocating and propagating a more hybrid Persian language with no bias against Arabic words.

However, resistance to the dominant ideology finds its strongest voice on the stage. The most recent play based on 'Rustam and Isfandiar' (directed by Pari Saberi), which was performed in January and February 2011, incorporates elements fundamentally at odds with an Islamic framework, namely, music and dance. Moreover, on the level of thematic perspective, 'Rustam and Isfandiar' – unlike 'Rustam and Sohrab', which is replete with nationalist and moralist themes – echoes with anti-autocratic and anti-aristocratic overtones. Firdausi, in this story, has shrewdly distinguished between the warriors, who represent opposing and autonomous wills, and the kings. Goshtasb, the king of Persia and Isfandiar's father, dispatches an army under the command of his son, to literally tie Rustam's hands for not being submissive enough to the kingship and to bring him to the king's court. Interestingly enough, Isfandiar, whose body, except for his eyes, is invulnerable, is known as the most ardent religious proselytiser, chosen by God to convert people to Zoroastrianism – then the newly acknowledged religion of Persia. Isfandiar, who represents the ruling power and the dominant ideology, challenges the rebellious figure, Rustam, who will not kneel before the king. His defeat in the battle with Rustam indicates the victory of the rebellious opposition over the religious ruling class. Staging this story and theatricalising it with dance and rapturous music in fact defies and challenges the austere representations favoured by the ruling elite.

## Conclusion

The adaptations of *Shahnameh* between 1920 and the present can be classified into three successive historical periods. In the first twenty years – the time of Reza Shah's rule – along with the predominant pro-aristocratic readings of the work, other kinds of adaptations of *Shahnameh* were produced by republicans, socialists and liberalists who, in spite of their slight political disagreements, furtively criticised the tyrannical Shah and the dependence of the kingdom on foreign powers. Ironically, although opposition groups were harshly suppressed on other grounds, they were at one with the ruling ideology in developing a sovereign Persian culture. In the reign of Mohammad Reza Shah, the above-mentioned theme was pervasive, but the seven-year period of a more open, political atmosphere at the beginning of his rule gave impetus to many prolific stage and film adaptations for both children and adults. Nevertheless, the goal of most of the adaptations was to prepare people for nationalism and at the same time to surreptitiously repudiate Islamic mores. In Post-Revolution Iran, because of transitions in political and social structures and the ever-increasing dominance of Islam, the stories of *Shahnameh* lost their power to attract. Thus, for about a decade, direct religious instruction replaced indirect pedagogical methods. After the Iraq-Iran war, with the spread of mass communication, the ruling elite's apprehension about cultural assault was aggravated and Islamic adaptations of *Shahnameh* sponsored by the government appeared. While they entertained children, these adaptations sought to moralise and provide religious instruction These productions presumably had the potential to confront 'un-Islamic' culture, to which the ruling class was antagonistic. In the last two decades, the number of adaptations of *Shahnameh* in the fields of literature, media, and entertainment has dramatically increased, proving the significance of *Shahnameh* as a means of inculcating and consolidating ideologies. What is common throughout this period is that the adapted texts have created a body of dynamic force, which, although it has perpetuated the name of the work and has kept it in the canon of literary classics, has also played havoc with the social effects the text was conceived to produce.

## Bibliography

### *Primary Sources*

#### *Books*

Bahar, M. 1975. *Jamshid Shah.*Tehran. Kanun Parvaresh Fekri Kudakan va Nojavanan.

Kashkuli, M. 1976. *Afsane-y Baran dar Iran* [The Myth of Rain in Persia].Tehran. Sazman Radio Television Meli Iran.

Parvizi, R. 1957. *Shalvarhaye Vasledar* [Patched Pants].Tehran. Amir Kabir.

Sha'bani, A. 2010. *Dastanha-y Shirine Shahanameh Firdausi* [Sweet Tales from Shahnameh]. Tehran: Nashre Peidayesh.

Taghi Beyg, M. 2010. *Majmueh Davazdah Jeldi az Shahnameh* [Shahnameh in Twelve Volumes]. Tehran: Gohar Andisheh.

Talbof, M.A. 1893. *Ketab-e Ahmed* [Ahmed's Book].Privately published.

## Films

*Firdausi.* 1985 [1933]. dir. Sepanta, A. Privately distributed.

*Chehel Sarbaz* [Forty Soldiers]. 2010 [2007]. dir. Nourizad, M. Moassesse Farhangi-Honari Shahid Avini.

*Izhdahak.* 2011. dir. Kasavanidi, A. Saba Studio.

*Siyavash in Persepolis.* 1966, dir. Fereydoun Rahnama.

## Plays

*Haft Khane Omid* [Omid's Seven Labours]. Directed by Mahmud Teimuri. Talare Honar, Tehran. 6 Sep. 2011, Performance.

*Qesehaye Man va To va Rustam va Shahnameh* [The Story of me and you and Rustam and Shahnameh]. Directed by Maryam Mo'etaref. Talare Honar, Tehran. 15 January 2010, Performance.

*Rustam va Isfandiar.* Directed by Pari Saberi. Teatre Shahr, Tehran. 7 November 2010, Performance.

## Secondary Sources

Ajudani, M. 2003. *Mashruteh Irani.* Tehran: Akhtaran.

Anonymous. 2008. 'Tahavolate Adabiate Koudak va Nojavan dar Salhaye Pas az Enghelab; Goftogou ba Nevisandegan va Sha'eran Adabiate Koudako Nojavan', in: *Ketabe Mahe Koudak va Nojavan.* Tehran: s.n., 81-93.

Akbarloo, M. 2009. '*Shahnameh*, Koudak va Yazdah Khan-e-Eghtebas Dramatic', in: *Namayesh* 120: 16-20.

Azhand, Y. 1985. *Adabiat Novin Iran (Persian Modern Literature).* Tehran: Amir Kabir.

Didar, M. 1988. *Bist Sal Talash! Kandokavi dar Ahdaf va Fa'aliathayeh 'Shorayeh Ketab-e Kudak', az 1341 ta 1361.* Tehran: Hozeh Honari.

Hanif, M. 2005. *Ghabeliathaye Nameyeshi-e Shahnameh.* Tehran: Sorush.

Hasheminasab, S.1992. *Kudakan va Adabiyat-e Rasmi.* Tehran: Sorush.

Mahdavi, S. 2006. 'Ruye Jadeye Namnak: Eghtebase Adabi dar Sinamaye Iran', in: *Hamshahri Newspaper,* 16 May 2006.

Rastegar Fasai, M. 2002. *Firdausi va HoviatShenasi Irani.* Tehran: Tarhe-nou.

Safa, Z. 1999. *Tarikh-e Adabiyat dar Iran va dar Qalamro-e zaban-e Farsi az aqaz-e Ahde Islami ta Doreyeh Saljuqi.* Vol 10. Tehran: Ferdos.

Sorrami, G. 2004. *Az Range Gol ta Ranje Khar; SheklShenasi Dastanhaye Shahnameh.* Tehran: Entesharat Elmi Farhangi.

Taslimi, A. 2009. *Gozarehai Dar Adabiat Moasere Iran.* Tehran: Akhtaran.

Vahed-doust, Mahvash. 2002. *Ruykardhaye Elmi be Ostureh Shenasi.* Tehran: Sorush.

Yahaghi, M.-J. 2007. *FarhangeAsatirvaDastanVareha.* Tehran: Farhange Moaser.

## Notes

1.  Before the Muslim conquest of Iran, the language of this region was Persian, but when the Arabs achieved dominance in the 7th century CE they tried to impose their own language. Yet they were largely unsuccessful and the outcome was a hybrid Persian language, which did not follow Arabic grammar or lexicography. However, the two languages, Persian and Arabic, have almost always been rivals, and at times of great national fervour different intellectuals have tried to purify the Persian language of Arabic words. Nationalism in Iran has usually had anti-religious and anti-Arab undertones. During the Constitutional Revolution (1907) such national feelings became so strong that Mirza Fath'ali Akhundzadeh, one of the most prominent Iranian intellectuals and social critics at that time, suggested the abolition of the current Arabic alphabet, and replacing it with a Western one (Ajudani 2003: 219-24).

# From Retelling to Adaptation

## Writing for Children against the Ideological Agenda of the GDR Cultural Sphere

### Sylvia Warnecke

This investigation into adaptations of the Prometheus myth for children in the German Democratic Republic (GDR)[1] – or East Germany – uncovers the multi-faceted, contradictory nature of the country's literary sphere and aims at overcoming over-politicised evaluations of its children's literature. The case study confirms that adapting this canonical myth for a state-initiated publishing project was shaped by the conflict between the socialist regime's idealistic objectives and its inclination to methodically supervise and control children's literature. The author, Franz Fühmann, goes beyond the objectives of the publishing project's initiators in that he experiments with literary themes and poetic styles. In doing so, he reflects upon central questions of Marxist-Leninist philosophy and their realisation in GDR society – thus re-evaluating the ideal of a socialist utopia. His most influential adaptation for children, the mythical novel *Prometheus*, exemplifies the shift from unequivocal assent to the translation of Marxist-Leninist ideology into children's literature to a steadily deepening rift between the author's convictions and the reality of the GDR. This novel is an example of bottom-up adaptation which deconstructs the pre-text and in turn deconstructs the receiving culture's sustaining beliefs and assumptions. It challenges the prevailing power structures, also in view of children's role in the socialist society. *Prometheus* reveals a complex conceptual system, incorporating key issues such as myth versus literary form, the natural versus the social aspects of human existence, reason versus intuition, myth versus ideology, and fairy tale versus myth. *Prometheus* shows artists embracing myth as a counter-movement to the official re-claiming of myth. Here myth is understood as the antithesis of ideology, as an interpretative category in the arts. Whereas the state had established ideology as the main category defining the arts, many artists' responses to this overwhelming emphasis on ideology was to highlight the inadequacy of this category and to bring back into play the non-rational, represented by myths. Fühmann's verdict on the state of human society led to the relative weighting of assenting and dissenting tendencies eventually tipping in favour of dissent. Yet the inter-relationship of these aspects resulted in an essentially new reading of myth diverging from its traditional interpretative patterns.

The first section of this study will introduce the historical-political context of writing for children in the GDR. The second section focuses on the development of Fühmann's unique approach to adapting myths and epics for children which shaped a generation of authors and readers. Section three revolves around the author's interpretative work, using examples such as the exemplification of the genealogy of power and its reflection in the socialist GDR. The fourth section illustrates the impact of the novel on readers, educationalists and critics using the example of a debate in *the* children's literature journal of the time. The conclusion will emphasise the impact of Fühmann's work, which helped to establish the notion of children as independent readers.

## Literature in an 'Educational Society'

In 1949, the GDR, devastated by war and the aftermath of the ideology of National Socialism, was desperately seeking to establish a changed set of ideological foundations for its society in order to make a new beginning. With the establishment of its rule, the state party of the GDR, the Sozialistische Einheitspartei Deutschlands (SED), which stylised itself as representing the working people, set out to turn the country into an '"educational state" GDR' (Barck, Langermann & Lokatis 1997: 99).[2] Siegfried Lokatis, a historian of GDR publishing and publishers, claims that 'according to the Soviet model the production of children's books was deemed particularly important in the 'educational state' GDR' (ibid.: 25; cf. infra).[3] This aim was brought about by the notion that on the one hand education would enable the working population to govern itself for the first time in German history and, on the other hand, that a carefully constructed and monitored education system would allow an all-embracing guidance and supervision of the people. In addition, adults and children were not considered to have very dissimilar needs when it came to education, since all GDR citizens were to become so-called socialist personalities through the education they received.[4] Socialist education was seen as a process that did not finish with the achievement of a degree and that was carried out continuously at all workplaces and in state institutions. The role literature was assigned in this context resulted from this understanding and the systematic instrumentalisation of literary life for educational purposes was to be guaranteed through this approach. And, just as in the Soviet Union, children's literature in the GDR developed very 'strong links with other agencies [as] a subdivision of the 'mass media', and was also closely intertwined with the agencies of education' (O'Dell 1978: 21; cf. infra).

One way of educating the nation was to make literary texts and traditions easily accessible and to encourage the people themselves to write. Therefore, the GDR's first Minister of Culture, Johannes R. Becher (1981), proclaimed the establishment of the 'literary society', which was to mark the dawn of a new era when literature within this socialist country should be written by everyone for everyone, and more importantly be freely discussed by every member of this society. Children's literature in particular was assigned the role of 'helping to educate children and young people to become responsible and active members of the socialist society' (Steinlein & Kramer 1999: 153).[5] Karin Richter, a renowned GDR researcher in the field of children's literature, confirms that this claim constituted 'a long-lasting and wholeheartedly shared consensus among most of those involved in the children's literature discourse' in the GDR (1996: 192).[6] As a result Richter identifies this as the reason why authors who worked in the sphere of children's literature in many cases felt less inclined to voice unconditional criticism of the so-called socialist experiment in the GDR. She states that this consensus 'barely provided scope for a non-conforming or at least compatible literature and this scope could only be achieved under extremely difficult […] conditions or in connection with 'accepted' deviations and dissent' (Richter 1996: 192).[7] This study sets out to illustrate how this consensus gradually disintegrated to create openings for a more realistic representation of children's experiences.

One of the outcomes of the endeavour to realise this utopian ideal of a literary society was an extreme degree of institutionalisation of the literary sphere. Since the concept of the 'literary society' was based on the democratic ideal of freedom of speech, it came into conflict with the government's urge for the supervision and control of any open expression of views. In order to counterbalance the potentially disruptive impact of the concept, the government established a highly complex network of institutions which monitored each other and strictly regulated all communication. This overview exemplifies the complexity of the process and the set-up of state-planned literary production in the field of children's literature. Figure 1 lists the institutions which were, in most cases, involved in the publication of a children's book.

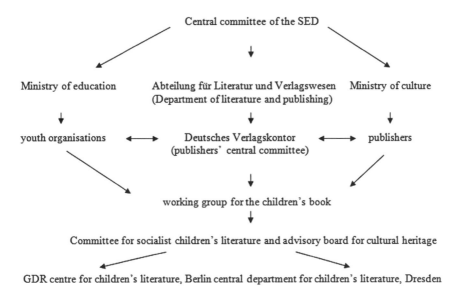

**Figure 1. Overview of institutions involved in the production, publication and reading of children's literature in the GDR**

Nevertheless, this network of institutions did not on every occasion function as a censoring tool or an obstacle; because of its sheer complexity and the intricacy of the production and publication procedures it frequently opened up scope for critical discussion as will be exemplified in the following sections.

## State-planned Literature for Children

One consequence of the establishment of a state-controlled and ideologically determined cultural sphere was the emergence of state-planned literary production.[8] The reality of working on such state-planned schemes was a rather open, disorganised and inventive process. This study examines a publishing project which, as well as many others in the history of GDR literature, is an example of interesting and ambitious plans that were in danger of being transformed into failures through inadequate planning and the dogmatic application of ideological premises. Since many officials' understanding of the role of literature in socialist society was a functional one, it set authors' as well as readers' needs aside. Consequently, generally positive intentions could seldom be put into practice without becoming political issues. Many authors in their individual ways did initially attempt the translation of the illustrated cultural-political postulates into literature. The story of the project tells the tale of the failure of such an approach to artistic work and reveals that the treatment of myths actually sparked dissent and criticism of government politics which eventually drove many authors to turn away from the reality of socialism in the GDR.

Being the most dynamic, successful and influential scheme in the context of state-planned literary production of its kind, this publishing project for the adaptation of literary traditions for children set many records. It ran for nearly thirty years, from 1960 to 1989, which is longer than any other state-initiated programme had ever lasted. It involved two publishing houses and twelve authors who represented a cross-section of the GDR literary sphere. It boasts 21 books as its literary output and 19 prizes were awarded to books written for this project.[9] The project was initially established to motivate authors to produce genuinely GDR-specific interpretations of myths from classical antiquity, old Germanic epics, sagas and the literature of the Christian Middle Ages.[10] The ideological objectives of this programme were expressed as follows:

> [It] is useful in the sense that these texts can communicate an idea of the experiences of people in the past to our children. Familiarity with these stories prevents our children from turning away from political problems to a surrogate reality[.] (Haase 1976: 595)[11]

This comparison was geared to pointing out that life in the socialist GDR was superior to the inequalities experienced by past societies. In addition, the project was to introduce younger generations to their literary heritage and to enable them to read the original texts as adults. In the wake of what turned out to be the most productive and controversially discussed plan for literary production, the heritage of fairy tales and myths came to represent a central issue in the debates revolving around the establishment of the canon of a genuine GDR national literature. In the spheres of children's and adult literature alike, the way many authors dealt with both traditions became an indication of their increasingly critical outlook on GDR society and their fundamental role as artists within it. Although the 'literary society'-construct burdened artists with immense educational responsibilities, it also provided artists with vast scope for expressing dissenting views more openly and consequently challenging the status quo.

Franz Fühmann was the most prolific contributor to the project. His contribution alone comprises six titles that won nine literary awards. He adapted the epic of Reynard the Fox, the myths of Odysseus' travels and the Trojan War, the Nibelungen saga and many more. All except one of his contributions to the project were published before any other contributors' adaptations. During the process of writing for the project, he established a ground-breaking approach to adapting myths for children, which is still relevant today. This study examines how he laid the foundations of his method and illustrates the way in which such classical texts can be reworked for a young readership without being simplistic or patronising. In addition, this case study will explore the unprecedented impact of the most influential book of this series – Franz Fühmann's adaptation of the Prometheus myth, *Prometheus: Die Titanenschlacht* ([Battle of the Titans], 1974), his final contribution to the project. Due to the socio-critical nature of his historical-philosophical approach to adapting myths, Fühmann came up against the limitations of a cultural sphere dominated by Marxist-Leninist doctrine during the writing, editing (and censoring) process of *Prometheus*. This circumstance eventually led him to give up the project altogether but not his deep-rooted belief in the socialist utopian ideal.

Although the mechanisms in the field of children's literature resembled those in the sphere of adult literature, many authors found greater scope for a critical debate in the field of children's literature, in spite of its initial appearance as being more restrictive. Censorship was less dogmatic here due to the fact that children were – officially – not considered independent readers. That is why many authors, who predominantly wrote for adults, like Franz Fühmann, Werner Heiduczek, Fritz Rudolf Fries and Günter de Bruyn, considered the project an opportunity for the critical discussion of the concept of a socialist utopia – an ideal many of these authors upheld in spite of their condemnation of the government's dogmatic attempts at its realisation.[12]

## Challenging Boundaries and Generating Artistic Scope

### *A Pioneering Approach to Adapting Myths for Children in a Socialist Context*

The reasons why Franz Fühmann's *Prometheus* became the most influential adaptation of the entire project are multi-faceted. His innovative approach to truly adapting rather than retelling traditional stories for children was not tainted by an ideological bias. Thus Fühmann shaped the aesthetic perspectives of the project when he moved from writing two-dimensional fairy tales to creating a multi-dimensional myth for children in his *Prometheus*.

He had started off writing his mythological novel as a fairy tale, as he had done in all his previous contributions to the project, but he soon realised that this would greatly limit his writing. In doing so he broke the taboo upheld by GDR educationalists that children's books had to adhere to the fairy tale structures of the conflict of 'good versus evil'. As a consequence, he abandoned the conflict solution of a happy ending in accordance with the typical fairy tale ending – a trend until then prevalent in GDR children's literature. The move from simplicity to complexity, from tradition to contemporary relevance on all narrative levels, signifies the author's changed outlook towards his work for children as well as his mode, the myth. In the novel itself, the shift from fairy tale to myth became perceptible in a number of aspects:

– external conflicts between two characters become internalised conflicts of one character, some of which are shown as impossible to solve;
– the text represents a multitude of layers of meaning;
– the gallery of characters increases dramatically;
– language is exposed as a tool to relate events and meaning as well as to manipulate others;
– the narration reflects the thoughts and the utterances of characters but more importantly forces the reader to take sides;
– the descriptions of surroundings are closely related to the feelings of characters;
– the style of the narration shifts from Homeric references to the language of the children of today.

By writing for children with such a complex conceptual framework Fühmann made a vital contribution to the progressive movement towards the blurring of the boundaries between children's literature and literature for adults.

The novel *Prometheus* also transcended the sphere of children's literature because it discussed highly topical philosophical matters many of which were considered contentious issues in the GDR. Among these themes are:

– human predestination and fate;
– the superiority of the child as the epitome of hope for any human society;
– the relationship between the human being and nature, morality and instincts;
– the genealogy of power interpreted as the succession of societal systems that eventually develop into a form of oppression of a majority by a minority which makes a total claim to power.

The following sections illustrate and examine this approach in more depth and analyse the author's journey from retelling fairy tales to his development of a novel perspective on writing for children in his societal context.

## *The Mythical Element in Literature*

In his essay 'Das mythische Element in der Literatur', based on a lecture for students of literature at the Humboldt University in Berlin in 1974, Fühmann stated that his method of appropriating traditional literary themes was the method of 'adaptation' as opposed to that of a 'retelling' (1993: 123). In the sphere of GDR culture this lecture represented a key study of the relationship between myths of classical antiquity and GDR literature at the time. It confirms that the reflection of artistic production went far beyond the realms of academic discussion in the GDR. The fundamental difference between the writers' and the scholars' approaches resides in the fact that artistic production and discussion reflected the contradictory nature of myths, whereas the majority of scholarly debates in the GDR up to that point avoided the issues of ambiguity and incongruity in mythical stories. The fact that Fühmann entitled his speech 'The mythical element in literature' is proof of this argument since he seeks to demonstrate that myths are not merely traditional artistic modes but an element of any kind of literature. A central aspect of any work of art is, according to the author's study, the 'mythical element', which exists independently of literary traditions, genres, or forms. Since Fühmann tackles the issue of myths from an artist's point of view, his reflections are dominated by the problems he encountered in his own artistic work.

According to the author, an adaptation is an idiosyncratic interpretation of the traditional story, whereas the 'retelling' adheres more closely to a previous version. An adaptation therefore has to be the modification of the theme of a myth or an epic in that it relates directly to the time and place of its creation. On the surface, the author's strategy appears to coincide with official cultural-political declarations. However, when Christian Emmrich, a prominent GDR children's literature scholar, notes that 'historicising myth and turning it into socialist literature happens by adapting it, which means by tailoring it to the needs of our socialist society', he has something else in mind than Fühmann (1979: 66).[13] Although his statement implies that the new version of the traditional story should be defined by the context of its creation, he claims that the story would have to be *tuned* to fit its function as an educational tool in socialist society.

Yet, Fühmann's conceptualisation presupposes that a traditional story cannot merely be functionalised in such a way. It is marked by the guiding principles of the place and time of its creation in that it *critically* evaluates these. In contrast, Emmrich lists three key methodological steps authors ought to take when adapting a traditional story according to GDR cultural policy: 'a) highlighting the rational within the fantastic as well as magical elements, b) uncovering the social causality, c) establishing proof of the historical stage of the development of humankind' (ibid.: 298).[14] This list displays clearly the primary concern of transforming a traditional story in order to highlight its political-ideological value for socialist literature.

Initially, this same principle was Fühmann's guideline when he produced his first two titles for the project, *Reineke Fuchs* ([Reynard the Fox], 1964) and *Das hölzerne Pferd: Die Sage vom Untergang Trojas und von den Irrfahrten des Odysseus* ([The Wooden Horse: The Saga of the Trojans' Fall and the Odyssey], 1968), whereas after 1968 his concept underwent a dramatic shift. When he maintains in the early 1970s that the adaptation of a myth is defined by the circumstances of its creation he does not imply that it conforms unconditionally to socialist cultural-political targets. The adaptation of a myth in socialist society, as in any other kind of society, is one author's account of this particular society at a certain time. When stating that 'Fühmann's adaptation technique is characterised by a method of treating myth that materialises the concept of fate', Emmrich points to a central theme in the author's approach which puts him in line with many modern, also pre-GDR adaptations of classical myths (1979: 66).[15] Yet Emmrich fails to recognise the actual novel aspect of Fühmann's adaptation technique and conceptualisation of fate. In Fühmann's children's books the mythical heroes discover that they need to take their fate into their own hands and cannot rely on the mercy of distant gods, a belief which reflects the author's atheist views and which to a degree echoes Marxist-Leninist philosophy.[16] Fühmann's interpretations revolve around the belief that planning and working can improve mankind's existence, again resonating with the foundations of socialist ideology.

Nevertheless, Emmrich's conclusion about the author's 'concept of fate' indicates his reluctance to admit the critical potential of such an outlook on the interpretation of myths of classical antiquity. His rationalisation of the outcomes of the project reflects a similar perspective to the one adopted by many GDR educationalists. In order to avoid confrontation with the socio-critical strength of myth and possible adverse effects on the readers' faith in socialist society, Emmrich characterises the adaptations of myths, epics and sagas produced within the framework of the publishing project as distinctly historical. He writes:

> The efforts of socialist society to uncover the influential myth-creating eras of human history, which gained depth and impact on a world stage, highlight: Socialism can […] absorb the old myths as cultural heritage and use them as art, as poetry for a new art. The historical-materialist method allows us to reveal the connections between myths and history and to identify myths as products of ancient fantastical-popular perception, as representations of a magical, holistic world in the same way as representations of societies riddled with conflict. We can discover and understand these through multiple artistic interpretations [.] (Emmrich 1979: 65)[17]

Emmrich's use of the term to absorb ('aufheben') is ambiguous. In Emmrich's sense it suggests both: to keep or to store as well as to do away with or to supersede. In both cases, the treatment of myth is supposed to be conducted from a safe distance, which allows the interpreter to omit the rigorous, critical edge of adapting a myth. Investigating the phenomenon of myths and the concept of fate from a historical perspective, as outlined in many a cultural-political declaration, presupposes that the targets of socio-critical references have been overcome and do not apply to the GDR.

Yet, Fühmann revealed the unequivocal potential of myths as opposed to any other expression of human thought as 'the representation of societal processes as fundamental and therefore as always historically defined' (1993: 123).[18] This characterisation is based on his insight that human beings in any society encounter conflicts due to the fact that they are shaped by being 'natural as well as societal creatures (ibid.: 111).[19] The crucial detail lies in what way man seeks to overcome such conflicts, whether this happens in a dogmatic, totalitarian or in a democratic, liberal fashion. The key factors in this context are communication, transparency, the involvement of every member of society in decision-making procedures and the appreciation of independent thinking. With his approach the author went far beyond the intentions of the initiators of the publishing project. Their objective had been to claim the *true ownership* of myths of classical antiquity as a socialist cultural heritage, thus providing easy-reading versions of these stories for children, aimed at making adult literature incorporating myths more accessible for future generations. Fühmann came to demonstrate the utopian-philosophical potential of myths in a socialist sense, i.e. neither anti-Marxist nor anti-communist. He criticised what he often referred to as the administrators of socialism in the GDR who in his view had lost sight of the fundamental ideas of Marxist philosophy.

## Locating the Untainted Version of the Myth

Three elements in Fühmann's work define the art of taking possession of the cultural heritage. Number one is his search for the sources of the stories he adapted that determined which of the versions he would accept as legitimate. This is significant in as much as it puts his work in a certain tradition. The second element is his adaptation of the stylistic features of earlier versions of these stories. He incorporated these as a means of bringing the ancient cultural tradition to life for children as well as to highlight his own aesthetic objectives. The third element is the author's reflection on how to adapt a particular myth for children.

Fühmann debated whether to adapt a myth in the form of a fairy tale, finishing with a 'happy ending' or whether he ought to be true to the nature of myths and attempt to confront his young readers with the insoluble conflicts they portray. If he chose the second option he would ask his readership to accept a potentially traumatising insight into human existence. In Fühmann's correspondence with Kurt Batt he summed up what being a child stands for. Batt had alluded to the author's portrayal of childhood as a period of disturbing and painful discoveries: 'Dear Doctor, in defining childhood as "the place where poetry and prose collide tragically" you summed up my work exactly and completely' (letter Fühmann to Batt cited in Heinze 1998: 120; cf. infra).[20] In view of this, Fühmann considered his children's books as a medium through which he was able to teach children about happy and frightful aspects of human existence. In an interview with Peter Gugisch, Fühmann explains further why his writing could help children grow up when he describes crucial incidents of his own childhood: 'Naturally, the cracks already appear in childhood, cracks of two kinds. [...] For example, one learns that adults are different from what one is supposed to think of them. Yet one also learns that they are different from how one wants to see them' (Gugisch interview with Fühmann, cited by Heinze 1998: 171).[21] The author therefore aimed to adhere to his principle of 'telling the whole story', a fact he became conscious of during his work on *Reynard the Fox* (Fühmann 1960: n.p.).[22]

The material in the Franz-Fühmann-Archiv Berlin illustrates vividly the author's search for the sources of the stories he adapted for children. This proves comparatively straightforward in the cases of his earlier contributions to the project *Reynard the Fox*, *Libussa* [Libuša], *Shakespeare-Märchen* [Four Shakespeare Plays as Fairy Tales] and *Das Nibelungenlied* [The Nibelungen Saga]. A key principle of the author's work can be detected even at the early stages of his treatment of traditional stories. For all his adaptations Fühmann sought to find the original of the story he undertook to tell for children. The author considered the oldest written or printed version accessible as the earliest or original version.[23] He sought to find the oldest available version of the story in order to discount all later versions so that he was able to produce a truly idiosyncratic interpretation.

In 1959, when his editor in the Kinderbuchverlag, Regina Hänsel, approached Fühmann with regard to the publishing project, he was instantly fascinated by the idea of adapting the Reynke story for children. He wrote a draft in which he set out the plan for his adaptation of the animal epic. Fühmann states: 'The original version is the essence which I want to bring out in my work, its content as well as its form. I believe that in this respect my approach is different from many a reteller's' (Sauter 1971: 52).[24] By reverting to the 'original or untainted' version, Fühmann sought to avoid the incorporation of values and attitudes that had been attributed to later versions of the story. The original was in the case of *Reynard the Fox* the Lübeck edition of 1498. *Reynke de vos*, the Low German version of the animal epic, is assumed to be a translation of the Low Dutch epic *Reinaerts Historie* by Hinrek van Alckmer. Fühmann also planned drawing on Goethe's rendering in hexameter verse and possibly even to include passages from Goethe's version in his children's book.[25] In addition, he drew on Karl Simrock's revised edition from 1845.

For his retelling of Homer's *Iliad* and *Odyssey*, published under the title *The Wooden Horse* in 1968, Fühmann was faced with an older and more extensive literary tradition of re-workings. Although he drew mainly on Homer's epic, he also named the works of Aeschylus, Sophocles, Virgil and Ovid as his sources. The passage in which he incorporates the character of Prometheus in *The Wooden Horse*, the chapter 'Thersites tells the story of Prometheus', indicates a paradigm shift in the author's attitude to the task of adapting a myth. Homer had not made any mention of the titan in his epic; Fühmann was so fascinated by the character that he decided to take the liberty of expanding Homer's tale by incorporating material from different sources, such as Aeschylus' tragedy *Prometheus Desmotes*.[26]

Including an additional myth into his adaptation of Homer's epic represents a first indication of the method which was to become the key principle of his adaptations: '[He] is bringing together a number of different interpretational strands which can even lead to an interpretation that is contradictory to the task' (Riedel 1980: 73).[27] The author adhered meticulously to Homer's work in his retelling of the *Iliad* but he alluded to the downfall of the Olympian gods at the end of his *Odyssey* adaptation, which represents a changed focus to Homer's epic. The author chose this interpretation of the story of the ancient gods in order to shed light on the fact that their social order was flawed and that a community based on the absolute power of one ruler cannot survive. Hence the retelling of the *Odyssey* was the starting point for Fühmann's revision of his concept of adapting myths of classical antiquity for children.

A third stage of the movement from retelling to adaptation was Fühmann's work on the Libussa saga.[28] Although the old Czech tribal saga had been published by the Kinderbuchverlag as the translation of the version by the Czech writer Jirásek as part of the anthology *Böhmens alte Sagen* [Old Bohemian Sagas] in 1957, Fühmann planned to produce a more contemporary adaptation of the saga in 1969. One reason for his choice was his great affinity with this particular subject matter because of his own life story. In the exposé for the Kinderbuchverlag he notes that he intends to offer children an insight into the matriarchal stage of the development of mankind. Fühmann's interest in the matriarchal stage of society as reflected in the Libussa saga resulted from his search for the portrayal of a very different type of society. This saga provided scope for the author to investigate the socio-historical potential and limitations of matriarchy and to find out what caused its collapse. Fühmann lists that Johann Gottfried Herder, Johann Karl August Musäus and Clemens Brentano along with Franz Grillparzer, all of whom belonged to the German Romanticism movement, incorporated motifs of the saga in their works. The oldest available version he found in the text of Cosma.[29] Fühmann hoped that this version could provide him with the means to move closer to the 'essence of the saga', which did not necessarily mean disregarding all other readings but having the opportunity to choose from the various lines of tradition and to eliminate unwanted interpretations and changes the story had undergone while being handed down (Seehase 1969: n.p.).[30]

With this approach the author laid the foundations for a different outlook on introducing the cultural heritage to children in the GDR. The fact that he neither sought to write a contemporary version in modern German of a well-known adaptation, such as Gustav Schwab's adaptations (1838-40), nor to create easy-reading, fairy tale-like stories incorporating mythological characters is a fundamental quality of the author's work on mythological stories. In contrast to the policy upheld by the Kinderbuchverlag in the 1950s, when the publisher brought out abridged versions of previous retellings, Fühmann aspires to create a novel way of conveying these stories to children.

During his search for the original version of the Prometheus myth the author was faced with an even more difficult task. In Hellenic and Roman times early versions of this myth were written which were essentially contradictory in their interpretation of the story of the Titan. Discussing the problems resulting from this circumstance, Fühmann states in his research documents:

> One wants to get to the core of the myth, which one then keeps to. But with this intention we end up like Peer Gynt. On the quest for the origin of this mythologem we will only find various versions instead[.] (Fühmann, Franz-Fühmann-Archiv [FFA], Sign. 98, Prometheus, Vorarbeiten: 1)[31]

During his search for the 'origin of the myth' Fühmann discovered seventy different versions. He lists contrasting perspectives taken in these interpretations of the Titan's story: First of all there was Aeschylus, who 'tells the story of an extraordinary uprising, of a conservative rebellion and of the exceptional emotionalism of the war against the Persians' (Fühmann, FFA, Sign. 99/10, Prometheus, Vorarbeiten: card 5).[32] Hesiod, on the other hand, tells the story 'of the one who brought a curse upon mankind, [...] who wanted to be shrewder than those in power, who [...] was a master in the art of deception' (ibid.: card 7).[33] Fühmann weighed up whether Hesiod's version, which is the older one, was closest to the roots of the Prometheus myth. Hesiod had drawn from Babylonian sources in his *Theogony*. Fühmann recalls that Plato tells the story of the Titan, who brought fire and wealth to mankind but did not provide mankind with any rules for the community or 'political virtues, which the Gods much later imparted to mankind' (ibid.: card 8).[34] Another source was Lucian, in whose work Prometheus' story is interpreted as 'a political conspiracy among rulers. Both parties are equally corrupt. [His story] is the chronicle of a scandal' (ibid.: card 9).[35] The author speculates: 'So – is it the brilliant rebel, the unwanted independent thinker, the member of a corrupt Duodeze regime?' (ibid.: card 9)[36]

The author's final decision on his choice of tradition was guided by the story he was planning to tell his young readers and by the consideration of the suitability of the story for this readership. In his preparatory work he states that the objectives of the initiators of the publishing project were insufficient for the creation of a genuine contemporary reading of the myth: 'if one tells a mythological story simply because it has been told by our predecessors the purpose of the new story is missing. […] If something ought to be more than a translation it has to have a clear purpose for us' (ibid.: card 12).[37] The key question Fühmann had to resolve was whether Prometheus had committed a crime by stealing fire from the gods and passing it on to mankind. He describes adapting a myth for children as 'a matter of taking sides par excellence' (Franz-Fühmann-Archiv [FFA], Sign. 98, Prometheus, Vorarbeiten: 2).[38] According to Karl Kerényi and Carl Gustav Jung, the corresponding elements of the numerous versions of a myth represent an amorphous supply of certain characters, actions and attributes, which only gain importance in the particular concrete structuring by an artist. This fact convinced Fühmann that he could neither simply follow one tradition nor create a new reading by collecting elements from many different versions. He needed to move in a third direction and create his individual interpretation. This insight goes hand in hand with his discovery of Johann Wolfgang von Goethe's and Percy Bysshe Shelley's versions of the myth as personifying elementary forces in the same way as the readings produced in Hellenic times and even prior to that. Fühmann thus declares that a 'myth can be considered a seed along with all the leaves it produces; its development is its life; stagnation in one form deemed the definitive one would be its death' (1993: 105). This insight encapsulates the author's personal understanding of Marxist philosophy. He claims: 'Myth is what needs to be transformed to survive. In this sense myth is linked to Marxism' (Fühmann, FFA, Sign. 99/10, Prometheus, Vorarbeiten: card 16).[39] This understanding of myths leads Fühmann to appreciate their utopian potential.

In this respect his retelling of *Reynard the Fox* was written with the same objective in mind as *Prometheus*, namely to further the good forces in society and to help promote the utopian ideal of a just community of men. However, what had changed since the early 1960s was his outlook on the educational value of children's literature. In this, Fühmann was part of a movement within the artistic community of the GDR which made a clear distinction between the 'real existing socialism' and the philosophical foundation of this society. He regarded the Marxist philosophical perspective on society as a true alternative to other conceptions of human civilisation and considered it a worthwhile cause – an understanding of Marxism that reflects the author's utopian thinking. However, this view was in conflict with the outlook of government officials on society. For this reason Fühmann reverted to myth in order to express his understanding of the future of humankind in the context of 'real existing socialism'. The author believed in the cathartic effect of reading literature and in the will of man to act 'with decency'.

Once Fühmann had decided that his approach to adapting myths would allow him to be unrestricted in his treatment of the numerous sources, he concluded that his favoured versions were Aeschylus' *Prometheus Desmotes* and Goethe's *Prometheus* poem along with the fragment of Goethe's *Prometheus* drama, because of their vitality and the positive forces represented by the Titan. By highlighting that humanity has to act in order to determine its own fate, the author brought his reading in line with the tradition favoured by the SED government. Fühmann did not take a purely historical outlook and undertook a further-reaching philosophical analysis of the foundations that determine the destiny of humankind.

## *Prometheus* – The Genealogy of Power and the Epitome of Hope

**Figure 2. The illustration depicts Kratos punishing his brother Bia to prove his loyalty to Zeus (Quevedo in Fühmann 1974: 195)**

It is one theme in particular that highlights the author's changing view of his society: the genealogy of power. Fühmann's description of this does not exclude the GDR and, in the posthumously published part II of the novel, he openly related his criticism of this tendency in human society to the reality of life in his country (1996). In *Prometheus: Battle of the Titans* (1974) no one is free under Zeus's rule but himself – yet his rule exudes a sense of justice whereas Chronos' exudes a sense of egotism. In the context of life in the GDR, Fühmann's interpretation of these power structures takes on another meaning: the idea that a new regime, though democratic in intention, can soon turn dogmatic and unjust reflects the author's doubts about any new leader's sincerity or even his own ability to rule justly. A potential comparison with the political strategies of the SED is possible, emphasised further when the reader discovers that Zeus uses his minions to spy on his brothers and sisters. Fühmann openly portrays the characters of these two brothers as resembling members of the GDR secret police. The adaptation is an attempt at describing in minute detail how power can corrupt and cause well-meaning leaders to manipulate and undeservedly punish others in order to stabilise their own power. Fühmann's poignant use of language is highlighted in the description of the characters. This table exemplifies how the attributes given to the three rules characterise their transformations.

| Kronos | Zeus | Prometheus |
|---|---|---|
| the Father | The Infant | Gaia's Favourite |
| The Strictest | the Conqueror | the awakening Titan |
| the One who rules alone | the unrestrained Ruler | the Dreamer |
| the Terrible | the Lout | the Creator |
| the Fallen | the Fool | the Blasphemer |

Table 1. This table exemplifies how the attributes given to the three rules characterises their transformations

In *Prometheus: Die Zeugung* [Prometheus: The Generation] even Prometheus cannot live up to his previously held ideal of leadership. Leipzig Germanist Jürgen Krätzer sums up the extent of the disillusionment symbolised in Prometheus' rule:

> The great fights have been fought, the ideals betrayed and the dreams dreamed: [...] even the Gods have to make do with this real existing triviality. [...] Incapacitation [in Prometheus' realm] leads to infantilisation and does not allow for development, the stagnant conflicts develop their own dynamics with suicidal consequences [.] (Krätzer 1996: 165)[40]

Issues like these were hardly ever touched upon in the public sphere of GDR literary life because they collided with the Marxist-Leninist theory of materialism. Further, they diverged from the concept of unbroken progress towards communist society and neglected the existence and influence of what researchers like C. G. Jung (1941; 2001), whom Fühmann drew on in his study of myths, called the 'soul' – human emotions, fears, predispositions that cannot be changed by the rules of a society.

A novel aspect of Fühmann's adaptation technique, particularly in view of the novel as a children's book, resides in the fact that in *Prometheus* the mythical heroes, which are often children (even by choice like Hermes), discover that they need to take their fate into their own hands and cannot rely on the mercy of distant gods. The child moves more and more into the focal point of the adaptation, not only as the envisaged reader but also as the main protagonist. At the same time Fühmann moves away from the use of Homeric stylistic idiosyncrasies in part II of *Prometheus* towards the contemporary language used by children; for example, the young goats – representative of children and a child-like way of thinking and speaking. The use of contemporary language indicates to the readers that the conflicts, emotions and ideas have moved closer to their own existence. They are not only expressed in the readers' language but also reflect the readers' reality. In the first volume of the novel, Fühmann had set out to reflect as closely as possible the language used in Homer's version of the myth. Yet he realised that to have an impact on today's children the characters must speak their language. In *Prometheus: The Creation*, the child-like characters are the ones that are the most current, progressive and lively, a fact that is clearly represented in their use of language. This table exemplifies the dramatic changes in the way in which characters speak and are described.

| Homeric stylistic features | Stylistic features directly addressing today's reader |
|---|---|
| Anaphora: 'Help us brothers! Help us sisters!' | 'Oh no, why do you let me snooze when finally there's something happening in this dull place?!' |
| Epithets: 'Prometheus – the one who sees the future' | 'Hey, this is sore, ouch!' |
| Allegories: 'her voice sounded like the sound of slowly falling rain' | 'Look at the big guy, dropping pieces of this stupid wall he's building... must even be too heavy for him.' |
| Asyndets: 'they grew out of the stumps of iron, of gold, of silver, of copper, of rock, of sand, of clay ...' | |
| Polysyndets: 'there were three giants... and each had one hundred arms and one hundred legs and fifty torsos and fifty heads ...' | |

**Table 2. Contrasting stylistic features**

Fühmann's *Prometheus* attributes a truly child-like nature to the Titan; in contrast to others, it focuses on the world-view of the child, which invariably has positive connotations and contrasts it to the world of adults in which the positive characteristics

**Figure 3. The illustration depicts young Prometheus looking into the future**
**(Quevedo in Fühmann 1974: 65)**

children embody rapidly vanish. The author – concurring with Carl Gustav Jung and Karl Kerényi's (1941) myth theory – depicted children as the epitome of hope for the survival of mankind. Prometheus, who cannot tolerate the slumbering existence of the other Titans, runs away to discover the world. In his world, Prometheus is the only one who bubbles over with an insatiable zest for life, laughs and cries out with happiness – something which is eventually prohibited by Chronos. Prometheus' laughter, which is not the laughter of sarcasm and vice, represents an allusion to his fate. He eventually disregards his duty, as dictated by Chronos, simply by desiring to experience life more intensely than his kinsfolk. It was his destiny to disregard the laws decreed by his ruler, and the novel states accordingly: 'He knew that Chronos had outlawed all of this but he simply could not act in any other way' (Fühmann 1974: 10).[41]

A further indication of the ground-breaking approach of this novel as an innovative, child-focussed reading is that the reader gets to know Zeus and all the other gods as babies and witnesses them growing up. Hermes is introduced as the god who is able to choose between the existence of an adult and a child, but favours going through his life as a child. Even in the animal kingdom it is the offspring, who personify happiness and joy. Fühmann alludes to the importance and otherness of the playfulness of children. According to Jung, Prometheus stands for a more light-hearted way of dealing with his surroundings; he is very closely related to the earth and to nature, he trusts in the potential of the future and actively takes part in shaping it (2001).

## Instigating Change by Giving Young Readers a Voice

**Figure 4. The illustration depicts Rhea hiding Zeus from Chronos in her mother, Gaia's, realm (Quevedo in Fühmann 1974: 43)**

*Prometheus* became a catalyst for the critical discussion of children's books in the GDR. The cultural-political context of the publication of *Prometheus* and subsequently the groundbreaking debate in 1975 on the adaptation and its illustrations by Nuria Quevedo in the *Beiträge zur Kinder- und Jugendliteratur* [Contributions to Children's and Youth Literature] sheds light on the complex and often contradictory relationship between artists, critics, cultural politicians and children as readers. In the early 1970s, reactions and approaches to publications of children's books in the public domain underwent a remarkable shift. Previously, literary criticism had been determined by a lack of transparency which meant that the public was not actively engaged in determining official interpretations of literary texts.[42] The task of literary criticism had been the selection of texts for the establishment of a literary-political and a literary-aesthetic canon. A cultural-political shift in 1971 marked the beginning of a short era when there was a thaw in the political climate which functioned as a stimulus for the emancipation of literature and provided scope for aesthetic concepts, sociological studies of literary criticism and the establishment of reception-based research projects. According to the revised cultural-political guidelines, the arts were to embrace the diversity of society and critically portray its ambiguities and contradictions. Expressions of this shift became visible in the fact that journals featured debates on cultural heritage and new approaches to reading literature, with a dialogue-like questioning that at times endorsed dissent (Ende 2005: 17).[43]

The way in which the debate on *Prometheus* was carried out in the leading GDR journal for children's literature, *Contributions to Children's and Youth Literature*, set new boundaries and generated fresh approaches to children as readers, as addressees of works of visual arts and as literary critics. It revealed a dramatic shift in the view of children from dependent to autonomous, from naïve to knowing, from imperceptive to intuitive. The debate brought to the fore the relation between visual arts and literary texts as well as the link between the history of twentieth century German literature and the history of modern art. Further, it made visible the pluralisation of literary and artistic traditions, methods of interpreting the correspondence of text and image, of tradition and current literary developments. Yet it also pointed to the fundamental conflicts between the government's need to control and the people's/artists' yearning for an open, productive dialogue.

The starting point for the debate was a letter to the editor by Julius Grau (1975: 37), who labelled himself an old cultural politician and representative of the dogmatic strand of GDR literary criticism. Gerhart Holtz-Baumert, editor-in-chief of the *Contributions*, printed this reaction to the publication of *Prometheus* and invited comments on the views aired by Julius Grau. He also drew attention to the form of such debates and highlighted the significance of the approach taken by children contributing to the debate:

> As opposed to Grau they give reasons for their disagreement and always express their lively interest in the illustrations. Apart from the issue of 'taste', which the children are naturally entitled to, their opinions pose crucial questions. We can learn a lot from them[.] (Holtz-Baumert 1975: 59; cf. infra)[44]

He thus called for a new culture of public debate that acknowledges the authors' as well as the readers' subjectivity. Grau criticised the depiction of the Greek gods in Quevedo's etchings as cool, crippled, pygmy-like beings (Grau 1975: 37). He demanded more beautiful and less uncompromising illustrations in the vein of Michelangelo's 'David'.[45] Grau neglected the children's ability and desire to relate to unusual images and claimed that Quevedo's figures lie outside the children's imagination and emotions.

Fühmann's reply drew attention to the mention of the supposed missing link between the illustrations and the literary text in Grau's scathing review (Fühmann 1975: 38). Observing children's reactions during readings, he had noticed that it was a challenge for young readers to make the connection between text and images, which he considered the most desirable and productive impact of a book. He added that Quevedo fully achieved her aim of placing the ancient and eternally new aspects of myths in the world of today's children and contested the call for a censor (ibid.: 39). Quevedo herself commented that 'coarse laughter' was an essential characteristic of ancient Greek culture, which she found represented in the depictions of gods in classical antiquity (Quevedo 1975: 40).[46] She stated that illustrating *Prometheus* was a challenge since she attempted to influence children's imagination and emotions in an essentially entertaining way.

Apart from identifying *Prometheus* as an outstanding children's book in which text and illustrations are humorous, archaic, original and energetic, other contributors took the debate onto the level of cultural policy. Fred Rodrian, editor-in-chief of the Kinderbuchverlag, highlighted that Quevedo reset the boundaries of book illustration for children (ibid.: 43). Her images supported new habits of perception in children and, importantly, in adults. Rulo Melchert, a literary critic, indicated that Quevedo's etchings convey a strong sense of realism and promote a 'naïve' approach to an image (ibid.: 46). He described her etchings as bizarre and highly satirical and claimed that they demonstrate that the world in *Prometheus* is not beautiful and pure in the classical sense. Melchert called for changes to the literary criticism of children's books, which would include illustrations. He advocated the turning away from a schematic and mechanical interpretation of children's literature. In view of the bias of cultural politicians, he emphasised that a degree of criticism does not mean total rejection but an active engagement with the issues (ibid.: 47).

Thomas Schleusing, a graphic artist, pointed out that more tolerance was needed towards graphic images as subjective as Quevedo's and that children's creative expression was often discouraged because a strict, schematic way of looking at their work was adopted in schools. He called for a change to the school curriculum with more scope for 'art education' as opposed to teaching 'drawing techniques', in order to provoke a better understanding of the diversity of forms of expression (ibid.: 52).

The journal lists a selection of eight letters by children between the ages of eleven and fifteen. Many described their first impressions as a combination of aversion and a feeling of curiosity, since the proportions somehow appear incorrect (Dressel 1975: 54).[47] They had difficulty relating to the portrayal of the gods' bodies. Jürgen wrote that he did not know why the artist decided to draw the gods with legs that are too short, since he could not find any explanation for this in the text (Auge referring to Fühmann 1974: 32). He did not reject the illustrations and was most impressed by the representation of the battle of the Titans (ibid.: 103), a terrifying image in which the characters appeared transparent (Auge 1975: 55).[48]

Some children would have preferred more colour in the illustrations. Others enjoyed the effects of the contrast between shades of black and white, and the light and dark tones of just one colour. Jeanette thought that colourful pictures tend to go with fairy tales but not with myths (Niendorf 1975: 58). Many stated that the pictures corresponded with the text (Dressel, 1975: 54). Some were disappointed that Quevedo had not illustrated the scenes they found most important and even made suggestions for possible illustrations. Jürgen (1975: 54) mentioned that he thought Chronos was portrayed as taller than the other gods because of his position as the ruler (Auge referring to Fühmann 1974: 32). Others identified landscape as an important feature but found Quevedo's landscapes too barren, although the narrator does mention a beautiful forest with birds singing in it (Stangel 1975: 57). Overall, the letters indicate that the children, who analysed the illustrations attentively, looked for familiarity and realism but were at the same time prepared to relate to these unusual, bizarre images.

The children's views represent a reversal of the process pedagogues assumed would happen; because Quevedo produced such – for children's books – atypical etchings, the children did not only look for the connection between the illustrations and the text but were also led towards a deeper understanding of the novel. Although they found it hard to accept unfamiliar forms of expression, these very honest, objective and thorough critics, made the link between the text and the image most pointedly. The call for scope for individual interpretations of visual images and texts clearly reflects the demand made in many public debates in the 1970s – the official acceptance of the fact that every citizen, child or adult, has the ability and the right to develop his or her individual way of interpreting works of art as well as to express views publicly. In writing *Prometheus,* Fühmann established that works of art from the past can only be adapted by developing individual approaches and readings. The reactions to his novel confirm this fact and go even further by asking for reform to the education system and the school curriculum. By instigating such a debate in the sphere of children's literature, *Prometheus* transcended this field doubly: it became reading material for adults but, more importantly, taught adults new lessons about the young audience's reading habits and approaches to works of art.

## Conclusion

This investigation into adapting the myth of Prometheus for children in the GDR has uncovered the multi-faceted, contradictory nature of the country's literary sphere and aimed at overcoming over-politicised evaluations of its children's literature. It has confirmed that writing an adaptation of this canonical myth for a state-initiated publishing project was shaped by the conflict between the socialist regime's idealistic objectives and its inclination to methodically supervise and control children's literature. Franz Fühmann, the most prolific and versatile contributor to this project, went beyond the objectives of the project's initiators in that he experimented with literary themes, poetic styles and reflections upon central questions of Marxist-Leninist philosophy, along with their reali-sation in GDR society. Thus he ended up re-evaluating the ideal of a socialist utopia. Fühmann's most celebrated contribution, the novel *Prometheus* (1974) for children, exemplifies the shift from unequivocal assent to the translation of Marxist-Leninist ideology into literature to a steadily deepening rift between many artists' convictions and the reality of life in the GDR. Whereas the state had set ideology as the main creative category, many artists' response to this overwhelming emphasis on ideology was to high-light its inadequacy and to bring the non-rational, represented by myths, back into play. Fühmann's mythical novel is an example of many GDR artists' approach to adopting myths that was in stark contrast to officially prescribed directives for appropriating cultural heritage. In the artists' view, myth became an essentially artistic matter, the

**Figure 5. The illustration depicts Poseidon racing across the seas
(Quevedo in Fühmann 1974: 238)**

antithesis of ideology. Fühmann's verdict on the state of human society as exemplified by *Prometheus* led to the relative weighting of assenting and dissenting tendencies eventually to tip in favour of dissent. Yet the inter-relationship of these aspects resulted in an essentially new reading of the myth, diverging from its traditional interpretative patterns and making children the central characters with the potential to change the world.

## Bibliography

Auge, J. 1975. 'Prometheus so?', in: *Beiträge zur Kinder- und Jugendliteratur* 36: 55-56.

Barck, S., M. Langermann & S. Lokatis. 1997. *Jedes Buch ein Abenteuer: Zensur-System und literarische Öffentlichkeiten in der DDR bis Ende der sechziger Jahre*. Berlin: Akademie-Verlag.

Becher, J.R. 1981. 'Von der Größe unserer Literatur', in: Becher, J.R. *Gesammelte Werke*. Vol. 18, *Publizistik 1952-1958*. Berlin: Aufbau, 499-534.

Dressel, P. 1975. 'Prometheus so?', in: *Beiträge zur Kinder- und Jugendliteratur* 36: 54.

Ende, D. 2005. 'Zur Neuprofilierung der *Weimarer Beiträge* Anfang der siebziger Jahre', in: *Weimarer Beiträge* 1: 5-40.

Emmrich, Ch. (ed.) 1979. *Literatur für Kinder und Jugendliche in der DDR*. Berlin: Kinderbuchverlag.

Fühmann, F. 1993. 'Das mythische Element in der Literatur', in: Fühmann, F. Vol. 8, *Essays: Gespräche: Aufsätze 1964-1981*. Rostock: Hinstorff Verlag, 82-140.

Fühmann, F. 1960. 'Letter to Schneider/DEFA-Trickfilmstudio', in: Stiftung Archiv der Akademie der Künste Berlin-Brandenburg. Franz-Fühmann-Archiv, Sign.: 101, 28 January 1960.

Fühmann, F. 1974. *Prometheus: Die Titanenschlacht*. Berlin: Kinderbuchverlag.

Fühmann, F. 1975. 'Prometheus so?', in: *Beiträge zur Kinder- und Jugendliteratur* 36: 38-39.

Fühmann, F. 1993. *Essays: Gespräche: Aufsätze*. Rostock: Hinstorff.

Fühmann, F. 1996. *Prometheus: Die Zeugung*. Rostock: Hinstorff.

Fühmann, F. 'Libussa Korrespondenz', in: Stiftung Archiv der Akademie der Künste Berlin-Brandenburg, Franz-Fühmann-Archiv, Sign.: 23.

Fühmann, F. 'Prometheus, Vorarbeiten', in: Stiftung Archiv der Akademie der Künste Berlin-Brandenburg, Franz-Fühmann-Archiv, Sign.: 98.

Grau, J. 1975. 'Prometheus so?', in *Beiträge zur Kinder- und Jugendliteratur* 36: 37.

Große, A. (ed.) 1970. 'Probleme der sozialistischen Rezeption des Erbes: Ein Rundtischgespräch', in: *Weimarer Beiträge* 2: 11-39.

Große, A. (ed.) 1971a. 'Lebendiges Erbe', in: *Weimarer Beiträge* 8: 5-10.

Große, A. (ed.) 1971b. 'Traditionsbeziehungen unserer Schriftsteller: Antworten auf eine Umfrage der Redaktion', in: *Weimarer Beiträge* 12: 89-103.

Haase, H. (ed.) 1976. *Literatur der DDR*. Berlin: Volk und Wissen.

Heinze, B. (ed.) 1998. *Franz Fühmann: Eine Biografie in Bildern, Dokumenten und Briefen*. Rostock: Hinstorff.

Hohendahl, P-U. (ed.) 1974. *Literaturkritik und Öffentlichkeit*. München: Piper.

Holtz-Baumert, G. 1975. 'Prometheus so?', in: *Beiträge zur Kinder- und Jugendliteratur* 36: 59.

Jung, C.G. 2001. *Archetypen*. München: dtv.

Jung, C.G. & K. Kerényi. 1941. *Einführung in das Wesen der Mythologie*. Amsterdam: Pantheon.

Kerényi, K. 1956. *Prometheus: Die menschliche Existenz in griechischer Dichtung*. Hamburg: Rowohlt.

Krätzer, J. 1996. 'Mythologie als Kammerspiel', in: *Neue Deutsche Literatur* 4: 163-165.

Krüger, B. (ed.) 2003. *Dichter sein heißt aufs Ganze aus sein: Zugänge zu Poetologie und Werk Franz Fühmanns*. Frankfurt a.M.: Lang.

Löffler, D., E-M. Scherf, D. Sommer & A. Walter. 1978. *Funktion und Wirkung: Soziologische Untersuchungen zur Literatur und Kunst*. Berlin: Aufbau.

Melchert, R. 1975. 'Prometheus so?', in: *Beiträge zur Kinder- und Jugendliteratur* 36: 46-47.

Niendorf, J. 1975. 'Prometheus so?', in: *Beiträge zur Kinder- und Jugendliteratur* 36: 57-58.

O'Dell, F.A. (1978). *Socialisation through Children's Literature: The Soviet Example*. Cambridge: CUP.

Quevedo, N. 1975. 'Prometheus so?', in: *Beiträge zur Kinder- und Jugendliteratur* 36: 40.

Richter, K. 1996. 'Kinderliteratur und Kinderliteraturforschung der ehemaligen DDR', in: Dolle-Weinkauff, B. & H.-H. Ewers (eds), *Theorien der Jugendlektüre: Beiträge zur Kinder- und Jugendliteraturkritik seit Heinrich Wolgast*. München: Weinheim, 191-209.

Riedel, V. 1980. 'Franz Fühmanns *Prometheus*', in: *Weimarer Beiträge* 2: 73-96.

Rodrian, F. 1975. 'Prometheus so?', in: *Beiträge zur Kinder- und Jugendliteratur* 36: 59.

Rolfes, B. 2005. *Helden(bilder) im Wandel: die Nibelungenhelden in neueren Adaptionen der Kinder- und Jugendliteratur*. Baltmannsweiler: Schneider-Verlag Hohengehren.

Sauter, J.-H. 1971. 'Interview mit Franz Fühmann', in: *Weimarer Beiträge* 1: 33-53.

Schleusing, T. 1975. 'Prometheus so?', in: *Beiträge zur Kinder- und Jugendliteratur* 36: 52-53.

Schmidt, U. 1991. 'Abschied von der "Literaturgesellschaft"?', in: Arnold, H.-L. (ed.), *Text + Kritik. Sonderband: Literatur in der DDR*. Munich: text + kritik, 45-52.

Seehase, I. 1969. 'Libussa Korrespondenz', in: Stiftung Archiv der Akademie der Künste Berlin-Brandenburg, Franz-Fühmann-Archiv, Sign.: 23.

Shelley, P.B. 1820. *Prometheus unbound. A lyrical drama in four acts. With other poems*. London: C. & J. Ollier.

Stangel, I. 1975. 'Prometheus so?', in: *Beiträge zur Kinder- und Jugendliteratur* 36: 56-57.

Steinlein, R. & T. Kramer. 1999. 'Überlegungen zu einem Projekt "Handbuch zur Kinder- und Jugendliteratur der SBZ/DDR 1945-1990"', in: *Zeitschrift für Germanistik* 3: 153-161.

Thomson-Wohlgemuth, G. 2007. *Translation under state control: The production and rewriting of books for young people in the German Democratic Republic (1961-1989)*. Guildford: University of Surrey.

von Goethe, J.W. 1990. *Prometheus*. Weimar: Nationale Forschungs- und Gedenkstätten der klassischen deutschen Literatur.

Wild, H. de 2003. *Bibliographie der Sekundärliteratur zu Franz Fühmann*. Frankfurt a.M.: Peter Lang.

# Notes

1.  The German abbreviation is DDR which stands for Deutsche Demokratische Republik.

2.  This type of society reflects the principles of a community which Siegfried Lokatis labels 'Erziehungsstaat', where all members of one society are considered equal in the sense that they are deemed to be in need of the same continuous instruction. All translations of quotations in this study are my own. All quotations in German have been translated for ease of access. The original extracts can be found in the endnotes.

3.  [d]em sowjetischen Modell folgend, wurde die Produktion von Kinderbüchern im 'Erziehungsstaat' DDR als besonders wichtig angesehen

4.  The term 'sozialistische Persönlichkeit' derives from the GDR educational policy of the Ulbricht-era in the 1960s. Officials used this term in order to summarise the objectives of education in the GDR. According to this concept, all children were to be brought up in a way that would enable them to feel deeply rooted in socialist society and to conceive of themselves as part of the great communist movement.

5.  Kinder und Jugendliche zu aktiven und verantwortlichen Mitgliedern der sozialistischen Gesellschaft erziehen zu helfen

6.  ein lange währender, freiwillig geteilter und getragener Grundkonsens der meisten am Kinder- und Jugendliteratur-Diskurs Beteiligten

7.  ließ eine nicht-systemkonforme oder zumindest kompatible Literatur nur unter außerordentlich erschwerten [...] Bedingungen oder aber im Zusammenhang 'anerkannter' (weil z.B. nicht mehr zu unterdrückender oder marginalisierender) Abweichungen/Dissidenz zu

8.  Gaby Thomson-Wohlgemuth's work *Translation under state control* (2007) on the production and rewriting of books for young people in the GDR gives a different perspective on this issue.

9.  The two publishers Kinderbuchverlag and Verlag Neues Leben were assigned the task of realising this project.

10. This list of the titles published as part of the project highlights the wide range of stories and traditions that authors attempted to cover:

    Fühmann, F. 1964. *Reineke Fuchs*. Berlin: Kinderbuchverlag.

    Fühmann, F.1968. *Das hölzerne Pferd: Die Sage vom Untergang Trojas und von den Irrfahrten des Odysseus*. Berlin: Verlag Neues Leben.

    Fühmann, F. 1968. *Shakespeare-Märchen*. Berlin: Kinderbuchverlag.

    Fühmann, F. 1971. *Das Nibelungenlied*. Berlin: Verlag Neues Leben.

    Fühmann, F. 1974. *Prometheus: Die Titanenschlacht*. Berlin: Kinderbuchverlag.

    Heiduczek, W. 1974. *Die seltsamen Abenteuer des Parzival*. Berlin: Verlag Neues Leben.

    Hermlin, S. 1974. *Die Argonauten*. Berlin: Kinderbuchverlag.

    Hüttner, H. 1975. *Beowulf*. Berlin: Kinderbuchverlag.

    De Bruyn, G. 1975. *Tristan und Isolde*. Berlin: Verlag Neues Leben.

    Meinck, W. 1976. *Das Ramayana*. Berlin: Verlag Neues Leben.

    Nowotny, J. 1976. *Die Gudrunsage*. Berlin: Kinderbuchverlag.

    Kreißig, H. 1976. *Der steinerne Mann und andere Erzählungen aus dem Orient*. Berlin: Kinderbuchverlag.

    Ruika-Franz, V. 1976. *Der Recke im Tigerfell: Eine alte Geschichte aus Georgien*. Berlin: Kinderbuchverlag.

    Hermlin, S., H. Hüttner, S. Kirsch, H. Kreißig, & J. Nowotny. 1977. *Sagen und Epen der Welt neu erzählt*. Berlin: Kinderbuchverlag.

    Schneider, R. 1978. *Die Abenteuer des Herakles*. Berlin: Verlag Neues Leben.

    Fries, F.R. 1979. *Verbannung und Sieg des Ritters Cid aus Bivar*. Berlin: Kinderbuchverlag.

    Hüttner, H. 1979. Herakles: *Die zwölf Abenteuer*. Berlin: Kinderbuchverlag.

    Holtz-Baumert, G. 1984. *Daidalos und Ikaros*. Berlin: Kinderbuchverlag.

    Hüttner, H. 1987. *Der Dank der Götter*. Berlin: Kinderbuchverlag.

    Heiduczek, W. 1989. *Orpheus und Eurydike*. Berlin: Kinderbuchverlag.

    Fühmann, F. 1996. *Prometheus: Die Zeugung*. Rostock: Hinstorff.

11. [Sie] ist in dem Sinne nützlich, da sie unseren Kindern in der Gegenwart eine Vorstellung von den Erfahrungen der Menschen in der Vergangenheit vermittelt. Sie schützt die Kinder davor, sich von politischen Problemen abzuwenden und sich in eine Ersatzrealität zu fliehen[.]

12. One characteristic of the publishing project was that many authors, who had not written a children's book before, became involved in this programme in the early 1970s in particular. This was a time when these well known writers, who could not publish their books for adults due to severe censorship, began contributing to the children's literature project.

13. die Historisierung des Mythos und seine Umwandlung in Poesie in der sozialistischen Literatur über die Adaption, d.h. über die Angleichung an die Erfordernisse unserer sozialistischen Gesellschaft [erfolgt]

14.   a) Verdeutlichung des Rationalen innerhalb des Phantastisch-Wunderbaren, b) Aufdecken der sozialen Kausalität, c) Nachweisen der zeitgegebenen Stufe des Humanen

15.   Für die Adaptionstechnik Franz Fühmanns ist z.b. eine Methode der Mythenbearbeitung charakteristisch, die den Schicksalsbegriff materialisiert.

16.   This position was one reason why contributions to the project won critical acclaim in the public domain. Yet the socio-critical potential regarding the GDR itself was not recognised by many of the cultural administrators.

17.   Die sich in den siebziger Jahren immer mehr vertiefenden und weltliterarisch ausweitenden Anstrengungen der sozialistischen Gesellschaft um die Erschließung großer mythenbildender Epochen der Menschheitsgeschichte verdeutlichen: Der Sozialismus […] kann die alten Mythen als Erbe aufheben und als Kunst gebrauchen, als Poesie für die neue Kunst. Die historisch-materialistische Methode ermöglicht, den Bezug der Mythen zur Geschichte zu erkennen und sie selbst als Produkte uralten, phantastisch-volkstümlichen Bewußtseins, als Abbilder einer magisch-ganzheitlichen Welt ebenso wie konfliktreicher Klassengesellschaften in mehrfacher künstlerischer Brechung zu erkennen und zu begreifen[.]

18.   die Darstellung gesellschaftlicher, und darum in der Realität immer als historisch konkret erscheinender Prozesse als elementarer

19.   Natur- und Sozialwesen

20.   Die Kindheit als 'der Ort, wo Poesie und Prosa aufeinanderstoßen, und zwar tragisch' – lieber Doktor, mit diesem Satz haben Sie meine Arbeiten exakt und vollständig auf einen Nenner gebracht.

21.   Natürlich beginnen die Brechungen schon in der Kinderzeit, Brechungen zweifacher Art. […] Man erfährt zum Beispiel, daß die Erwachsenen anders sind, als man sie sehen und nehmen soll. Aber man erfährt, daß sie auch anders sind, als man sie sehen und nehmen will.

22.   das Ganze [zu] erzählen. Fühmann, F. 1960. 'Reineke Fuchs, letter to Schneider/DEFA-Trickfilmstudio, 28 January 1960', in Stiftung Archiv der Akademie der Künste Berlin-Brandenburg, Franz-Fühmann-Archiv, Sign.: 101.

23.   This approach is problematic in that it discounts all previous oral and lost printed or handwritten versions of a traditional story.

24.   Das Original ist die Grundsubstanz, die ich mich bemühe, in meiner Arbeit spürbar zu machen, inhaltlich natürlich, aber auch formal. Ich glaube, daß ich mich gerade hierin von manchem Nacherzähler unterscheide.

25.   See Johann Wolfgang von Goethe, *Reineke Fuchs* (Frankfurt a.M.: Insel, 1975).

26.   'Thersites erzählt von Prometheus'. Fühmann had read Karl K. 1956. *Prometheus: Die menschliche Existenz in griechischer Dichtung*. Hamburg: Rowohlt, 60-66.

27.   [Er] führt verschiedene Überlieferungsstränge zusammen, was sogar zu einer dem Anliegen entgegengesetzte[n] Aussage führen kann.

28.   The children's book remained unfinished. The more than 10 000 pages Fühmann produced for this adaptation are kept in the Franz-Fühmann-Archiv at the Akademie der Künste Berlin-Brandenburg.

29. Fühmann referred to Václav, V. von Tomek (ed.) 1859. *Die Grüneberger Handschrift: Zeugnisse über die Auffindung des 'Libusin soud'*: zusammengestellt von W.W. Tomek: Aus der böhmischen Museumszeitschrift übersetzt von Jakob Malej und Václav Vladivoj Tomek. Prague: published by the museum. A further source was Grigorovitza, E. 1901. *Libussa in der deutschen Literatur*. Berlin: Duncker.

30. Ingrid Seehase comments on Fühmann's draft, on 24 January 1969. She posits that the new approach to eliminate all interpretations of the saga could only be realised by the author in a socialist society, since the socialist attitude to the cultural heritage allowed the search for an entirely new and unaffected reading of traditional stories. As Fühmann proves in his analysis of the function of mythological stories, no interpretation of such a story can be considered as *the* true or only valid interpretation, it is defined by the circumstances it was produced under [emphasis added].

31. Man will zum Kern der Sage stoßen, an den man sich getrost halten kann. Aber mit diesem Vorsatz ist man in der Lage Peer Gynts. Auf der Suche nach dem Ursprung eines Mythologems werden wir immer nur auf Fassungen stoßen[.]

32. [von] einer grandiosen Auflehnung, [von] einer konservativen Rebellion und [dem] unerhört[en] Pathos der Kämpfe gegen die Perser [erzählt]

33. von dem, der den Fluch über die Menschen gebracht hat, […] der schlauer sein wollte als die Macht, der […] die Kunst des Betrügens [beherrschte]

34. politische Tugenden, die ihnen erst [später] von den Göttern gewährt wurden

35. eine Kabinettsintrige unter Herrschenden. Beide Seiten sind gleichermaßen vorgekommen. [Seine Geschichte] ist eine Skandalchronik

36. Also was: der unerhörte Rebell, der unerwünschte Krummdenker, der Konsumideologe, der Angehörige eines verrotteten Duodezregimes?

37. wenn man mythische Geschichten erzählt, bloß weil sie die Alten erzählt, so fehlt der Zweck des Neuen. […] Soll etwas nicht Übersetzung sein, so muß es für uns einen Zweck haben.

38. eine Sache der Parteinahme par excellence

39. Mythos ist das, was umgeformt worden ist, damit es lebe. In diesem Sinn [verbindet sich] Mythos [mit] Marxismus.

40. Die großen Kämpfe sind ausgefochten, die Ideale verraten und die Träume ausgeträumt: […] selbst die olympischen Götter haben sich in diese real existierende Banalität dreinzuschicken. […] Entmündigung [in Prometheus' Reich] führt zur Infantilisierung und läßt Entwicklung nicht zu, die gestockten Widersprüche entwickeln eine Eigendynamik von (selbst)mörderischer Konsequenz[.]

41. Er wußte, daß Kronos dies alles verboten hatte, allein er konnte einfach nicht anders.

42. The term 'transparency' is my attempt at an adequate translation of the German term 'Öffentlichkeit', which Hohendahl (1974) used to define degrees of public awareness of societal processes. It refers to the actual involvement as well as significance of the readership in the course of determining officially approved interpretations of literary texts.

43.  The journal *Weimarer Beiträge* published a series of debates on the issue of the cultural heritage of the GDR. See the debates edited by Große (1970: 11-39); (1971a: 5-10) and (1971b: 89-103).

44.  Im Unterschied zu Grau begründen sie ablehnende Haltungen und äußern stets ihr genaues Interesse an den Illustrationen. Über den mehrfach zitierten »Geschmack« hinaus, den selbstverständlich auch Kinder in Anspruch nehmen können, werfen diese Kindermeinungen eine Reihe bedeutender Fragen auf. […] Da wäre auch für unsere Diskussion viel zu lernen[.]

45.  The image that accompanies Grau's letter is the least controversial of Quevedo's illustrations and depicts the scene when Apollo meets Aphrodite (Fühmann 1974: 137).

46.  derbes Lachen

47.  The illustration depicts the scene in which Rhea presents Chronos with her first baby. The image is reproduced here (Fühmann 1974: 32).

48.  The illustration depicts the 'Hundertarmigen' [the ones with one hundred arms], fierce and powerful monsters, the Titan's brothers, whom Chronos controls with his Belt of Gravity.

# PART 2

# SOCIO-CULTURAL ASPECTS OF

# ADAPTATION

# 'A translation far worse'

## Canonisation and Adaptation in the Early Dutch and English Translations of the Brothers Grimm's *Kinder- und Hausmärchen*

### Vanessa Joosen

In critical as well as popular discourse, adaptations are often treated with disdain: they always come second, and '[t]he idea of fidelity [...] is often what drives any directly comparative method of study' between the source and the adaptation (Hutcheon 2006: xiii). Does the adaptation remain true to the original, that is, does it faithfully reproduce the content, style and 'spirit' of the first work? The history of fairy tales, however, thrives on imitations and adaptations, and ideal standards of originality, purity and faithfulness are more likely to produce frustration than insight in the study of this genre. If we assume that today's most popular fairy tales have their roots in oral tradition, then any original is beyond retrieval. There are no 'firsts', only seconds, thirds, fourths and so on.[1] And if we compare older versions of tales such as 'Sleeping Beauty' and 'Little Red Riding Hood', it turns out that the former was impregnated by her prince charming during her sleep (in Giambattista Basile's tale), and the other died in the stomach of the wolf (in Charles Perrault's version). It is clear that adaptation has been vital for the inclusion of these tales in the canon of children's literature.[2] This article departs from the question of what role adaptation has played in the international dissemination of the Brothers Grimm's *Kinder- und Hausmärchen* ([Children's and Household Tales],1812-1857) in the early nineteenth century. I will discuss the divergent selection and translation strategies of the first Dutch and English translations of the Grimm tales and consider their role in the equally divergent reception of these two works.

### 'A translation far worse' (Jacob Grimm)

The first Dutch collection of Grimm tales appeared in 1820 under the title *Sprookjes-boek voor kinderen* [Fairy-Tale Book for Children] with G.A. Diederichs from Amsterdam, a publisher specialised in German literature. Three years later *German Popular Stories* came out, the first and initially anonymous English translation of a selection of Grimm's fairy tales. It would later be revealed that they were translated by Edgar Taylor, in cooperation with David Jardine.[3] In 1824, Jacob Grimm mentioned the two translations in a letter to his friend Karl Hartwig Gregor von Meusebach. In comparison to the English translation, which he had received from Taylor a year before, Jacob Grimm called the Dutch version 'a translation far worse' (cited in Van de Zijpe 1975: 168). Readers and critics apparently agreed with Jacob Grimm. *Fairy-Tale Book for Children* received an extremely negative review in the leading critical journal from the Netherlands, *Vaderlandsche Letteroefeningen* ([Exercises in National Literature], 1821):

> With respect to the highly intellectual *German* publishers and book critics, and the most learned, but linguistically not very capable *Dutch* translator also, we have not for a long time held a more foolish little book with more repulsive illustrations in our hands. Some farm woman from *Nieder-Zwehrn* put the most and most beautiful (!) fairy tales in their heads! Maybe we do not understand the elevated purpose of these stunningly beautiful curiosities; but this we know, that the brains and quiet sleep of our sweet little ones are too dear to us than that we should ever expose both to the fear-imposing impression of such ghostly illustrations and red-riding-hood, bluebeardlike tales. (Anonymous 1821: 46; emphasis in original)[4]

Moreover, *Fairy-Tale Book for Children* also proved hard to sell (Van de Zijpe 1975: 178). The second volume that the preface announced never appeared. The book was probably reprinted only once, half a century later, under the title *Sprookjes uit de nalatenschap van Moeder de Gans* ([Fairy tales from the Legacy of Mother Goose], Grimm 1870). This second edition will be briefly discussed in the conclusion of my article.

The first English translation, in contrast, was received with the greatest enthusiasm. 'The immediate success of *German Popular Stories* as a best-seller can be measured by the fact that it was reissued in the same year, and was then reprinted a third and fourth time in 1824 and 1825', writes Martin Sutton (1996: 9).[5] A second volume of tales appeared in 1826, and both volumes were reprinted in 1839 in the highly prolific collection *Gammer Grethel* (Alderson 1993: 67). Taylor's translation is still available in the Puffin edition of *Grimm's Fairy Tales* today (Grimm 1994). Already with their first translation, the Grimm tales seemed secured of a place in the English canon of children's literature, whereas in Dutch their introduction went rather unnoticed. How can the divergent reactions in these geographically and linguistically close countries be explained?

There are extra-textual features from which Edgar Taylor benefited when *German Popular Stories* appeared. Although Gillian Lathey notes 'an excitement across Europe' in the early nineteenth century 'at the innovative and imaginative change of direction taken by writers of the German Romantic movement' (2010: 82), the interest in Romantic literature, German literature and fantasy appears to have been substantially larger in England than in the Netherlands. If David Blamires writes that in the United Kingdom 'the time was certainly ripe' (2006: 165), it is clear that in the Netherlands it was not yet so: 'with some exceptions, there was a rather resentful attitude towards the boundary crossings on various levels that were advocated by Romanticism' (Van den Berg & Couttenier 2009: 21).[6] The review from *Exercises in National Literature* certainly illustrates the resentment of the folk spirit, when it describes the idealised Dorothea Viehmann as 'some farm woman from *Nieder-Zwehrn*', and the reviewer's concern about the sleep of small children signals his scepticism of the scary, sinister stories that were so highly valued by Romanticism. In this review, fantasy is equaled with nonsense. Taylor's translation, in contrast, 'met a growing interest among the English reading-public of the time in the fantasy world of folk- and fairy-tale' (Sutton 1996: 9). In terms of translated literature, Willem van den Berg and Piet Couttenier also describe a growing interest in the Netherlands in English literature and culture at the beginning of the nineteenth century, more than in French or German books (2009: 31). Blamires notes the reverse in England, considering Taylor's translations to be 'part of the growing English interest in German literature and culture' (2006: 165) to which there seems no direct counterpart in the Dutch language area. As for children's literature, Dutch children's books lay under the strong influence of philanthropic, Enlightenment-inspired pedagogues at the beginning of the nineteenth century – they were averse to fairy tales, and had a strong influence on what children were allowed to read (Buijnsters & Buijnsters-Smets 2001: 15; 19). Although fairy tales were circulating – often anonymously – they would generally remain considered unsuitable reading material for children until several decades after the first Grimm translation appeared.

Although the literary and cultural context must have been a decisive factor in determining the contrasting successes of the two translations, there are additional textual factors that would have reinforced these books' potential attraction (in Taylor's case) or lack of it (as for the Dutch version). In what follows, I will therefore shed light on how the divergent reception of the first Dutch and English translations of Grimm's fairy tales can also be explained by the content, style and implied audience of the books themselves.

## Adapting Adaptations

Both the first Dutch and English translations are based on the same source text: the 1819 edition of the *Children's and Household Tales*, a two-volume collection of 161 tales and nine legends.[7] This edition was already an adaptation to at least the second degree in its own right. The Grimms had not invented their tales themselves, but borrowed and adapted them from oral and written sources (see a.o. Rölleke 2000; Zipes 2002). Inevitably, some form of adaptation took place at this stage, especially since several stories were presented in multiple variants, and the Grimms used the process of 'contamination' to combine these into one printed tale.[8] Wilhelm Grimm continued to revise the tales, fine-tuning the so-called Gattung Grimm or typical Grimm style. There are some striking differences between the first and second editions of the *Children's and Household Tales*, such as the infamous deletion of Rapunzel's pregnancy and the replacement of Snow White's malicious mother with a stepmother. The 1819 version of the 'Frog Prince', a tale which will be discussed in detail below, was a combination of two tales in the 1812 edition, 'The Frog Prince' and 'The Frog King' (Zipes 2009: 90). Wilhelm Grimm's alterations were motivated by the discovery of new variants, by the wish to make the collection more coherent, and by an effort to appeal to a younger audience and their parents (see a.o. Rölleke 2000; Kamenetsky 1992).

Ruth Bottigheimer warns against the 'very human tendency to project the experience of the present onto the past, that is, to graft the extraordinarily broad twentieth-century acceptance of the [*Children's and Household Tales*] onto its nineteenth-century reception' (1993: 80). Her research of letters and sales figures indicates that in the early years, the Brothers Grimm's fairy-tale collection did not sell well at all times. Although the sales of the first volume were reasonably good, the second volume of the first edition was 'a publishing flop' and the second edition of 1819 sold even less (ibid.: 83-84).[9] The early German reactions to the Grimm tales 'were mixed at best and heartlessly critical at worst' (ibid.: 79).[10] Maria Tatar points out that 'the Grimms waited in vain for reviews from such luminaries as Goethe' while minor scholars in the field 'seized the chance to get even' after the Grimms had written highly critical reviews of their work (2003: 15). This initial lack of enthusiasm for the Grimm tales in both German and Dutch raises the question all the more urgently of what made Taylor and Jardine's translation so successful. Selection and adaptation prove to be two important factors.

## Selection of Tales

The German Grimm collection of 1819 contains a great variety of tales: animal tales, comic anecdotes, royal tales, legends, and so forth. Some only consist of a few lines, others go on for pages. A few are in dialect, others have a high, formal register. Both the Dutch and English translations present only a small selection of the 170 stories from 1819. There are 31 tales included in English and 20 in Dutch:

| Dutch 1820 | | English (Taylor) 1823 | |
|---|---|---|---|
| 1. | The Frog Prince | 1. | Hans in Luck |
| 2. | Mary's Child | 2. | The Travelling Musicians |
| 3. | The Ungrateful Son | 3. | The Golden Bird |
| 4. | The Son Who Wanted to Travel | 4. | The Fisherman and his Wife |
| 5. | The Four Artful Brothers | 5. | Tom-Tit and the Bear |
| 6. | The Six Servants | 6. | The Twelve Dancing Princesses |
| 7. | The Water of Life | 7. | Rose-Bud (Briar Rose) |
| 8. | Fairy Tale of One Who Could Not Be Scared | 8. | Tom Thumb |
| 9. | The Little Earthmen | 9. | The Grateful Beasts |
| 10. | The Magic Coat | 10. | Jorinda and Joringel |
| 11. | The Young Giant | 11. | The Wonderful Musician |
| 12. | The Singing, Springing Lark | 12. | The Queen Bee |
| 13. | The Merry tale of Little Frits and his Fiddle | 13. | The Dog and the Sparrow |
| 14. | The Good Sale | 14. | Frederick and Catherine |
| 15. | The Crows | 15. | The Three Children of Fortune |
| 16. | Faithful John | 16. | King Grisley-Beard |
| 17. | The Twelve Brothers | 17. | The Adventures of Chanticleer and Partlet |
| 18. | The White Snake | 18. | Snow-Drop |
| 19. | The Queen Bee | 19. | The Elves and the Shoemaker |
| 20. | Doctor Know-it-all | 20. | The Turnip |
| | | 21. | Old Sultan |
| | | 22. | The Lady and the Lion |

| Dutch 1820 | English (Taylor) 1823 |
|---|---|
| | 23. The Miser in the Bush |
| | 24. The King of the Golden Mountain |
| | 25. The Golden Goose |
| | 26. Mrs Fox |
| | 27. Hansel and Gretel |
| | 28. The Giant with the Three Golden Hairs |
| | 29. The Frog-Prince |
| | 30. The Fox and the Horse |
| | 31. Rumpelstiltskin |

**Table 1. Selection of tales**

The selection for the two translations is radically different, and they share no more than three tales: 'The Frog Prince', 'The Springing, Singing Lark' and 'The Queen Bee'.

If we look at recent popularity polls and indexes of reprints, the same, small canon of tales appears over and over again, with slight variations. For the top ten below, I have combined the results of a pop poll with a panel of 750 Dutch participants in 1999 (Meder 2000: 37) and a small survey that I made of the most frequently included Grimm tales in a selection of Dutch fairy-tale collections since 1995:

| Most popular and reprinted Grimm tales | Taylor & Jardine 1823 | Dutch 1820 |
|---|---|---|
| 1. Snow White | X | |
| 2. Hansel & Gretel | X | |
| 3. Cinderella | (II) | |
| 4. Little Red Riding Hood | | |
| 5. Sleeping Beauty | X | |
| 6. Frog Prince | X | X |
| 7. Brave little taylor | | |
| 8. Mother Holle | (II) | |
| 9. Rapunzel | | |
| 10. Wolf and the seven kids | | |

**Table 2. Most popular and reprinted Grimm tales**

Of these ten tales, four are already included in the first English volume, and two more in Taylor's second volume. The Dutch scores low with only one. Of course *German Popular Stories* is likely to have contributed to the establishment of the international fairy-tale canon as the highly successful and influential introduction of the Grimms into English. But what was the appeal in its selection of tales?

In my shortlist of most popular and reprinted tales, one type of fairy tale is clearly dominant: half of the stories listed describe a young princess who goes through an ordeal and marries a prince ('Snow White', 'Cinderella', 'Sleeping Beauty', 'The Frog Prince' and 'Rapunzel'). By the early nineteenth century, this romantic fairy-tale type had already been internationally established by Charles Perrault and Madame Leprince de Beaumont, something that the Dutch translator acknowledges in the preface when he or she writes: 'Which of you has not heard speak of Mother Goose? Which of you has not, in their playtime, enjoyed themselves with her stories?' (Grimm 1820: n.p.)[11] Yet on the romantic fairy-tale type that Perrault had made popular in his Mother Goose tales, the Dutch translation scores particularly low, including only three examples. Taylor has six romantic fairy tales, and these are again still the most popular. That neither translation includes 'Cinderella' and 'Little Red Riding Hood' may be because these tales were already known in Perrault's version, from which the Dutch preface clearly distinguishes itself. After making reference to Mother Goose, the preface continues: 'Then the fairy tales that you are offered here have so far been unknown to you for sure' (ibid.).[12] Taylor does include 'Rose Bud', the Grimm variant of 'Sleeping Beauty' that was also present with Perrault.

A second striking difference between the selections of tales in the two translations, is the high number of animal tales in *German Popular Stories*. By including so many animal tales and by stressing their moral potential in his introduction, Taylor found alliance with the then popular genre of the fable, in which fantasy served as a moral lesson (Sutton 1996: 15). The Dutch collection, in contrast, includes no animal tales.

From the twenty Dutch tales, remarkably few are still part of the contemporary fairy-tale canon. Except for 'The Frog Prince' and, to a lesser extent, 'The Twelve Brothers' and 'The Six Servants' none are still regularly reprinted.[13] There is a clear preference in the Dutch translation for tales that feature a young hero who completes tasks (usually in competition with a few others) and is rewarded with a young princess. 'The Water of Life' and 'The Queen Bee' belong to this type, among others. If we compare the selections in the two translations in terms of gender, the majority of the Dutch tales features a male protagonist (sixteen out of twenty or 80%). Three tales have a female protagonist, and one has a mixed pair of a boy and girl. In my top ten of most popular and reprinted tales, the situation is reversed: seven tales have a female protagonist, and then there is one with a male protagonist ('The Brave Little Taylor'), one with a mixed pair ('Hansel and Gretel') and one animal tale ('The Wolf and the Seven Kids'). In *German Popular Stories*, the selection is more balanced in terms of the protagonists' gender.

Another striking aspect in the selection of tales is the preference for tales from the second volume of the *Children's and Household Tales* in the Dutch translation: only eight tales come from the first volume (40%), eleven are borrowed from the second volume (55%) and one tale stems from another author (Albert Ludwig Grimm). The tales in Dutch are selected in certain clusters: six tales come from the first nine in the *Children's and Household Tales*, five others come from the tales numbered 88-98. In the English translation, three quarters of the tales are borrowed from volume I. This difference matters because the two volumes are somewhat different in character:

> Wilhelm Grimm's basic editorial principles began to change between the first and second volumes of the first edition, that is, between 1812 and 1815. In terms of provenance, content, and style, the first volume was bourgeois,

whereas the second volume of the first edition began to reflect the folk tone and content that the entire collection ultimately embodied. (Bottigheimer 1993: 81)

The Dutch publisher and translator seemed to have realised this difference, stressing the folk aspect of the Grimm collection in the preface and selecting the tales accordingly. This was not the best commercial choice, however. Not only did the critic from *Exercises in National Literature* ridicule the folk origin of the fairy tales, the sales indicate that 'the book-buying public voted decisively with its purse in favor of the "bourgeois" tales and against the "folk" ones' (ibid.). Bottigheimer's conclusion proves to be valid not only for Germany, but also for the Netherlands and the UK.[14] The relatively small number of bourgeois tales in the Dutch translation may help explain why this book did not catch the imagination of the public. The preference for tales from the first volume is also reflected in the contemporary fairy-tale canon: all the tales in my list of most popular and reprinted tales appear in the first volume.

It is remarkable, finally, that the Dutch translation, as well as Taylor's second volume, contained stories that were not included in the *Children's and Household Tales*, but were borrowed from other authors and collectors. The Dutch translation included the tale 'Het vrolijke sprookje van den kleinen Frits met zijne vedel' [The Merry Tale of Little Frits with his Violin] in a version by Albert Ludwig Grimm, even though the Grimm collection held a similar tale, 'The Jew in Thorns'. Not a relative of the Brothers Grimm, Albert Ludwig Grimm had published a book called *Kindermärchen* in 1808 ([Children's Fairy Tales], Tatar 2003: 13), and during the 1810s a disagreement had developed between Albert Ludwig on the one hand and Jacob and Wilhelm Grimm on the other. They disagreed, among other things, on the quality, pedagogical value and child-friendliness of fairy tales (Buijnsters & Buijnsters-Smets 2001: 101-102; Tatar 2003: 16-18). None of the Grimms must have liked the confusion with their namesakes, and the fact that the Dutch collection added one of Albert Ludwig Grimm's tales to the Brothers', may have increased Jacob Grimm's irritation about this translation.

## Fairy-Tale Book for Children?

Not only in their selection of fairy tales, but also in their dominant translation strategies, the first Dutch and English translators of the Grimm tales took a radically different approach. In general, the Dutch translation is a very literal one, to the point that it contains a high number of German constructions that feel unidiomatic in Dutch. Van de Zijpe speculates that there may have been two translators at work, including one who was not a native speaker of Dutch, but of German (1975: 175).[15] Taylor not only managed to reproduce a more fluent English text but also made both small and large-scale adaptations to fit a younger target audience and their parents and teachers. As Taylor and Jardine admit in the preface: 'In those tales which they [the translators] have selected they had proposed to make no alteration whatever; but in a few instances they have been compelled to depart in some degree from this purpose' (Grimm 1823: xi-xii). Although the Dutch translation places the child more centrally in its title than Taylor's – 'Fairy-Tale Book for *Children*' (emphasis added) versus *German Popular Stories* – it is clear that Taylor places children more centrally in the actual text. In comparison, both titles are thus in fact misleading: the Dutch text is more popular (in the sense of folkloric) than the English, and the English text is more child-friendly than the Dutch.

Even more than the source text, Taylor's translation fitted the bourgeois image of childhood and poetics of children's literature: 'Evidently Wilhelm [Grimm]'s censorship was not severe enough in the eyes of the Grimms' first English translator', Martin Sutton writes (1996: 56). If we recall the negative review of the Dutch translation in *Exercises in National Literature*, it is clear that its anonymous critic also found that the adaptations were insufficient to make the text suitable for a young audience.[16] Some of the most scary and cruel tales are rendered faithfully in *Fairy-Tale Book for Children*, for example the ghost tale 'The Fairy Tale of One Who Could Not Be Scared' or the sinister story 'The Crows'. A short and rather coarse tale is featured with 'The Ungrateful Son', in which the protagonist is punished by getting a toad stuck on his face. It is rendered faithfully, unhappy ending and coarse language included. In contrast, several tales in *German Popular Stories* have been altered: references to sexuality and bodily functions were avoided and several violent scenes were deleted (Sutton 1996: 22; 52), even though to later standards, a high degree of violence was still allowed. Brian Alderson notes that the approach that Taylor took ultimately led to its success:

> One can indeed argue that the Grimms – as they themselves recognized – were well served by this translation. For although it is deeply conservative in its response to the originalities of the *Kinder- und Hausmärchen*, and although it is cavalier over the precise matching of words – as the Grimms also recognized – it is nevertheless a version with a proper feeling for the rhythms of English prose. (Alderson 1993: 66)

To these observations, I wish to add two others, which link up with my comparison of the selection of tales in Dutch and English. Taylor not only includes more bourgeois princess stories but also makes them more romantic. Moreover, in his selection of tales as well as in his adaptations, Taylor seeks alliance with existing literary models and themes. I will illustrate this by focusing on the three tales that the translations share: 'The Frog Prince',[17] 'The Queen Bee', and 'The Singing, Springing Lark'.

## 'The Singing, Springing Lark'

The Brothers Grimm's 'The Singing, Springing Lark' is a variant of the so-called 'animal groom' tale type, to which 'The Frog Prince' also belongs. It opens with a father who departs on a journey and asks his three daughters what they want as a gift. The eldest ask for jewelry, but the youngest, modest daughter wants only a small bird, a lark. When the father encounters such a bird in a forest and tries to have his servant obtain it, he is captured by a lion. When the daughter is sent to replace her father, the lion turns out to be a charming prince. They get married, have a child, and live through another long series of adventures before the tale concludes with a happy ending.

In Taylor's translation, this tale is renamed 'The Lady and the Lion'. This title marks it more clearly from the start as a bourgeois variant on the animal groom type, putting the lady central and establishing a titular analogy with 'The Beauty and the Beast'. Moreover, Taylor combines the first part of 'The Singing, Springing Lark' with a variant from the Grimm 1812 edition, 'The Summer and Winter Garden'.[18] Hence, the youngest daughter asks her father not for a lark, but for a more romantic gift: a rose. This has consequences for how the gift is retrieved. Whereas the father had a servant climb the tree to catch the lark, he now discovers an enchanted garden where it is half summer and half winter. In the summer part grows the rose. Taylor thus opts for the romantic symbol of love and for the more imaginative setting of a garden with two seasons. In doing so, he finds alliance with Madame Leprince de Beaumont's 'The Beauty and the Beast' once more.

In the Grimms' 'Summer and Winter Garden', the father is not threatened by a lion but by a wild animal. This is the point where Taylor returns to the version of 1819, opting for a lion. Later in this long episodic tale, Taylor seeks alliance with existing stories once again. At a certain point, the lion is separated from his wife, and when she finds him again, he is fighting with a tapeworm. This episode is hard to visualise, and the tapeworm is a strange animal to feature in a fairy tale. Taylor replaces it with a creature known from myths, legends and medieval romance stories: the dragon. Another odd figure in the Grimm tale is the *Vogel Greif*, a lesser known mythological bird, which carries the reunited couple over the sea. Taylor deletes the two episodes in which the *Vogel Greif* features from the tale, shortening the rather long story by a few lines. Further, small alterations seem to be informed by prudishness: the pigeon that the princess has to follow drops only white feathers, and not red blood drops, as in Grimm. When she wishes to retrieve her husband from a false princess, she asks only to speak to the prince, not to sleep in his room.

The Dutch translator, in contrast, keeps all the oddities and sexually suggestive scenes, making only minor stylistic changes. As in several other tales, he or she deletes a few images which add to the visionary liveliness of this tale. It is described, for example, how the princess 'opzag' ([looked up], 77) instead of how she 'die Augen aufschlug' ([cast up her eyes], Grimm 2004: II.10); the wind is said to blow through 'alle gaten en reten' ([all holes and gaps], 78) instead of 'durch alle Bäume und unter alle Blätterchen weg' ([through all trees and under all small leaves], ibid.: II.10); the father no longer leaves the lion 'mit traurigem Herzen' ([with a sad heart]; ibid.: II.7), and the translator deletes the image that the prince felt 'als rausche der Wind draußen in den Tannenbäumen' ([as if the wind was rustling through the pine trees outside], ibid.: II.12) when the princess talks to him in his sleep. The register of the Dutch translation is also more formal than the English one, although both introduce a moment of slightly more affection for the plagued heroine: in the English text she is called 'our poor wanderer' (121), in Dutch 'ons meisje' ([our little girl], 79). In short, the Dutch provides a literal translation of the 1819 edition, keeping in the oddities, such as a fight with a tapeworm. Taylor adapts the tale by combining it with an earlier, different tale, and by seeking alliance with existing fairy tales. He deletes oddities and instead adds romantic images.

## 'The Queen Bee'

If we compare the Dutch and English translations of 'The Queen Bee', similar differences surface. Like many tales in the Dutch collection, 'The Queen Bee' is a story about three princes facing a challenge. The youngest, Dummling or Simpleton, distinguishes himself from the others through his kindness to animals – ducks, ants and bees. When the three arrive at a castle, Simpleton can release the castle from its enchantment and win the fairy-tale princess with the help of the animals he has saved before. The changes in the Dutch translation are minor, and mostly limited to shifts in word order. In English, one major change is introduced in the opening, with regard to the identity of the protagonist. The German tale opens as follows:

> Two king's sons once upon a time set out on an adventure, and fell into a wild, untamed life, so that they didn't return home at all. The youngest, called Simpleton, went out to find his brothers: but when he found them, they mocked him, that he with his simple nature would want to get on in the world, when both of them wouldn't come through and were much smarter. (Grimm 2004: I. 344)[19]

With Taylor, the opening goes:

> Two king's sons once upon a time went out into the world to seek their fortunes; but they soon fell into a wasteful foolish way of living, so that they could not return home again. Then their young brother, who was a little insignificant dwarf, went out to seek for his brothers: but when he had found them they only laughed at him, to think that he, who was so young and simple, should try to travel through the world, when they, so much wiser, had been unable to get on. (Grimm 1823: 86)

The Dutch translator retains the opening: 'The youngest son of the king, called stupid'[20] – a more or less literal translation of the German, that only adds the repetition of 'king' and thus stresses that Simpleton is the son of the king too. This is a rather rare combination for a fairy tale, because mostly simpletons feature in more jokey fairy tales (Ó hÓgáin 2008: 865), and usually they are poor as well as stupid. In contrast to most of his namesakes in the Grimm collection, the Simpleton that is the protagonist of 'The Queen Bee' does not commit any dumb acts in the tale. He is merely pictured as kinder and less wild and opportunistic than his brothers, which eventually makes him more successful. The brothers appear as much more vain and foolish in undertaking tasks which they cannot perform. From what we can derive from the tale itself, those who named Simpleton made a mistake.

Taylor changes the defining features of the tale's protagonist, making him 'a little insignificant dwarf'. In this version, the protagonist's identity is asserted by a voice with more authority, that of the narrator. This boy is not just called a dwarf, he is defined by the narrator as being a little dwarf and insignificant. The text, however, will also prove the narrator wrong. With the choice of a dwarf rather than a simpleton, Taylor departs from the more folkloric tradition of the simpleton who proves to be smart, seeking alliance with another tradition. In the history of German literature, dwarves had already featured in the classic *Nibelungenlied* (Burke 2006: 7). Moreover, they fitted better in Taylor's view of the Grimm tales as Northern tales with a wild nature. Dwarves feature amply in Norse mythology (ibid.: 8; Stephens 2008: 286), albeit that many of those are of a wilder and less kind nature than this one. Taylor here marks 'The Queen Bee' more clearly as a Northern tale of magic, once again seeking alliance with existing models, albeit that he introduces a new oddness to the fairy-tale world by giving a dwarf the status of a prince and, at the end of the tale, making the dwarf a king. Taylor's dwarf is also extremely benign, and stands out from his brothers as being more controlled. From a Nordic dwarf one would have expected a more savage nature. As John Stephens writes, '[i]n folktale collections and retellings from the seventeenth to nineteenth centuries, dwarfs are mostly creatures of dubious purpose (as in "Rumpelstiltskin") or quite evil (Marie Catherine d'Aulnoy's "Le nain jaune" [The Yellow Dwarf])' (2008: 286). However, Stephens also points out that the Grimms themselves break this stereotype by introducing a group of entirely benevolent dwarfs in 'Snow White', a tale that Taylor also includes in *German Popular Stories*. The change from Simpleton to dwarf is signaled in Taylor and Jardine's notes, and even deplored:

> We have here the favourite incident of the despised and neglected member of the family, who bears the name of 'Dummling,' setting out on his adventures, and overcoming all disadvantages by talent and virtue. (See note on 'The Golden Goose,' in which story we have left the hero his name, as perhaps we ought to have done here). (Grimm 1823: 226)

Why Taylor opted for a dwarf rather than a simpleton is not explained. Perhaps Taylor sought alliance here with the 'Tale of Tom Thumb' that he refers to in his preface (1823: vi) and his notes (235), drawing the comparison between *Dummling* (simpleton) and *Däumling* (little Tom Thumb). Generic content affiliation seems the most logical explanation.

## 'The Frog Prince'

As with 'The Singing, Springing Lark', Taylor also combines two tales from the first edition of the *Children's and Household Tales* for his version of 'The Frog Prince',[21] instead of using the 1819 edition, where the Grimms had integrated these two tales themselves. The source text of the Dutch translation is only the 1819 tale, which is again translated mostly literally.[22] Yet, the difference in source text alone cannot account for a few striking differences between the English and the Dutch translations. Rather, what we see is a different approach to the content and structure of the fairy tale and to its readership. More than the previous two examples that I have discussed, 'The Frog Prince' is a tale that might have raised some eyebrows in the early nineteenth century, especially considering it as children's literature. The story is well-known: a princess drops her golden ball in a pond, and a frog offers to dive in to retrieve it for her if she promises to let him be her companion, eat from her plate and sleep in her bed. As soon as the princess has her ball back, she runs home and forgets her promise. The frog comes after her, however, and when the king hears of his daughter's promise, he makes her keep it. The princess yields, up to the moment where the frog wishes to sleep in her bed. She throws him at the wall, and finds him transformed into a charming prince. Then they fall happily asleep together. The next day they ride home, together with the prince's loyal servant Iron Henry. The latter had been so sad about the prince's transformation that he had to put three iron bars across his heart, so that it wouldn't burst. While they ride home, the three bars break because of his joy at his master's release, and that's the end of the Grimms' story.

Like most animal groom tales, 'The Frog Prince' can be interpreted as a tale about the fear of sexual union, as psychoanalysts such as Bruno Bettelheim have argued:

> It is difficult to imagine a better way to convey to the child that he need not be afraid of the (to him) repugnant aspects of sex than the way it is done in this story. The story of the frog – how it behaves, what occurs to the princess in relation to it, and what finally happens to both frog and girl – confirms the appropriateness of disgust when one is not ready for sex, and prepares for its desirability when the time is ripe. (Bettelheim 1976: 290)

When the young girl's fear is overcome, what was once repulsive becomes something beautiful. Although Bettelheim does not give a satisfactory explanation for why the frog transforms at the moment of the princess' most intense disgust and rebellion, suggestions of a sexual interest of the frog in the princess can indeed be distinguished in Grimm, especially when he asks to sleep in her bed.

In Dutch, some mild censorship of the sexual dimension in the story can be detected. The Dutch frog does not ask to be the princess' companion, but is content to be her 'speelgenootje' [playfellow]. Also, the sentence is omitted that her bed is 'schön und rein' [nice and clean] (4), which hints at her virginity. Some moments of innuendo are retained, however. The princess complains in German that the frog 'will zu mir herein' – meaning that he wants to enter her house, but taken literally it says that he wants to get inside of her. In Dutch she says that he wants to come to her, with possible sexual implications.[23] The scenes where she throws him against the wall and where they sleep together are retained. The translator only deletes the word 'vergnügt' [happy] when the princess and her newly transformed prince fall asleep together.

Taylor, in contrast, has substantially adapted this story. While deleting many allusions to sexuality, he puts greater emphasis on romantic courtship. Taylor's frog not only wants to be the princess' companion, but he asks her to *love* him (Grimm 1823: 206). Taylor also repeats the verse that the frogs says at the princess' door and makes it more romantic:[24]

Open the door, my princess dear,
Open the door to thy true love here!
And mind the words that thou and I said
By the fountain cool in the greenwood shade.
(ibid.: 208)[25]

The German verse is more factual, as the literal translation shows:

Princess, youngest,
Open the door to me!
Don't you know, what yesterday
You said to me
By the cool water in the well?
Princess, youngest,
Open the door to me.
(Grimm 2004: I.3)[26]

Taylor turns the frog from an assertive animal into a dedicated suitor who tries to win the princess' heart and describes the location of their first encounter in highly romantic terms. The German text is more factual and may even be interpreted as being rather coarse – after all, 'mach mir auf' may hint at more than 'open the door to me'. Taken more literally, it means: open (yourself) to me.

It is at the point when the frog wants to sleep in the princess' bed, that Taylor substantially alters the course of events, removing the most loaded parts. Taylor has the frog sleep in the princess' bed for three nights, but makes it clear that the frog sleeps on the pillow and stays there (Grimm 1823: 209), avoiding the possibility that he moves closer to the princess. In the Grimms' version (1819), her disgust is too intense to allow him into her bed at first. They describe how 'she began to cry, truly bitterly, and was afraid of the cold frog, she didn't dare to touch it and now it would be sleeping in her nice, clean little bed' (Grimm 2004: I.4)[27] – her disgust at this moment is much more intense than when he wanted to eat from her plate. Taylor removes this description of her revulsion, as well as her forceful reaction, when she throws the frog against the wall. In the English text, the princess simply finds the frog transformed into a prince when she wakes up on the third morning. Whereas they consequently fall asleep together in Grimm, Taylor increases the physical distance between prince and princess, placing him 'at the head of her bed' (Grimm 1823: 209). The prince explains that he was enchanted by a hag – this being an explanation that the Grimms would later add themselves, under Taylor's influence – and a marriage proposal immediately follows: 'I will marry you, and love you as long as you live' (ibid.). Even as he says this, a coach drives up to take them to his kingdom. The Grimm's coda on the prince's faithful servant Henry is reduced to a mere sentence, as Taylor opts for a different, more romantic ending: 'Then all set out full of joy for the prince's kingdom; where they arrived safely, and lived happily a great many years' (ibid.: 161).[28]

## Conclusion

Jack Zipes (2006) has noted the non-recognition of translation in the popularity of fairy tales. Yet, various critics stress that the first English translation has proven vital for the international dissemination of the Grimm tales. Martin Sutton writes that it is

> conceivable that some of the revisions introduced by Wilhelm Grimm to later editions of the *KHM* [short for *Kinder- und Hausmärchen*, V.J.] follow the example of changes made by Taylor himself to the Grimms' original text. [These are] improvements which Wilhelm Grimm either copied knowingly or independently made of his own accord, seeing the same flaws that Taylor had seen and corrected before him. (Sutton 1993: 57)

With its lauded illustrations by George Cruikshank, *German Popular Stories* even inspired the Brothers Grimm themselves to publish a small edition of their tales in 1825, specifically aimed at and adapted for children, and with illustrations by their brother Ludwig Emil Grimm (Tatar 2003: 19-20). By the mid-nineteenth century, the Grimm tales had taken the place in the English canon of children's literature that they have not lost since, with various translators following in Taylor's footsteps. In Gillian Lathey's words, he opened 'the floodgates' for a wave of translations of Grimm tales (2010: 92). In Dutch literature, the gates would remain closed until at least the 1860s, when translators such as Jan J.A. Goeverneur selected different tales from the ones included in *Fairy Tale Book for Children*, and made more fluent translations with more adaptations (see a.o. Goeverneur 1861 and 1871). The textual comparison and early reactions show that selection and adaptation have been vital in the introduction of the Grimms' fairy tales abroad. For some critics, Taylor's adaptations are considered to be a loss. As Linda Hutcheon argues, 'the morally loaded discourse of fidelity is based on the implied assumption that adapters aim simply to reproduce the adapted text' (2006: 7). Indeed, in his analysis of Edgar Taylor's English translation of 'Snow White', Martin Sutton describes several adaptations in the text as a 'failure', primarily made out of 'fear' (1996: 52). Whatever Taylor's motivations were, the reception of his work does show that he was a more skilful linguist than his Dutch counterpart and made a better assessment of what his target culture lacked and found acceptable. This moment in the history of fairy tales therefore supports Hutcheon's point on adaptations that 'to be second is not to be secondary or inferior, likewise, to be first is not to be originary or authoritative' (2006: xiii). Taylor's translation influenced the small editions of the *Children's and Household Tales*, which in turn influenced the large editions, which in turn influenced numerous new translations and adaptations, and so on. The history of fairy tales seems indeed to be a never-ending story that would not be as rich without its many impurities and creative adaptations.

In this context, it is important to note that in 1870 *Fairy-Tale Book for Children* was reissued in Dutch under the title *Sprookjes uit de nalatenschap van Moeder de Gans* [Fairy Tales From the Legacy of Mother Goose] with A.W. Seithoff. This was a time when the Grimms had experienced some fame through their scientific work as linguists and specialists in the history of German literature, and their tales had received praise from influential critics, such as Nicolaas Beets (1867: 46-55). In this new context, the first Dutch translation apparently offered Seithoff the possibility to retrieve a selection of still lesser known tales that readers interested in the Grimms might wish to read in addition to the tales that had been introduced from other books. The adaptations that the translator and/or publisher made in the second edition show an awareness of the critique of *Fairy-Tale Book for Children* in *Exercises in National Literature*. First, the anonymous illustrations of the first edition have been replaced by new, colored ones by Gerardus Johannes Bos. It is clear, though, that he has been inspired by his predecessor, choosing several similar scenes and illustrating them in strikingly similar ways. Second, the preface, with its reference to Dorothea Viehmann, has been deleted. Third, the text has been stylistically revised, which results in a high number of small adaptations of sentence order, and sometimes rephrasing. For example, the word for pearls, 'Perle', becomes 'paarlen' in the first Dutch translation, strongly resembling the German, and is replaced with the more common plural 'parels' in the revised edition. The word 'koningsdochter' [king's daughter], derived from the German 'Königsdochter', is replaced with the more common 'prinses', derived from French 'princesse'. Nouns are no longer capitalised, as is common in German and was done in the first edition. Fourth, one tale is deleted in the second edition: 'Our Mary's Child'. Even though several references to God are retained, the revision also includes the deletion of several references to religion and praying, e.g. in 'The Crows' and 'The Twelve Brothers'. These deletions follow a strategy already practiced by Taylor. One tale in particular is more strongly adapted than the others. To the coarse tale of 'The Ungrateful Son', the revised edition adds a newly invented coda: when the ungrateful son asks forgiveness from his father, he is released from the obnoxious toad that in Grimm resides on his face for the rest of his life. These comparisons reveal a response to the criticism formulated in *Exercises in National Literature* and an acknowledgment of a bourgeois poetics of children's literature. These minor adaptations were not enough, however, to compete with the more adequately selected and heavily adapted collections of Grimm tales that had started to circulate in the late nineteenth century. Like *Fairy-Tale Book for Children*, the new edition *Fairy Tales From the Legacy of Mother Goose* did not make a big impression, and did not manage to save from oblivion the majority of the nineteen tales that it contained. Instead, the canonisation of the Grimms in Dutch went through other translators and publishers.

## Bibliography

Alderson, B. 1993. 'The Spoken and the Read: *German Popular Stories* and English Popular Diction', in: D. Haase (ed.), *The Reception of Grimms' Fairy Tales: Responses, Reactions, Revisions*. Detroit: Wayne State University Press, 59-77.

Anonymous. 1821. 'Review of *Sprookjes-boek voor kinderen*', in: *Vaderlandsche Letteroefeningen*: 45-46.

Basile, G. 2001 [1634]. 'Sun, Moon, and Talia', in: J. Zipes (ed.), *The Great Fairy Tale Tradition: From Straparola and Basile to the Brothers Grimm*. New York: W.W. Norton & Company, 685-688.

Beets, N. 1867. *Verscheidenheden, meest op letterkundig gebied. Vol III*. Haarlem: De erven F. Bohn.

Bettelheim, B. 1976. *The Uses of Enchantment*. London: Thames and Hudson.

Blamires, D. 2006 [1989]. 'The Early Reception of the Grimms' *Kinder- und Hausmärchen* in England', in: G. Lathey (ed.), *The Translation of Children's Literature: A Reader*. Clevedon: Multilingual Matters, 163-174.

Bottigheimer, R. 1993. 'The Publishing History of Grimms' Tales: Reception at the Cash Register', in: D. Haase (ed.), *The Reception of Grimms' Fairy Tales*. Detroit: Wayne State University Press, 78-101.

Buijnsters, P.J. & L. Buijnsters-Smets. 2001. *Lust en leering: geschiedenis van het Nederlandse kinderboek in de negentiende eeuw*. Zwolle: Waanders.

Burke, J. 2006. 'Dwarfs', in: J. Zipes (ed.), *The Oxford Encyclopedia of Children's Literature*. Vol. II. Oxford: Oxford University Press, 7-8.

Goeverneur, J.J.A. 1861. *Oude sprookjes: Opnieuw verteld*. Schiedam: H.A.M. Roelants.

Goeverneur, J.J.A. 1871. *Daar was 'ereis...: Sprookjes en vertelsels voor jonge kinderen*. Groningen: Noordhoff en Smit.

Grimm, A.L. 1921 [1806]. *Kindermärchen*. Hildesheim: Olms-Weidmann.

Grimm, J. & W. 1820. *Sprookjes-boek voor kinderen*. Amsterdam: G.A. Diederichs en Zoon.

Grimm, J. & W. 1823. *German Popular Stories*. London: C. Baldwin.

Grimm, J. & W. 1870 [1820]. *Sprookjes uit de nalatenschap van Moeder de Gans*. Leiden: A.W. Seithoff.

Grimm, J. & W. 1994 [1823]. *Grimms' Fairy Tales*. London: Puffin.

Grimm, J. & W. 2004 [1819]. *Kinder- und Hausmärchen*. 3 vols. Hildesheim: Olms-Weidmann.

Haase, D. 1999 [1993]. 'Yours, Mine, or Ours? Perrault, the Brothers Grimm, and the Ownership of Fairy Tales', in: M. Tatar (ed.), *The Classic Fairy Tales*. New York: W.W. Norton & Company, 353-364.

Hutcheon, L. 2006. *A Theory of Adaptation*. New York: Routledge.

Kamenetsky, C. 1992. *The Brothers Grimm and Their Critics*. Athens: Ohio University Press.

Kyritsi, M. 2005. 'Taboo Or Not To Be? Edgar Taylor and the First Translations of the Grimms' *Kinder- und Hausmärchen*', in: V. Joosen & K. Vloeberghs (eds.), *Changing Concepts of Childhood and Children's Literature*. Newcastle: Cambridge Scholars Press, 195-208.

Lathey, G. 2010. *The Role of Translators in Children's Literature: Invisible Storytellers*. New York: Routledge.

Meder, T. 2000. 'Nederlandse sprookjes in de negentiende en twintigste eeuw: Verteld, verzameld, gedrukt', in: B. Dongelmans (ed.), *Tot volle waschdom: Bijdragen aan de geschiedenis van de kinder- en jeugdliteratuur*. Den Haag: Biblion, 31-46.

Ó hÓgáin, D. 2008. 'Simpleton', in: D. Haase (ed.), *The Greenwood Encyclopedia of Folktales & Fairy Tales*. Westport: Greenwood Press, 865-867.

Perrault, Charles. 2001 [1697]. 'Little Red Riding Hood', in: J. Zipes (ed.), *The Great Fairy Tale Tradition: From Straparola and Basile to the Brothers Grimm*. New York: W.W. Norton & Company, 745-747.

Rölleke, H. 2000. *Die Märchen der Brüder Grimm: Quellen und Studien. Gesammelte Aufsätze*. Trier: Wissenschaftlicher Verlag Trier.

Stephens, J. 2008. 'Dwarf, Dwarves,' in: D. Haase (ed.), *The Greenwood Encyclopedia of Folktales & Fairy Tales. Vol. I*. Westport: Greenwood Press, 286-287.

Sutton, M. 1996. *The Sin-Complex: A Critical Study of English Versions of the Grimms' Kinder- und Hausmärchen in the Nineteenth Century*. Kassel: Brüder Grimm Gesellschaft.

Tatar, M. 2003 [1987]. *The Hard Facts of the Grimms' Fairy Tales*. Second edition. Princeton, Oxford: Princeton University Press.

Van de Zijpe, R. 1975. 'Die erste niederländische Übersetzung Grimmscher Märchen von 1820', in: L. Denecke (ed.), *Brüder Grimm Gedenken*. Vol. II. Marburg: N.G. Elwert, 168-182.

Van den Berg, W. & P. Couttenier. 2009. *Alles is taal geworden: geschiedenis van de Nederlandse literatuur, 1800-1900*. Amsterdam: Bakker.

Zipes, J. 2002. *The Brothers Grimm*. Second edition. New York: Palgrave Macmillan.

Zipes, J. 2009. *Relentless Progress: The Reconfiguration of Children's Literature, Fairy Tales, and Storytelling*. New York: Routledge.

# Notes

1. On the ownership of fairy tales, see Haase (1999).

2. I am referring here to Giambattista Basile's variant of 'Sleeping Beauty', called 'Sun, Moon, and Talia' (1634), and to Charles Perrault's version of 'Little Red Riding Hood' (1697).

3. Translations of children's literature frequently appeared anonymously in the nineteenth century, because of the low literary status of this genre (Sutton 1996: 3; Lathey 2010). Even Taylor's name was not publicly revealed until the end of the nineteenth century, seven years after his death (Sutton 1996: 10).

4. Met verlof van de hooggeleerde *Duitsche* Uitgevers en Boekbeoordeelaars, en den zeer geleerden, maar niet zeer taalkundigen, *Nederlandschen* Vertaler tevens, hebben wij in lang geen zotter boekje met misselijker prentjes in handen gehad. Eene *Nieder-Zwehrnsche* boerin spelde hun de meeste en schoonste (!) sprookjes op de mouw! Misschien verstaan wij den verhevenen zin van deze wonderschoone rarigheden niet; maar dit weten wij, dat ons de hersenen en de geruste slaap van onze lieve kleinen te zeer ter harte gaan, dan dat wij beide aan den schrikwekkenden indruk van zulke spookachtige prentjes en roodkousige, blaauwbaardige vertelseltjes immer zullen wagen (all translations by Vanessa Joosen, unless mentioned otherwise).

5. See also Blamires (2006: 171).

6. Zo stond men in Noord-Nederland, enkele uitzonderingen daargelaten, vrij afwijzend tegenover de grensoverschrijdingen op talloze terreinen die door de Romantiek werden gepredikt.

7. These included an elaborate preface by the Brothers Grimm. A third volume with scholarly notes appeared in 1822, two years after the Dutch and a year before the English translation.

8. As Jack Zipes explains, 'in folklore terms, to contaminate means to mix different variants of a known tale to form either a new variant or an ideal tale type based on different variants. […] So, the Grimms were not merely collectors of "pure" folk tales, they were creative "contaminators" and artists' (Zipes 2002: 31).

9. See also Tatar (2003: 11-15).

10. Bottigheimer's and Tatar's research thus proves wrong the claim to success in Germany that the Dutch translator refers to in his or her preface as a reason for introducing *Die Kinder- und Hausmärchen* in the Netherlands. See also Van de Zijpe (1975: 172).

11.    Wie toch, van ulieden, heeft niet van Moeder de Gans hooren spreken? Wie heeft zich, in zijne speeluren, niet met de lezing van hare vertellingen verlustigd?

12.    Dan de sprookjes, welke u hier worden aangeboden, zijn tot dusverre voorzeker aan ulieden onbekend gebleven.

13.    Conversely, the tales that are included in *Sprookjes-boek voor kinderen* are no longer popular today. Only four of the twenty tales still featured in recent collections of favourite fairy tales (not counting the complete translations of the entire collection).

14.    Kyritsi adds that 'Taylor's selection of tales is based on the literary canon of his time, where the importance of "moral education" […] superseded the pleasures of fantasy and imagination' (2005: 198).

15.    See also Buijnsters & Buijnsters Smets (2001: 104).

16.    Taylor left out religious tales and references to religion, such as prayers or the mention of the devil. In contrast, the religious tale 'Marienkind' is included in Dutch.

17.    For an evolution of this tale in the Grimm collection, see Zipes (2009: 90).

18.    The Grimms replaced this tale in the next edition with 'The singing, springing lark', possibly because 'The Summer and Winter Garden' came very close to Madame Leprince de Beaumont's 'The Beauty and the Beast'.

19.    Zwei Königssöhne gingen einmal auf Abentheuer, und geriethen in ein wildes, wüstes Leben, so daß sie gar nicht wieder Haus kamen. Der jüngste, welcher der Dummling hieß, ging aus und suchte seine Brüder: aber wie er sie fand, verspotteten sie ihn, daß er mit seiner Einfalt sich durch die Welt schlagen wolle, da sie zwei nicht durchkämen und wären doch klüger (344).

20.    De jongste zoon des Konings, domoor geheeten

21.    Partly from the 1812 edition and partly from an 1815 variant.

22.    The Dutch translator gives this tale the somewhat misleading title 'The King of Frogs', which the Frog King is not. It renders the tale almost word by word, with only minor stylistic changes in word order and sentence length. See also below.

23.    wil tot mij komen (3)

24.    In Grimm (1812) and (1819) he says it only once.

25.    The verses are also reminiscent of the first printed variant of the tale, which Zipes locates in *The Complaynt of Scotland* (c. 1550): 'Open the door, my hinny, my hart, / Open the door, mine ain wee thing: / And mind the words that you and I spak / Down in the meadow, at the well-spring!' (Zipes 2009: 100).

26.    Königstochter, jüngste, / mach mir auf, / weißt du nicht, was gestern / du zu mir gesagt / bei dem kühlen Brunnenwasser? / Königstochter, jüngste, / mach mir auf.

27.    Da fing die Königstochter an zu weinen, gar bitterlich, und fürchtete sich vor dem kalten Frosch, den getraute sie sich nicht anzurühren und der sollte nun in ihrem schönen, reinen Bettlein schlafen.

28. Zipes notes similar adaptations in the Grimms' editorial process: Wilhelm Grimm gradually 'de-eroticized the story he heard (and probably other variants as well) so that the princess appears to be a child, and the frog never enters her bed' (2009: 92).

# Cinderella's Godmother Disenchanted

## The Fairy's (Dis)Guises in the Light of the (Implied) Translator's Ideology in Dutch 'Cinderella' Translations

### Lien Fret

During the past three centuries, hundreds of Dutch authors have been enticed into adapting classic stories into children's books, at times leaving their readers with nothing but a few recognisable story elements. Yet Charles Perrault's fairy tale 'Cendrillon ou la petite pantoufle de verre' [Cinderella or the Little Glass Slipper] (first published in *Histoires ou contes du temps passé. Avec des moralitez* [Stories or Tales of Times Past with Morals], 1697) seems to have survived the ravages of time very well. Maybe because the story not so much stimulates translators to manipulate its relatively concise text as it invites them to fill in its telling gaps. One of its poorly developed characters beats all the others when it comes to her potential for gap filling. Where Cinderella's fairy godmother is concerned, Perrault gives the reader particularly little to go on. Information about the fairy's age, looks or motives is withheld and it is not until the explicit moral at the end of the fairy tale that the reader's attention is drawn to the character's significance outside of the magical 'chronotope': a beautiful young lady's good traits may prove to be useless if she does not have a godfather or a godmother to make them count. Yet this limited information is what allowed for such a rich array of interpretations. In Dutch versions alone the fairy appears in the guise of a goddess, a beggar woman, a witch, a grandmother, Mother Goose herself and many more variations on these guises. Some translators turned the fairy into a more rounded character because the genre or the intended audience required them to. Others did so because they seem to have appreciated the potential of this flat but influential character to instil (implicitly or explicitly) the implied translator's ideas not only into Cinderella's mind but also vicariously into that of the reader, provided that the character is developed more fully.

In this article I will draw on Emer O'Sullivan's communicative model of translation which identifies the implied translator as the intratextual agency that generates the implied reader of the target text, who in turn is seen as a time-specific and culture-specific entity (2005: 105-106). When we are looking to identify the beliefs and values of that implied translator, or what O'Sullivan refers to as 'the discursive presence of the translator' (ibid.: 109), we can either examine paratexts such as prefaces, or, as such *explicit* renderings of the translator's views became less and less customary, *implicit* traces can be found in the texts themselves, for instance in the textual elements added in the target text in order to fill gaps in the source text. Where Dutch 'Cinderella' translations are concerned, we find these traces in the guises that Cinderella's fairy godmother adopts.

This article will look into those different (dis)guises within the selected corpus of five Dutch translations published between the end of the eighteenth and the end of the twentieth century. It will explore how the translators' interpretations of Perrault's character reveal child images and reflect prominent tendencies in the development of children's literature in the Netherlands and Flanders. The term 'translation' will be used for both target texts that are equivalent to the source text, or at least create the illusion of being so, and target texts that deal with those source texts more freely. As such there is no strict line between translations and adaptations, which I prefer to see not as opposites but as positions on a scale.

## Out with Well-To-Do Godparents, in with True Love

The first Dutch translation of Perrault's fairy tales was published anonymously in The Hague in 1754 and was meant, as the subtitle states, 'for the youth to practise their French and Dutch'.[1] It contains Perrault's French text as well as its Dutch translation and is one of the most faithful translations of Perrault's fairy tales ever published in the Dutch-speaking regions. As such it contrasts quite strongly with a second, entirely new translation which was most likely published some 25 years later, around 1770. The first translation to find fault with Perrault's moral, in the preface added in the second edition as well as in the fairy tale itself, was the 'Cinderella' translation of *Vermakelyke Vertellingen Van Den Oude Tyd, Of zo genaamde Sprookjes Van Het Rood Kousje. Nieuwelyks uit het Frans Vertaald. Met Zeede-Leszen en Aanmerkingen verrykt* [Amusing Tales of Old Times, or So-called Fairy Tales of Little Red Stocking. Newly Translated from French. Improved with Morals and Remarks]. As such it is an excellent first illustration of how the character of the fairy, or in this particular case her absence from the moral of the story, shows traces of the implied translator's ideology. Because, although the 'Cinderella' translation is relatively faithful as a whole, its moral – aptly called 'Remark'(Anonymous n.d.: 74)[2] – is not. There is no mention of godmothers or godfathers. At least they *seem* to be absent because the anonymous translator *is* in fact very much concerned with what those godparents stand for, namely the means to bring someone to the throne. He writes: 'Because for money, nor for goods,/did virtue ever touch one's heart./ […] Cinderella was full of virtues,/and so the Prince was swift to take her;/for if her manner had not pleased him,/he would never have asked for her again' (ibid.: 75).[3] It is Cinderella's virtues, her beauty and good soul that enchant the prince, not money or the influence of a well-off godmother.

In this moral the translator seems to condemn the societal practice that Perrault refers to in his moral, when he writes that a young lady's talents cannot bring her success without the blessing of a godparent. 'But all of these [talents] may prove useless/And you may indeed need others/If you think you can have success/Without godfathers or godmothers' (Perrault 1697: 148; translation Jack Zipes 2001: 454).[4]

The first Dutch translation of 1754 made this reference to well-to-do godparents much less open for interpretation by adding the adjective 'rich', stating that young people who are looking for success can only obtain it when they have *rich* godfathers or godmothers:

'Yet these gifts [wit, courage, good sense and birth] rarely make/a young person aspiring advancement/very successful without *rich* Godfathers or Godmothers/to make them count'(Anonymous 1754: 101; emphasis added).[5]

The 1770s translation dismisses the idea of wealth as a determining factor for a marriage altogether. The beliefs behind this fundamental change to the core message of the source text are discussed in the quite extensive preface to the second edition of the fairy tale collection in which the anonymous author both adheres to and dismisses some of the ideas of early enlightenment, proving to be an advocate of a more sensitive kind of enlightenment, influenced by sentimentalism. The author claims to believe in the ability of fiction 'to playfully educate the young' (Anonymous n.d.: 2):[6] when fiction diverts while edifying, it has the potential to develop the reader's intellect (ibid.: 4).[7] This claim immediately calls to mind John Locke's ideas on education, published in *Some Thoughts Concerning Education* in 1693. Although the book was translated into Dutch five years later, the Netherlands had to wait 55 more years, until 1753, for a second and much more influential translation to be published. That translation by Pieter Adriaen Verwer seems to have influenced, among others, Hieronymous van Alphen, who is often called the founder of Dutch children's literature and who introduced ideas into the Netherlands that had already been in vogue in other parts of Europe for quite some time. Some call him a precursor of Romanticism (among others P.J. Buijnsters 1973: 113) but in his pedagogical views the influence of the Enlightenment is unmistakable. One of his most famous poems 'Het vrolijk leeren' [The Cheerful Learning], published in 1778 in *Proeve van kleine gedigten voor kinderen* [Example of Little Poems for Children] bears testimony to the influence of Locke's pedagogical ideas in the Netherlands: 'My playing is learning, my learning playing,/so why should learning be weary?/I take pleasure in reading and writing' (van Alphen 1778: 25).[8]

Although the author of the preface of the *Amusing Tales* adheres to these ideas on education, making a plea for 'edifying pleasure',[9] he departs from Locke's ideas when it comes to the kind of books he himself considers to be suitable for the purpose of playful learning, namely books on true love. According to him, the subject had been banned from literature, along with other subjects familiar to bourgeois society, because it was in discord with 'Reason'. In his view 'it is certain that true and unfeigned love should be the foundation of any respectable marriage' (Anonymous n.d.: 3-4)[10] because in marriages arranged for reasons of 'Wealth, Honour or State'(ibid.)[11] discord ruled. And so in the 'Cinderella' translation that this preface precedes, the well-to-do fairy godmother in the end has to yield her role or at least part of her role in the realisation of Cinderella's marriage for true love. In what looks like an attempt to edify youngsters while diverting them, the translator adapted Perrault's moral, stripping the fairy not of her magic but of her earthly powers.

## Mercy and Resignation Lead to Heaven

Another firm believer in the power of literature to educate and edify is Dr. Pieter Jan Heije, one of the most well-known Dutch children's poets of the nineteenth century. After the separation of Belgium from the Netherlands in 1831, he seems to have considered it his duty to awaken the Dutch people, cultivate their good qualities and fight national vices.[12] Furthermore the poverty problem was assuming such vast proportions that members of the upper-middle class felt obliged to take a stand on the issue. And so did Heije: not only in a lecture on poverty, but also in a 'Cinderella' translation titled *Asschepoester. Een sprookje uit de oude doos* ([Cinderella. A Fairy Tale of the Olden Days], 1865)[13] that reflected the views expressed in that lecture.

In his lecture *De grondslag van de Maatschappij der Toekomst* [The Foundations of the Future Society] published in 1850, Heije proposed two approaches to the poverty issue. He first of all considered love for one's fellow man (which can be seen as a broader concept than Christian charity) to be the key to solving the social problems. According to his biographer Alphons Julianus Maria Asselberghs, Heije secondly defended the idea of a class society ordained by God (1966: 49). Throughout his oeuvre we find a 'cult of resignation' – explicitly promoted in paratexts or incorporated within the stories themselves – that propagates the message that resigning oneself to one's god-given lot in life will lead to heaven. Heije underlines 'the bliss, found in being poor, when one subjects oneself to God's will, like a child; [...] the joy of the needy, who have gathered great treasures in Heaven through their suffering, their hunger and their thirst' (Heije 1850 quoted in Asselberghs 1966: 49).[14]

Both views, or virtues that one should pursue – mercy (as a solution for poverty) and resignation to one's god-given lot – resurface in Heije's 'Cinderella' translation, both in the explicitly expressed views of the fairy who acts as a representative of God, on the one hand, and in the tests that she puts Cinderella through on the other. Those tests are no novelty in the history of Dutch 'Cinderella' translations. From the nineteenth century onwards several Dutch translators seem to have found Cinderella's humble acceptance of her dire fate insufficient proof of her virtue. An extra test in the shape of an old lady or the odd old man begging for food[15] was meant to emphasise Cinderella's good nature just a little more. In Heije's translation Cinderella can hardly prove to be any more virtuous than she already is since she is not only 'generous', 'obliging', 'docile', 'ever-contented', 'never envious', 'patient', 'compassionate', 'merciful', 'pious', 'humble', 'good', 'virtuous', 'gentle', 'kind', 'sweet', 'intelligent' and 'obedient',[16] her piety is also unparalleled: she prays to be tall and strong so that she can do an even better job for her stepsisters (Heije 1865: 5).[17] And yet Heije also submits her to a test that she obviously passes with flying colours. When the fairy comes to Cinderella disguised as a poor old lady 'shivering with the cold, the elbows through her sleeves' (ibid.: 10),[18] the girl offers her her last piece of bread, pretending not to be hungry at all. After which the lady announces: '"[...] The grace of Heaven will be showered upon you! – /I know, that our Dear Lord/rewards mercy,/and that his Host of angels preserve those/who are pious and humble and good!/And so it will preserve You;"' (ibid.: 12).[19] Because of her mercy for the beggar woman, the compassion that she has shown for someone who is even worse off than she is, Cinderella finds herself protected by God *and* rewarded on earth, by the fairy who grants her a night at the ball.

As C.J. Spat aptly remarks in his review of the translation, Cinderella at this point proves to be 'not insensitive to the pleasures of life'(1866: 520),[20] a small flaw that he evaluates as one of the positive aspects of the book, making Cinderella a very 'natural' character. From a present-day perspective, the character can hardly be called natural but Heije, too, seems to have deemed Cinderella flawed and found that one test was insufficient proof of her virtue. So he puts her through a second test, after which the true reward awaits. That second test is unique for Heije's translation and does not take shape until the very end of the story: '"and through your modesty/you passed the last test …/because if you had not waited humbly,/until the slipper was brought to you,/but had gone to the court yourself,/ then you too/(that much is clear!)/had *not* fitted the slipper!"' (Heije 1865: 59).[21]

Acceptance of her dire fate, of what Heije mentioned in his lecture, namely 'the suffering, the hunger and the thirst', secures Cinderella a reward. If she had not waited humbly for God to reveal his plans to her, she would have missed out on her chance to be part of the royal family, and in this particular translation, replace the prince's dead sister and continue to do good for the poor. The festivities in honour of Cinderella's acceptance into the royal family last but a few weeks but her acts of charity for the poor last a lot longer because: 'she (who had once endured so much hardship/herself)/knew, how much it hurts,/when everyone forgets us/and we have to suffer so forlorn!' (ibid.: 67-68).[22]

Children who, just like Cinderella, can relate to this feeling of loneliness, are the implied readers or listeners of the frame story in which Heije embedded his 'Cinderella' tale. On the first page of the book, children, poor children in particular, are invited to vicariously experience what Cinderella lives through when she sees her stepsisters leave for the ball and is left behind. This is because, just like Cinderella, the addressees see a peer – Klaartje, the neighbours' daughter dressed in her Sunday clothes – leave for a ball, while the narrator assures them that they should not be jealous of her since:

> [a] pleasant evening by the fireside,/spent with sweet song and beautiful stories/is worth much more/than the most exquisite ball or meal./And children, even if you have nothing,/pray envy, spite or sorrow/for what someone else possesses/will never creep into your heart. (ibid.:1)[23]

This extract characterises Heije as the 'Enlightened moralist with Romantic impulses'[24] that Petrus Jacobus Buijnsters and Leontine Buijnsters-Smets call him (2001: 115). The frame story allows readers to experience the importance of both domesticity and of resigning oneself to one's fate *from within*. But it also clearly propagates Enlightenment ideas, stressing the importance of literature on a more metatextual level and clarifying what this translation is to achieve. Heije has been called a 'functional' writer (Stroop 2002: 241) because he firmly believed in the power of literature and song to educate and edify the lower classes as well as children. And which genre was better fitted to edify both groups than the fairy tale, provided that it was adapted to their level of comprehension and included a moral? Heije considered a moral to be an indispensable part of poetry for the lower classes as well as for children. In a letter to Jan Pieter de Keyzer sent on January 3, 1866 he grants that in 'pure lyrical poetry' morals are a mistake, but in 'poetry for the working classes and children a moral is almost a virtue, at least an inevitable, necessary means to an end' (quoted in Asselberghs 1966: 110),[25] the end being to educate and elevate. This assumption also seems to apply to Heije's fairy tales like 'Cinderella' and 'De Gelaarsde Kat' ([Puss in Boots], [1867]) which are both overtly moralising. In his review of Heije's 'Puss in Boots' translation of 1868, Simon Gorter criticises the translator for making the now elderly Mother Goose preach (187).[26] And this preaching is also present in his 'Cinderella' translation. Contemporary critics criticised Heije for sacrificing the literary qualities of his work to the message that he wanted to spread, although his 'desire to cultivate good qualities and fight national vices'(J.G. Frederiks & F.J. van den Branden 1888-1891: 332)[27] was greatly appreciated.

Heije seems to have considered the incorporation of his message of mercy and resignation into his story, by means of a fairy godmother who acts as his and God's spokeswoman, insufficient. In what seems like an attempt to 'touch the tender chords of children's hearts', as Spat puts it (1866: 521),[28] Heije embedded his tale into a frame story that allows the implied reader to experience the moral of the fairy tale from within.

## Humour, Humanity and Diligence

Despite Jan Pieter Heije's attempts to bridge the emotional distance between him and his young readers, he never quite managed to do so. Whereas he, as a patronising author trying to instil his bourgeois morals, kept towering over the reader, the author of *De sprookjes van moeder de gans* [The Fairy Tales of Mother Goose] published in 1866 made a few more well-considered attempts to bridge the gap with the child reader. Agatha, a pseudonym for Reynoudina de Goeje, marks the beginning of a new era in Dutch children's literature. During the second half of the nineteenth century, when, as Buijnsters & Buijnsters-Smets claim, writers who had to live up to their literary name no longer wrote children's books (2001: 287), the overall attitude towards children's literature had changed. Whereas in the first half of the nineteenth century Dutch children's books were mainly meant to emancipate the child as quickly as possible, propagating enlightened ideas and morals, authors for children now seemed to realise books did not have to be 'useful, learned and tedious' (Hildebrand 1837: 346)[29] for them to 'contribute to their education' (Agatha [1866]: 1).[30] Children's books published during that second half of the nineteenth century had to be amusing and diverting, in line with poetical ideas expressed by prominent authors and critics such as Petrus Augustus de Génestet (1858)[31] and Nicolas Beets (1867),[32] who felt that children's literature had to be more playful and the child characters more childlike.

As a well-known writer of some hundred books for infants, young girls and young ladies, publishing one book after the other because she was dependent on her writing income, Agatha is responsible for a large part of Dutch children's literature published during the second half of the nineteenth century. The new mentality, which includes a new child image, shows in Agatha's entire oeuvre, but is particularly reflected in her 'Cinderella' translation included in *The Fairy Tales of Mother Goose*. Agatha's concern for the child readers and their involvement in the story can be noticed in some very small changes and additions to the source text that the translator identifies in her preface as 'Contes de

Perrault' (Agatha [1866]: 1). Examples are the explicit link made between text and illustrations in the words 'as can be seen in the picture' (ibid.: 15)[33] and the exchange of 'orange and lemon segments' that the prince offers Cinderella at the ball into 'pistachios and sugared almonds' (ibid.: 16).[34] But the new mentality is much clearer in two more fundamental changes to the source text which, again, involve the fairy godmother. It can first of all be seen in the comic relief that was added to the story in the shape of the fairy's good sense of humour, and secondly in the very subtle way in which Cinderella's godmother allows her godchild to be more human. In the preface to her fairy tales Agatha explicitly claims that she wants to correct the 'unchildlike' aspects of the *Contes de Perrault* (ibid.: 1).[35] One of those aspects may be Cinderella's almost superhuman stamina in the face of her ordeal. Agatha's fairy godmother allows her godchild to no longer be the ever-virtuous and patient push-over that she used to be. She gets to complain about her arms getting stiff from all the ironing and makes a witty remark about the thin waists that her stepsisters want to obtain no matter what, the irony of which the elder stepsister fails to catch: '"She [the beautiful princess at the ball] must have been delighted about your thin waists, I should think," Cinderella remarked, mockingly. "I believe so too," said Javotte, "she seemed very fond of us"' (ibid.: 17).[36]

Her godmother bears this remark about the sisters' vanity in mind when she eventually deals with their outrageous behaviour in a very humorous way:

> 'You misbehaved and you will be punished severely.' 'Have mercy, have mercy,' the sisters begged, but the fairy would not budge and waved her wand over the sisters, as she said: 'one favour I will grant you. You will keep your thin waists, because you love them so much,' and she turned them both into wasps, that flew away buzzing[.] (ibid.: 22)[37]

Apart from her work as a writer of fiction (for children), Agatha was closely involved in what one of her reviewers called 'the female question' (J.C.H. Heijse 1874: 373).[38] She was an editor of one of the first feminist women's magazines of the Netherlands, *Ons streven* [Our Ambition], and published several books on the issue of the position of women in society, such as *Onze werkkring* ([Our Working Environment], 1868) in which she fulminates against 'the young ladies of our class who do not do anything but wait for a marriage!' (quoted by J. Hoek 1868: 405).[39] It is surprising that this involvement is not reflected in the 'Cinderella' versions that Agatha wrote because the fairy tale is, after all, very much concerned with the position of women in society. What we do find in her fairy tale book of 1866 is a moral that promotes diligence as a way to reach happiness. Because if a girl or boy is as diligent as Cinderella, he or she will be rewarded by the fairy: 'Be as kind and friendly,/as diligent and helpful,/then I can vouch for it,/that the goddess of luck,/will offer you so much joy in your heart/that you can hardly imagine it' (Agatha [1866]: 23).[40]

Cinderella's godmother did in fact, intentionally or unintentionally, test that diligence before sending her godchild to the ball in an episode included in almost every Dutch 'Cinderella' translation that bears resemblance to Perrault's version. Perrault and most Dutch translators make Cinderella come up with the idea of checking the trap for a rat to turn into a coachman, all by herself. Agatha, on the other hand, makes the fairy wonder out loud where she can get a coachman, as if to test Cinderella:

> That coach with those six horses was a pretty sight. 'But how do I ever get a coachman?' the godmother asked. 'Shall I check whether there are any rats in the trap?' Cinderella asked. 'Good thinking,' said the godmother pleased and changed the rat that was caught in the trap into a coachman[.] (ibid.: 13-14)[41]

Cinderella passes the test with flying colours, receiving praise for her diligence from her godmother and being rewarded with a night at the ball.

By means of her humour, a more human main character and a call for (female) diligence Agatha set more than one trend in the history of Dutch 'Cinderella' translations.

## Working through a Cinderella Complex

During the next decades, authors of children's literature continued to explore the possibilities of more 'natural' child characters and around the turn of the century more and more explicit attention was given to children's feelings. This trend is reflected in the next translation which is an excellent example of what Dutch critic Anne de Vries called 'the sentimental genre' (2000: 31),[42] a genre that became popular in Dutch children's literature almost a century after the heyday of sentimentalism in the Netherlands and that comprised touching stories about poor children who nevertheless triumphed in the end.

As a story about virtue in distress in the widest possible sense, the 'Cinderella' tale can serve the main purpose of mainstream sentimental literature, namely teaching a moral lesson by effectively appealing to the readers' feelings. In order to induce readers to respond to the story almost physically, the translator just has to add to Cinderella's suffering and highlight her emotions. During the nineteenth century and at the beginning of the twentieth several Dutch translators recognised the fairy tale's potential as a source of 'tragic pleasure' (Anonymous 1863: 93).[43] This led them to increase Cinderella's suffering, thereby creating textual possibilities for the reader to suffer vicariously, while at the same time reassuring that reader with the prospect of a happy ending. But most of those translators denied Cinderella any kind of 'human' reaction to her increased suffering, still portraying the character as an impassive, unchildlike paragon of virtue. Apart from just a few exceptions, it is not until the interbellum that Cinderella is allowed to be flawed. Johanna Wildvanck is one of those translators who turned Cinderella into a sentimental character that readers can respond to almost physically but she also allows her protagonist a human response. Just like Agatha's Cinderella, Wildvanck's character does not stay impassive in the face of her ordeal.

In her 1917 'Cinderella' translation, Wildvanck's additions to Cinderella's suffering seem endless: the evil stepsisters become Cinderella's actual sisters, who deprive her of all love and contact with fellow human beings, forcing her to befriend animals instead. It almost goes without saying that in this romantic translation Cinderella is able to speak the language of the doves, the mice, the rats and the lizards (Wildvanck [1917]: 6).[44] The appropriate tear-jerking reaction to this ordeal is a lament that takes up almost two entire pages, in which Cinderella shows her human, childlike side; imagining herself to be much too ugly and stupid to show herself to the world, she thinks: '"O, how horrible is my destiny," […]. "I actually wish I was dead"' (ibid.: 9).[45]

Later on she repeats these words to her godmother, complaining that she gets absolutely nothing out of life, at the same time realising that someone as ugly and stupid as she is should just crawl away into a corner. 'She sat down in front of the fire place and, as a real Cinderella, stared into the remains of the fire […]' (ibid.: 36).[46]

This metafictional reference to the 'real Cinderella' seems to suggest that Wildvanck's Cinderella considers the dependent fairy tale character that is unable to make something of her life on her own, some kind of ideal worth imitating. The fairy helps Cinderella work through her Cinderella complex, thereby implicitly pointing out the flaws of her godchild's literary role model to the reader. Like a real therapist, she allows her godchild to talk through her hardships. And this talk therapy seems to work like magic because 'Cinderella was starting to forget her sorrow' (ibid.: 13).[47] But it is the fairy's actual magic that allows the girl to finally feel entitled to the prince's hand in marriage: instead of wallowing in self-pity and not taking any initiative, as do women suffering from the Cinderella complex, Wildvanck's Cinderella eventually overcomes her fears.

## Curing Alzheimer's to Accommodate the Implied Reader

In my final example it is not Cinderella but the fairy godmother herself who is humanised. In 1950 Disney released its animated film *Cinderella* and soon afterwards dozens of Dutch 'Cinderella' books featuring the Disney illustrations flooded the market. A small number of those books are translations of English text versions of the Disney film. But much more interesting in the context of this article are the Dutch versions that combine the Disney illustrations with the authors' own versions of the story, or, as the cover of the first Dutch Disney translation puts it, 'retell the story based on information from the film' (Belinfante [1950]: 1).[48] Those authors seem to have had the liberty to handle that 'information' quite freely because some deviate considerably from the path paved by Disney, again especially when it comes to a character on which Disney left its very recognizable mark: the fairy godmother.

Marina Warner is right to argue that in Disney's *Cinderella* '[a]uthentic power lies with the bad women, and the plump cosy fairy godmother […] seems no match for them' (1994: 207). Plump cosy fairy godmothers are however no novelty in the history of Dutch 'Cinderella' translations. Before Disney left its mark on the character – a mark that has inevitably influenced later Dutch translations – the fairy had already appeared in all kinds of guises, in some Dutch versions as an extremely powerful and frightening woman, in others as a charming plump old lady with limited magic powers. But Disney *is* the first to fill a telling gap in Perrault's tale that all Dutch 'Cinderella' versions published before 1950 had left open. After providing Cinderella with a coach, a coachman and footmen, Perrault's fairy stops doing magic, obliging her godchild to explicitly ask her for a new set of clothes: 'Then the fairy said to Cinderella, "Well, now you have something to take you to the ball. Are you satisfied?" "Yes, but am I to go in these dirty clothes?"'(Perrault 1754; translation Zipes 2001: 451).[49]

Some Dutch versions subsequently have the fairy wonder how she could be so forgetful but none *explain* that her forgetfulness may or may not be intentional. The fairy could, for instance, be conjuring up another test for Cinderella to see how much (or little) initiative she shows. Disney filled that gap (of the lack of explanation for the fairy's forgetfulness) by cursing Cinderella's godmother with the early symptoms of Alzheimer's, turning her into a slightly demented old lady who keeps forgetting where she left her wand, thereby rendering her even more harmless than she already was and at the same time providing some comic relief.

Not all Dutch authors who worked with the Disney illustrations seemed to agree with this extensive 'humanisation' of the fairy, perhaps *because* it adds to an issue that Warner has drawn attention to, namely the 'disequilibrium between good and evil' in the Disney version of 'Cinderella' (1994: 207). The prevalence of evil throughout the story may have conflicted with the clear code of right and wrong that several Dutch and Flemish critics demanded after the two world wars, out of a concern for the perceived moral decay of youth (de Vries 2000: 39). On the other hand Dutch translators may have expected the humanised fairy to not quite live up to the readers' expectations, which is what the author of a Dutch Disney book published in 1951 seemed to anticipate. The book is a chromo-graph album in which children could paste the 125 chromo trade cards (lithographs in colour) of Disney's *Cinderella* that they could find in boxes of De Beukelaer biscuits. Unable to change the fairy's physical traits shown in the illustrations, the translator created an implied reader who is surprised to encounter such a human fairy.

> When Cinderella lifts her head, she sees a very sweet elderly lady standing next to her in a circle of bright lights. 'Who are you?' she asks, sobbing. 'I am your godmother. I am a fairy.' 'A fairy?' the girl asks surprised. Because a fairy usually looks quite different. Not that motherly and simple. A fairy is usually quite untouchable. You can look at her for a moment and then your eyes sting. You can't talk to her like you would to your brother or sister[.] (Anonymous [1951]: 20)[50]

Another series of books for 'young readers', *Sprookjes Parade: De 17 beste verhalen voor jonge lezers* ([Fairy Tale Parade: The Best 17 Stories for Young Readers], 1973), *Walt Disney Assepoester*, ([Walt Disney Cinderella], 1976) and *Walt Disney's leesboek* ([Walt Disney's Reading Book], 1976), simply undoes Disney's humanisation of the fairy. She is not only no longer Cinderella's godmother rather than just a fairy, but she is also extremely lucid and efficient, finishing her magic job in no time. Cinderella does not even have to ask for a new dress: 'Now it was Cinderella's turn. The fairy kept on doing magic. Shoes, a dress, long gloves, earrings, she conjured up everything for Cinderella' (Walt Disney Studio & J. G. Steur 1973: n.p.).[51]

This characterisation of the fairy could, again, be linked to the intended audience of the fairy tales, as the books, that are meant as reading material, clearly identify their addressees, stating that 'the choice of words and syntax are adapted to the young readers' reading proficiency' (ibid.).[52] With its extensive humanisation of the fairy, Disney had cleared the path for some very successful fairy tale versions featuring variably 'human' fairies, in animation as well as in literature. DreamWorks Animation Studio turned the 'Fairy Godmother' into the main antagonist of its computer-animated film *Shrek 2* (2004). As a scheming opportunist on a diet, the fairy could hardly become any more human. Yet in contrast to Disney this humanisation empowered the character, as does a trend in fiction. 'Cinderella' versions that turn the fairy into Cinderella's lover empower the character *sexually* because they enable her not only to exercise *magic* power over her godchild but also to strengthen the emotional ties with Cinderella. In fairy tale versions for an older intended audience, this trend of having a sexually powerful fairy was established well before the character ever made her way into children's literature. We find an example in Emma Donoghue's 'Tale of the Shoe', published in *Kissing the Witch* in 1997 and translated into Dutch as *Een kus voor de heks* in the same year. But the Netherlands also had their very own potent fairy, put on stage in both a magic melodrama and a ballet-pantomime, written around 1865 by Wilhelmus Nicolaas Peypers. They both show the fairy, disguised as an old beggar woman, caressing and trying to seduce the footman sent around the world to find Cinderella. It took almost two centuries for this sexually potent fairy to make it from the stage into Dutch children's literature: a picture book published in 2010, *Roodkapje was een toffe meid. Stoere sprookjes om te rappen* [Little Red Riding Hood was a Fabulous Chick. Cool Fairy Tales to Rap] by Marjet Huiberts, shows Cinderella standing the prince up, leaving with the fairy instead.

These examples are just a few illustrations of a trend followed by dozens of Dutch 'Cinderella' translations that humanise the fairy but, in contrast to Disney, in doing so also empower her. Disney's disempowering humanisation did not find a ready acceptance with Dutch translators. The authors of the Dutch Disney books that I discussed most likely cured the fairy's incipient Alzheimer's to accommodate the implied readers of the translations who needed recognisable characters and a superhuman counterweight for the evil stepmother.

## Conclusion

Cinderella's fairy godmother is not always who we imagine her to be. When disenchanted through literary analysis, the character of the fairy shows her true colours, revealing traces of the translator's ideology in every guise that she adopts. At the end of the eighteenth and in the first half of the nineteenth century the fairy, replaced by middle-class ideals in the anonymous 1770s translation, or acting as a representative of God in Heije's tale, conformed with ideas of the Enlightenment, propagated virtues and, in doing so, edified the young. Although Cinderella still played an exemplary role in 'Cinderella' translations published in the *second* half of the nineteenth century, she no longer had to be an absolute paragon of virtue. Agatha's godmother allowed her to be more human and this humorous translation with its new child image met the demand for more child friendly children's books. Children's feelings kept gaining importance and Johanna Wildvanck's sentimental translation showed children and parents alike how to deal with those emotions, by means of a fairy godmother whose main purpose was to cure Cinderella of her negative self-image. Finally none of the previous translations humanised the fairy like Disney did, so much so that Dutch translators felt the need to dehumanise her. But whether she is portrayed as almost divine or down-to-earth, empowered or disempowered, forcing Cinderella in her turn to be almost superhuman or allowing her to be human instead, in all of these Dutch translations the fairy godmother seems to have fulfilled her potential.

# Bibliography

## *Primary Sources*

Agatha. [1866]. *De sprookjes van moeder de gans. Op nieuw verhaald. Door Agatha. Met vele Houtgravuren*. Leiden: Van den Heuvell & Van Santen.

Agatha. 1868. *Onze werkkring*. Haarlem: Bohn.

Anonymous. N.d.. *Vermaaklyke Vertellingen van den Ouden Tyd, of zogenaamde Sprookjes van het Rood Kousje; zynde de Vertellingen van Moeder de Gans uit het Fransch vertaald. Met Zede-Lessen en Aanmerkingen verrykt. Den Tweeden Druk*. Amsterdam: Erve de Weduwe Jacobus van Egmont.

Anonymous. 1754. *Contes De Ma Mere L'Oye./Vertellingen Van Moeder De Gans. Met negen kleurlyke koopere Plaatjes, zeer dienstig voor de Jeugdt om haar zelve in het Fransch en Hollands te oeffenen*. The Hague: Pierre van Os.

Anonymous. [ca. 1770]. *Vermakelyke Vertellingen Van Den Oude Tyd, Of zo genaamde Sprookjes Van Het Rood Kousje. Nieuwelyks uit het Frans Vertaald. Met Zeede-Leszen en Aanmerkingen verrykt*. Amsterdam: Erve de Weduwe Jacobus van Egmont.

Anonymous. 1865. *Asschepoetster, of het glazen muiltje. Nieuw, Groot, Phantastisch Ballet-Pantomine, in vier bedrijven, of dertien tafereelen, vrij gevolgd naar de vertelling van moeder de gans*. Amsterdam: De erven H. van Munster & zoon.

Anonymous. [1951]. *Album Assepoester 125 chromos*. Antwerp: De Beukelaer.

Belinfante, R. [1950]. *Walt Disney's Assepoester*. Amsterdam: L.J. Veen.

Donoghue, E. 1997. *Een kus voor de heks*. Amsterdam: Atlas. (Translation of: Donoghue, E. 1997. *Kissing the Witch: Old Tales in New Skins*. London – New York: Hamish Hamilton – HarperCollins.)

Heije, J.P. 1846. *Sprookjes uit de oude doos*. Amsterdam: J.H. & G. Van Heteren.

Heije, J.P. 1865. *Asschepoester. Een sprookje uit de oude doos, op rijm gebragt door J.P. Heije. Met Hoogduitsche Vertaling, door Mevr. Henriette Heinze-Berg*. Amsterdam: J.H. & G. Van Heteren.

Heije, J.P. [1867]. *De gelaarsde kat (der gestiefelte kater) Een sprookje uit de oude doos. op rijm gebragt door J.P. Heije. Allen frommen deutschen Kindern zu Liebe, aus dem hollaendischen des Dr. J.P. Heije Uebersetzt von Henriette Heinze-Berg*. Amsterdam: G.L. Funke.

Huiberts, M. 2010. *Roodkapje was een toffe meid. Stoere sprookjes om te rappen*. Ill. W. Panders B. Linger (CD) Haarlem: Gottmer.

Perrault, C. 1697. *Histoires ou contes du temps passé. Avec des moralitez*. Paris: Barbin.

Peypers, W.N. N.d.. *Asschepoester en het glazen muiltje. Groot toovermelodrama in acht tafereelen, met een tusschenspel in zeven tableaux; naar aanleiding van het sprookje van 'moeder de gans'. Tweede druk.* [S.l.: s.n.].

van Alphen, H. 1778. *Proeve van kleine gedigten voor kinderen.* Utrecht: Wed. Jan van Terveen en Zoon.

Visser, P.H.J. N.d.. *De nieuwe Asschepoetster.* Leiden: Noothoven van Goor.

Walt Disney Studio & J.G. Steur 1973. *Walt Disney's Sprookjes Parade. De 17 beste verhalen voor jonge lezers.* Antwerp – Harderwijk: Zuid-Nederlandse Uitgeverij – Centrale Uitgeverij.

Walt Disney Productions & J.-M. Mink. 1976. *Walt Disney's leesboek.* Antwerp: Zuidnederlandse Uitgeverij.

Walt Disney Productions. 1976. *Walt Disney Assepoester.* [Antwerp]: [Zuidnederlandse Uitgeverij].

Wildvanck, J. [1917]. *Asschepoester naverteld door Johanna Wildvanck Teekeningen van Sijtje Aafjes.* Amsterdam: Scheltens & Giltay.

## Secondary Sources

Anonymous. 1863. 'De sprookjes van Perrault', in: *De Nederlandsche Spectator* 28 februari: 66-67.

Asselberghs, A. J. M. 1966. *Dr. Jan Pieter Heije, of: De kunst en het leven.* Amsterdam: Vereniging voor Nederlandse Muziekgeschiedenis.

Beets N. 1867. 'Over kinderboeken. Gesprek met Crito', in: N. Beets, *Verscheidenheden, meest op letterkundig gebied III.* Haarlem: De erven F. Bohn, 1-66.

Buijnsters, P.J. & L. Buijnsters-Smets. 2001. *Lust en leering. Geschiedenis van het Nederlandse Kinderboek in de negentiende eeuw.* Zwolle: Waanders.

Buijnsters, P.J. 1973. *Hieronymus van Alphen (1746-1803).* Assen: Van Gorcum & Comp.

de Génestet, P.A. 1858. 'Over kinderpoëzy', in: *Nederland* 1: 239-282.

de Vries, A. 2000. *Van Hiëronymous tot heden.* The Hague: Letterkundig Museum.

Frederiks, J.G. & F.J. van den Branden. 1888-1891. 'Jan Pieter Heije', in: *Biographisch woordenboek der Noord- en Zuidnederlandsche letterkunde.* Amsterdam: L.J. Veen, 332-333.

Gorter, S. 1868. 'De gelaarsde kat', in: *De Gids* 32.1: 177-189.

Hildebrand. 1837. 'Vooruitgang', in: *De Gids* 1.1: 345-351.

Heije, J.P. 1850. *De Grondslag van de Maatschappij der Toekomst. Eene voorlezing (uitgegeven ten voordeele van het Volks-Zangonderwijs te Amsterdam.).* Amsterdam: J.H. en G. van Heteren.

Heijse, J.H.C. 1874. 'Op eigen wieken drijven. Novellen uit het Hoogduitsch door Agatha. Schiedam, van Dijk & Cº, 1872', in: *De Gids* 1.38: 364-376.

Hoek, J. 1868. 'Onze werkkring, door Agatha. "Aide-toi, et Dieu t'aidera"', in: *Vaderlandsche Letteroefeningen*: 404-409.

Locke, J. 1693. *Some Thoughts Concerning Education.* London: A. and J. Churchill.

O'Sullivan, E. 2005. *Comparative Children's Literature.* London: Routledge.

Spat, C.J. 1866. 'I. Fraaie Letteren: Al de volksdichten; Asschepoester', in: *Vaderlandsche Letteroefeningen*: 513-521.

Stroop, J. 2002. 'De nieuwe koers van Dr. Heije', in: *Literatuur zonder leeftijd* 16.58: 241-253.

Verwer, P.A. 1753. *Over de opvoeding der kinderen.* Amsterdam: K. van Tongerlo en F. Houttuin.

Warner, M. 1994. *From the Beast to the Blonde: on Fairy Tales and their Tellers.* London: Chatto & Windus.

Zipes, J. 2001. *The Great Fairy Tale Tradition: From Straparola and Basile to the Brothers Grimm.* London/New York: W.W. Norton & Company.

# Notes

1.  zeer dienstig voor de Jeugdt om haar zelve in het Fransch en Hollands te oeffenen (all translations by Lien Fret, unless otherwise indicated).

2.  Aanmerking

3.  Want voor het Geld, noch voor het Goed,/Kwam nooit de Deugd in het Gemoed./[…] Aschepoester vol Deugden was,/Daarom zo nam de Prins haar ras;/Want had haar omgang niet behaagt,/Hy had 'er nooit weêr na gevraagt.

4.  Pour votre avancement ce seront choses vaines /Si vous n'avez, pour les faire valoir, /Ou des parrains, ou des marraines.

5.  Doch deeze gaven [geest, moed, oordeel en geboorte] maken zelden/Dat eenig jong persoon, die na bevordring streeft,/Heel verre komt, indien hy, om ze doen gelden,/Geen Ryke Peetooms of geen Petemoeyen heeft.

6.  om de Jeugd al speelende te onderwyzen

7.  […] dat ze [Schryvers] de Jeugd al stichtende leeren en vermaaken. Dus oordeel ik dat zulke Verdichtsels, (men mag 'er van zeggen wat men wil,) verstand kunnen bijbrengen […] [[…] that they [writers] edifyingly teach and divert the youth. So I judge that such fiction (one may say of it what one wants,) can develop the intellect […]]

8.  Mijn speelen is leeren, mijn leeren is speelen,/En waarom zou mij dan het leeren verveelen?/ Het lezen en schrijven verschaft mij vermaak.

9.  de Jeugd al stichtende leeren en vermaaken [to teach and entertain the youth while edifying them] (Anonymous [ca. 1770]: 4)

10. […] dat het zeker is dat eene oprechte en ongeveinsde Liefde de grondslag van een onberispelyk Huwelyk zyn moet

11. Rykdom, Eer en Staat

12. In a letter written in 1867 Heije (quoted by his biographer A.J.M. Asselberghs 1966: 139) writes: 'k Ben […] zóó innig overtuigd van 't éénig nóódige voor ons Volk – "aesthtische en morele verheffing" naar binnen *én naar buiten* […]' [I am […] so profoundly convinced of the one thing néeded for *our* Nation – 'esthetic and moral edification' inwards *ánd outwards*? […]]

13. The *Cinderella* translation was first published in 1846 in *Sprookjes uit de oude doos* [Fairy Tales of the Olden Days], a collection of four translations of Perrault's fairy tales that included 'Roodkapje' [Little Red Riding Hood], 'De gelaarsde kat' [Puss in Boots] and 'Klein Duimpje' [Little Thumb].

14. […] het geluk, dat er in gelegen is arm te zijn, wanneer men zich kinderlijk onderwerpt aan Gods beschikkingen; […] de vreugde des behoeftigen, die zich door zijn lijden, zijn hongeren en dorsten, groote schatten in den Hemel vergaderd heeft[.]

15. In *De nieuwe Asschepoetster* [The New Cinderella] published around 1870 by P.H.J. Visser a beggar with a long beard rewards Cinderella for her compassion.

16. 'gul', 'gedienstig', 'gedweê', 'altijd weltevreê', 'zonder nijd', 'geduldig', 'vol meêlij', 'barmhartig', 'vroom', 'nedrig', 'goed', 'zedig', 'zacht', 'vriend'lijk', 'lieflijk', 'verstand[ig]' and 'braaf'

17. Dan bad ze: 'Och, maak mij, Lieve Heer!/Och, maak mij spoedig groot en sterk,/Opdat ik toch eens goed mijn werk/Kan doen […]' [Then she prayed: 'Oh, Dear Lord, make me!/Oh, soon make me tall and strong/so that I can do a good job for once […]']

18. bibbrend van de koû,/En de ellebogen door de mouw

19. '[…] Des Hemels gunst daal' op u neêr! – /Ik weet, dat bij ons' Lieven Heer/Barmhartigheid belooning vindt,/En dat zijn Englenschaar behoedt/Wie vroom en nedrig is en goed!/Dat zal ze ook U doen;'

20. niet ongevoelig voor 't genot des levens

21. 'en door uw zedigheid/De láatste proef doorgestaan …/Want hadt ge, nedrig, niet gewàcht,/Tot U het muiltje werd gebràgt,/Maar waart ge Zelv' naar 't Hof gegaan,/Dan had ook U/(en dit stond vast!)/Het glazen muiltje niet gepast!'

22. […] zij (die zelve zoo veel leed/Eens doorstond)/Wist, hoe zéer het doet,/Wanneer een ieder ons vergeet/En men zo eenzaam lijden moet!

23. Een prettige avond aan den haard,/Bij zoet gezang of mooi verhaal/Gesleten, is wel méer nog waard'/Dan 't prachtigst bal of 't lekkerst maal./En hadt ge ook, kinders! niêmendal,/Dan sluip' toch nimmer in uw hart/De nijd, de wangunst of de smart,/Omdat een ànder 't hebben zal.

24. een verlicht moralist met romantische bevliegingen

25. […] Moraal – komt mij voor in het volks- en kinderdicht bijna een *deugd*, althans een onvermijdelijk nóodig *middel* ter *bereiking* van het doel te zijn.

26. Moeder de Gans [is] […] op haar ouden dag aan het preeken gezet

27. 'zucht tot aankweking van goede eigenschappen in ons volk en bestrijding van nationale ondeugden

28. de teedere snaren te treffen van 't kinderlijk gemoed

29. De kinderen onzer dagen lezen allerhande nuttigheid, geleerdheid, vervelendheid. Zij lezen van volwassenen, die zij niet begrijpen, en van kinderen, die zij niet zouden durven navolgen. [The children of our days read all kinds of usefulness, learnedness and tediousness. They read about adults, whom they don't understand, and about children, whom they would not dare to imitate.]

30. medewerken tot hunne vorming

31. In 'Over kinderpoëzy' [On Children's Poetry] P.A. de Génestet claims: 'Kinderen moeten met kinderlijke versjes worden opgevoed, ook om later natuurlijke en kinderlijke menschen

te worden.' (1858: 338) [Children need to be raised with childlike rhymes, so that they can grow up to be natural and childlike people.], 'Want kinderen moeten kinderen, jongens moeten jongens wezen, en kinderpoëzie [...] geen schoolsche moraal.' [Because children need to be children, boys need to be boys, and children's poetry [...] no schoolish moral.] (1858: 341-342), 'al die vroege naarstigheid, geleerdheid, wijsheid [is] schadelijk [...] voor lichaam en geest' [all that early diligence, knowledge and wisdom are harmful [...] for body and mind] (1858: 343)

32.   In 'Over kinderboeken. Gesprek met Crito' [On Children's Books. Discussion with Crito] Nicolaas Beets (pseudonym Hildebrand) makes a plea for fairy tales, especially those of the brothers Grimm, because they are 'niet kinderachtig, maar in den reinsten en edelsten zin kinderlijk' [not childish, but in the most pure and noble sense childlike] (1867: 54).

33.   zooals op het plaatje te zien is

34.   pistaches en suikerbonen

35.   Het is niet te ontkennen dat de 'Contes de Perrault' bij veel schoons, ook veel onkinderlijks bevatten. Ik heb getracht dat in deze bewerking te verbeteren. [It cannot be denied that the 'Contes de Perrault', besides much beauty, also contain many unchildlike aspects. In my adaptation I have tried to correct those]

36.   'Zij [de schone prinses op het bal] was zeker opgetogen over uwe dunne middeltjes, denk ik,' merkte Asschepoester spottend aan. 'Dat geloof ik ook,' zeide Javotte, 'zij scheen zeer op ons gesteld te zijn.'

37.   '[...] Gij hebt veel misdaan en zult er zwaar voor boeten.' 'Genade, genade,' smeekten de zusters, maar de toovergodin liet zich niet verbidden en zwaaide haar wonderstaf over het zusterpaar heen, terwijl zij zeide: 'een gunst zal ik u bewijzen, namelijk, om u dunne middeltjes te laten, omdat gij daar zooveel van houdt,' en zij veranderde ze beiden in wespen, die brommende wegvlogen.

38.   de vrouwen-quaestie

39.   de jonge dames uit onzen stand [die] niets doen dan wachten op een huwelijk!...

40.   Weest maar even lief en aardig,/Even ijvrig en hulpvaardig,/Dan sta ik er vast voor in,/Dat u de geluksgodin/Zooveel vreugd in 't hart zal schenken,/Als gij u haast niet kunt denken.

41.   't Was een mooi gezicht die koets met die zes paarden. 'Maar hoe kom ik nu aan een koetsier?' vroeg de petemoei. 'Wil ik eens kijken of er ook ratten in de val zijn?' vroeg Asschepoester. 'Goed bedacht,' zeide de petemoei tevreden en veranderde de rat die in de val zat in een koetsier[.]

42.   het 'sentimentele genre'

43.   het verschrikkelijke, als element van tragisch genot voor de kleinen mag volstrekt niet worden weggelaten [the horrific, as a source of tragic pleasure for the little ones, can absolutely not be left out]

44.   Duiven, muisjes, ratten, hagedissen, allen spraken met haar, want van allen kende zij de taal [...] [Doves, mice, rats, lizards, they all spoke with her, because she knew their languages [...]]

45.   'O, hoe vreeselijk is toch mijn lot,' [...]. 'Ik wou eigenlijk maar dat ik dood was.'

46.    Ze ging voor de schouw zitten en staarde, als een echte Asschepoester, in de restjes van 't vuur [...]

47.    Asschepoester [was] bezig om haar verdriet te vergeten

48.    Naar gegevens uit de film 'Cinderella' opnieuw verteld door Renée Belinfante

49.    La fée dit alors à Cendrillon: 'Eh bien! voilà, de quoi aller au bal: n'es-tu pas bien aise? – Oui, mais est-ce que j'irai comme cela, avec mes vilains habits?'

50.    En als Assepoes het hoofd oplicht, ziet ze daar een zeer lieve oude dame naast zich staan in een kring van felle lichtjes. 'Wie zijt U?' vraagt ze in een snik. 'Ik ben je petemoei. Ik ben de goede fee.' 'Een fee?' verwonderd [sic] het meisje zich. Want een fee ziet er gewoonlijk toch anders uit. Niet zo moederlijk en eenvoudig. Een fee, die staat gewoonlijk zo ver van je af. Daar kun je alleen even naar kijken en dan prikken je ogen reeds. Daar kun je niet zo maar mee praten lijk met je broer of zus.

51.    Nu was Assepoester aan de beurt. De fee toverde en toverde maar. Schoentjes, een jurk, lange handschoenen, oorbellen, alles toverde ze voor Assepoester.

52.    Woordkeus en zinsbouw zijn afgestemd op de leesvaardigheid van jonge lezertjes.

# How Immortal is Disney's *Little Mermaid*?

## The Disneyfication of Andersen's 'The Little Mermaid'

### Jan Van Coillie

'Langt ude i Havet er Vandet saa blaat, som Bladene paa den deiligste Kornblomst og saa klart, som den reneste Glas[.]' [Far out in the ocean the water is as blue as the petals of the loveliest corn flower, and as clear as the purest glass.][1]

This is how Hans Christian Andersen's fairy tale 'Den lille havfrue' [The Little Mermaid] begins, but how does it end? Ask any child and it will probably answer: the bad sea witch was killed and then of course Ariel and the prince married and lived happily ever after. It would be very surprising if a child answered: after the little mermaid had discovered that the prince loved someone else, she threw herself into the sea. There she was welcomed by the daughters of the air, awaiting an immortal soul. Nevertheless, this is how Andersen's fairy tale ends. The other version is Disney's.[2] The ending, however, is only a portion of Disney's changes. This study focuses on Disney's adaptation of Andersen's fairy tale, trying to reveal and interpret some essential characteristics of its so-called 'disneyfication'.[3]

## Adaptation as Interpretation

Andersen's 'Den lille havfrue' appeared in 1837 in the first volume (third book) of his *Eventyr fortalte for Børn* [Fairy Tales Told for Children]. Over time, it has been published in many languages and forms. Disney's *The Little Mermaid* was released in 1989. The Disney studios adapted Andersen's story[4] for the screen. 'Adaptation' has several meanings here. Disney adapted the fairy tale to another medium (from book to screen; from written text to audio-visual text) and to a new audience: children and their parents living in another time and place.

Linda Hutcheon defines adaptation in a broad sense as 'an extended, deliberate, announced revisitation of a particular work of art' (2006: 170). More specifically, film adaptation is defined by Brian McFarlane as a form of intersemiotic translation, as 'the matching of the cinematic sign system to a prior achievement in some other system' (1996: 21). McFarlane continues to say that adaptation always implies the 'appropriation of a meaning from a prior text' (ibid.: 21). Adaptation, in other words, is always a form of interpretation. It reveals the 'vision' of the filmmaker, his or her views on (the functions of) film and his or her world view or ideology.[5] In studies of Disney's films, his vision or 'revisitation' of existing tales is seen as a kind of disneyfication.

## Comparative Analysis and Narratology

For this study, a comparative analysis of Andersen's fairy tale and Disney's film adaptation will be carried out. This analysis is based on concepts taken from narratology. The advantage of this discipline is that it can be applied to literature as well as to film. Both literary texts and films are narratives. Or, as Seymour Chatman states in his pioneering article 'What Novels Can Do that Films Can't (And Vice Versa)': 'One of the most important observations to come out of narratology is that narrative itself is a deep structure quite independent of its medium' (1980: 435).

This study of disneyfication focuses not only on what is narrated or presented, but also on how this is done. While literature and film can use similar strategies, they use different techniques. The study of these strategies and techniques is important, because they determine how the receiver is manipulated into forming certain views about the story and its meaning. In a film, for instance, a high angle shot (the camera looking down on a character) can manipulate the spectator into seeing the character as vulnerable or weak.

The analysis presented in this article focuses on changes in plot, characterisation, time, setting and perspective. Changes can be omissions, additions, substitutions or modifications and rearrangements. Events, characters, periods, settings can be omitted, added, substituted (replaced by another with similar characteristics or functions) or modified (changes within the presentation of an event, character or setting). Rearrangements affect the structure or sequencing of the film. Due to the limited scope of this study, a complete analysis of all these changes is not possible. The focus will be on the changes affecting the main character, the little mermaid. In both story and film she plays a central role in a series of events that form the nub of the narrative. Deep down in the ocean, the sea king lives with his daughters, the youngest of whom is different because she is fascinated by the human world. One night she sees a prince on a ship. When a storm starts to rage, she saves the prince from drowning. She leaves him behind on the beach but longs to see him again and goes to visit the sea witch, asking her to change her into a human being. In return, the witch wants her beautiful voice. Once human, the little mermaid sees the prince again on the mainland and tries to win his love.

A detailed comparison of the plot of the original fairy tale and the film makes very clear that the differences are much more striking than the similarities. The following table, giving a survey of the first fifteen scenes and first ten events,[6] immediately makes clear how dramatically Disney changed Andersen's story, omitting and adding scenes. Parallel scenes always contain changes, too, as will become clear in the analysis.

| Andersen | Disney |
|---|---|
|  | Introduction of Eric, Grimbert and Max on the ship |
| Introduction, describing the setting | Titles, while the merpeople converge on the sea king's palace |
| Introduction of the sea king and his family | Concert with introduction of Triton and his daughters |
|  | Ariel and Flounder explore a sunken ship |
|  | Ariel and Flounder visit Scuttle on his island |
|  | Ursula plans her revenge |
|  | Triton warns Ariel and forbids her to go to the surface again. |
| Description of the little mermaid's garden | Ariel sings in her cave |
| Grandmother's explanation of the transition ritual |  |
| Little mermaid's yearning |  |
| First sister rises up out of the ocean |  |
| Second sister rises up |  |
| Third sister rises up |  |
| Fourth sister rises up |  |
| Fifth sister rises up |  |
| Interest in the sisters diminishes |  |
| The little mermaid is prepared by her grandmother to rise up out of the ocean |  |
| Birthday party on the prince's ship, the little mermaid sees the prince | Birthday party on the ship, the little mermaid sees the prince |
| The little mermaid saves the prince during a storm | Ariel saves the prince during a storm |
| On the shore | On the beach |

**Table 1. Comparison of scenes/events**

## From Tormented Young Woman to Rebellious Teenager

In both Andersen's fairy tale and Disney's film version, the little mermaid is the main character. The comparative analysis focuses on her outer appearance, personality, thoughts and feelings.

What does Andersen write about the little mermaid's looks? In fact, very little:

> [B]ut the youngest was the most beautiful of them all. Her skin was soft and tender as a rose petal, and her eyes were as blue as the deep sea, but like all the others she had no feet. Her body ended in a fish tail.

Typical of Andersen's style are the similes to render the skin and eyes special: they cannot be 'translated' directly into film. Film cannot combine the skin and the rose petal in one image. Andersen stresses the little mermaid's beauty time and again, but mostly in general terms. Once she becomes human, he mentions her 'beautiful white legs and arms'. What does Disney make of these few elements?

In the very first shots of Ariel, her distinctly childlike face immediately attracts attention. The unusually big, round eyes, set wide apart, have been a popular characteristic of the sweet child in illustrated children's books since the end of the nineteenth century (Van Coillie 2008: 25-26). Ariel's sidekick and best fish friend, Flounder, looks like a cuddly toy and has a baby face. He accentuates her 'cuteness'. In this scene, where she searches through the sunken ship, she also behaves like a child: she is extremely curious and excited when she finds something new. On the other hand, she is not afraid at all (contrary to Flounder).

Her language too can be characterised as childlike in this scene: 'Isn't it fantastic […] Oh my gosh! Oh my gosh! Have you ever seen anything so wonderful in your life?' Further on in the story, she again behaves like a child: she disobeys her father's rules, she plays with soap bubbles in the bath and she hangs upside down under the carriage.

At the same time, Ariel clearly is an attractive young lady: she has an extremely slim waist and a pronounced hourglass figure. The contour of her bosom is accentuated by the purple seashell bra and the thin line in the middle. Her haircut accentuates her femininity.

It is no surprise then that Eric cannot stay insensitive to her beauty, as opposed to the prince in Andersen's fairy tale. In Andersen's story, the prince is only once said to be impressed by the little mermaid, more precisely when she dances for him. But even then, he does not see her as a beautiful woman, but rather as a soul mate or a child: 'She charmed everyone, and especially the prince, who called her his dear little foundling'. Further on, he again calls her his 'dear, dumb foundling' and even a 'dumb child'. In Disney's film, Eric explicitly states how beautiful Ariel is when she enters the dining room in a lovely dress: 'You look – wonderful.' The effect of his words is enhanced by the soft music and Ariel coming out of the shadow. Her posture expresses a mixture of shyness (the curves of the eyebrows and her hands folded in her lap) and sensuality (her red lips, long hair, naked shoulders and the contour of her bosom). Upon receiving the compliment, Ariel bows. This recurrent combination of shyness and sensuality in the film firmly shapes the viewer's image of Ariel.

In terms of character, the little mermaid is described by Andersen's authorial narrator as 'a strange child, quiet and thoughtful'. Several times it is stressed that she listens, watches and thinks. She stays utterly passive in her relation with the prince, even though the sea witch and her grandmother made it quite clear that she had to win the love of a man in order to gain an immortal soul. In the film, the spectator must infer Ariel's character from what she does and says (or sings) and what others say about her. However, she is not quiet or thoughtful at all: she is extrovert, (hyper)active and rebellious and sometimes even reckless. While Andersen's narrator mentions that the little mermaid dares more than her sisters, Disney magnifies this trait. She has to flee from a shark when she searches a sunken ship and she jumps into the sea wanting to swim to Eric's ship in order to prevent Ursula from marrying the prince, although her legs prevent her from swimming so far.

The crab, Sebastian, Triton's court musician, calls Ariel 'a headstrong teenager'. She doesn't listen to him at all. When he reprimands her, she swims away. And what is worse, she repeatedly disregards her father's prohibition against contact with humans. This leads to a hot dispute, with Ariel answering back in a way that is very recognisable for today's audience:

> Ariel: 'I'm sixteen years old – I'm not a child anymore.'
> Triton: 'Don't you take that tone of voice with me young lady. As long as you live under my ocean, you'll obey my rules!'
> Ariel: 'But if you would just listen.'
> Triton: 'Not another word – and I am never, NEVER to hear of you going to the surface again. Is that clear?'

Whereas Andersen's little mermaid hardly says a word – she only speaks three times (105 words in all, in the Danish version) – Ariel speaks/sings in fifteen scenes and some of her utterances are quite long. Andersen's little mermaid keeps her words inside: in no less than nineteen passages, her thoughts receive attention. Moreover, her thoughts and feelings fundamentally differ from Ariel's. After a conversation with her grandmother, the little mermaid starts yearning for an immortal soul. In order to get it, her grandmother adds, a human being has to fall in love with her. Even then, the little mermaid does not think of the prince. He only becomes part of her desire during the ball. From that moment onwards, she carries a double yearning for the prince's love and an immortal soul. This is mentioned no less than eight times and, each time her longing is not met, her grief grows. Ariel's love, on the contrary, is much more down to earth. When she sees the beautiful prince on the ship, she is literally struck by love at first sight and she wants to be with Eric and marry him. The changes in the pronouns and modal verbs in the song she sings before and after she sees the prince are quite telling in this respect: '*Wish* I could be part of *that* world' (before she sees the prince); '*Wish* I could be part of *your* world' (after); 'Some day I'*ll* be part of your world' (end of the song; emphasis added). Disney makes her lovesickness very recognisable for the (young) public: 'Ariel: (Picking petals off a flower) "He loves me … hmmm, he loves me not … He loves me! I knew it!"'

Not only do the thoughts of the little mermaid and Ariel differ, but also their feelings differ radically. This becomes most clear in the motif of the tears. From the start, Andersen stresses that a mermaid has no tears, 'and therefore she suffers so much more.' Whereas the grief of the little mermaid sits deep inside, Ariel's grief looks more superficial: she cries no less than five times in the film. Further, not her grief but her whole personality appears superficial. Andersen's little mermaid, on the contrary, is a complex being, tortured by conflicting feelings. When she sings at the ball in her father's palace, the narrator states that

> for a moment, her heart was happy, because she knew she had the loveliest voice of all, in the sea or on the land. But her thoughts soon strayed to the world up above. She could not forget the charming prince, nor her sorrow that she did not have an immortal soul like his. (Paull 1875)

When the prince first meets the little mermaid in her human form, Andersen writes that her 'deep blue eyes looked at him tenderly but very sadly'. In Disney's version of this first meeting, there is no sorrow or pain. The viewer hears romantic, soft music. Ariel's body language and facial expression are clearly seductive. She puts up her hair, her eyes seem bigger than ever and she bites her lip. Seconds later, she moves her right shoulder towards Eric. Immediately afterwards a switch of perspective suggests intense contact: first we see Ariel's face in close-up, then we get a shot of Eric, seen from Ariel's higher angle (she sits on a rock). Both shots are linked by a medium shot of the couple. In this scene, too, Ariel is brought to the fore as a child-woman. When she tries to make clear that she cannot speak, her pantomime appears funny and she literally ends up in Eric's arms. However, her innocent and helpless looks are replaced by a knowing glance at Scuttle the seagull and Flounder, when Eric says he will help her.

How can these dramatic changes in plot, characterisation, setting and perspective be explained? The key question is in how far these changes can be explained as inevitable differences caused by the transfer from text to screen or whether they are due to the process of disneyfication.

## Inevitable Changes through Film Adaptation

Chatman called the essential difference between novels and films a difference between 'showing' and 'telling': 'So, in its essentially visual mode, film does not describe at all but merely presents; or better, it depicts, in the etymological sense of that word: it renders in pictorial form' (1980: 128). This fundamental difference has consequences for the plot, time, setting, characters and point of view.

Andersen's story has 7964 words. A film has to present this story in approximately one hour and a half. This difference in discourse-time necessarily entails changes. In the first part of Andersen's story, each of the five older sisters rises up out of the ocean on her birthday and her experiences are described. Disney drops these scenes, probably because they depart too much from the central story line. From the little mermaid's birthday onwards, the pace slows down: while the experiences of the five sisters are summarised in approximately two pages, the youngest sister gets three pages. Here and also further on, the narrator enters at length into her thoughts and feelings, so that time slows down considerably. Because films have more difficulties with slowing down than novels (film is more bound to real duration; Peters 1980: 89-90), most of these passages have been omitted. Another reason for these omissions is that the filmic rendering of thoughts is problematic. Film has to 'externalise' thoughts. Sometimes, we see Ariel think, for instance, before she enters Ursula's dwelling. However, you don't know what she thinks. To express thoughts, Disney uses songs. A striking example is Ariel's song in which she expresses her longing to become human. But even during this song, a great deal of activity is going on (Sebastian the crab is struggling around, finally crashing down).[7]

The setting, too, has to be made concrete in the film (Peters 1980: 93). Although Andersen describes his settings in an elaborate and detailed way, Disney still has to add details in order to visualise them. An author can never achieve an exhaustive description. In his description of the prince's palace, for instance, Andersen does not tell us how many columns, pillars, towers or staircases there are, or how high it is. It is conspicuous that Disney rarely keeps the details Andersen gives, but moulds the settings with his own fantasy. Eric's palace looks very romantic, with red roofs and golden towers. Andersen's descriptions of settings are also highly metaphorical. Metaphors cannot be copied as such in films. Filmmakers will have to use other techniques to create similar effects. The following description, rich in imagery, is taken from the first paragraph of Andersen's fairy tale:

> Far out in the ocean, where the water is as blue as the prettiest cornflower, and as clear as a crystal, it is very, very deep; so deep, indeed, that no cable could fathom it: many church steeples, piled one upon the other, would not reach from the ground beneath to the surface of the water above. (Paull 1875)

Disney creates a similar effect of depth by having the camera follow a small fish that flops out of the hands of one of the sailors on the prince's ship.

In Andersen's tale, the authorial and personal narrator constantly alternate, the little mermaid being the main personal narrator and focaliser. The reader 'sees' many situations from her point of view. Films traditionally make more use of an 'authorial' camera angle because it is more difficult to narrate from an internal focus (Bordwell 1988: 116). However, film has its own techniques to simulate a personal point of view, such as the point-of-view shot or the over-the-shoulder-shot, combined with zooming and changing camera angles or shot sizes. Disney uses them frequently, for instance when conveying Triton's growing anger before he punishes his disobedient daughter (low-angle-shot) and his remorse afterwards (high-angle-shot).

## Disneyfication: Reduction of Revitalisation?

Apart from these technical operations, Disney also has a strong impact as regards content, in that he adapts Andersen's story to suit his own world view. Many scholars have condemned Disney's adaptations for simplifying, reducing, sentimentalising and Americanising the original stories (Bettelheim 1976: 24; Walz 1998: 51; Wasko 2001: 126; Inge 2004: 140). On the other hand, disneyfication has undoubtedly revitalised the old stories (Brode 2004). As Hutcheon stresses, an adaptation can keep a prior work alive, 'giving it an afterlife it would never have had otherwise' (2006: 176). For M. Thomas Inge, Disney retold the old stories 'with such consummate skill that he made them the modern definitive versions and the best-known ones worldwide' (2004: 140). Whatever attitude one adopts towards disneyfication, Disney's films exert an undeniable influence on the (young) audience. According to Henry A. Giroux, they play a powerful role 'in shaping individual identities and controlling fields of social meaning through which children negotiate the world' (1996: 96). In my reading of Disney's adaptation of Andersen's 'The Little Mermaid', I discern three cornerstones of disneyfication: entertainment, romance and moralism, which are responsible for the most dramatic changes.

## *Humour and Suspense: It's All Entertainment*

Disney's stress on entertainment provokes two important changes in Andersen's fairy tale. He adds humour and suspense, the two 'great seducers' for children (Van Coillie 2007: 111) and he removes grief and pain from Andersen's story.

Janet Wasko gives an accurate description of Disney's typical humour:

> The classic Disney Style came to be typified by light entertainment, punctuated with a good deal of music and humour which revolved round physical gags and slapstick, relying heavily on anthropomorphized (human-like) neotenized (childlike) animal characters[.] (Wasko 2001: 111)

Most of the new characters in Disney's *The Little Mermaid* are humorous or responsible for comic situations and entirely new scenes are based on this humour. Flounder creates examples of humour, based on superiority. Children could thereby see themselves as more clever or braver than Ariel's little companion. The crab Sebastian is a sympathetic boaster who gets himself in trouble time and again, creating some of the funniest scenes, such as the kitchen scene with cook Louis trying to grab him. In the end, Louis' moustache is on fire, his face is covered with sauce and the kitchen is a complete mess. The wild chase takes place to the tune of the French cancan. Scuttle, the seagull, is a totally comic character. His over-enthusiastic reactions, his made-up explanations and his tumbling around turn him into a clown. The final scene, with Vanessa, the sea witch in disguise, being attacked by the animals, is an example of humour that can release tension: the villain is defeated by slapstick with clear taboo-breaking actions: birds fly under her dress, a seal throws her upside down into the wedding cake and, finally, Max the dog bites her in the buttocks.

Other characters and scenes are added in order to create suspense. This is true of Flotsam and Jetsam, Ursula's accomplices, whose appearance is always accompanied by threatening music. Their mean eyes function as a kind of magic glass for Ursula. The extra scene where Ursula is introduced creates suspense right away. The sea witch utters a curse to Ariel and the king. While doing so, she emerges from the dark, a well-established ploy in animation for introducing the villain.[8] Another scene introduced in order to enhance suspense is where Ursula changes herself into Vanessa. The final scene, where Ursula becomes enormous and grotesque and threatens to destroy Ariel and Eric, is equally full of suspense.

The essence of disneyfication leaves no room for sad feelings or a negative ending, as Vyrna Santosa concludes: 'It seems that all Disney animated films are only made to sell happiness and dreams' (Santosa 2003: 196). Disneyfication thus provokes a radical change to the essence of Andersen's fairy tale. Suffering and pain are central motives in many of Andersen's fairy tales, such as 'The Snow Queen', 'The Ugly Duckling', 'The Wild Swans', 'Thumbelina', 'The Little Match Girl', 'The Princess and the Pea' and 'The Red Shoes'. Many scholars link the motif of pain to Andersen's personal life. It is seen as a symbol of the humiliation and emotional pain he suffered in his youth. His career in the theatre failed because he lost his voice and his lower class status pursued him, even when he became famous and was invited into the highest circles (Bredsdorff 1975: 7; Sells 1995: 177). The little mermaid's grief and pain are central motifs in Andersen's story. The author uses the word 'bedrøvet' [sad] or a synonym nine times and mentions the little mermaid's pain eight times, comparing it with piercing knives or a sword. Disney eliminates all those references. There is no trace left of either the heroine's tormented soul or her unbearable physical pain.

## *Romance and the Power of the Female Body*

Romance is the second cornerstone of disneyfication. As Cummings states: 'Disney strips the traditional fairy tale of anything but the romantic trajectory [...] by focussing narrative attention on courtship as plot advancement and marriage as denouement' (1995: 22). The romantic turn has consequences for the plot. First of all, it explains the changed opening scene. Andersen opens his fairy tale in a traditional way, typical of the genre, by introducing the heroine, her family and her living environment. Disney, however, introduces the prince right away, suggesting that he is the real hero and awakening expectations with the audience as to the romantic story line. As we have seen, Disney radically changes the end of the story and adds several scenes to enhance romance. The boat trip on the lake, for instance, is clearly inserted to give the romantic story line a boost. It is a telling example of how cinematic techniques can create a certain mood. Disney pictures a romantic lake with an immense willow under a full moon. The light is dimmed, with blue, purple and rosy shades. The circle is the central motif, with fireflies circling around the couple and the boat turning round and round. Long shots, medium shots and close-ups alternate, the camera zooming in for the final kiss. All this makes of this location a typical romantic topos.[9]

The romantic turn causes the most dramatic changes in the characters. Whereas for Andersen's little mermaid love is a means to a higher end, for Ariel love *is* the end. The major part of the film focuses on getting Eric and Ariel to kiss each other. In the end, of course, 'true love' wins, culminating in no less than three kissing scenes. Ariel's and Eric's helpers, too, support the theme of romance. Flounder, Scuttle and Sebastian do everything they can so that Ariel and Eric can kiss each other before the third day has passed. Grimsby, Eric's manservant and confidant, encourages the prince to marry and even Eric's dog, Max, recognises 'the one and only'. He can't speak, but he barks cheerfully whenever he spots Ariel.

In this context of Ariel's love for the prince, feminist critics have noted that, even though Ariel demonstrates more agency and strong will than other Disney heroines, she is still defined by male standards and goals. Her ultimate aim is for a romantic relationship with a dream prince, and as such she continues to promote the cultural logic that a woman's destiny is defined by men (Trites 1991: 145; Bell et al. 1995: 108; Wasko 2001: 116; Lacroix 2004: 225). Moreover, it is Ariel's father (again a man) who makes it possible for Ariel to marry the prince by finally turning her into a human.

Both in Andersen's tale and in Disney's film it is the little mermaid who has to win the prince's love, and she has to do that without her lovely voice. In both stories, the sea witch stresses the importance of body language for a woman to win a man, but Ursula pays much more attention to this. When Ariel asks how she can win the prince without her voice, Ursula answers: 'You'll have your looks! Your pretty face! Don't underestimate the importance of body language! Ha!' In the song she sings in order to convince Ariel to give up her voice, she expands her argument:

> The men up there don't like a lot of blabber
> They think a girl who gossips is a bore
> Yes, on land it's much preferred
> For ladies not to say a word
> And after all, dear, what is idle prattle for?
> Come on, they're not all that impressed with conversation
> True gentlemen avoid it when they can
> But they dote and swoon and fawn
> On a lady who's withdrawn
> It's she who holds her tongue who gets her man.[10]

This may sound deeply sexist, but it is important to notice that it is the witch who utters these words, which makes them suspect, as she is a malicious and unreliable character. Spectators are not likely to believe what she says.

However, it is not only Ursula who stresses the power of female body language. By accentuating Ariel's sensuality through her looks, posture, movements and outfits, the Disney animators strongly suggest that female power is the power to seduce or 'enchant' men. It is no coincidence that Ariel looks so seductive. As Bell et al. state, 'Disney animation is not an innocent art form: nothing accidental or serendipitous occurs in animation as each *second* of action on screen is rendered in twenty-four different still paintings' (1995: 108). According to Santosa, this physical side of romance makes Disney's films equally appealing to adults (2003: 189).

## *Good versus Evil – Daughter versus Father: The Pedagogic Turns*

Moralism is the third cornerstone of disneyfication, implying two 'pedagogic turns'. The first has to do with the conflict between good and evil and the second with the education of children.

In the classic Disney films the moral is clear: good is rewarded, evil is punished. Characters are either good or bad. Their good or evil personality is exemplified by their looks, living environment, helpers and behaviour. As in most Disney films, the heroine is slim and attractive, while the villain is fat and ugly.[11] Moreover, animation makes it easy to elaborate evil or good traits. As Lee Artz states, '[v]illains are drawn with sharp angles, oversized and often darkly' (2004: 130). Moreover, he declares that '[a]nimation has available the same artistic capacity as illustration, where color, shape, and size evoke certain psychological responses and attitudes towards an object' (ibid: 118). Music and light can be added to this list as typical 'manipulators' in animation film. Thomas A. Nelson asserts that Disney mostly placed good and evil 'in ready-made conventions which he and his public understood' (1978: 101). Ursula's tentacles are a clear example of this. Ariel's goodness on the other hand is enhanced by her cuteness and innocence, both of which show in her childlike face with the extra big eyes, incarnating a romantic child image. According to Gene Walz, Disney's classic films are essentially 'cute' or 'charming' (1998: 52). Wasko, too, calls innocence one of the typical values in Disney's work. She quotes Walt Disney himself, who links it to his dual audience:

> I do not make films primarily for children. I make them for the child in all of us, whether we be six or sixty. Call that child 'innocence'. The worst of us is not without innocence, although buried deeply it might be. In my work I try to reach and speak to that innocence [...]. (Wasko 2001: 118)

Wasko continues, quoting Giroux, who considered Disney's universe to be defined by a 'pedagogy of innocence [...], teaching children specific lessons through beguiling and pleasurable entertainment' (ibid.).

Several changes in the plot support the final conflict between good and evil. The main change concerns the end of the story. Whereas Andersen's little mermaid sacrifices herself so that the prince can marry his beloved, Disney's Ariel marries the prince after he has killed the evil sea witch in a heroic battle. In the logic of Disney's classic films, good must triumph over evil and order must be restored.

In the end, Andersen's little mermaid has to make a fundamental choice between good and evil. She can only save her life by killing the prince. When she realises that the prince truly loves his bride, she hurls herself into the sea. While the battle between good and evil is fought inside the little mermaid, in Disney's version the battle is external, it is a fight between 'Good' and 'Evil' in the universe and the characters are stereotypical symbols of one or the other, which makes it easier for the audience to feel sympathy for the good ones and antipathy for the evil forces.

But there is more to this story. After the little mermaid's self-sacrifice, Andersen adds a long passage, linking this dramatic act to her longing for an immortal soul and indirectly giving a lesson to his young audience. The little mermaid is welcomed by the daughters of the air who tell her that they can gain an immortal soul and enter 'the kingdom of God', provided they do all the good that they can for three hundred years to come. For each day they find 'a good child who pleases his parents and deserves their love', God is willing to shorten the term. But each time they see 'a naughty, mischievous child', one more day is added. Obviously the little mermaid's dramatic sacrifice did not fit Disney's vision, and neither did the 'airy' moral of the daughters of the air and the very explicit and old-fashioned lesson to a young readership.

Disney's second pedagogic turn stems from his views about educating children. It clearly affects the plot and the characters. Disney adds conflicts between Triton and his rebellious daughter and omits the moral lessons and good advice from the sea king's mother. Moreover, Disney fundamentally changes the relation between the little mermaid and her father. Andersen's fairy tale resembles a Bildungsroman. It focuses on the little mermaid's quest that turns her into a woman, who learns to accept her fate and is forced to make fundamental choices. It is a quest full of grief and pain. Her father, the sea king, does not play an important role in this process. In fact, he even lets his mother educate his daughters. Triton, on the contrary, is one of the main characters in Disney's film. He is the king of the sea, but above all, he is Ariel's father and as such tries to keep his 'headstrong teenager' firmly in line. Finally, however, he changes his mind, giving Sebastian the opportunity to present a crucial message, framing the story in terms of the American way of life: 'children have got to be free to lead their own lives'. He decides to accept his daughter's wish, even when he knows that he will miss her. But he is rewarded with her declaration 'I love you Daddy'.[12]

## Under the Rainbow

It should have become clear from this contribution that Andersen's 'The Little Mermaid' changed dramatically in the hands of the Disney animators. The comparative analysis has revealed drastic changes in the plot, characterisation, time, setting and point of view. Complete events, characters and settings have been omitted or added and what is 'borrowed' (the nub of the story) has been changed to a large extent. Characters are given another personality or role, in many scenes the pace has been increased, settings such as the sea witch's dwelling, the prince's palace or the beach are shown in the film with many more (and different) details and, finally, the point of view is more omniscient.

Some of these changes are due to inevitable differences between text and screen. Because of the film's adaptation, duration and pace differ because a film has more difficulties with slowing the pace than a novel. The period that elapses is a lot shorter in the movie, probably because film has to put more effort into capturing and keeping the audience's attention. This goes hand in hand with a fundamental change in the character of the little mermaid. Whereas in Andersen's story the focus is on her inner life, in Disney's film it is on the action, which is a logical consequence of the shift from telling to showing. This shift implies that the settings and outer appearance of characters are made much more concrete, with many details added. Finally, in the film the narration is conveyed from an omniscient perspective since personal perspectives are much harder to achieve in this medium.

However, the most dramatic changes are a result of Disney's vision, by means of which he 'disneyfies' the classic stories. Of course, this ideological adaptation goes hand in hand with the technical possibilities and restrictions of film animation.

First and foremost, Disney's films provide entertainment. Giving his (young) public what it wants, he lightens Andersen's deadly serious story with humour, making the evil characters look ridiculous. Animation offers special opportunities here. The animator can easily create humorous effects by means of caricature or anthropomorphism. Disney not only adds humour, but also suspense for the purpose of entertainment. Here, too, he skillfully manipulates the spectators, using specific camera angles, shot-sizes, lighting and especially music. A drastic consequence of Disney's stress on entertainment is the elimination of pain and suffering, two central motifs in Andersen's fairy tale.

Romance, the second cornerstone of disneyfication, fundamentally changes Andersen's tragic story of thwarted desire into a romantic musical, culminating in a dream marriage. This change reveals a specific view of women and intersexual relations. Although Ariel is more active and rebellious than former Disney heroines, she eventually conforms to male norms and values. Moreover, her body language in the film suggests that female power lies in physical charms. She is presented as a child-woman, combining childish enthusiasm with seductiveness and shyness. Because these characteristics do not necessarily conflict, she is a simple character, not as complex as Andersen's little mermaid, who is forced to make a fundamental choice in the end.

Andersen's fairy tale contains a fairly explicit (religious) lesson. His twofold moral, that an immortal soul is more important than mortal love and that children have to please their parents, probably did not fit into the American view of education in the 1980s. Disney keeps the implicit message of the classical fairy tale that good is rewarded and evil punished, but sharpens the conflict. Ursula is a lot meaner than Andersen's sea witch: she does not warn the little mermaid of the consequences of her desire and is clearly driven by revenge and hatred. Good and evil are made very clear by the looks of the characters, their living environment, helpers and behaviour. As a consequence, the public's sympathy and antipathy are strongly manipulated. Spectators will sympathise with Ariel's innocence and her sacrifice for love, and with Eric's courage, which again fortifies traditional role models. More explicit is the piece of wisdom Sebastian gives to Triton in the final scene: 'children have got to be free to lead their own lives'. With a sigh, Triton gives his daughter her human legs and her freedom, illustrating a changed view of education, a view no longer based on power and respect, but on freedom and responsibility.

In the final scene, the disneyfication is at its clearest, combining suspense, humour, romance, the triumph of good over evil and a moral directed at a dual audience. It is this combination that seems to make Disney's version of 'The Little Mermaid' immortal, though not in the religious sense that Andersen had in mind. And yet… One never knows. In the finale of Disney's version, a rainbow appears. Traditionally a symbol of hope and of a new beginning, the rainbow is also a Christian symbol of God's everlasting covenant with mankind. Can it be explained in that sense? The final word is from Walt Disney himself: 'We make pictures and then let the professors tell us what they mean.' (quoted by Wasko 2001: 108)

## Bibliography

Andersen, H.C. 1835-1837. *Eventyr fortalte for Børn. Første Samling*. Kopenhagen: C.A. Reitzel.

Andersen, H.C. 1836. *Den Lille Havfrue*,
    <http://www.hcandersen-homepage.dk/eventyr_den_lille_havfrue.htm.>
    Accessed 21/12/2010.

Andersen, H.C. *Hans Christian Andersen's Fairy Tales*. Translated by Henry H.B. Paull. London: Warne & Co [1875].

Andersen, H.C. *The little mermaid*. Translated by Jean Hersholt,
<http://www.andersen.sdu.dk/vaerk/hersholt/The LittleMermaide.html.>
Accessed 03 January 2011.

Artz, L. 2004. 'The Righteousness of Self-Centered Royals: The World According to Disney Animation', in: *Critical Arts Journal* 18.1: 116-146.

Bal, M. 1980. *De theorie van vertellen en verhalen: inleiding in de narratologie*. Muiderberg: Coutinho.

Bal, M. 1997. *Narratology: Introduction to the Theory of Narrative*. Toronto: University of Toronto Press.

Bell, E. et al. (eds) 1995. *From Mouse to Mermaid: The Politics of Film, Gender and Culture*. Bloomington: Indiana University Press.

Bettelheim, B. 1976. *The Uses of Enchantment: Meaning and Importance of Fairy Tales*. New York: Knopf.

Bordwell, D. 1988. *Narration in the Fiction Film*. London: Routledge.

Bordwell, D. & K. Thompson. 2010. *Film Art: An Introduction*, 9th ed. New York: McGraw-hill.

Bredsdorf, E. 1975. 'Andersen: What was he like?' *Danish Journal, special issue*: 6-17.

Brode, D. 2004. *From Walt to Woodstock: How Disney Created the Counterculture*. Austin: University of Texas Press.

Bryman, A.E. 2004. *The Disneyization of Society*. London: Sage Publications.

Chatman, S. 1980. 'What Novels Can Do that Films Can't (And Vice Versa)', in: *Critical Inquiry* 7.1: 121-140.

Cummings, J. 1995. 'Romancing the plot: The real beast in Disney's Beauty and the beast', in: *Children's Literature Association Quarterly* 20.1: 22-28.

Dundes, L. & A. Dundes. 2000. 'The Trident and the Fork: Disney's "The Little Mermaid" as a Male Construction of an Electral Fantasy', in: *Psychoanalytic Studies* 2.2: 117-129.

Fowler, R. 1981. *Literature as Social Discourse: The Practice of Linguistic Criticism*. London: Batsford Academic.

Furniss, M. 1998. *Art in Motion: Animation Aesthetics*. Sidney: John Libbey & Company Limited.

Giroux, H.A. 1994. *Disturbing Pleasures: Learning Popular Culture*. New York: Routledge.

Giroux, H.A. 1996. 'Animating Youth: the Disneyfication of Children's Culture', in: H.A. Giroux, *Fugitive Cultures: Race, Victim and Youth*. New York: Routledge, 89-113.

Hutcheon, L. 2006. *A Theory of Adaptation*. New York/London: Routledge.

Inge, M.T. 2004. 'Art, Adaptation and Ideology: Walt Disney's "Snow White and the Seven Dwarfs"', in: *Journal of Popular Film & Television* 32.3: 132-142.

Lacroix, C. 2004. 'Images of Animated Others: The Orientalization of Disney's Cartoon Heroines from The Little Mermaid to the Hunchback of Notre Dame', in: *Popular Communication* 2.4: 213-229.

McFarlane, B. 1996. *Novel to Film: an Introduction to the Theory of Adaptation*. Oxford: Clarendon.

Maio, K. 1998. 'Disney Dolls', in: *New Internationalist* 308: 12-14:
<http://www.newint.org/issue308/dolls.html.> Accessed 02/12/2010.

McCallum, R. & J. Stephens 2011. 'Ideology and Children's Books', in: S.A. Wolf, K. Coats, P. Encisco & C.A. Jenkins (eds), *Handbook of Research on Children's and Young Adult Literature*. New York/London: Routledge, 359-373.

Nelson, T.A. 1978. 'Darkness in the Disney Look', in: *Literature Film Quarterly* 6.2: 94-103.

Peters, J.M. 1980. *Van woord naar beeld: de vertaling van romans in film*. Muiderberg: Coutinho.

Propp, V. 1968. *Morphology of the Folktale*. Austin/London: University of Texas Press.

*Treasures Untold: The Making of Disney's 'The Little Mermaid'*. 2006. Bonus material from *The Little Mermaid: Platinum Edition*. 1989. Directed by R. Clements & J. Musker. Walt Disney Pictures, Walt Disney Studios Home Entertainment, 2006, DVD.
<http://en.wikipedia.org/wiki/The_Little_Mermaid_(1989_film)>. Accessed 29/12/2010.

Santosa, V. 2003. 'The Grammar of Disney Long Animations: a Structuralist Reading', in: *K@ta* 5.2: 187-198.

Sells, L. 1995. 'Where Do the Mermaids Stand? Voice and body in "The Little Mermaid"', in: E. Bell, L. Haas & L. Sells (eds), *From Mouse to Mermaid: The Politics of Film, Gender and Culture*. Bloomington: Indiana University Press, 175-192.

*The Little Mermaid: Platinum Edition*. 1989. Directed by R. Clements & J. Musker. Walt Disney Pictures, Walt Disney Studios Home Entertainment, 2006, DVD.

Trites, R. 1991. 'Disney's Sub/Version of Andersen's "Little Mermaid"', in: *Journal of Popular Film and Television* 18.4: 145-152.

Van Coillie, J. 2007. *Leesbeesten en boekenfeesten: Hoe werken (met) kinder- en jeugdboeken*. Leuven: Davidsfonds/Infodok.

Van Coillie, J. 2008. 'Van Blauwbaard tot Roodlapje. Een aanzet tot de illustratiegeschiedenis van het sprookje in Nederland en Vlaanderen (1)', in: *Literatuur zonder leeftijd* 22.77: 10-29.

Verstraeten, P. 2006. *Handboek filmnarratologie*. Nijmegen: Uitgeverij Vantilt.

Walz, G. 1998. 'Charlie Thorson and the Temporary Disneyfication of Warner Bross Cartoons', in: K.S. Sandler (ed.), *Reading the Rabbit: Explorations in Warner Bross Animation*. New Brunswick: Rutgers University Press, 49-66.

Wasko, J. 2001. *Understanding Disney: The Manufacture of Fantasy*. Cambridge: Polity Press.

Wells, P. 1998. *Understanding Animation*. New York/London: Routledge.

Whelehan, I. 1999. 'Adaptations: The Contemporary Dilemmas', in: D. Cartmell & I. Whelehan (eds), *Adaptations: From Text to Screen, Screen to Text*. New York/London: Routledge, 3-19.

Windling, T. 2003. 'Hans Christian Andersen: Father of the Modern Fairy Tale', in: *Realms of Fantasy*,
<http://www.endicott-studio.com/jMA03Summer/hans.html>. Accessed 20/10/2010.

Zukin, S. 1995. *The Cultures of Cities*. Oxford: Blackwell Publishing.

# Notes

1. The English quotations are taken from the translation by Jean Hersholt (published on <http://www.andersen.sdu.dk>, the site of the Hans Christian Andersen Center) which is a fairly 'literal' translation. In one instance, Mrs. Herny H.B. Paull's version (Paull 1875) is given, when her translation stays closer to the source text. The quotations from the film script are taken from the original transcription by Corey Johanningmeier (1989), consulted on <http://www.imsdb.com/scripts/Little-Mermaid,-The.html>.

2. When a reference is made to Disney's *The Little Mermaid*, his studios are meant. The film was released in 1989, 23 years after Walt Disney's death (1966).

3. The term 'disneyfication' is used to describe the transformation of culture or society as a whole to resemble the Disney theme parks or more generally to adapt it to Disney's world

vision. Sharon Zukin (1996) uses the term in her book *The Cultures of Cities*. The synonym 'disneyization' was popularized by Alan Bryman in *The Disneyization of Society* (2004).

4.   It is most unlikely that the Disney studios based their film on Andersen's original text in Danish. Disney's practice was rather to develop a script from a concept, not a specific pre-text. According to information from the bonus material on the DVD (*Little Mermaid* 1989), Ron Clements, who presented a two-page draft of The Little Mermaid to the Walt Disney studios in 1985, got the idea after having discovered a collection of Andersen's fairy tales while browsing a bookstore. In fact Clements revitalised an old idea of Disney's, for he had planned a full feature film based on Andersen's fairy tales back in the thirties.

5.   In this article, the definition of ideology is taken from Roger Fowler: 'the set of values, or belief system of a social group, communicated by language' (1981: 130). In cultural products (books as well as films) the ideology can be communicated explicitly or implicitly. According to McCallum and Stephens '[t]he implicit presence of a writer's assumptions in a text arguably has a more powerful impact in so far as such assumptions may consist of values taken for granted in the society that produces and consumes the text, including children' (2011: 362). This implicit presence will be the focus of attention in this study of disneyfication.

6.   To compare the plot of fairy tale and film, each has been split up into events and scenes. The classification of events/scenes is not absolute, for sometimes the researcher has to draw the line. Normally, a new event or scene is marked by a change in setting or a new action or happening in the same setting. In Andersen's fairy tales, the paragraphs often (but not always) correspond with events. In Disney's movie, most of the scenes are marked by means of cuts or fades.

7.   In one instance, Disney uses a special technique to 'externalise' Ariel's thoughts. In an over-the-shoulder-shot the viewing audience sees Ariel staring at the ship in the light of the setting sun while she 'hears' Ursula's voice in her head: 'Before the sun sets on the third day.'

8.   For more information about the effect of colour in animation film, see Furniss 1998: 71-75.

9.   It is typical for Disney that he mixes the romantic mood with humour. Scuttle, too, tries to 'create a little vocal romantic situation' – quoting Sebastian – but his bad singing misses its aim completely. The incongruous combinations of animals in the orchestra create visual humour too.

10.   Fragment of the song 'Poor Unfortunate Souls', lyric by Howard Ashman (1988).

11.   This relation between moral and physical characteristics has also been condemned by feminist critics (Trites 1991: 148; Wasko 2001: 116).

12.   This father-daughter relation drew the attention of psychoanalysts who explain the film as a rendering of the Electra complex (Dundes & Dundes 2000: 128).

# (De)Canonisation Processes

# E.T.A. Hoffmann's 'The Nutcracker and the Mouse King' and the Interfaces between Children's and Adult Literature

## Bettina Kümmerling-Meibauer

The history of canonisation processes in children's literature in general and the development of a canonical theory of children's literature in particular are new areas of research in need of further exploration. Although some scholars advocate investigating these aspects in more detail, so far only a few studies dealing with this demanding topic have been published. Among them is Beverly Lyon Clark's seminal monograph *Kiddie Lit: The Cultural Construction of Children's Literature in America* (2003), which focuses on the marginalisation of children's literature in the US by the mainstream critical establishment and in the academic world. Clark demonstrates that children's literature was highly regarded by the nineteenth-century cultural elite, but that since the beginning of the twentieth century many critics and scholars have been dismissive of this topic, downplaying children's literature as 'kiddie lit'. This derogatory term reveals fundamental shifts in the assessment of the literary value of books read by both children and adults, leading to an increasing divergence of 'highbrow' and 'lowbrow' literature.

This issue is also the starting point of my study *Kinderliteratur, Kanonbildung und literarische Wertung* ([Children's Literature, Canon Formation and Literary Evaluation], 2003) that illuminated the changing attitudes towards children's literature and childhood in Germany over the course of two centuries. Based on examination of primary materials such as reviews and articles in scholarly journals, literary histories, lists of recommended books, anthologies and textbooks, this monograph demonstrates the mutual relationship between decreasing appreciation of children's literature since the beginning of the nineteenth century and distanced respect for research on children's literature in the academic sphere.

As a complement, the volume edited by Anja Müller *Adapting Canonical Texts in Children's Literature* (2013) mostly focuses on the adaptation processes in the realm of children's literature, accessing both historical and transcultural adaptation in relation to the underlying concepts of childhood. As these studies apparently show, the analysis of historical canon processes and their impact on the changing assessment of children's literature is still in the fledgling shoes[1] and in strong need further investigation. In this article I firstly give a short overview on the canon processes in German children's literature from the Enlightenment until the present, before delving into the variegated reception of E.T.A. Hoffmann's Romantic fairy tale 'Nußknacker und Mausekönig' ([The Nutcracker and the Mouse King], 1816). Initially conceived as a literary work for a child audience, this fairy tale was soon – against the author's intention – consigned as literature for adults. This attitude led to a shift in the appraisal of 'The Nutcracker and the Mouse King' which culminated in its de-canonisation, thus denying its character as suitable reading matter for children. It will be shown how this discussion influenced the assessment of Hoffmann's fairy tale over the course of two hundred years and how diverse adaptations, ranging from picturebook versions and ballet scenarios up to animated films, largely contributed to a re-consideration of this work as part of the children's literature canon.

## Canonisation Processes in German Children's Literature

While children's literature was considered worthy reading matter during the Enlightenment in Germany, in the second half of the nineteenth century the Romantic era's ambivalent attitude towards children's literature and the misuse of children's books for nationalist and political purposes contributed to a vehement rejection of children's literature by teachers, educationalists, literary critics and scholars. This attitude was strongly influenced by an adult-centered perspective that regarded childhood as a stage of immaturity that had to be overcome. Another reason for the lack of interest of literary scholars in this topic is that it was mainly librarians and educationalists who were concerned with children's books; most of them were women, whose work was largely dismissed by the male-dominated academic world.

The German teacher Heinrich Wolgast played a decisive role in this context. His pamphlet *Das Elend unserer Jugendliteratur* ([The Misery of our Youth Literature], 1896) greatly influenced the increasing disregard for children's literature in Germany since the end of the nineteenth century. Wolgast was mainly concerned about the relationship between literature and the education of children: he asserted that only literature written for adults constituted suitable reading matter in schools, instead of the mainstream children's books popular since the second half of the nineteenth century. According to Wolgast, convenient literature was either the so-called 'authentic literature' offered by folk tales and the fairy tales written by the Brothers Grimm (for the early school grades) or, for older children, classics of adult German literature by famous authors such as Johann Wolfgang von Goethe, Friedrich von Schiller, Theodor Storm, and Adalbert Stifter.

In this respect, and contrary to the general scholarly opinion that children's literature usually goes unmentioned in literary histories, my detailed study of literary histories revealed that the discussion about appropriate reading matter for children and the literary assessment of children's book authors are constituent parts of many literary histories, and contribute greatly to the (de)canonisation of children's literature in Germany (2003). This analysis is based on 120 literary histories from 1790 to the present day, concentrating largely on the historical development of German literature and including sections on children's literature. Detailed examination of this corpus shows that the literary evaluation of children's literature is subject to historical change, with attitudes ranging from high regard to defamatory denigration.

On the whole, academics have long since considered children's books to be inferior and beneath serious literary consideration. Accordingly, literary value was no longer associated with children's literature. This is also shown by the evaluation of children's books in literary histories: children's literature, often conflated with women's literature, was either regarded as useful mainly for the child's socialisation, or it was seen as being written by authors who merely wanted to earn a living. These prejudices increased to a remarkable degree in the second half of the twentieth century. Even contemporary German literary histories tend to consign children's literature exclusively to the categories of light fiction and popular literature. Conversely, excellent children's books such as E.T.A. Hoffmann's 'The Nutcracker and the Mouse King' or Erwin Strittmatter's *Tinko* (1954) are generally classified as works written for adults, although both books were regarded as children's books by the authors themselves. As a result, by the end of the twentieth century, children's literature was even more invisible in literary histories than it had been in the nineteenth and at the beginning of the twentieth century.

## Norms and Reasons for the Devalorisation of Children's Literature

On closer examination, there are four essential norms that determine the assessment of children's literature in German literary histories. The most important norm, which appears in every literary history, identifies children's literature with educational literature. In this case the main purpose of children's literature is to promote knowledge and transmit moral, religious and political values. As a result, children's book authors are characterised as 'Erziehungsschriftsteller' [educational authors] (Baur 1790: VII), and their books are regarded as 'educational novels' or 'didactic works' (Gedike 1787: 6). This instructive trend became the focus of attention from the end of the eighteenth century onwards, and obstructed the acceptance of other norms. However, in the course of the nineteenth century two other norms emerged in literary histories: firstly, children's literature had to be suitable for children, taking into consideration the child's limited knowledge and cognitive abilities, and secondly, children's literature was interpreted as a revival of folk literature. Poems written for children, in particular, were considered as standard texts that fulfilled the norm of suitability for children. The most frequently mentioned essential features of suitability were naivety, simplicity and humour, which already built a bridge to folk literature. However, the main difference between folk literature and children's literature consists in the attribution of 'pure childishness' to children's books (Baur 1790: IX). In addition, proximity to folk literature is an important feature of children's literature. Poetry for children, fairy tales, girls' stories and the sentimental stories written by Biedermeier authors such as Christoph von Schmid or Gustav Nieritz were regarded as typical genres that satisfied this condition.

A further norm, although seldom mentioned in literary histories, is the demand that children's literature should be distinguished by its aesthetic quality. However, a strict demarcation is drawn here between literature for children and literature for adults. In general, the aesthetic quality of children's books is limited by the child's abilities. Just a few books written for children – such as Johanna Spyri's *Heidi's Lehr- und Wanderjahre* ([Heidi], 1880) or the *Kinder- und Hausmärchen* ([Children's and Household Tales], 1812-1815) by the Brothers Grimm – are regarded as convincing works of art comparable to highly respected works intended for an adult readership. However, the poetic or aesthetic value of children's books is always relative with regard to adult literature. Literary historians generally deny the aesthetic value of children's books. They strongly refute the idea of classifying children's literature as an autonomous body of literature on a par with adult literature.

These four norms have different priorities in literary histories. While the first norm appears in every literary history, often combined with the second and/or third norm, the last one is found very rarely. This generally denies the literary status of children's literature and contributes to the process of its de-canonisation.

To sum up, there are five reasons for the marginalisation of children's literature on the one hand and the absence of children's books in the literary canon on the other hand. The primary reason is the supposedly inferior quality of children's literature, which stresses its inadequate contribution to the child's developing literary taste. Secondly, children's literature is regarded as a minor genre, equivalent to light fiction and popular literature. The third reason is the undervaluation of children's book authors by using negative stereotypes, for example the literary devalorisation of Johann Bernhard Basedow, Joachim Heinrich Campe and Christian Felix Weiße, authors from the Enlightenment period. The fourth reason is the lack of detailed knowledge about literary traditions in the realm of children's literature. While almost every literary history referred to children's books of the Enlightenment era, Romantic children's literature – with the exception of the Grimms' fairy tales – was either omitted or categorised as adult literature. This reason is strongly connected with the fifth reason for the lack of representation of children's literature in the general literary canon: the categorisation of high quality children's books as works written for adults. This tendency mainly relates to the fairy tales written for children by Clemens Brentano, Ludwig Tieck and E.T.A. Hoffmann, who paved the way for the development of modern fantasy for children (Kümmerling-Meibauer 2003: 251-257). This assumption has hampered a thorough analysis of children's literature in literary histories up to the present day, since aesthetically demanding children's books usually have been regarded as books written for adults, although authors such as Hoffmann and Brentano permanently insist that their fairy tale collections were directed towards a child audience. Whenever positive aspects of children's literature are acknowledged, this is normally restricted to sub-genres like songs, fables and fairy tales intended for pre-school children with a special emphasis on their didactic intention. Children's books for school children and young adults, especially stories and novels, are either regarded as educational literature or as light fiction, which denies them any aesthetic value.

As a result, a multi-perspectival reading of children's literature was out of the question. Innovative aspects of thematic topics or narrative techniques, evident in Romantic children's literature or children's books influenced by New Realism during the 1920s and

1930s, generally went unremarked in literary histories. In addition, certain features of adult literature, such as unreliable narration, open endings, intertextuality, irony or combining of different genres, were not regarded as characteristics possible in children's literature, although they occur in many sophisticated children's books. Literary histories generally lack any intrinsic analysis of children's literature that reflects the abilities and needs of the intended audience. The occasional criticism of the poor quality of many children's books has not led to a thorough reflection on the necessary criteria for a challenging kind of children's literature, nor initiated an objective comparison between high quality children's books and mass-produced children's literature.

## Hoffmann's 'The Nutcracker and the Mouse King' as a Romantic Fairy Tale for Children

To demonstrate the impact of canonical studies on the evaluation of children's literature in more detail, the following sections will focus on the mechanisms of (de)canonisation processes. Our main example is a case study of E.T.A. Hoffmann's 'The Nutcracker and the Mouse King' (1816),[2] which was vigorously rejected as adequate reading matter for children by literary critics and historians in the nineteenth and twentieth century, but is regarded today as an international children's classic (Kümmerling-Meibauer 1999).[3] In this fairy tale, which was written for the children of Hoffmann's publisher, Hitzig, the author tried to reveal the interior world of a 'lively imaginative' child. The fairy tale consists of a frame story and three inner stories. The frame story starts on Christmas Eve and is located in the apartment of a bourgeois German family at the beginning of the nineteenth century. Although the cover illustration of the first edition, which was created by Hoffmann himself,[4] concentrates on the title figures, the main protagonist is a seven-year-old girl, Marie Stahlbaum.

Since the original version has often been abridged or updated, even in recent editions such as *The Nutcracker* (2010), with illustrations by Alison Jay, I will summarise the main plot in order to demonstrate the complex narrative structure.

On Christmas Eve, Marie and her siblings receive many Christmas presents from their parents and Marie's godfather, Droßelmeier, who is a keen clockmaker. Although he has made an amazing doll's house with moving dolls, Marie is more attracted by a nutcracker hidden under the Christmas tree. Unfortunately her brother Fritz damages the nutcracker, so that Marie scolds him and feels obliged to protect it. After the family goes to sleep Marie continues playing with her dolls and the nutcracker. But when the clock strikes midnight, the toys come to life and a fierce mouse king with seven crowned heads suddenly appears with his army to fight the nutcracker and the other toys. Terrified by the fighting, Marie smashes a glass cabinet and hurts her arm, but she manages to rescue the nutcracker and his allies by throwing her shoe at the mouse king. The next morning Marie develops a traumatic fever. Her parents refuse to believe her account of the events of the night before. Afterwards the mouse king threatens Marie that he will destroy her beloved nutcracker unless she gives him all her sweets and Christmas presents. While her parents and siblings believe that Marie is confused because of her serious illness, Droßelmeier

**Figure 1. Illustration by E.T.A. Hoffmann for the first edition of 'The Nutcracker and the Mouse King' (1816)**

supports her. He is the narrator of the 'Story of the Hard Nut', a story within a story told on three consecutive evenings, which makes a link between the nutcracker, the mouse king and Marie's nocturnal adventures. By means of revenge for her subjects who have been killed, the mouse queen, Mauserinks, transforms the beautiful princess Pirlipat into a horrible monster resembling a nutcracker. Her father requests the court astronomer and clockmaker Droßelmeier to find a way to turn her back into a princess. A horoscope predicts that only the golden nut Krakatuk will succeed in releasing the princess from her monstrous appearance. The nut should be cracked by a young man who has not yet worn boots nor been shaved. After a fifteen-year quest, Droßelmeier returns with his nephew from Nuremberg. When the nephew cracks the golden nut, he steps backwards and accidentally kills the mouse queen, who casts a spell transforming him into an ugly nutcracker. The now-beautiful princess refuses to marry him despite his services. On the contrary, the nephew and his uncle are chased away. The curse can only be lifted under two conditions: the nutcracker has to kill the mouse king and he has to gain the love of a girl despite his deformity.

After hearing this story, Marie is convinced that both her godfather and the clockmaker on the one hand, and the nutcracker and the transformed nephew on the other hand, are the same figures. The following night Marie promises the nutcracker that she will support him. He asks for a sword with which he kills the mouse king. Then he offers Marie the mouse king's seven crowns and takes her to his kingdom, the gingerbread country. The next morning Marie wakes up in her bed and tells her family the story of her adventures. Everybody believes it was a dream, even after Marie has shown them the little crowns, because her godfather claims that he gave the crowns to Marie as a birthday present. Marie falls silent and behaves like a somnambulist from then on. However, as she whispers to the nutcracker that she would have married him, she feels a blow and falls off her chair. Her mother comes in and introduces the godfather's nephew from Nuremberg. He discloses his identity as the former nutcracker, redeemed by Marie's love, and proposes to her. After their marriage he takes Marie in state to his kingdom.

## The Constitution of a New Image of Childhood

Hoffmann radicalised the late Romantic pattern of the 'dualistic fairy tale', which already hinted at the dualism between magical and empirical events in fairy tales, and created a new type of fairy tale described as a 'realistic fairy tale', which is regarded by many literary scholars as the precursor of modern fantasy children's literature (Apel 1978; Vitt-Maucher 1989). The action is no longer shifted to an undefined place but gives an insight into the daily routine of children belonging to the urban upper-middle class at the beginning of the nineteenth century. The children's world of play is described in detail, as well as their family life and their parents' educational strictures. The representation of daily life is arranged according to the laws of modern psychological realism which, strictly speaking, exclude the magical. The key figure is seven-year-old Marie Stahlbaum, brooding increasingly over her fantasies and nightmares, which alienate her from her family. Her parents embody the principle of enlightened reason, whereas the girl goes through experiences that give her access to another level of reality. Marie's age is not chosen accidentally: according to research by Jean Piaget and in modern cognitive psychology, children aged from five to seven have to learn to distinguish between fantasy and reality (Schikorsky 1995: 528). This developmental stage is evidently illustrated in Hoffmann's fairy tale. Hoffmann gives another interpretation of Marie's strange behaviour in the second volume of his collection *Die Serapionsbrüder* ([The Serapion Brethren], 1819-1822). The narrator of the frame story characterises Marie as a 'little somnambulist' (ibid.: 331) who is guided by mysterious, unknown powers (Neumann 1997). The clash between the experience of reality and the experience of wonder becomes ambiguous: it can be interpreted as dream, illusion, reality or crisis of consciousness. Moreover, the ambiguity is emphasised by the multiple transformations of toys into living beings, of human beings into toys or machines, and of the shifting identities of the protagonists. For instance, Droßelmeier is Marie's godfather in the frame story and an astronomer in the inner story. In addition, he is transformed into a small toy-like figure sitting on the mantelpiece during the battle between 'The Nutcracker and the Mouse King'.[5] Both approaches to experience, i.e. the experience of reality and the experience of wonder, happen in the girl's inner world, mirroring her mental conflict. Since her parents express doubts about the truth of Marie's experience and disapprove of her superstition, the girl is depressed, weighed down by a sense of increasing isolation which cannot even be reduced by Droßelmeier. He is the only adult who shows some understanding of her situation. The narrator also seems to stand by Marie, but on closer examination he points to the story's ambiguity with its counterbalance between a childlike and an adult point of view (Miller 1975). From the adult's standpoint, the fairy tale appears as a gloomy tale of disease, while from the child's angle the story changes into an optimistic fairy tale. This ambiguity is also evident in the last scene. The marriage and the retreat into a gingerbread country can either be interpreted as the euphemistic depiction of a delusion or as a happy fairy tale ending.

With this pessimistic view of the dangers to which 'lively imaginative children' (Hoffmann 2001 [1819-21]: 306) are exposed on account of their parents' lack of understanding, Hoffmann created an image of childhood that radically contrasted with the pre-Romantic utopias of childhood (Alefeld 1996; Baader 1996; Ewers 1989; Ewers 2001). The crucial novelty of Hoffmann's literary discourse consists in taking the child's perception and imagination seriously, thus denying the interpretation of abnormal behaviour in the sense of Enlightened middle-class rationality. In this fairy tale a new literary poetics of the strange and uncanny is developed in connection to the hardly known dimension of the child's imagination.[6] This concept is diametrically opposed to the predominant, pedagogical-rhetorical aesthetics of pre-Romantic children's literature that contests the presentation of horrors and magical events in reading matter for children (Steinlein 1999). In Hoffmann's case, literary critics disapproved of his work because of its strangely disturbing representation of the child's inner life. They also denied that 'The Nutcracker and the Mouse King' was a fairy tale for children, arguing that the intended readership would certainly be incapable of understanding the complicated narrative structure and ambivalent ending.

Hoffmann included this fairy tale in his four-volume collection, *The Serapion Brethren*, and tried to argue for its status as children's literature in the frame story:

> In my opinion it is generally a great misunderstanding to believe that lively imaginative children, about whom we are talking, are satisfied with shallow drivel presented as fairy tales. Oh! They probably demand something better, and it is astonishing with what precision and liveliness they grasp some things which totally escape many a very intelligent father. Learn this and show respect! (Hoffmann 2011: 337)[7]

With this assertion the narrator of the frame story, who could be seen as the author's mouthpiece, defends the fairy tale against the reproach that it should be regarded as meaningless 'drivel'. Contradicting the mainstream opinion that children's literature should be simple and straightforward, Hoffmann stresses that children's literature is complex and demanding and expresses a poetics of the fairy tale that aims at the transgression of the border between children's literature and adult literature, which anticipates twentieth-century ideas (Grenz 1990). While Hoffmann admits that children cannot fully grasp this 'fairy tale for big and small children' (Hoffmann 2001 [1819-21]: 306) down to the last detail, he argues that they have access to this story thanks to their imagination, which probably even surpasses the understanding of an adult reader.

Accordingly, the child, with his or her ascribed affinity with poetry and magic, serves as an example for the adult. Behind these ideas, Hoffmann's concept of an ideal childhood is revealed. It is not bound to any biologically determined stage of life, but can be preserved as an infinite possibility in the mind. This childhood image is mirrored in Hoffmann's so-called 'serapiontical principle' that also applies to 'The Nutcracker and the Mouse King'. This principle states that a higher reality, usually regarded as madness, develops out of the poet's visionary power (Kremer 1993: 40ff.). However, the fantastic world of the imagination is not allowed to break free, but has to remain in contact with reality. Hoffmann fleshes his arguments out by referring to aesthetic, psychological and reception-oriented criteria. Although children are disadvantaged because of their limited literary knowledge, they still have cognitive abilities that might compensate for this deficit, even beyond the comprehension of common adult readers. Here, Hoffmann hints at the proximity of childhood and poetry, a topic prevalent in Romantic thought. The author goes on to draft an aesthetic programme that emphasises the advancement of literary competence by means of ambitious children's literature. At the same time he stresses that his fairy tale consists of multiple levels of meanings, thus addressing children and adults alike.

Despite this plea, contemporary reviews published in renowned journals such as *Morgenblatt für gebildete Stände* [Morning Gazette for Educated Classes] and *Jenaische Allgemeine Literaturzeitung* [General Literary Journal from Jena] considered this fairy tale as clear evidence for the author's inability to successfully write for children.[8] Although Hoffmann promised to create another fairy tale that would take the main points of criticism into consideration, his fairy tale 'Das fremde Kind' [The Strange Child], which was published in the subsequent volume of *Kinder-Märchen* [Fairy Tales for Children] in 1817, introduced another innovative image of childhood that influenced the development of international children's literature for years to come. The strange child as main protagonist is unusual because of its properties and characterisation: it has magical abilities, its look goes back to the tradition of the Romantic genius, it has a mysterious family situation and is characterised by its loneliness and lack of education. What particularly distinguishes this child character is its ambiguous gender status. The strange child's gender neutrality leads to a reversal of the binary gender pattern, since it implies both sexes. These gender perspectives and the refusal to grow up are responsible for the melancholic ending of the story, delivering the strange child into a state of growing isolation. This motif is repeatedly varied in Romantic and modern children's literature, ranging from George Sand's *Histoire du veritable Gribouille* ([Story of the True Gribouille], 1850) to J.M. Barrie's *Peter and Wendy* (1911), Antoine de Saint-Exupéry's *Le petit prince* ([The Little Prince], 1943) to Astrid Lindgren's *Pippi Långstrump* ([Pippi Longstocking], 1945), Michael Ende's *Momo* (1973) and Peter Pohl's *Janne min vän* ([Johnny my Friend], 1985) (Kümmerling-Meibauer 1996: 33-35; 2003: 220-229).

## The Influence of 'The Nutcracker and the Mouse King' on International Children's Literature

In any case, Hoffmann's fruitless attempts to highlight the innovative traits of 'The Nutcracker and the Mouse King' led to a divergence in the reception of this fairy tale. While it was only published in editions for an adult readership in Germany until the middle of the twentieth century, 'The Nutcracker and the Mouse King' had a resounding impact on the creation of modern fantasy for children in a number of other European countries. It is curious that Hoffmann's fairy tale has been de-canonised as children's literature in Germany, whereas it has been considered a seminal contribution to international children's literature in other countries.

'The Nutcracker and the Mouse King' was translated into almost every European language and influenced the development of Romantic children's literature in Denmark, England, France, Sweden and Russia for a long period. In his early fairy tales, the Danish author Hans Christian Andersen referred primarily to Hoffmann's image of childhood. For example, Andersen's story 'Den lille Idas Blomster' ([Little Ida's Flowers], 1835) has a number of features in common with 'The Nutcracker and the Mouse King'. The nocturnal adventure of the middle-class girl, Ida, who learns about the true nature of the wilted flowers and is allowed to participate with her doll, Sophie, in a festive flower ball in her parents' living room, leaves an open question as to whether her experience is a dream or reality. In contrast to Hoffmann's model, Andersen's fairy tale lacks the feelings of seriousness and menace. Andersen describes an idyllic childhood and takes the edge off the child's ambivalent experience typified by Hoffmann's Marie Stahlbaum. Andersen's *Eventyr, fortalte for børn* ([Fairy Tales Told for Children], 1835-1848) are famed for their aesthetic sense of childhood. The author not only portrays the child's immediate surroundings, marked by an exact description of place and landscape, but also integrates the child's faculty of speech. Furthermore, Andersen consciously adopts the child's point of view by placing ordinary small things at the centre of the story. In these 'fairy tales of things', inanimate objects like toys or household articles, which are characterised by childlike qualities, dominate the action.

The allegorical fairy tale 'Sneedronningen' [The Snow Queen], which is notable for its subtle combination of realistic and fantastic events, demonstrates his outstanding skill. This story is often classified, together with Hoffmann's fairy tale, as the precursor of children's fantasy literature. Andersen succeeded in reconciling his deistic worldview with ideas of the Romantic image of childhood. After many trials, the selfish love of the girl, Gerda, overcomes the Snow Queen, who personifies abstract reason, and she liberates the boy Kay from the Queen's magic spell. Through their experience, both children become more mature, even almost adult, but deep down they are still children and preserve childlike qualities such as a faith in God, love of nature and artistic leanings (Kümmerling-Meibauer 2008: 194). The fairy tale's philosophical expressiveness is enhanced by bringing the story into the narrator's immediate present with the last sentence: 'Og det var sommer, den varme, velsignede sommer' [And it was summer, warm, wonderful summer] (1995 253; translation B.K.M.).

Inspired by Andersen, the Swedish-speaking author Zachris Topelius, who is regarded as the founder of Finno-Swedish children's literature, took a serious interest in Hoffmann's fairy tale poetics. The initial result was his fairy tale collection *Sagor* ([Fairy Tales], 1847), but Topelius indicated his own poetical view only in the preface to his eight-volume anthology *Läsning för Barn* ([Reading Matter for Children], 1865-96). He expounded a programme of aesthetic poetry for children, combining Romantic ideas of childhood, especially Hoffmann's concept of the 'lively imaginative child', with an anthropomorphic view and initial attempts at a pedagogic system concentrating on the child's point of view.

In Russia, Antony Pogorelsky, a renowned expert on the German Romantics and a great admirer of E.T.A. Hoffmann's works, took up where the Romantics had left off with his fairy tale for children, *Chernaya kuritsa, ili podzemnye zhiteli* ([The Black Hen, or the Underground People], 1992 [1829]). As in Hoffmann's 'The Nutcracker and the Mouse King', the story centers on a lonely, sensitive child who often daydreams and is misunderstood by adults. In this story it is not clear at all whether the fantasy incidents actually happen or whether they should be interpreted as dreams. The things which the main character Alyosha gets from fantasy figures contribute to the reader's uncertainty. Although a link is made to a story of disease (the fantasy episodes hint at the child's madness), Pogorelsky decided against an open ending. He conformed to the literary conventions of his time by dealing with the loss of the child's world of dreams and imagination and, at the same time, presenting Alyosha's transformation into a self-conscious boy who has both feet firmly on the ground. The loss of the world of imagination is accompanied by a melancholic atmosphere already indicated in the introduction to the story, where the narrator wistfully describes the vista of the city and suburbs of St. Petersburg at the beginning of the nineteenth century and complains about the loss of familiar places from his youth.

The tendency to adopt themes and motifs from 'The Nutcracker and the Mouse King', but to minimise the ambivalent message and to present an unambiguous, harmonious solution instead of an open ending, characterises almost all post-Romantic fairy tales. Typical examples are the Swedish children's classic *Lille Viggs äventyr på julafton* ([Little Vigg's Adventures on Christmas Eve], 1875) by Viktor Rydberg, or the fantastic children's novel *The Cuckoo Clock* (1877) by Mary Louisa Molesworth.

For some time there was no reaction to the idea of the role of the 'lively imaginative child' as a victim in fantastic children's literature, except in realistic Romantic children's literature, such as the short story collection *I Brønden og i Kjærnet* ([In the Well and in the Lake], 1851) by the Norwegian author Jørgen Moe. The six stories describe the adventures of a sister and brother, Beate and Viggo, whose character exhibits qualities similar to Marie and Fritz Stahlbaum in 'The Nutcracker and the Mouse King'. The book's title refers to two dramatic events: Beate falls into the well and is saved from drowning by holding on to her doll at the well's edge. Remarkably, the doll is as important to her as the nutcracker is to Marie Stahlbaum. Later, Viggo breaks through the frozen surface of the lake while ice-skating and is saved by his dog. Some analogies are obvious:

Beate's and Viggo's rescue by their best friends (doll, dog) and the place of danger (well, lake). This anthology of stories is defined by a contrast between two literary movements. Whereas the stories about Beate were influenced by the Romantic movement, the stories about Viggo display features of naturalism. Beate experiences a discrepancy between her hopes and reality and finally gives up. This process is particularly evident in 'Den flydende ø' [The Flying Island]. At first sight this is the story of an idyll characterised by innocent play and daydreams. However, Beate disturbs the peacefulness of nature because of her lack of attention. Her feeling of guilt is reinforced by the loss of her doll and by her father punishing her. Beate submits to social demands and gradually falls into the role of victim. Her brother, however, who is a steady, sensible character and vigorously takes the initiative, has a great future ahead. Although Moe clearly demonstrates his sympathy for the female character, he already indicates a certain skepticism towards the self-assertion inherent in the Romantic image of childhood.

Romantic concepts of childhood also come to light in Jules Michelet's *Mémorial* ([Memorial], 1820-22) and in Alphonse Daudet's *Le petit chose* ([The Small Thing], 1865). Although these two works were not originally intended for children, they eventually gained acceptance as reading matter for the young. Michelet's widow revised his autobiography after his death and published it as a children's book with the title *Ma jeunesse* ([My Youth], 1875). The abridgements and revisions resulted in an over-simplified version reminiscent of the Romantic myth of childhood. Catering to predom-inant pedagogical expectations, ironic passages were cut out so as to emphasise the exemplary nature of the main character. Despite this apologetic tendency, Michelet's autobiography remained a realistic and moving representation of a child's physical and psychological sufferings. For this reason we can classify the novel in relation to the literary motif of the child as a misunderstood victim of adults, as established by E.T.A. Hoffmann.

This pattern is even more evident in Daudet's autobiographical novel *Le petit chose*. Here, the main character is not even granted a proper name. With the deprecatory epithet 'small thing', the child is deprived of its individuality and its gender – in order to conceal from the reader for a long time that the story is about a boy. The uneasy claustrophobic atmosphere and the adults' lack of sympathy for the child's interests contribute to the novel's gloomy mood. Due to its modern and radical views, which were unrivaled at that time, the work is seen as a continuation of Hoffmann's late Romantic concept of childhood as expressed in 'The Nutcracker and the Mouse King' (Kümmerling-Meibauer 2008: 196).

The aftermath of Hoffmann's Romantic image of childhood is more clearly evident in European children's literature, starting with the nonsense books of Lewis Carroll (*Alice's Adventures in Wonderland*, 1982 [1865]) and William Thackeray (*The Rose and the Ring*, 1964 [1855]), the children's novels by Charles Kingsley (*The Water Babies*, 1862), George MacDonald (*At the Back of the North Wind*, 1871), Edith Nesbit (*The House of Arden*, 1908), progressing to John Masefield (*The Midnight Folk*, 1927), Astrid Lindgren (*Mio, min Mio* [Mio, My Son], 1954), Mary Norton (*The Borrowers*, 1952), and Michael Ende (*Die Unendliche Geschichte* [The Never-ending Story], 1979), and including the picture books by Elsa Beskow (*Puttes äventyr i blåbärsskogen* [Little Hans in the Blueberry Wood], 1901) and Maurice Sendak (*Outside Over There*, 1981). Even in contemporary children's literature the fascination for Hoffmann's Romantic image of childhood seems not to have diminished. Proof of this influence comes in the successful children's novels of, among others, David Almond (*Skellig*, 1998), Jostein Gaarder (*Sofies verden* [Sofie's World], 1991), Philip Pullman (*His Dark Materials* trilogy, 1995-2000) and Neil Gaiman (*Coraline*, 2002). Each text demonstrates the extent to which the project of writing for children is influenced by Romantic thought in general, and by Hoffmann's literary child characters in particular (Kümmerling-Meibauer 1996: 40; 2008: 199).

## Reception of Hoffmann's Fairy Tale in Germany

By contrast, there was no reaction to Hoffmann's 'The Nutcracker and the Mouse King' in children's literature during the nineteenth century in Germany. Only Erich Kästner picked up the thread with his children's fantasy novel *Der 35. Mai oder Konrad reitet in die Südsee* ([The 35th of May or Conrad's Ride to the South Seas], 1931), which intertextually continued the dialogue with Hoffmann's fairy tale. After the Second World War, a renaissance of Hoffmann's story in Germany was initiated by the reception and translation of Anglophone fantasy for children, such as the books by Pauline Clarke, Kenneth Grahame, A.A. Milne and Pamela Travers. The fantasy novels by Michael Ende, James Krüss and Otfried Preußler contributed to fantasy becoming accepted in German-speaking countries. Moreover, since the 1950s several illustrated editions of 'The Nutcracker and the Mouse King' have been published in various countries,[9] most of them in German editions as well. The 1990s became a turning point for a renewed reception of Hoffmann's fairy tale in Germany, as several publishers, such as Dressler (1993) and Arena (1995) included the story in their children's classics series.

There are several reasons for the lack of a response to Hoffmann's fairy tale for children in Germany up until the mid-twentieth century. Firstly, the innovative image of childhood at that time differed radically from the images of childhood in the early Romantic era. As a result, contemporary literary critics disapproved of Hoffmann's fairy tale. They argued that the demanding literary style, complex narrative structure, literary allusions, and ambivalent ending of the work made it too difficult to be understood by children at all. Although Hoffmann defended 'The Nutcracker and the Mouse King' as suitable reading matter for 'lively imaginative children' (2001 [1819-21]: 306), its vehement repudiation by educationalists and critics meant that the fairy tale was not regarded as children's literature of any kind. The gist of Hoffmann's discourse about childhood consists in taking the perception and imagination of children seriously, refraining from the common opinion of Enlightenment thinkers who interpreted these capacities as bad behaviour that had to be curbed. Hoffmann developed a poetics of children's literature that emphasised the importance of strangeness and the uncanny as essential characteristics of the child's imagination. But the representation of the disturbing inner life of the child led to vehement rejection of 'The Nutcracker and the Mouse King'.

This negative evaluation becomes strikingly obvious if we consider my comprehensive analysis of 120 German literary histories published from 1822 up to the present day (2003).[10] While 54 literary histories do not mention Hoffmann at all, 75 of the histories examined include largely negative opinions of the author, and 29 of the histories feature positive judgments. Only eight of the literary histories in the survey mention that Hoffmann wrote two fairy tales for children. However, from the 1830s onwards – after Hitzig published the first biography of Hoffmann – literary critics and scholars tended to see a relationship between Hoffmann's life and works. As Hoffmann was known for his eccentric way of life marked by sharp breaches and alcoholic excesses, many of his contemporaries claimed that Hoffmann's works reflected his lifestyle. Georg Gottfried Gervinus characterized Hoffmann's writings as 'feverish dreams created by a sick brain' (1842: 685), while Rudolph Gottschall described them as 'dreams of a drunkard' (1875: 420), and Otto Roquette claimed that Hoffmann's authorship had been influenced not by the muse of poetry, but by the champagne bottle (1863: 501). Other literary historians even maintained that Hoffmann sometimes was so frightened by his own stories that his wife had to be nearby to prevent horrific nightmares (Scherr 1854: 139). Joseph von Eichendorff's dictum, '[h]e wrote in order to drink, and he drank in order to write' (1857: 189), became a *topos* in German literary histories of the nineteenth century. The majority of these accounts claimed that Hoffmann was a dubious character haunted by nightmares and hallucinations induced by alcohol abuse. Although some literary historians conceded that Hoffmann's ideas and style were quite brilliant, they undermined their positive verdict by arguing that the author's strange behaviour and habits justified his demotion from the status of a prominent representative of German Romanticism. Karl Goedeke insisted that Hoffmann's works completely lacked veracity and deep insight; he said they might only be useful as case studies for psychiatrists (1859: 414). In the long run, the defamation of Hoffmann led to the author's exclusion from the literary canon in the nineteenth century. This lasted until the beginning of the twentieth century, when Hoffmann's contribution to international literature began to be acknowledged.

These ambivalent, even negative statements also influenced the reception of 'The Nutcracker and the Mouse King'. This fairy tale is usually subsumed under the category of a 'Romantic fairy tale' written for adults; in all, only seven literary histories mention that 'The Nutcracker and the Mouse King' was written for children. The first detailed examination of this story was by Eichendorff, but he denied that it was a fairy tale for children. He argued that the philosophical reflections and the conflict between nature and society contradicted the expected naivety of children's fairy tales (1970 [1857]: 450). In general, literary historians are almost skeptical about the childlike character of this work. They argue that children are unable to grasp the ironical remarks and the complex structure, implying that Hoffmann misjudged the cognitive and linguistic abilities of children. Even the first literary histories that focus on the history of German children's literature are somewhat ambivalent about Hoffmann. Hobrecker describes 'The Nutcracker and the Mouse King' as a fussy and abstruse fantasy (1924: 58), Fronemann claims that the fairy tale is too complicated for a child audience (1927: 98), Prestel denotes it as '*kindfremd*' [strange for children] (1933: 63), Rüttgers refers to 'Nutcracker' as a pure, funny fantasy story without any intellectual depth (1944: 71), and Graebsch concludes that the work can only be understood by a minority of clever children (1967: 100). It is no wonder that from the 1980s onward 'The Nutcracker and the Mouse King' has not been mentioned in German literary histories at all, although this fairy tale was rediscovered as seminal in the development of modern fantasy for children and has been re-issued in more than thirty editions since the mid-1980s. While scholars working in the field of children's literature research stress Hoffmann's importance for the development of fantasy for children and contribute to the author's international acclaim, their conclusions are to this day not reflected in modern German literary histories. 'The Nutcracker and the Mouse King' is still seen as a fairy tale written for adults, and regarded as a minor contribution to the genre in comparison to Hoffmann's fairy tale 'Der Goldene Topf' [The Golden Pot]. The de-canonisation of Hoffmann as an author for children is still prevalent, especially in German-speaking countries. This attitude towards Hoffmann's fairy tales for children is particularly evident in academia. In monographs which offer an overview of literary history, these fairy tales in particular are either not mentioned at all or are referred to as marginal works (Kümmerling-Meibauer 2003: 258-263).

## Media Versions and New Editions of Hoffmann's Fairy Tale

As we can see, not every scholar working in the realm of children's literature research acknowledges Hoffmann's seminal position with regard to modern fantasy for children. This is mainly due to bad translations, adaptations, and different media versions, especially films. A case in point is Alexandre Dumas' French version *L'histoire d'un casse-noisette* ([The Story of a Nutcracker], 1845). Up until now many scholars have mistakenly classified Dumas' fairy tale as a faithful translation of Hoffmann's story. However, *L'histoire d'un casse-noisette* goes far beyond mere translation, being adapted for an upper-middle-class audience in France, in shifting the realistic frame story to the magical, in reducing the grotesque, in incorporating moral comments, in adjusting the tale to fit the tradition of the French fairy tale and, finally, in the altered happy ending. In comparison with Hoffmann's original, Dumas' adaptation is actually a step backward in so far as Dumas adapted his image of childhood to suit the pedagogical demands of his time. The fallacy that both fairy tales are practically identical is one reason why the modernity of Hoffmann's works is usually underestimated. This reception was further highlighted by the famous ballet *The Nutcracker* (1892) by the Russian composer Peter Tchaikovsky, whose libretto was based on Dumas' version. The numerous performances of this ballet worldwide have meant that the adapted version is mistakenly seen as Hoffmann's original work, in spite of all the radical changes made by the French author.

Furthermore, the numerous film versions of the story of 'The Nutcracker and the Mouse King' are based on Dumas' adaptation, although many producers and directors claim that their version derives from Hoffmann's fairy tale. However, they appear unaware of the innovative conceptualisation and content of the original story. Unfortunately, the short cartoon films such as *The Nutcracker* (directed by Jesse Winfield; released 1999), the animated film versions *Katya and the Nutcracker* (directed by Alistair Graham, 2001),

*Barbie in the Nutcracker* (directed by Owen Hurley, 2001) and *The Nuttiest Nutcracker* (directed by Harold Harris, 1999), to name just a few, transmit an adulterated version of Hoffmann's fairy tale, reducing the original work to a sentimentalised story often embellished with slapstick sections, funny, cute minor characters, and a happy ending. These films are produced in the USA, but they are distributed in other countries as well (via Amazon, for example). All this contributes to obscuring the ambivalent undertones of the Romantic fairy tale. *The Nuttiest Nutcracker*, for instance, tells the story of a group of fruits and vegetables trying to help the nutcracker army to mount a star on a Christmas tree before midnight, and to stop a hostile army from destroying the Christmas festival. This cartoon film is clearly only loosely connected to the original story. The same applies to *Barbie in the Nutcracker*, where Barbie tries to comfort her younger sister, Kelly, who is afraid of going on stage to perform a ballet dance. Barbie tells Kelly the story of Clara and the ugly nutcracker that turns into the charming Prince Eric after Clara confesses her love to him. Clara, meanwhile, is revealed as the former Sugarplum Princess. This animation is supplemented by live-action film clips showing ballet performances from the renowned Bolshoi Ballet. These films clearly demonstrate that the producers and directors are influenced by Tchaikovsky's balletic version, although the front credits and/or end titles claim that the screenplay is based on Hoffmann's story and never mention Dumas.

We might assume that these changes are typical features of media transformation processes; however, a survey of the editions of 'The Nutcracker and the Mouse King' published as children's books during the last few decades reveals that even modern editions often do not contain the original text, but an abridged, modernised version or a retelling of Hoffmann's fairy tale. A case in point is Germany, where more than thirty editions have been published since the 1980s. These editions differ in format and illustration. While most of them appear in a picture book format, some editions are printed in the typical format of a children's book, containing only black-and white illustrations. Apart from the format, the range of artistic style in the illustrations is varied. Several editions were illustrated by famous artists such as Roberto Innocenti, Eva Johanna Rubin, Adrienne Ségur, Maurice Sendak, Gennady Spirin, and Lisbeth Zwerger.[11] While these special editions show a profound understanding of Hoffmann's fairy tale, with sophisticated illustrations that clearly allude to the implied meanings in Hoffmann's work,[12] a detailed analysis of the editions and translations shows that only twelve publications are based on his original text. The other eighteen editions, among which are recent ones from 2008 and 2009, show significant variations. The text was abridged in order to squeeze it into a picture book format with 32 pages, or a standard format for 'beginner readers'. According to the blurb of an Austrian edition from 2003, the editor regrets that the original edition is 'too long' (Hoffmann 2003: n.p.). The French editions such as *Histoire d'un Casse-Noisette* (1955), with illustrations by Adrienne Ségur, usually have the following information on the front matter: story by Hoffmann, retold (or translated) by Alexandre Dumas. In other words, French children are used to Dumas' tame version, and usually do not know the original text. This is all the more surprising if we recall that Hoffmann was highly estimated among Romantic authors and the bourgeois readership in France during the nineteenth century. Regarded as an innovator in the realm of fantastic stories, he had a great influence on French authors such as Charles Nodier and George Sand (Hoffmeister 1990).

Furthermore, Hoffmann's style was modernised, the narrator's comments were omitted, and those passages that hint at the ambiguity of the events described were rewritten to clarify their meaning – which is always an interpretation by the editor and/or publisher, since they are afraid that children, and perhaps even adults, may refuse to read a book that lacks a happy ending and a clearly defined interpretation. 'The Nutcracker and the Mouse King' consequently mutates into an exciting Christmas tale, stressing the mysterious atmosphere at this time of year.

It is interesting to note that the age of the protagonist, Marie, is often concealed because the marriage between a seven-year-old girl and a nutcracker prince might arouse suspicion about the credibility of the story. In other editions, the time span between the proposal of marriage and the wedding ceremony is extended to several years, to achieve a more convincing ending. To illustrate the far-reaching impact of these abbreviations and changes, readers should compare the final chapters of different editions. In some of them, the last chapter, which is approximately ten pages long, has been deleted. An older German edition from 1909 that was re-issued in 1991 would be a typical example. After Marie has informed her parents and older siblings about her daydreams and nightmares, her family calls her a dreamer. This version finishes with the words: 'Ja, in der lieben frohen Weihnachtszeit träumen die Kinder wunderliche Dinge! Und schöne Träume sind auch die Märchen, wie das vom Nußknacker und Mausekönig' [Of course, at this lovely, happy Christmas time children always dream funny things! And fairy tales such as 'The Nutcracker and the Mouse King' are also wonderful dreams!] (1991 [1909]: 82; translation B.K.M.). No wonder that even brand-new editions, such as the above-mentioned picture book version, *The Nutcracker* (2010), more or less retell the story based on the libretto for the ballet production. The phrase in the front matter, 'based on the story by E.T.A. Hoffmann', is quite deceptive. Consequently, we can assume that Hoffmann's fairy tale has obviously not lost the innovative character and challenging potential that contradict common pedagogical assumptions about texts suitable for children up to the present day.

## Conclusion

In sum then, a thorough analysis of these different strands of reception highlights the multiple (de-)canonisation processes that Hoffmann's fairy tale has undergone in almost two hundred years. Five reasons are responsible for the marginalisation of Hoffmann's children's literature on the one hand, and for the non-existence of his children's books in the literary canon on the other hand. The main reason is the seemingly inferior quality of children's literature, thus stressing its insufficient contribution to the child's developing literary taste. In addition, children's literature is regarded as a minor genre, equivalent to light fiction and popular literature. A third reason is the devaluation of children's book authors by means of negative stereotypes. The fourth reason is concerned with adult critics' imperfect knowledge about literary traditions in the realm of children's literature.

Whereas almost every literary history made statements on children's books of the Enlightenment era, Romantic children's literature – with the exception of the Grimms' fairy tales – is either not included or ascribed to adult literature. This tendency mainly concerns the fairy tales written for children by E.T.A. Hoffmann, who paved the way for the development of modern fantasy for children. This aspect leads to the fifth reason for the missing representation of children's literature in the general literary canon: the categorisation of high quality children's books as works written for adults, as is the case with E.T.A. Hoffmann's 'Nutcracker and the Mouse King' (1816). This makes it impossible to pursue a multi-perspectival reading of children's literature. In addition, certain features of adult literature, like an open ending, intertextuality, irony or a combination of different genres, were not taken into consideration as possible features of children's literature, although they occur in many sophisticated children's books, including Hoffmann's works.

Moreover, the shifting classification of 'The Nutcracker and the Mouse King' as either a book suitable for children or a challenging work for an adult readership highlights the importance of the theoretical approach of crosswriting (or crossover fiction) for prospective studies on canonical research, emphasising the interface between adult literature and children's literature in general (Knoepflmacher & Myers 1997). An insightful reading of Hoffmann's work will help to emphasise the significance of competing discourse in the process of canon formation and its connection to crosswriting, since Hoffmann is both an author for adults and for children, and he addresses children and adults alike by creating multiple levels of meaning in his fairy tales for children. What makes these facts so interesting, however, is that they obviously influence the reception and (de-)canonisation of an author and his/her works in different media and in the academic world. This means that analysis of canonical processes must be taken into account when considering the history of children's literature research. It will certainly help readers interested in cultural history in achieving a better understanding of changing attitudes towards children's literature and childhood.

# Bibliography

## Primary Sources

Almond, D. 1998. *Skellig*. London: Hodder Children's Books.

Andersen, H.C. 1995 [1835-1848]. *Eventyr, fortalte for børn*. Copenhagen: Gyldendal.

Barrie, J.M. 2008 [1911]. *Peter and Wendy*. Oxford: Oxford University Press.

Beskow, E. 1901. *Puttes äventyr i blåbärsskogen*. Stockholm: Bonnier.

Carroll, L. 1982 [1865]. *Alice's Adventures in Wonderland*. Oxford: Oxford University Press.

Daudet, A. 1977 [1868]. *Le petit chose*. Paris: Gallimard.

Dumas, A. 1845. *L'histoire d'un casse-noisette*. Paris: Hetzel.

Ende, M. 1973. *Momo*. Stuttgart: Thienemann.

Ende, M. 1979. *Die Unendliche Geschichte*. Stuttgart: Thienemann.

Gaiman, N. 2002. *Coraline*. New York: HarperCollins.

Gaarder, J. 1991. *Sofies verden*. Oslo: Aschehoug.

Grimm, J. & W. Grimm. 1985 [1812-1815]. *Kinder- und Hausmärchen*. Frankfurt: Deutscher Klassiker-Verlag.

Hoffmann, E.T.A. 1909 [1816]. *Nußknacker und Mausekönig*. Ill. O. Bauriedl & E. Kutzer. Wien/ Leipzig: Gerlach.

Hoffmann, E.T.A. 1955. *Histoire d'un Casse-Noisette. Un conte d'Hoffmann. Raconté par Alexandre Dumas*. Ill. A. Ségur. Paris: Flammarion.

Hoffmann, E.T.A. 1977. *Nussknacker und Mausekönig*. Ill. E. J. Rubin. Berlin: Kinderbuchverlag.

Hoffmann, E.T.A. 1984. *Nutcracker*. Ill. M. Sendak. New York: Crown Publishers.

Hoffmann, E.T.A. 1987. 'Nußknacker und Mausekönig', in: H.-H. Ewers (ed.), *Kinder-Märchen. Von C.W. Contessa, F. de la Motte Fouqué, E.T.A. Hoffmann*. Stuttgart: Reclam, 66-144.

Hoffmann, E.T.A. 1993. *Nußknacker und Mausekönig*. Ill. U. Mühlhoff. Hamburg: Dressler.

Hoffmann, E.T.A. 1995. *Nußknacker und Mausekönig*. Ill. H.G. Schellenberger. Würzburg: Arena.

Hoffmann, E.T.A. 1996. *Nutcracker*. Ill. R. Innocenti. Mankato: Creative Editions.

Hoffmann, E.T.A. 1996. *The Nutcracker*. Ill. G. Spirin. New York: Stewart, Tabori & Chang.

Hoffmann, E.T.A. 2003. *Nussknacker*. Ill. L. Zwerger. Salzburg: Neugebauer.

Hoffmann, E.T.A. 2010. *The Nutcracker. Based on the story by E.T.A. Hoffmann. Retold by Ann Marie Anderson*. Ill. A. Jay. New York: Penguin Group.

Hoffmann, E.T.A. 2001 [1819-1822]. *Die Serapionsbrüder*. W. Segebrecht (ed.), Frankfurt/M.: Deutscher Klassiker-Verlag.

Hoffmann, E.T.A. 2011. *The Serapion Brethren*. Trans. A. Ewig. San Francisco: Bottom of the Hill Publ.

Kästner, E. 1931. *Der 35. Mai oder Konrad reitet in die Südsee*. Berlin: Williams.

Kingsley, C. 1862. *The Water Babies*. London: Macmillan.

Lindgren, A. 1954. *Mio min Mio*. Stockholm: Rabén & Sjögren.

MacDonald, G. 1871. *At the Back of the North Wind*. London: Blackie & Son.

Masefield, J. 1927. *The Midnight Folk*. London: Heinemann.

Michelet, J. 1971 [1820-22]. *Mémorial*, in: P. Viallaneix (ed.), *Œuvres completes*. Vol. 1. Paris: Flammarion.

Michelet, J. 1883. *Ma jeunesse*. Paris: Flammarion.

Moe, J. 1972 [1851]. *I Brønnen og i Kjærnet*. Oslo: Aschehoug.

Molesworth, M. 1877. *The Cuckoo Clock*. London: Macmillan.

Nesbit, E. 1908. *The House of Arden*. London: Fisher Unwin.

Norton, M. 1952. *The Borrowers*. Harmondsworth: Penguin.

Pogorelsky, A. 1992 [1829]. *Chernaya kuritsa, ili podzemnye zhiteli*. Moscow: Russkaya kniga.

Pohl, P. 1985. *Janne min vän*. Stockholm: Rabén & Sjögren.

Pullman, P. 1995-2000. *His Dark Materials*. 3 vols. London: Scholastic.

Rydberg, V. 1980 [1875]. *Lille Viggs äventyr på julafton*. Stockholm: Bonniers.

Saint-Exupéry. A. de. 1988 [1943] *Le petit prince*. Paris: Gallimard.

Sand, G. 1990 [1850]. *Histoire du véritable Gribouille*. Paris: Flammarion.

Sendak, M. 1981. *Outside Over There*. New York: Harper & Row.

Spyri, J. 2002 [1880]. *Heidis Lehr- und Wanderjahre*. Hamburg: Dressler.

Strittmatter, E. 1954. *Tinko*. Berlin: Kinderbuchverlag.

Thackeray, W.M. 1964 [1855]. *The Rose and the Ring*. Harmondsworth: Penguin.

Topelius, Z. 1847. *Sagor*. Stockholm: Albert Bonnier Forlag.

Topelius, Z. 1865-1892. *Läsning för Barn*. Stockholm: Albert Bonnier Forlag.

## Films

*Barbie in the Nutcracker*. 2001. dir. Hurley, O. Lions Gate.

*Katya and the Nutcracker*. 2001. dir. Graham, A. IMC Vision.

*The Nutcracker*. 1999. dir. Winfield, J. Disney Studios.

*The Nuttiest Nutcracker*. 1999. dir. Harris, H. Sony Pictures.

## Secondary Sources

Apel, F. 1978. *Die Zaubergärten der Phantasie. Zur Theorie und Geschichte des Kunstmärchens*. Heidelberg: Winter.

Alefeld, Y-P. 1996. *Göttliche Kinder: Die Kindheitsideologie in der Romantik*. Paderborn: Schöningh.

Baader, M.S. 1996. *Die romantische Idee des Kindes und der Kindheit. Auf der Suche nach der verlorenen Unschuld*. Neuwied: Luchterhand.

Baur, S. 1790. *Charakteristik der Erziehungsschriftsteller Deutschlands. Ein Handbuch für Erzieher*. Leipzig: Fleischer.

Brunken, O., B. Hurrelmann & K.-U. Pech (eds). 1998. *Handbuch zur Kinder- und Jugendliteratur. Von 1800 bis 1850*. Stuttgart/Weimar: Metzler.

Clark, Beverly Lyon. 2003. *Kiddie Lit. The Cultural Construction of Children's Literature in America*. Baltimore: The John Hopkins University Press.

Drux, R. 1986. *Marionette Mensch. Ein Metaphernkomplex und sein Kontext von Hoffmann bis Büchner*. Munich: Fink.

Elling, B. 1996. 'E.T.A. Hoffmanns Rezeption in den Literaturgeschichten des 19. Jahrhunderts', in: C.A. Bernd, I. Henderson & W. McConnell (eds), *Romanticism and Beyond: A Festschrift für John F. Fetzer*. New York: Peter Lang, 133-163.

Ewers, H.-H. 1989. *Kindheit als romantische Daseinsform: Studien zur Entstehung der romantischen Kindheitsutopie im 18. Jahrhundert: Herder, Jean Paul, Novalis und Tieck*. Munich: Fink.

Ewers, H.-H. 2001. 'Kinderliteratur als Medium der Entdeckung von Kindheit', in: I. Behncken, & J. Zinnecker (eds), *Kinder – Kindheit – Lebensgeschichte. Ein Handbuch*. Seelze-Velber: Kallmeyersche Verlagsbuchhandlung, 48-62.

Fronemann, W. 1927. *Das Erbe Wolgasts*. Langensalza: Beltz.

Gedike, F. 1789. *Einige Gedanken über Schulbücher und Kinderschriften*. Berlin: Unger.

Gervinus, G.G. 1842. *Geschichte der poetischen National=Literatur der Deutschen*. Vol. 5. Leipzig: Engelmann.

Goedeke, K. 1859. *Grundrisz zur Geschichte der deutschen Dichtung*. Hannover: T. Ehlermann.

Gottschall, R. 1875. *Die deutsche Nationalliteratur des 19. Jahrhunderts*. Vol. 3. Fourth edition. Breslau: E. Trewendt.

Graebsch, I. 1942. *Geschichte des Jugendbuches*. Zurich: Atlantis.

Grenz, D. 1990. 'E.T.A. Hoffmann als Autor für Kinder und für Erwachsene', in: D. Grenz (ed.), *Kinderliteratur – Literatur auch für Erwachsene?* Munich: Fink, 65-74.

Heintz, G. 1974. 'Mechanik und Phantasie. Zu E.T.A. Hoffmanns Märchen 'Nußknacker und Mausekönig'', in: *Literatur in Wissenschaft und Unterricht* 7: 1-15.

Hobrecker, K. 1924. *Alte vergessene Kinderbücher*. Berlin: Mauritius.

Hoffmeister, G. 1990. *Deutsche und europäische Romantik*. Stuttgart: Metzler.

Knoepflmacher, U.C. & M. Myers. 1997. 'Cross-Writing and the Reconceptualizing of Children's Literature Studies', in: *Children's Literature* 25: VII-XVII.

Kremer, D. 1993. *Romantische Metamorphosen. E.T.A. Hoffmanns Erzählungen*. Stuttgart, Weimar: Metzler.

Kümmerling-Meibauer, B. 1996. 'Identität, Neutralität, Transgression: drei Typen der Geschlechterperspektivierung in der Kinderliteratur', in: G. Lehnert (ed.), *Inszenierungen von Weiblichkeit. Weibliche Kindheit und Adoleszenz in der Literatur des 20. Jahrhunderts*. Opladen: Westdeutscher Verlag, 29-45.

Kümmerling-Meibauer, B. 1999. *Klassiker der Kinder- und Jugendliteratur. Ein internationales Lexikon*. Stuttgart, Weimar: Metzler.

Kümmerling-Meibauer, B. 2003. *Kinderliteratur, Kanonbildung und literarische Wertung*. Stuttgart, Weimar: Metzler.

Kümmerling-Meibauer, B. 2008. 'Images of Childhood in Romantic Children's Literature', in: B. Dieterle, M. Engel & G. Gillespie (eds), *Romantic Prose Fiction*. Amsterdam: Benjamins, 183-203.

Kuznets, L. 1994. *When Toys Come Alive. Narratives of Animation, Metamorphosis and Development*. New Haven, London: Yale University Press.

Miller, N. 1975. 'E.T.A. Hoffmanns doppelte Wirklichkeit. Zum Motiv der Schwellenüberschreitung in seinen Märchen', in: H. Arntzen (ed.), *Literaturwissenschaft und Geschichtsphilosophie. Festschrift für Wilhelm Emmrich*. Berlin: de Gruyter, 357-372.

Müller, A. (ed.) 2013. *Adapting Canonical Texts in Children's Literature*. London: Bloomsbury.

Natov, R. 2003. *The Poetics of Childhood*. New York: Routledge.

Neumann, G. 1997. 'Puppe und Automate. Inszenierte Kindheit in E.T.A. Hoffmanns Sozialisationsmärchen "Nußknacker und Mausekönig"', in: G. Oesterle (ed.), *Jugend – ein romantisches Konzept?* Würzburg: Königshausen & Neumann, 135-160.

Prestel, J. 1933. *Geschichte des deutschen Jugendschrifttums*. Freiburg: Herder.

Richter, K. & L. Jahn. 2006. *Bildwelten zu E.T.A. Hoffmanns "Nußknacker und Mausekönig"*. Baltmannsweiler: Schneider Verlag Hohengehren.

Roquette, O. 1863. *Geschichte der deutschen Literatur, von den ältesten Denkmälern bis auf die neueste Zeit*. Vol. 2. Stuttgart: Ebner & Seubert.

Rüttgers, S. 1914. *Die Dichtung in der Volksschule*. Leipzig: Dürr.

Scherr, J. 1854. *Allgemeine Geschichte der Literatur*. Berlin: Weidmann.

Schikorsky, I. 1995. 'Im Labyrinth der Phantasie. Ernst Theodor Hoffmanns Wirklichkeitsmärchen "Nußknacker und Mausekönig"', in: B. Hurrelmann (ed.), *Klassiker der Kinder- und Jugendliteratur*. Frankfurt/M.: Fischer, 520-539.

Schmidt, R. 2006. *Wenn mehrere Künste im Spiel sind: Intermedialität bei E.T.A. Hoffmann*. Göttingen: Vandenhoek & Ruprecht.

Steedman, C. 1995. *Strange Dislocations: Childhood and the Idea of Human Interiority, 1780-1930*. London: Virago Press.

Steinlein, R. 1999. 'Kindheit als Diskurs des Fremden: Die Entdeckung der kindlichen Innenwelt bei Goethe, Moritz und E.T.A. Hoffmann', in: A. Honold & M. Köppen (eds), *"Die andere Stimme". Das Fremde in der Kultur der Moderne. Festschrift für Klaus R. Scherpe zum 60. Geburtstag.* Cologne, Weimar, Vienna: Böhlau, 277-297.

Vitt-Maucher, G. 1989. *E.T.A. Hoffmanns Märchenschaffen. Kaleidoskop der Verfremdung in seinen sieben Märchen.* Chapel Hill, London: University of North Carolina Press.

von Eichendorff, J. 1970 [1857]. *Geschichte der poetischen Literatur Deutschlands*, in: W. Mauser (ed.), *Sämtliche Werke.* Vol. 9. Regensburg: Habel.

Wild, R. (ed.) 2008. *Geschichte der deutschen Kinder- und Jugendliteratur.* Third edition. Stuttgart, Weimar: Metzler.

Wolgast, H. 1896. *Das Elend unserer Jugendliteratur.* Hamburg: Selbstverlag.

# Notes

1.  For a comprehensive overview, see the introduction by Sylvie Geerts and Sara Van den Bossche, this volume.

2.  The German title is usually translated as 'The Nutcracker and the Mouse King,' but there are variations such as 'Nutcracker and the Mouse King'; 'Nutcracker and the King of Mice'; or simply 'Nutcracker.'

3.  Brunken, Hurrelmann & Pech (1998) barely acknowledge Hoffmann's pioneering contribution to international children's literature. Even Wild (2008) fails to explain Hoffmann's seminal role in detail.

4.  Hoffmann was an all-round artist: an author, painter, composer, and musician. See Schmidt (2006) for further information.

5.  The metamorphosis of figures is investigated in Drux (1986) and Heintz (1974). Kuznets (1994: 62-68) also refers to these transformations; however, she conflates Hoffmann's original story with the rewritten, tame version by Alexandre Dumas.

6.  For this reason Natov categorises Hoffmann's tale as 'dark pastoral' (2006:130-132).

7.  Es ist überhaupt meines Bedünkens ein großer Irrtum, wenn man glaubt daß lebhafte fantasiereiche Kinder, von denen hier nur die Rede sein kann, sich mit inhaltsleeren Faseleien, wie sie oft unter dem Namen Märchen vorkommen, begnügen. Ei – sie verlangen wohl was Besseres und es ist zum Erstaunen, wie richtig wie lebendig sie manches im Geistes auffassen, dass manchem grundgescheuten Papa gänzlich entgeht. Erfahrt und habt Respekt! (2001: 306)

8.  More information about the reception of Hoffmann's fairy tales at the beginning of the nineteenth century can be found in the epilogue written by Hans-Heino Ewers in Hoffmann (1987: 300-302).

9.  A French translation with illustrations by Adrienne Ségur was published in 1953 by Flammarion (Paris). A children's book edition, illustrated by Eva Johanna Rubin, appeared in 1976 in the former GDR (Berlin: Kinderbuchverlag). The Austrian illustrator Lisbeth Zwerger illustrated two separate editions for Neugebauer Press (Salzburg) in 1987 and 2003. The success of the American translation with illustrations by Maurice Sendak (New York:

Crown Publ., 1984) was complemented by the editions illustrated by Roberto Innocenti (Mancato: The Creative Company, 1996) and Gennady Spirin (New York: Stewart, Tabori & Chang, 1996).

10.  Compare Elling (1996), who studied the reception of E.T.A. Hoffmann in 85 German literary histories published in the nineteenth century.

11.  Richter & Jahn (2006) investigated the impact of different illustrated versions (Innocenti, Zwerger, Spirin, Sendak) on primary school students. They acknowledged that it was largely the illustrations that stimulated the students' emotional and aesthetic reactions.

12.  Maurice Sendak, for instance, openly refers to his picturebook *Where the Wild Things Are* (1965) in a wordless picture sequence showing Marie's journey to the land of gingerbread. Marie sits in a boat and feels quite frightened by strange beings waiting on the shore. With this reference, Sendak is probably emphasising that both journeys (Max's and Marie's) could be interpreted as imaginative dreams.

# PART 3

# TRANSMEDIAL ASPECTS
# OF ADAPTATION

# Stories in Transition

## Observations at Grassroots Level

### Franci Greyling

'Literature is seamless at the edges', according to Ruth Finnegan (2005: 180). At these edges – at the intersection between orality and literacy, between cultures, languages, genres and semiotic systems – 'ordinary people' are involved in the telling, retelling and remediation of stories.

Canonisation is inherently centrifugal with the focus on work that has stood the test of time and attained prominent status in a particular field. In literature the concept of canonisation is generally used with reference to printed texts – oral texts and literature for children are seldom considered to be part of the central canon. Cultural globalisation further contributes to this somewhat narrow view of literature and literature creation, as Richard Alain and Flora Veit-Wild observe:

> In our era of cultural globalization, literary productions tend to get streamlined; they are determined by marketing strategies that control the content and forms of cultural creation. [...] Literary globalization also tends to place a strong emphasis on the genre of the novel and to neglect and suppress most other types of literary production. (Alain & Veit-Wild 2005: ix)

The consequence is that large parts of the literary practice – amongst which are the so-called 'grassroots writing and reading' (ibid.: x) – are ignored or for the most part function relatively unnoticed.[1] Grassroots literature is often distinguished by its temporal and local character, and the particular context in which it is created and appreciated. This form of literature is characterised by hybridity and intertextuality – including a blend of traditional, local and personal elements; the combination of modes, media, forms and semiotic systems; and diverse genres. These forms can incorporate traditional storytelling or performance, cultural forms such as African oral praise poetry, as well as contemporary forms such as rap or the popular novel. Grassroots literature often fulfils a significant function in the community (ibid.).

As a creative facilitator and mediator, I am involved in diverse projects regarding the creation and reception of texts, among others community-based projects and literature at grassroots level. This involvement necessitates a careful consideration of and reflection on the creative dynamics with regard to text and context. I am especially interested in the transitional dynamics in this 'seamless' space and how the complex interaction of the diverse aspects that are involved can be analysed, described and understood. This article focuses on the genre of the folktale, particularly the fairy tale, which is often encountered in grassroots literature. The recognisable features of this genre provide a unique opportunity for analysis, description, comparison and reflection. A theoretical framework in the first part of the article serves as a background for the discussion with reference to three variations of wonder tales ('Cinderella', 'How Six Travel through the World' and 'Three Magic Gifts') encountered in grassroots literature in Namibia and South Africa.

## Framework

More and more researchers, such as Ruth Finnegan (1982: 29; 2005: 182) and Walter Ong (1982: 8), have drawn attention to the diverse elements which play a role in the creation and reception of any recorded or printed version of an oral narrative and the importance of recognising the complex dynamics involved. This holistic approach is also observed in modern folk narrative research. However, much more research is needed in this regard, as Siegfried Neuman points out:

> Of course, narrative research is no longer just interested in the narrated material itself, but also in the narrator and audience, in the context and motivation of the narrative event, and in the role of storytelling in the intellectual and cultural life of people today. In this respect we have achieved so far only limited results that – in the distant wake of the Grimms – urgently need further study and elaboration. (Neuman 2001: 977-978)

In an attempt to understand and describe the complex dynamics involved in the creation and reading of the peripheral texts under discussion, I draw on six interlinked aspects, namely the primary ways of cultural transference in a community and modes of representation; the narrative chain; the particular context; the role and identity of the mediator and the 'skopos'; and finally, the multidimensional character of literature. Due to the scope of the article and the complexity of the interaction, I will concentrate only on aspects relevant to my argument.

### *Primary Means of Cultural Transference in a Community and the Modes of Representation*

Régis Debray, a contemporary French philosopher, distinguishes between three media spheres, namely the 'logo sphere', 'grapho sphere' and the 'video sphere'. The foremost feature of each sphere respectively is that cultural transmission mainly occurs through the spoken word ('*logo* sphere'), written word ('*grapho* sphere') and the image ('*video* sphere'). Gunter Kress refers to speech, writing and image as 'modes of representation' (2003: 137). The three media spheres broadly correspond with Walter Ong's distinction between 'primary orality', 'literacy' (chirographic and orthographic culture) and 'secondary orality' (1982: 15). Primary orality refers to the 'pristine orality of mankind untouched by writing or print which remains still more or less operative in areas sheltered to a greater degree from the full impact of literacy and which is vestigial to some degree in all of us' (ibid.: 13). Orality is strongly associated with performance as a narrative mode, with qualities such as immediacy and temporality. Although some communities can be considered as basically primary oral cultures in many ways, they are to a lesser or larger degree modified by contact with secondary orality (ibid.: 14). Secondary orality, which entails electronic technology such as the radio and television (and by implication the internet), is to varying degrees literate and is totally dependent on writing (ibid.: 18-19): 'In fact, a residual primary orality, literacy, and secondary orality are interacting vigorously with one another in confusing complex patterns in our secondarily oral world' (ibid.: 19).

The division between the 'logo-', 'grapho-' and 'video spheres' – between 'primary orality', 'literacy' and 'secondary orality' – is relatively fluid. Even in cultures where the oral tradition is prominent (such as in the South Pacific, as Finnegan has demonstrated), there is interaction between orality and literacy: written notes, for example, serve as a mnemonic for oral performance. Since there is a potential 'feedback' from written sources in oral forms, a simple division or distinction between oral and literary formats is not straightforward (Finnegan 1982: 29). The so-called pristine oral texts, untouched by the printed text or digital media, are very much an illusion. This is to a large extent also the case in Southern Africa, as there are hardly any communities left that practice a 'pure' oral culture (Loubser 2002: 34). Nonetheless, Francis Abiola Irele emphasises that orality is still the dominant mode of communication in Africa (2001: 11), and points out that '[d]espite the undoubted impact of print culture on African experience and its role in the determination of new cultural modes, the tradition of orality remains predominant and serves as a central paradigm for various kinds of expression on the continent' (ibid.: 31). In countries such as South Africa, rather complicated relationships exist between the different modes of transfer (Brown 1999: 9); multiple and multidimensional interfaces of orality and literacy are apparent; and there is a large domain of cultural forms that cross the boundaries between the written and the oral, the foreign and the indigenous (Alain & Veit-Wild 2005: xii).

This intricate relationship between orality and literacy is also a feature of the European folkloric tradition. Even though folktales originated in oral cultures (Fludernik 2009: 63), Lewis Seifert, in discussing the origin of the fairy tale, points out that orality and literacy were to a greater degree interwoven in the folkloric tradition than is generally acknowledged:

> Literary fairy tales are usually defined as written narratives based, in however minimal a way, on folktales, the oral narratives preserved and told by literate and non-literate groups alike. However, to conclude that the folkloric tradition was exclusively oral would be an over-generalization, for the historical study of folkloric tale-types and motifs has revealed that it is often impossible to separate written from oral versions. As they were told and retold, tales were transformed, truncated, and combined with other motifs or tale-types in accordance with both printed and oral narratives. (Seifert 2001: 904)

Stories have always been retold and adapted in new contexts – new contexts which include the travelling and transmittance between continents, countries, languages and generations (Ewers 1992: 174; Finnegan 1982: 29, 33; Willemse 2004: 69). Such retellings are often integrated into local styles, forms and insights (Finnegan 1982: 22; Ewers 1992: 174). This vitality of the folktale can, amongst other things, be attributed to special characteristics of orality which enable the transference of stories. According to Irele, in oral culture there is always a 'minimal text' and often a 'master text' (2001: 37). The recognisable and memorisable motives, characters and story structures enable narrators to retell the story or to use it as a basis for new stories.

In his discussion of the origin of the literary fairy tale, Jack Zipes highlights the role of the 'oral wonder tale tradition' ('Zaubermärchen' [magic tale], or the 'conte merveilleux' [marvellous tale]). The literary fairy tale was a continuation of the oral wonder tale, but the genre's conventions, motifs, *topoi*, characters and plots were modified to address a reading public formed largely by the aristocracy and the middle class (Zipes 2001: 847). In his seminal work on folklore, Vladimir Propp discusses the narrative structure of the wonder tale in detail. In essence

> [a] wondertale begins with some harm or villainy done to someone […] or with a desire to have something […] and develops through the hero's departure from home and encounters with the donor, who provides him with a magic agent that helps the hero find the object of the search. Further along, the tale includes combat with an adversary [..], a return, and a pursuit. (Propp 1984: 102)

All these experiences lead to the transformation of the protagonist and the reversing of the wheel of fortune. Zipes explains the functions, dynamics, characteristics and vitality of the wonder tale as follows:

> The significance of the paradigmatic functions of the wonder tale is that they facilitate recall for teller and listeners. Over hundreds of years they have enabled people to store, remember, and reproduce the plot of the tale and to change it to fit their experiences and desires due to the easily identifiable characters who are associated with particular social classes, professions, and assignments. The characters, settings, and motifs are combined and varied according to specific functions to induce *wonder* and *hope* for change in the audience or listeners/readers, who are to marvel or admire the magical changes that occur in the course of events. It is this earthy, sensual, and secular sense of wonder and hope that distinguished the wonder tales from other oral tales such as the legend, the fable, the anecdote, and the myth; it is clearly the sense of wonder that distinguishes the *literary* fairy tale from the moral story, novella, sentimental tale, and other modern short literary genres. (Zipes 2001: 848; emphasis in original)

Zipes is of the opinion that it is this 'celebration of miraculous or fabulous transformation in the name of hope' in the oral wonder tale (and by implication in the literary fairy tale) that accounts for its major appeal (ibid.). As will be illustrated in the latter part of the article, this 'sense of wonder and hope' is not only applicable to the audience, but might also apply to the narrator as such.

The rediscovery of narrative genres such as fairy tales, myths, legends and merry tales during the Romantic period in Europe, and the collection of these narratives by Charles Perrault and by Wilhelm and Jacob Grimm, resulted to a certain extent in the ossification of these stories, and their increased association with children's literature (Ewers 1992: 170). These collections and narratives gradually spread to other parts of the world, where one often encounters variations of and motifs from these oral wonder tales and literary fairy tales. Although the printed form, especially in the case of the Grimms' tales, over time became the norm and container of the canon, the re-interpretation and remediation continued through the ages, as a magnitude of variations in diverse forms and media testifies (Neumann 2001: 978).

## *The Narrative Chain*

The retelling in new contexts presupposes a mediator and a creative act, in other words, a creative (re-)interpretation. This process – the constant retelling of the story through different mediators for different receivers in diverse contexts – I call the narrative chain. In a simplified manner, it can be presented as follows (Figure 1):

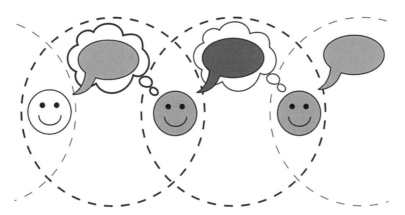

**Figure 1. The narrative chain.**

Each individual involved in the narrative chain – whether as a performer, 'renarrator', author, scribe, translator, illustrator, editor, etc. – is engaged in a creative activity which establishes a new version of the text.

However, this schematic presentation is an oversimplification, because it implies a linear progression. In reality, there is an interweaving of narrations that can originate at any point in the simplified narrative chain and that can result in a new narrative chain. Continuing the metaphor of the chain, the result can then be presented as a loose interlacing of chains (similar to the medieval 'chain mail'). The metaphor of weaving also corresponds with the origin of the word *text*, namely *texere* – to weave.

A story is retold multiple times and texts are intuitively adapted to the narrator's social circumstances and lived experience – the *social fabric of story* is always part of it in one way or another. With the repeated retelling of a story in a certain community (especially the oral variations), it increasingly becomes part of the community, with characteristic cultural, spatial, social and identity markers that give the story a unique local feeling. The oral tradition of a story is so flexible precisely because there is no fixed form. J.A. (Bobby) Loubser explains the process and result as follows:

> During oral-aural communication, intertextual reference can only come from memory. Because memory is in a permanent state of flux, such references are usually adapted to the present needs of the audience to such an extent that the original context becomes obscured. (Loubser 2002: 39)

Because of the temporality of the spoken story ('orality') as related to retelling or *performance*, it survives beyond the context of the moment only through the process of *mediation* (Brown 1999: 4). This mediation involves, among other things, that the text is captured in some way, for example through sound recordings, filming or transcription. Transcription is, however, not a neutral act, but has the potential to largely influence an original narrative (ibid.: 4-5). As soon as other modes and media are involved, it also implies that the semiotic system changes – for example *verbal* narration which changes to *writing*, as in the case of transcription. The oral text is usually transferred to a printed form through the agency of a literate *intermediary*, who is often in a position of political or publishing power over the performer or informant. This situation also applies to some extent to *grassroots reading and writing*, when an outsider introduces the text to a wider audience.

The more formal process of publication also implies functions such as selection and editing. Although the mediator may not influence much of the *content* of the text in this regard, selection and editing can have significant consequences. These mediators can also determine the place (context) of publication, which can have a great influence on the text and its reception. Transcription, re-interpretation and remediation *per se* imply a kind of cultural translation. Making texts accessible outside their specific language and cultural context involves translation in the more traditional sense of the word. Because the texture of a text is intertwined with language, translation is necessarily associated with the loss of meaning and qualities that are unique to a certain language, including vocabulary, metaphors, rhythm and sound associations.

The processes of selection, transcription and editing have, however, always been part of the process of the recording and retelling of folktales and fairy tales in different contexts. Different manuscripts and publications of the brothers Grimm, for example, show that the texts were edited, and that they were further shaped and refined in preparation for publication (Zipes 1983: 47; Dollerup 1999: 29). In subsequent publications, the narratives were also revised, expanded and adapted for the *envisaged readers* (Neumann 2001: 971-973; Zipes 1983: 48). Finnegan stresses that, although it is important to take the limitations of transcriptions into account, in practice such 'translations, trans-formations and interchanges' constantly take place between different modes of literary formulation, and that they are part of the 'unending cycles of human creation' (2005: 177-178).

## Context

As argued in the introduction of this volume, stories are invariably influenced by the specific context in which they are narrated or published. The process of retelling traditional narratives is necessarily 'influenced by the "attitudes and ideologies" which characterise the new context' (Geerts & Van den Bossche with reference to Stephens & McCallum 1998, this volume). Narrations always take place in a certain context and are construed for a specific audience. Karin Barber highlights the importance to establish 'as accurately as possible [...] what the text *could have meant* or, rather, *could have been taken to mean*, in the context of its double relationship to its original author and audience'(1999: 27; emphasis in original). In the instance of an oral narration, the audience is not only present, but also influences the narration in various ways (Dollerup 1999: 28; Finnegan 2005: 172). Stories can therefore only be properly understood in the context of the specific constellation of narrators and audiences in which they are being told (Johnstone 1991: 40; Barber 1999: 27). The narration is, however, also embedded in an expanding context, for instance the personal circumstances of the narrator; the narrative context (for example, whether it is a spontaneous narration, forms part of a ritual, or – as is sometimes the case in folk narrative research – is being told to relative strangers); the specific as well as the wider socio-cultural, political and ideological contexts and the historic period in question.

With regard to printed texts, the context can also involve the origin of the text, the specific publication (such as the format, scope and physical appearance of the text or the publication as a whole), as well as other relevant aspects of the publication system. With grassroots literature, which often functions beyond the literary publication system, texts are sometimes acquired, initiated or collected by outsiders, who then further introduce and publish them. This context must also be taken into consideration when texts are being scrutinised, because it can influence the text in different ways.

Each situation or context, in which a story is retold to a different audience, creates new possibilities in which the text can be read and interpreted. The reader, like the author, is part of a specific conjuncture, society and community, and each brings his or her background, expectations and values to the text, and understands and interprets it in the light of this code (Machet 1996: 32). This implies that readers will invariably read and understand the texts differently.

## The Identity of the Mediator

Identity – including personal, narrative, language and cultural identity – is always interwoven in a narrative, and the identity of each of the participants in the narrative chain (be it the narrator, performer, commissioner, transcriber, author, translator, illustrator, publisher or reader) exerts a certain influence on the narrative. Since identity is constantly shifting and changing, it is impossible to pin down (Martin 2000: 113); nevertheless, it is possible to make inferences regarding identity when it is represented in some way or another. In every community there exist certain levels of cultural identity – symbols, heroes, rituals and values – which are embodied through *practices* (Hofstede 1991: 19).

Through a closer look at these practices, actions and artefacts, it is possible to identify attributes of individuals or communities which in themselves are difficult to pinpoint, and to make inferences regarding identity. Narratives are one of these practices which reflect distinctive qualities indicative of the identity of an individual or community. It is, however, important to recognise that identity is multilayered, multifaceted and constantly changing (Hall 2000: 57). Personal narratives provide one with access to the reality of one's own life. Furthermore, personal narratives are not only a way to tell life stories, but also a way through which identities are shaped (Greyling & Combrink 2008: 244).

The constant interpretation and re-interpretation of narratives are both a means by which individuals or communities respond to change as well as a manner in which change can be accomplished. Maureen Whitebrook explains the process of narrative structuring as follows:

> Narrative structuring allows that narratives may be revised, reinterpreted – to incorporate other('s) stories; unexpected events can be assimilated; stories can be reconstructed – on the basis of remembrance, memory or invention; and identities can be retold in reaction to previous narratives of identity. Recollection and memory are essential to the narrative process – remembering the past in order to tell and retell and revise narrative identity. Because narrative is processual there is constant revision and editing allowing the assimilation of untoward events, the unexpected: the story is shaped and reshaped as it is being told. (Whitebrook 2001: 38)

According to Stuart Hall, '[i]dentity is not something which is formed outside and then we tell stories about it. It is that which is narrated in one's own self' (2000: 49). The variations of stories, as well as the particular uses and features of specific texts, can consequently provide insight into the identity of individuals or communities. In this regard, re-interpretation of the same narrative, or of a corpus of recognisable narratives or motives such as is the case with the fairy tale, could serve as a valuable basis to compare and assess variations of a text or genre, whether by different individuals, in diverse modes, media, formats or semiotic systems, within different contexts, or over time.

## *'Skopos' and Addressee*

Karin Barber explains that '[e]very text, like every other utterance, bears the marks of its orientation towards an addressee, revealing an expectation of being interpreted' (1999: 27). The process of telling, retelling, re-interpretation and remediation in a narrative chain implies a continuous awareness of and orientation towards an addressee. Sometimes this retelling, re-interpretation or remediation is carried out by the creator of the 'original' text, for example when a writer reworks his or her own short story into a play; in other cases, another mediator may be performing the retelling, for example a parent telling a story to a child or an artist illustrating a text. In addition, in the publishing process, diverse functions such as compiling, editing and translating are conducted with particular audiences in mind. This orientation towards an addressee exerts an inevitable influence on the text.

To a certain extent, the process of retelling and re-interpretation can be regarded as translation, since both a source text and a target text are involved. Renowned children's book illustrator Piet Grobler, for example, argues that illustration can also be interpreted as a form of translation (2004: 130). In keeping with Grobler's position, it can be argued that the remediation of any text amounts to a kind of translation of that text, with the result that a 'skopos' is involved (Greyling & Combrink 2008: 251). Vermeer's 'skopos theory', which originated within translation studies and according to which the *function* or 'skopos' of the target text is taken into consideration, can therefore be of great value in describing and understanding the interactions between texts. The skopos of a translation is the *instruction*, the commission given by oneself or by someone else, stating the *goal and purpose* of the translation or remediation and the *target readership or recipients*.

As indicated, each context in which a story is retold to a different audience creates new possibilities of reading and interpreting. Naturally, the perspective and identity of the reader will determine how a text is experienced and interpreted. When the addressee acts with his/her own frame of reference as a mediator and 'translates' the story further, a new 'skopos' is implied, which again exerts an influence on the text.

## *The Multidimensional Character of the Text*

When considering the text, diverse features come into play, namely the modes of representation (speech, writing, and image), the medium, genre, format and semiotic systems – and the unique combination of these. It is thus paramount that the particular 'format' of the narrative also be taken into consideration, concurrently with its content.

As has been pointed out, the distinction between orality and literacy is not clear-cut. In the words of Finnegan: 'Written and oral forms can overlap and intermingle, and are related in manifold and variegated ways rather than existing as distinctive modes having hard-edged properties' (2005: 169). Finnegan, who prefers the term 'display' for all forms of literary texts, including oral literature, investigates how the concept of 'performance literature' can contribute not only to a better understanding of literature from Asia and Africa, but also to any literary forms of which performance is a part. Orality, and by implication performance, is a feature of folktales, fairy tales and the genre of children's literature (Ewers 1992: 169-170). Finnegan points out that performance is in essence multisensory: 'visual, kinesic [sic], acoustic, proxemic, material, tactile, moving, and embodied' (2005: 172). In her discussion of the unique qualities of performance, she warns against a binary division between orality and literacy and comes to the conclusion that essentially 'all literary performance is in one way or another multidimensional' (ibid.), and that writing, too, is multimodal and contextualised. This multidimensionality is observed through attributes within the text itself – such as the typographic format, pictorial image, colour, the materiality of the 'display' – and through acoustic elements – such as rhythm, rhyme, emphasis. Other attributes are created through the 'reader's art', whether in silent or vocalised reading and in the 'resonances of auditory speech' (ibid.: 173-175).

This multisensory intertextuality also applies to the aspect of media. Loubser refers to the 'media texture' of a message which can be observed by 'considering the media properties that influence the production, format, distribution and reception of the text' (2002: 42). The particular medium – including technology – is one of the fundamental reasons why texts exhibit peculiar characteristics (ibid.: 28), and also provides the opportunity to develop unique storytelling capabilities (Ryan 2009: 264). Marie-Laure Ryan notes that '[t]he properties of narratives produced in a certain medium are often due to a combination of cultural, technological, and semiotic factors' (ibid.: 269). An awareness of this multidimensional character of texts, the multisensory intertextualities inherent in a text, the possible influence of the medium, and the conventions of genre and form can contribute to the appraisal of grassroots literature.

Of special interest for this discussion is the occurrence of orality in literary narratives. In her contribution on conversational and oral narration in the *Handbook of Narratology*, Monika Fludernik distinguishes four prototypes of oral narrative, viz. spontaneous conversational narrative, oral poetry, traditional storytelling and pseudo-oral discourse (2009: 64-65): 'Pseudo-orality occurs in two forms in literary (and sometimes in non-literary) narratives: the representation of dialect or foreign speech in written dialogue and the evocation of an oral narrator persona' (ibid.: 65). The latter includes the use of a 'pseudo-oral narrative voice', 'a teller figure whose style suggests that the discourse has been uttered rather than written down' (ibid.). This effect of orality can be achieved through a combination of various aspects, for example vocabulary, syntax and diverse narrative markers such as interjections, interruptions and the familiar addressing of an active listener or audience. These techniques can be used deliberately, as is the case with skilled authors, but in grassroots literature the effect of orality is most likely due to a more unconscious transference of oral narrative conventions to writing. Discourse study and discourse analysis can provide the necessary structure for the assessment of conversational narrative and narrative structure in texts, for example Labov's (1972) basic structure and narrative clauses.

## Discussion

I wish to illustrate the aforesaid with three examples of grassroots literature noted in Namibia and South Africa respectively. These three instances of different orality-literacy contexts demonstrate the functioning of the narrative chain, the role and influence of diverse mediators and contexts in furthering the narrative, and the multidimensionality of texts. In all cases, the type of narratives are fairy tales.

### *Example 1: Oral Performance – 'Cinderella'*

In his article 'The politics of narrating Cinderella in Namibia', Hein Willemse discusses two variations on 'Cinderella' as performed by two female narrators from Namibia (2004: 69-70).[2] He explains that the research 'took place within a performance framework that explored individual and communal communicative events and the socio-political contexts of these articulations' (ibid.: 69). Both variations of Cinderella were recorded on a field trip in Namibia during March and April 1994. The two informants lived in meagre circumstances in isolated communities in two small towns close to the eastern border between Namibia and Botswana, on the edge of the Kalahari Desert. The majority of Willemse's randomly selected informants had either no schooling or less than five years of schooling and could either barely read or not at all. Less than 5% of the rural households had access to electricity; in Aranos the majority of informants had access to radio broadcasts. All the informants spoke Afrikaans, and a third were bilingual (Afrikaans-Nama) (ibid.: 71). It could be concluded that the informants were part of a primarily oral society.

The stories, which were performed in Afrikaans, were recorded and transcribed and later translated into English. The performances depended on the 'Cinderella' master narrative – that of the persecuted heroine – classified by Antti Aarne and Stith Thompson as Type 510. It is also related to Type 510B – 'Cap o' rushes', and the motif 'Love like salt', which sometimes appears as a separate tale, Type 923 (Thompson 1977: 128). This motif is prominent in the two informants' versions.

Willemse observes that in the retelling (remediation) of the European fairy tales, the storytellers intuitively adapt the story to their own social circumstances and authentic, lived experience, constructing their experience of life in colonial circumstances and under apartheid (2004: 73). Some examples are the depiction of the social distance characteristic of the domestic servant-master relationship, and references to housing, clothing, behaviour, skin colour and social habits indicative of social differentiation (ibid.: 75-76). This resulted in texts that portray local political, gender and social matters: 'It was in the retelling that these storytellers were defining their own values, contesting established ones and determining their own, if intuitive, visions of the future' (ibid.: 82). Integral to the performance is the use of language, as the performers' use of expletives, modes of address, exclamations, interjections and repetition also resonate with their lived experience. The way in which the storytellers apply language is to a great extent entangled with social, cultural, geographical and historical circumstances, with the result that it is not always fully appreciated or comprehended by outsiders and impossible to translate in all its nuances.

## Example 2: Oral Performance – 'How Six Travel through the World'

As part of a project which was aimed at promoting an interest in storytelling, writing and publication in communities, Anneretha Combrink recorded stories told by master storyteller Gert Hendriks (aged 54) on a farm in the rural community of Rysmierbult, North West Province, South Africa (2010).[3] Hendriks, a handyman and manual labourer, grew up in the Eastern Cape, South Africa, but later relocated to the provinces of Gauteng and North West. Before he settled in the Rysmierbult area, he worked on an ostrich farm where he entertained tourists by racing ostriches and where he also played minor roles in documentary films (Hendriks 2006a: 40). In his life story, he talked about his love for stories, a teacher who used to tell stories to the children and the fun of sharing these and other stories (Hendriks 2006b: 53). Circumstances forced him to leave school in grade five, but he still loved to read stories and was a passionate radio listener – he especially listened to a local Afrikaans radio station, where he presumably encountered some of his stories. Hendriks is an example of someone moving between the 'logo-', 'grapho-' and 'video spheres', vested in the oral storytelling tradition, but who is also familiar with the 'secondary orality' of radio and television (Combrink 2010: 297).

The farm workers in the North West Province are generally poor and semi-literate. On the farm where Hendriks resided, the workers and their families have access to electricity and are able to watch TV if they own a TV set. Due to a lack of readily available and affordable public transport, they are relatively isolated from the nearby towns. The mother tongue of the majority of the people in the district is Setswana. Afrikaans and, to a lesser degree, English, serve as languages of communication in the work environment. Gert Hendriks, a Xhosa, told his stories in Afrikaans (ibid.).

One of Hendriks' stories is a variant of 'How Six Travel through the World' or 'The Land Water Ship/The Ship That Went on Sea and Land' (Aarne-Thompson Types 513A and 513B; Grimm No. 71 – 'Sechse kommen durch die ganze Welt'). The story is distinguished by the extraordinary companions with special endowments enabling them to perform tasks set for the hero (Thompson 1977: 53-54). In Hendriks' (2006c) variation, 'Die goue skip met vlerke' [The Golden Ship with Wings], the king declares that his daughter will marry a man who can bring him a flying ship with golden wings. The two eldest sons of a woodcutter, while chopping wood in the bushes, are confronted by a deformed old man who requests to share their food. This they refuse. The third and under-valued son shares his food with the old man and is rewarded with the flying ship. On his way to the king, he meets five helpers with special qualities: a swift runner, a sharp shooter, a man with excellent hearing, one with a huge appetite, and a soldier who can miraculously turn a bag of sticks into soldiers. The king, who does not want his daughter to marry the poor man, confronts him with several challenges. With the aid of his friends, the youngest son ultimately succeeds. He is joined by his parents and two brothers, marries the princess and inherits half the king's fortune.

The story structure and motifs are similar to known variations of the narrative. This specific narrative, however, displays features which contribute to its unique texture. Aspects of the narrative which are clearly localised include socio-cultural references, such as to food, the description of the stranger in the wood, the three sons' respective reactions to the stranger and their attitude to their tasks. Furthermore, the style of narration, use of language, metaphors and vocabulary are characteristic of oral storytelling and idiosyncratic to this specific narrator. It is clear that the informant is a natural storyteller who enjoys the act of storytelling and has a well-developed sense of narrative structure and creation of suspense. The transcription and especially the translation of Gert Hendriks' stories resulted in some loss of the unique qualities of the narrator that were realised through his use of language and diction.

## *Example 3: Written Text to Publication – 'Three Magic Gifts'*

The third example to be discussed in more detail is a variant of Aarne-Thompson Type 563: 'Three Magic Gifts/ The table, the ass, and the stick' (Grimm No. 36 – 'Tischen deck dich, Goldesel und Knüppel aus dem Sack') by Godfrey van Rooyen (age 17). The text was written in a project that was aimed at promoting an interest in storytelling, writing and publication in communities.[4]

The Promosa township is situated on the outskirts of Potchefstroom, a small university city in the North West Province of South Africa. The township used to be a largely Afrikaans-speaking community of people living in formal housing. Since the abolition of the Group Areas Act,[5] however, the compound of Promosa has become more diverse due to, among others, the increase of Setswana-speakers in the township, as well as the increase of informal housing. Most people in the community have access to electricity and communication media such as radio, television and cellular phones, but personal computers and access to the internet are luxuries. This particular project focused on the Afrikaans-speaking community in Promosa, which can be considered as both a *developing community* and a *literary minority*. The actual project involved three age groups (namely primary school children, teenagers in secondary school and elderly people) who participated in different sub-projects adapted for the particular age group. The project as a whole took place in three phases: sharing stories, making a book, and the subsequent publication of the stories in a community publication (Greyling 2005: 166-170).

Godfrey van Rooyen's story was written in the high school sub-project, which consisted of a writing competition and a creative writing workshop. The original text was entered for the competition under the topic *Die dag in my lewe wat ek nooit sal vergeet nie* [The Day in my Life that I Will Never Forget]. For publication in the community volume, the editors changed the title to *Kierietjie, kierietjie, trek weg!* [Go, Kierietjie, Go!]. The text was also adapted as a picture book and two versions of the text were digitally published on the internet. Although the text was remediated in different media and formats (chirographic and orthographic; picture book; on the internet) and involved diverse mediators (author, editors, illustrator), the same text was used throughout. Changes observed in the versions can thus be attributed to the influence of the specific mediator, the context in which it was published and the multidimensionality of the literature. The different versions of the text make it possible to observe the dynamics of the narrative chain in this particular case.

This story (A-T Type 563: 'Three Magic Gifts'), which already appears in a collection of Chinese Buddhist legends in the sixth century CE, has a very extensive distribution, including Europe, Asia, North and South America and India, and is told throughout Africa (Thompson 1977: 72). In the story, a collective of poor characters (often three brothers) departs on a quest, is required to perform certain tasks, acquire certain skills and meet people, and is rewarded with magic gifts. These gifts are an animal (ass, goat, sheep, duck or cock) which supplies money or precious stones; a table, tablecloth or flask which provides food; and a stick (a club or cudgel) which beats somebody on demand. These gifts are stolen (by an inn-keeper or a neighbour) and are repossessed through punishing the thief by means of the magic stick. Order is restored and the protagonist's status elevated. The Grimms' variation is combined with the story of the talking goat (Ashliman 2011; Meder 2011; Thompson 1977: 72).

In van Rooyen's story, similar themes and motifs are found. What is significant in this variation is that the author, van Rooyen, depicts himself in the text as the first-person narrator and main character. In the story, the eleven year old Godfrey van Rooyen lives with his grandmother in poverty-stricken circumstances, where wood chopping is one of his daily chores. One day there is no wood left on the pile at home and he decides to collect wood from the *veldt*, and during his search he encounters an old man on a rubbish dump. Godfrey takes pity on the old man and is rewarded with a magical cane (*kierie*) which he should use when in danger. On this journey he also meets a shepherd, from whom he receives a lamb that is able to spit out coins, which drastically changes the circumstances in which Godfrey and his grandmother live. However, after two years of prosperity, thugs discover Godfrey's secret and both Godfrey and his lamb are abducted. Fortunately he remembers to use his magical cane and he succeeds in getting rid of the villains. This story has a happy ending.

Godfrey's story is particularly interesting because of the use of form and content. In his story, he combined *reality*, *fiction* and *his own life history* in a tale based on folklore. In the process, his story reflects the space and social reality of this particular community at this particular time. According to Meder, this fairy tale, 'Tafeltje dek je' [Three Magic Gifts], is a reflection of elementary human needs in the past: the need for food, money and security – needs which in the time of supermarkets, social grants and visible policing are taken for granted (2011). Apparently Meder made this remark with reference to modern Europe, but in the community of Promosa these needs are still very pertinent, with many people living in meagre circumstances and often struggling for survival. This story of a boy living with his grandmother and having to help with the provision of their livelihood, portrays localised socio-economic circumstances quite typical of life in the townships:

> I, Godfrey van Rooyen lived with my grandma, I was eleven and my grandma was already fifty-four years old. We lived in a four-room;[6] it was a little uncomfortable for my grandma and me, but because of the circumstances we couldn't afford a better one.
>
> My responsibility was that I had to cut wood; we had a big log of wood behind our house and I had to hit that log with an axe until there were crumbs of wood. But as time passed, the log got used up and I, as a young boy, had to look for another plan, because we depended on a little fire, on the fire a little porridge we used to get from people, a little milk we bought once a week – that was our daily living. (Van Rooyen 2004; translation A. Combrink)[7]

In *Go, Kierietjie, Go!* the social and physical space has been localised to encompass the writer's own experience of reality. For example, the incident where Godfrey meets the old man on the rubbish dump portrays the complexity of the social relationships in the community. This old man was banned from his home by his wife and children when they discovered that he had fathered a child with another woman. From this old man he received the *kierie* (a cane also used as a weapon) and from the shepherd a magic lamb. The money spat out by the lamb enabled his grandmother to enrol Godfrey in the primary school; they also acquired the services of an architect who designed a large brick house for them. The need for security and social status is manifested in localised symbols of prosperity such as education, brick houses, medical aid and sufficient food (Greyling & Combrink 2008: 249).

By depicting himself as the first-person narrator and main character, Godfrey van Rooyen in essence creates a narrative identity for himself (Bruner 2002: 66; Greyling & Combrink 2008: 259). It is striking that, regardless of the circumstances in the story, the narrator does not portray himself as a victim, but as the victor who is able to provide for his own and his grandmother's needs and to act as caretaker of the family. In this way, van Rooyen creates not only a positive image of himself, but also positive expectations for his future – inducing *wonder* and *hope for change* in the audience, but, more importantly, also in himself as the narrator.

Godfrey's story shows characteristics of both the written and oral storytelling tradition. Several examples of the oral tradition are present in his text, in terms of style of narration, syntax, choice of words, and the use of Labov's narrative clauses as indications of natural storytelling. Examples of syntactic indications of the oral narrative include long, complex sentences, narrative structures such as the regular use of 'and then', as well as the use of dialogue and dramatisation. Inherent in the narrative is the unique use of language (both the particular dialect of the community, as well as the author's idiolect). Expressions peculiar to the specific community and distinctive words and phrases are other markers of orality in the text.[8] Godfrey van Rooyen's writing gives the reader the impression that he spells words as he hears them pronounced in the community, which again emphasises his heavy reliance on the oral tradition (Greyling & Combrink 2008: 250).

The second version of Godfrey van Rooyen's story is included in the community volume, *Die soetsuur lemoen: die hartseer en geluk van Promosa* [The Sweet-Sour Orange: The Sorrow and Joy of Promosa]. The 'skopos' of the publication was to compile a volume of stories from the community in a participatory project, which can be read and enjoyed by the participants of the project, as well as the community of Promosa, in order to encourage an interest in storytelling, writing and publication. Participants acted as the editorial team who compiled the volume, did some basic editing, and made illustrations. The organisers of the project, however, had the final say in the compilation of the volume, detailed text editing, page layout and publication. These editorial interventions, as well as the context of the volume (including the format, contents and compilation), the contents of the stories and the variety of voices, influence each of the texts that were included, and also the way readers read and interpret the volume. As such, it reflects the identity of both the community and the organisers (and of the editors as mediators) of the project. *Go, Kierietjie, Go!* was the final story in the volume in the section *Fluit, fluit, my storie is uit* [This Is the End of my Story]. Using this phrase, a *coda* typical in oral tales, as section heading implies that this particular narration is fiction, and also that the story (and book) has come to an end. As is the case in the first version of Godfrey van Rooyen's story, the writers and the intended readers share the same socio-cultural space. Because of the 'skopos' and its specific application, the editing resulted in naturalisation – the community could identify with the volume and its content, and the participants took ownership thereof (ibid.: 252).

The third rendition of Godfrey's story is in the form of a picture book, *Go, Kierietjie, Go!* (Van Rooyen & Bornoff 2005). As part of a course assignment, Emily Bornoff and Janita Holtzhausen, two postgraduate students in Publication Studies at the University of Pretoria, developed Godfrey van Rooyen's story into a picture book. The assignment ('skopos') was to compile a publication which would fulfil the need for additional reading matter for learners of primary schools in coloured Afrikaans-speaking communities, with special reference to the community of Eersterust, Pretoria. This book further illustrates the dynamics of the narrative chain and the influence of diverse mediators in furthering the text.

Emily Bornoff, an international student, was born and educated in England. As an illustrator, part of Bornoff's task was therefore to 'translate' a text to readers whose socio-cultural frame of reference is vastly different from her own. It can be expected that the depiction of the story would be influenced by her expertise and training as an illustrator, as well as her own frame of reference. Since Bornoff does not speak Afrikaans, Holtzhausen, the co-compiler and text editor, told her the story in English. Apart from the illustrator and the editor, the supervisor and commissioner[9] also played a part in the final product, and recommended, amongst other things, that the illustrations should be stylistically realistic, and both support the text and be relevant to the readers. The illustrations in *Go, Kierietjie, Go!* meet these conditions by being realistic, in a naive style and containing little perspective and few details. The physical circumstances, emotions and relationships between characters are portrayed through their facial expressions, posture, appearance and use of colour and frames. Poverty and hardship are, for example, suggested by the clothing (the boy goes barefoot) and the facial expressions of the characters (Figure 2). In many of the illustrations, the main character's back is turned towards the reader/viewer, which reinforces the notion of the character as an observer and narrator (Greyling & Combrink 2008: 254-255).

Diverse worlds are established through the portrayal of space. For example, the technique of newspaper-collage and the use of shades of brown establish a rather sombre mood at the rubbish dump scene, which closely reflects the grandfather's circumstances (Figure 3).

The large green and blue surfaces of the *veldt* suggest and strengthen the feeling of space and freedom. Here the well-dressed shepherd conveys a European theme (Figure 4).

It is also significant that an idealised African space is established by placing animals (impala, lizards, squirrels, bats and insects) in the landscape. The magic cane does not look like a traditional *kierie*, but rather resembles an Aboriginal design. Through the repetition of the lamb and cane themes in the illustrations and decorative page numbers, their magical elements are enhanced.

Figure 2. 'With grandma' in: Godfrey Van Rooyen, Emily Bornoff. 2005.
*Kierietjie, kierietjie, trek weg!*, 11.

Figure 3. 'At the rubbish dump' in Godfrey Van Rooyen, Emily Bornoff. 2005.
*Kierietjie, kierietjie, trek weg!*, 3.

**Figure 4. 'Shepard' in: Godfrey Van Rooyen, Emily Bornoff. 2005.**
*Kierietjie, kierietjie, trek weg!*, **8.**

Complementary to the word text, the illustrations dealing with the kidnapping and assault are not presented in an upsetting manner. The faces of the perpetrators are not shown and only their shadows and silhouettes are drawn. The feeling of impending catastrophe and menace is conveyed through the use of colour. When the villains are attacked by the magic cane, they appear in the background as stickmen, while Godfrey and his lamb are watching them from the safety of a tree, surrounded by the animals, and a crescent moon (Figure 5). In the end, the boy and his grandmother are placed in a photo frame, reinforcing the idea of safety, love, togetherness and security (ibid.: 255-255).

With regard to the *word text*, the 'skopos' required the style to stay unchanged in order to enable the reader to hear the authentic voice of the community. Editing mainly entailed the shortening of sentences, as well as a few cases where sentence construction was slightly adapted. Local expressions, which could possibly lead to confusion, were clarified: the word 'four-room' was, for example, changed to 'four-room house'. Some words and sentences were deleted. These omissions were most probably done to accommodate the text to picture book format, but could also be attributed to the specific target reader. The reason why the old man was banned from his house was also omitted because children were the target readers. For the same reason, the death of the lamb was not mentioned (ibid.: 255-255).

**Figure 5. 'Nightscene' in: Godfrey Van Rooyen, Emily Bornoff. 2005.**
*Kierietjie, kierietjie, trek weg!*, **19.**

The story was, therefore, removed from the context of the community volume, isolated as a single story and illustrated and presented in a specific format. Readers who encounter Godfrey van Rooyen's story for the first time in the picture book read the story together with the illustrations, which was in essence a creation of a new version of the story. Although the illustrated version was submitted to a publisher, it was not accepted for publication. Possible reasons could be that the book would be too expensive for the target market, as well as that it was too culture-specific for a broader market. To sell the book successfully on the open market, grammar and contents would, most probably, have to be adapted and the text would need to be edited according to standard conventions. Consequently, the story would be stripped of culture-specific as well as personal references, which would deprive the text of many of its unique characteristics (ibid.: 256).

In an effort to expose Godfrey van Rooyen's story to a wider audience, the story was published on Storiewerf, a website aimed at promoting children's books, as well as young writing talent (Van Rooyen & Bornoff 2006). Two versions of the story were published, namely the story with selected illustrations from the volume of stories, and the picture book format. The flexibility of the internet made it possible to revise the story and correct some transcription oversights. The publication of the story on Storiewerf created a totally new context, as the posting of the story on a website for children's books implied that the target audience was younger readers. The story was also published in the category *Lapastories* [camp-fire stories], which is a category created to accommodate traditional (oral) narratives, as well as non-mother tongue speakers of Afrikaans. To the discerning reader, the specific format can therefore also be a determining factor in the reading and interpretation of the text. Texts posted on the internet have potential readers from all over the world, and in this instance the original target readers (the communities of Promosa and Eersterust) and the subsequent target readers are literally and figuratively worlds apart. The codes shared by the author and the readers could differ vastly, which would establish new interpretations of the text and of identity – and new possibilities for re-narration (Greyling & Combrink 2008: 256-257).

## Conclusion

In this discussion I have endeavoured to demonstrate something of the ebb and flow of literature at the 'seamless space' characteristic of grassroots reading and writing, and shown how a consideration of the primary ways of cultural transference in a community and the modes of representation, the narrative chain, the identity of the mediator, the context, the 'skopos', and the multidimensionality of texts can contribute to an appreciation of the text at hand, and a better understanding of the complex dynamics involved. Due to the familiarity and recognisable features of fairy tales, the study of fairy tales (oral wonder tales) provides ideal opportunities for comparison.

In a sense, the manifestation of these familiar themes and motives in grassroots literature in diverse cultures, languages and formats, confirms the canonical status of the oral wonder tale and of the literary fairy tale. It also illustrates the dynamic furthering of these tales in the seamless space of grassroots literature – where ordinary people make these age-old narratives their own, inducing wonder and hope for change in narrator and audience alike.

## Bibliography

Ashliman, D.L. 1996-2011. *Folklore and Mythology Electronic Texts*. <http://www.pitt.edu/~dash/folktexts.html> Accessed 16 December 2010.

Barber, K. 1999. 'Obscurity and Exegesis in African Oral Praise Poetry', in: D. Brown (ed.), *Oral Literature & Performance in Southern Africa*. Oxford: James Currey, 27-49.

Brown, D. 1999. 'Introduction', in: D. Brown (ed.), *Oral Literature & Performance in Southern Africa*. Oxford: James Currey, 1-17.

Bruner, J. 2002. *Making stories: Law, Literature, Life*. Cambridge, Massachusetts: Harvard University Press.

Combrink, A. 2010. *Die rol van oraliteit en identiteit in die bevordering van gemeenskapseie woordkuns in Suid-Afrika*. Disseration (unpublished). Potchefstroom: North-West University.

Dollerup, C. 1999. *Tales and Translation*. Amsterdam: John Benjamins.

'Grass roots'. n.d., in: *Webster's Online Dictionary*: <http://www.websters-online-dictionary.org/definitions/Grass+roots> Accessed 15 October 2011.

Ewers, H. 1992. 'Children's Literature and the Traditional Art of Storytelling', in: *Poetics Today* 13.1: 169-178.

Finnegan, R. 1982. 'Oral Literature and Writing in the South Pacific', in: *Pacific Quarterly Moana, Oral and Traditional Literatures* 7.2: 22-36.

Finnegan, R. 2005. 'The How of Literature', in: *Oral Tradition* 20.1: 164-187.

Fludernik, M. 2009. 'Conversational Narration/Oral Narration', in: P. Hühn, J. Pier, W. Schmid & J. Schönert (eds), *Handbook of Narratology*. Berlin: Walter de Gruyter, 63-73.

Greyling, F. &. A. Combrink. 2008. ''n Storie met baie stories: Identiteit en konteks in die interpretasie en re-interpretasie van "Kierietjie, kierietjie, trek weg!"', in: *Mousaion* 25.10: 241-260.

Greyling, F. 2005. 'Oor grense heen: 'n Deelnemende projek ter bevordering van skryf in ontwikkelende gemeenskappe', in: *Stilet* XVII.2: 155-181.

Grobler, P. 2004. *'n Ondersoek na die betekenis in prenteboeke vanuit 'n vertaalteoretiese perspektief*. Dissertation (unpublished). Stellenbosch: University of Stellenbosch.

Hendriks, G. 2006a. 'Die lekkerte van stories', in: A. Combrink (ed.), *Die pad deur Rysmierbult*. Potchefstroom: Vakgroep Skryfkuns, North-West University, 53-55.

Hendriks, G. 2006b. 'Gert Hendriks se storie', in: A. Combrink (ed.), *Die pad deur Rysmierbult*. Potchefstroom: Vakgroep Skryfkuns, North-West University, 40-41.

Hendriks, G. 2006c. 'Die goue skip met vlerke', in: *Lapastories*: <http://www.storiewerf.co.za/lapastories/goue_skip_1.htm> Accessed 26 May 2011.

Hall, S. 2000. 'Old and New Identities, Old and New Ethnicities', in: A.D King (ed.), *Culture, Globalization and the World-System: Contemporary Conditions for the Representation of Identity*. Minneapolis: University of Minnesota Press, 41-68.

Hofstede, G.H. 1991. *Cultures and Organisations: Software of the Mind: Intercultural Cooperation and its Importance for Survival*. London: Harper Collins.

Irele, F.A. 2001. *The African Imagination*. Oxford: Oxford University Press.

Johnstone, B. 1991. *Stories, Community and Place*. Bloomington, IN: Indiana University Press.

Kress, G. 2003. 'Interpretation or Design: From *The World Told To the World Shown*', in: M. Styles & E. Bearne (eds), *Art, Narrative and Childhood*. Stoke on Trent: Trentham Books, 137-153.

Labov, W. 1972. *Language in the Inner City*. Philadelphia: Univ. of Pennsylvania Press.

Loubser, J.A. 2002. 'Many Shades of Orality and Literacy: Media Theory and Cultural Difference', in: *Alternation* 9.1: 26-45.

Machet, M. 1996. 'Literacy in a Multicultural Environment', in: M. Machet, S. Olen & T. van der Walt (eds), *Children's Literature Experiences*, *Vol. 3*. Pretoria: Unisa Press, 32-45.

Martin, D.C. 2000. 'The Burden of the Name: Classifications and Constructions of Identity. The Case of the 'Coloureds' in Cape Town (South Africa)', in: *African Philosophy* 13.2: 99-125.

Meder, T. 'The table, the Ass, and the Stick.' <http://www.verhalenbank.nl/lijst_lexicon.php?act=detail&volksverhaal_type=AT 0563.> Accessed 5 May 2011.

Neumann, S. 2001. 'The Brothers Grimm as Collectors and Editors of German Folktales', in: J. Zipes (ed.), *The Great Fairy Tale Tradition: From Straparola and Basile to the Brothers Grimm*. New York: W.W. Norton & Company, 969-980.

Ong, W.J. 1982. 'Literacy and orality in our times', in: *Pacific Quarterly Moana, Oral and Traditional Literatures* 7.2: 8-21.

Propp, V. 1984. *Theory and History of Folklore (Theory and History of Literature, Vol. 5)*. Manchester: Manchester University Press.

Richard, A. & F. Veit-Wild. 2005. 'Introduction: Local Literatures Versus Global Culture', in: A. Richard & F. Veit-Wild (eds), *Interfaces Between the Oral and the Written: Versions and Subversions in African Literatures Vol 2*. Amsterdam: Editions Rodophi, ix-xiv.

Ryan, M. 2009. 'Narration in Various Media', in: P. Hühn, J. Pier, W. Schmid & J. Schönert (eds), *Handbook of Narratology*. Berlin: Walter de Gruyter, 63-73.

Seifert, L. 2001. 'The Marvelous in Context: The Place of the *Contes de Fees* in late Seventeenth-Century France', in: J. Zipes (ed.), *The Great Fairy Tale Tradition: From Straparola and Basile to the Brothers Grimm.* New York, W.W. Norton & Company, 902-933.

Thompson, S. 1977. *The Folktale.* Berkeley: University of California Press.

Van Rooyen, G. 2004. 'Kierietjie, kierietjie, trek weg!', in: F. Greyling & A. Combrink (eds), *Die soetsuur lemoen: hartseer en geluk van Promosa.* Potchefstroom: Skryfkuns, North-West University.

Van Rooyen, G. & E. Bornoff. 2005. *Kierietjie, kierietjie, trek weg!* (Unpublished.) Pretoria: Departement van Inligtingkunde van die Universiteit van Pretoria.

Van Rooyen, G. & E. Bornoff. 2006. *Kierietjie, kierietjie, trek weg!* in: *Lapastories:* <http://www.storiewerf.co.za/lapastories/kierie_voor.htm> Accessed 8 May 2008.

Whitebrook, M. 2001. *Identity, Narrative and Politics.* London: Routledge.

Willemse, H. 2004. 'The politics of Narrating Cinderella in Namibia', in: *Tydskrif vir letterkunde* 41.2: 69-98.

Zipes, J. 1983. *Fairy Tales and the Art of Subversion.* New York: Routledge.

Zipes, J. 2001. 'Cross-Cultural Connections and the Contamination of the Classical Fairy Tale', in: J. Zipes (ed.), *The Great Fairy Tale Tradition: From Straparola and Basile to the Brothers Grimm.* New York: W.W. Norton & Company, 845-869.

# Notes

1.  The noun grassroots (literally the roots of grass) usually refers to 'the essential foundation or source' and 'the common people at a local level (as distinguished from the centers of political activity)' (Webster's Online Dictionary).

2.  Katriena Louw (aged 72) and Martha Frederik (age unknown). Katrina Louw was illiterate while Martha Frederik could be considered functionally illiterate since she only had the 'barest smattering of education'.

3.  The project, *Our own stories: Books by the community – Rysmierbult* (2006), was presented to the community of Rysmierbult, district Potchefstroom, by the Department of Creative Writing at the North-West University, South Africa.

4.  The project, *Our own stories: Books by the community – Promosa* (2004), was presented to the community of Promosa, Potchefstroom, by the Department of Creative Writing at the North-West University, South Africa.

5.  Act No 41 of 1950 which forced physical separation between races by creating different residential areas for different races.

6.  'four-room': local expression for a house consisting of four rooms.

7.  Ek, Godfrey van Rooyen het saam met my ouma gebly, ek was elf jaar oud en my ouma was al vier en vyftig jaar oud. Ons het in 'n viervertrek gebly, wat 'n bietjie ongemaklik was vir ek en my ouma, maar weens die omstandighede kon ons nie 'n beter een bekostig nie.
    My plig was dat ek moes hout gekap het, ons het 'n dik stomp gehad agter onse huis en ek moes met 'n byl daardie stomp geslaan het tot daar krummels van houtjies is. Maar soos die tyd gegaan het, het die stomp klaar geword en ek moes 'n ander plan gekyk het as jong seun, want ons het gelewe van 'n vuurtjie, op die vuurtjie 'n potjie met 'n bietjie pap wat

ons by mense kry, 'n bietjie melk wat ons een keer 'n week koop, dit was ons daglikse lewe.

8.  Examples of these include 'onse huis' [our's house]; 'as gevaar spring' [when danger pounces]; 'ek moes 'n ander plan gekyk het' [I had to look for another plan], 'hy skep eers wind' [he first catches some wind], and 'ou oupa' [old grandfather].

9.  Prof. Maritha Snyman.

# Mishmash, Conceptual Blending and Adaptation in Contemporary Children's Literature Written in Dutch and English

## John Stephens & Sylvie Geerts

Contemporary adaptations in the field of children's literature are apt to demonstrate an imaginative combination of sameness and difference which reflects what Fauconnier and Turner (2002) refer to as the mind's capacity for *conceptual blending*. If, indeed, the mind were not constantly engaged in integrating apparently incompatible mental patterns (Turner 2003: 118), radical adaptations could be neither imagined nor comprehended. In this study, we will examine processes of adaptation of traditional stories and story motifs which, while evoking recognisable pre-texts, adapt their source material in ways that are considerably more disruptive than familiar processes of retelling. Although this kind of writing has emerged only recently, it is quickly becoming quite widespread across various children's literatures, and the innovative adaptations of familiar narratives we discuss here, four drawn from Dutch and five from English literature, indicate a need for a new (and international) theory of adaptation in the field. Retellings and adaptations in children's literature became a focus of particular interest in the 1990s, with the first general theory of retellings in the area, *Retelling Stories, Framing Culture*, by John Stephens and Robyn McCallum, appearing in 1998. There had been many iconoclastic retellings of fairy tales by that time, especially feminist revisions using postmodernist strategies of playful deconstruction, but similar strategies were not as strongly evident in other areas of retelling or adaptation. Looking back from the present, we now perceive a different picture, for two main reasons.

First, while many retellings still function to keep traditional stories alive in culture, there is now a growing awareness that a particular retelling is not necessarily an adaptation of some original text, but part of a larger process of adaptation in which many other retellings and intertextual affiliations lie between a common source text, such as Ovid's Golden Age Latin retelling of the story of Medusa (*Metamorphoses,* IV. 779ff), and twentieth-century adaptations. Such blending applies both to adaptations that strive to preserve its ethos, such as Roger Lancelyn Green's *Tales of the Greek Heroes* (1958), and to more recent re-versions such as Els Pelgrom's feminist interpretation of the story in *Donder en bliksem* ([Thunder and Lightning], 2007) or Rick Riordan's modernised reshaping of the story in *Percy Jackson and the Lightning Thief* (2005). Although the *Metamorphoses* is undoubtedly the most common source for retellings of this myth, when published in 8 C.E. it was already a late adaptation of a Greek myth that had circulated for more than eight centuries. Ovid's version might therefore be regarded as part of an ongoing *Medusa-script* – that is, 'a knowledge representation in terms of which an expected sequence of events is stored in the memory' (Herman 2002: 10). Scripts are part of our everyday comprehension of life processes, but this comprehension also extends to the stories we tell and are told, which may be expressed and interpreted on the basis of very few cues. The *Medusa-script* after Ovid consists of four core schemas: the transformation of a beautiful woman into a monster; the particular characteristics and effects of her monstrosity; the reason and manner of her death; and the uses of her monstrous head after her death. The transmission of stories as scripts then enables a modern adaptation to take a drastically new form while remaining constant to the script. Thus when the questers in *Percy Jackson and the Lightning Thief* are lured into 'Aunty Em's Garden Gnome Emporium' (Riordan 2010: 171-187), the story follows an everyday script of a visit to a roadside purveyor of statuary and its café, but gradually, as their host's identity as Medusa emerges, it unfolds into a version of the *Medusa-script* and evokes all four core schemas of this script.

Quite disparate stories may be perceived to share a script because they share a structure, and hence apparently incompatible mental patterns may be blended, as in this quite explicit example from Imme Dros's *De reizen van de slimme man* ([The Journeys of the Clever Man], 1992):

> Mr Frank had told me about the journey of the clever man from his island back to his island and it was also his own journey from Amsterdam back to Amsterdam. The stories ran into each other. The cave of the giant with only one eye was a cellar without candles. The enemies were outside and the door was closed. It was war and the eye of the enemy saw everything. (Dros 1992: 110-11)[1]

In blending the story of Odysseus' encounter with Polyphemus (Homer's *Odyssey*, Book 9) with the Nazi persecution of Jews in The Netherlands in the 1940s, Dros neatly demonstrates how stories, once assigned to 'places in a single conceptual "frame"' (Turner, 2003: 120), can be adapted to modern circumstance and how, in this case, a script about enclosure, fear and monstrosity underlies these disparate stories in such a way that each intensifies the emotional impact of the other as the processing mind blends them.[2] The connection of the two narratives at this moment also functions as a mise en abyme. It encapsulates how the text of *The Journeys of the Clever Man* uses script and schema to embed an individual's coming of age story within an interplay of sameness and difference that ranges from Homer's *Odyssey* to everyday domestic scenes:

> The three of us sit there together. Perhaps our room in Amsterdam looked like this, the same lamp, the same plants, the radio on, my mother singing to herself as she stirs her drink. (Dros 1992: 134)[3]

In contrast to the previous example, in which a script discloses the compatibility of quite different stories, the schema for companionable family life employed here enables a reader's mind to grasp the narrator's remembrance that links moments in the past and the present and perceives deep significance in the present moment. The former example, however, has a greater bearing on the process of adaptation, in that, as Turner observes, 'Human beings go beyond merely imagining stories that run counter to the present story.

[…] we connect two stories that should be kept absolutely apart, and we then blend them to make a third story' (2003: 119).

A sustained conceit in *The Journeys of the Clever Man* is that when the reclusive Mr Frank reads Homer's Odyssey aloud to Niels, the narrator, he reads in Greek, which Niels does not know, and yet Niels both grasps and imagines the story. In other words, the text enacts the process by which any source text, at any stage of transmission and remaking of its story component, becomes a script. Conceptual blending of variants, compatible scripts and apparently incompatible scripts then entails an imaginative leap to produce the 'third story'.

In contemporary children's texts, the transformation of 'sources' into scripts seems to entail a very significant increase in playfulness in the form of parodic and deconstructive adaptations. Adaptation was thus to take a heavily comedic turn from around the turn of the century, when the pleasure an audience takes in retellings of familiar stories had focused on playful or even iconoclastic modes. Comic action originates in disruption and discord, and hence comedic retellings characteristically disrupt familiar scripts and forms as a dialogue between recognition and defamiliarisation, while the comedic trajectory towards harmony and reconciliation implies that in the 'third story' disruption will have moved toward a new kind of positive outcome. An audience thus derives transgressive pleasure from rethinking the relationships of canonical texts to social ideology and practice, such that the final version of social harmony may emerge as an overt *textual* construct and the teleology of the text is thereby exposed for scrutiny. Not all contemporary retellings are playful, but the large number that are suggests that their contribution to the modelling of possible life-worlds, which is part of the business of children's literature, now takes a more interrogative stance towards the ideologies inhering in scripts, canonical texts and genres.

## Multimodal Texts and Adaptation

The second main reason that the nature of adaptations has changed since the end of the twentieth century is because the types of text which are increasingly prominent in the daily experience of children and young people are, as Victoria Carrington observed, now 'multi-modal (rather than printed), intertextual (rather than isolated and bounded) and politically charged (rather than rendering childhood as an ideological or commercial 'neutral zone')' (2003: 95). Because of the multimodal nature of online texts, young people experience meaning-making differently from their experiences with print-based texts, and many authors of print texts now write with an awareness that their readers are likely to engage with these texts in a multi-modal or hypertextual context. Herein lies something of a paradox: first, many stories which were once a part of everyday culture somewhere are no longer recognised; second, a curious reader can use a search engine such as Google or Yahoo and in a few minutes find out more about such a story than their parents are likely to have known; and third, there are still oblique forms of intertextuality, such as script structures and other kinds of isomorphic relation, which are impervious to search engines. Yahoo and Google were developed in the mid-1990s (Yahoo was launched in 1995, and Google in mid-1996), and these sophisticated search engines have transformed both the production and reception of adaptations of all kinds. For example, Peter Van Olmen's *de Kleine Odessa* ([Little Odessa], 2009), a novel about the quest of a little girl, Odessa, for the identity of her parents, overtly signals the hypertextual possibilities opened up to readers. The story starts in the recognisable setting of a contemporary city, from which, as a result of strange and magical incidents, Odessa sets out on a journey to the secondary world of 'Scribopolis'. In this city where all writers live together in immortality, Odessa befriends a girl named Wiki,[4] whose character and role in events function as a metaphor for the novel's hypertextual possibilities. The following fragment shows how information is gradually and fragmentarily imparted to Odessa and hence to readers:

> 'Who is he?' she whispered to the girl next to her. […]
> 'You must be new here? That is Dostojevski! One of the greatest writers ever. You really don't know him? He writes thick books full of human drama. But you'd better not get into a fight with him. He is very hot-tempered. Everyone is afraid of him. […] The one all tarted up, with the green carnation in his lapel, is Oscar Wilde. And that one, with the big walrus moustache, can you see him, who leans backwards and drums on his belly? That's Flaubert. The thin one with the flap-ears and the black eyes, that's Kafka. Now that's what I call a strange fellow, he always comes up with rules no one understands.' (Van Olmen 2009: 117-8)[5]

To assign a name, however, is not necessarily to assign a significance, and few young readers will have any associations for most, if any, of these authors. Further, citation of iconic attributes (a boutonnière, a dandyish mode of dress, incomprehensible rules) does not offer an explanation but an invitation to seek further explanation, and the figure of Wiki serves as a cue for readers to take up an active role in this process of inquiry. Wikipedia – one of the best known Wikis – features a photograph of Flaubert which can reasonably be assumed to stand as the source of this description (see Figure 1). A richer and more pleasant reading experience thus awaits those who accept the proffered role and leave the linear narrative to search for the information on the Internet.

Hypertext also invites readers to take up an even more active role: that of writer (Landow 2006: 7-9). Although not to the same extent as in 'fan fiction', readers of *Little Odessa* are given the possibility to take up an active role by leaving their comments and experiences on the blog on the book's website.[7] The idea of readers-as-writers is equally pursued in the book, where the inhabitants of Scribopolis can enter books and be part of the stories described in them, just as actual world readers can enter a Wiki and write collaboratively. Odessa herself ends up in Homer's *Odyssey* in the cave of the Cyclops. Her presence in the scene changes the course of the events:

> ~~The men found a stake and sharpened it and hardened it in the fire.~~
> Why had they crossed out that sentence? What were the men going to do with that stake? Why weren't they allowed to use it anymore? […] She was in a cave between rough men who smelled like sweat and cheap wine, and stared

**Figure 1. The Wikipedia image of Gustave Flaubert[6]**

in the fire. The cave was large and high. She heard sheep. Through the door she could see the hairy leg of a giant. The cyclops. He sat on a rock, in the middle of a flock of sheep. […]

'What! Because you have to go through a test in another world, we risk our lives? Who do you think you are? Now you save us!' (Van Olmen 2009: 322-24)[8]

The relation between reader and writer is further explored through the dangerous creation of a magical book, named 'Boekus', by the 'evil' writer Mabarak. Everything written in Boekus happens in reality. Hence the writer of Boekus gets the power to rule the world. Eventually Mabarak is defeated by his own daughter Odessa, and Boekus locked away safely. The end of the novel hints at the importance of free will and agency as Odessa writes in Boekus:

> *People are master of their own story*
> *and nobody will ever change that.*
> (ibid.: 461; italics in original)[9]

In the course of the novel we follow Odessa's development from unknowing to knowing and we see her gradually gaining more agency. The bits and pieces are imparted to readers in the same gradual manner and they, too, are prompted to take up an active role – as reader as well as in reality.

Daniel Pinkwater's *the Yggyssey* (also published in 2009) likewise combines an adaptation of a traditional quest narrative form (and hence a linear narrative) with a hypertext environment, but cues this less overtly than does *Little Odessa*. A metaphor for navigating this textual situation is embedded at one point in the novel, when the four child protagonists are attempting to cross a river in a coracle that has been built 'from pictures in an encyclopedia' (Pinkwater 2009: 159):

> The coracle had a tendency to spin and it careened all over the river. After a while we started to get the hang of it. With two people paddling and two others using their paddles as rudders at the front and back of the boat – assuming it had a front and back – we could get it to go more or less in one direction. (ibid.: 158-59)

Pinkwater's narrative is likewise very apt to careen all over the place, and does this because there is an assumption – largely implicit – that its readers will at numerous points turn aside from the narrative to investigate some of its references. As in the case of the coracle, the model for doing this is print media (an encyclopedia), and this is the inevitable model here because the novel is set in 1953 (with some anachronisms). Shortly afterwards (ibid.: 161), one of the characters, Big Audrey, quotes an obvious encyclopedia entry about coracles. A reader who checks will find it has been synthesised from Wikipedia, and by looking will find other sites about coracles, and then will know that the children are trying to paddle their coracle quite incorrectly: their solution is a joke. So what seems to be happening here is that Pinkwater knows his readers like surfing the net and uses this modern practice to open up other avenues of pleasure for them, to position his own text within multi-modal textuality (even though it is print), and to create a culturally dense and rich reading experience. Further, allusions to fiction in *the Yggyssey* (*Alice in Wonderland*; *The Wizard of Oz*) have the same textual status as allusions to actual events, such as the Korean War, and to how the parallel universe in the novel makes reference to this-world things: for example, while characters walk down the road in the parallel universe, as in *The Wizard of Oz*, they sing old songs which can be listened to on YouTube:

> Swinging our arms, we walked four abreast along the road, singing songs as the miles went by. Besides 'The Cry of the Wild Goose', we sang 'Mule Train', and the song from the movie *High Noon*. All good walking songs. (ibid.: 193)

Readers of Terry Pratchett's novels, which are also thick with allusion, will have noticed that Pratchett has for many years also depicted characters *who look things up*. In the case of *the Yggyssey*, readers who play the game will end up knowing a surprising amount about popular culture and world history in the early 1950s.

## Adaptation and the Fluidity of Scripts

What does this expectation about reader curiosity tell us about adaptations? It proposes a conception of adaptation that is more fluid than that proposed by, for example, Linda Hutcheon in *A Theory of Adaptation*. In particular, it sets aside three key tenets of Hutcheon's position: that an adaptation is an acknowledged transposition of a recognisable other work or works, a creative *and* an interpretive act of appropriation/ salvaging, and an extended intertextual engagement with the adapted work. She specifically excludes 'allusions to and brief echoes of other works' because these don't qualify as 'extended engagements' (Hutcheon 2006: 9). Further, the principle that adaptations intended for young readers, or which include young readers in their audience, draw on scripts rather than any single recognisable text and employ a discourse which embeds schemas intertextually involves an extension of what might be classified as an adaptation. 'Extended intertextual engagement' may be replaced by shorter units of text, and texts may incorporate brief allusions that form a pattern that evokes a particular chronotope – in other words, they are adaptations of the producing culture as well as of its texts – or else they pastiche cultures at different historical points or social levels. Pinkwater refers to this process as 'mishmash' in a metafictive conversation that occurs in the third volume of the series (*Adventures of a Cat-whiskered Girl*, 2010: 188-89). Predominantly a pejorative term, in the discourse of adaptation *mishmash* has developed a positive resonance as a descriptor of a semiotic mode which disrupts audience assumptions about stories, representations and perspectives, refuses simple binary oppositions, and encourages meanings to proliferate.[10]

In *Adventures of a Cat-whiskered Girl*, mishmash is explained as an intellectually unmotivated appropriation of whatever bits and pieces are found lying around, as when a TV company has 'half enough cowboy costumes, and half enough Nazi costumes. They just write a script about a world where there are Nazis and cowboys. It's a cheap device used in movies too' (ibid.: 189). And then, with a big wink, as it were, to readers, the passage concludes: 'Pretty soon fiction writers will start using it in books' (ibid.). Books, however, are not dependent on material props and costumes in the same way visual media are, and hence comparable blending in verbal narrative is more apt to be grounded in play with cognitive perception of objects, with metamorphosis, and destabilisation of schemas. This strategy occurs frequently in Pinkwater's previous book, *the Yggyssey*, as in these examples of 'people' encountered in another plane of existence:

> There was a girl, about our age, but taller and wider. She had long brown hair, nice eyes, and whiskers like a cat. (2009: 133)
> [Labrador retrievers] make good cops. They're polite and friendly, never give up, and they don't mind getting wet. (ibid.: 134)

In each case, the core schema is destabilised by unexpected components. The schema of a friendly peer is familiar in 'girl', 'our age', 'long brown hair', 'nice eyes', but the cognitive processing of the schema must deal with 'taller and wider' and 'whiskers like a cat'. Likewise, the police, who at the same time are and are not Labrador retrievers, are a clear case of conceptual blending, and the schema constructed here combines attributes of a good police officer (politeness and persistence) with an attribute essential to a working retriever dog (doesn't mind getting wet). *The Yggyssey* not only generates multiple examples of this kind as part of its narrative fabric, but also generates a quasi-hypertext structure as it mingles fact and legend and morphs from one adaptation to another in unfolding its overarching quest narrative.[11] Even as a ghost story, many of its ghosts did once live (Rudolf Valentino, the La Brea woman), but others are the ghosts of invented people, such as the three marching figures in Archibald Willard's iconic American kitsch painting, *The Spirit of '76*. Further, the notion of a 'haunted hotel' is important to Hollywood tourist sites and dark tourism in the USA in general (see Levitt 2010: 64). Once a reader's curiosity is aroused, he or she may feel prompted to check every place-name, every urban legend, every song title, even any object named, in order to confirm whether or not it exists or has existed, and if so, what exactly it is. In *Little Odessa,* mythology, literary fiction, popular culture (Odessa screams 'beam me up, Dosti' to instruct Dostojevski to take her out of the Cyclops' cave) and historical and geographical facts are referred to in the same manner. For example, a quick 'wiki search' reveals that the mine 'Gwynfynydd', where Mabarak went to fetch the material for the only pen that can write in Boekus, is a historical place in Wales. In contrast, other characters and places are pure inventions (Ergolas Verktaki) or refer to other fictions (Gnorks are based on Tolkiens Orks). The list of 'Dramatis Personae' at the end of the novel explains some of the references, but it equally places fact and fiction at the same level. As such, these two novels probably represent the loosest and most encompassing form of mishmash adaptation, and can be ludically infuriating in their processes. *The Yggyssey* overtly adapts familiar texts such as *Alice in Wonderland, Hansel and Gretel, Millions of Cats, The Wind in the Willows, The Wizard of* Oz (both book and film versions), and so on, but also functions as a confluence of pre-texts inferred by audiences on the basis of minimal data and hence inferred in different ways and as different stories. To a great extent it is an adaptation of genre within which are embedded transpositions of recognisable other works and specific allusions (see Figure 2).

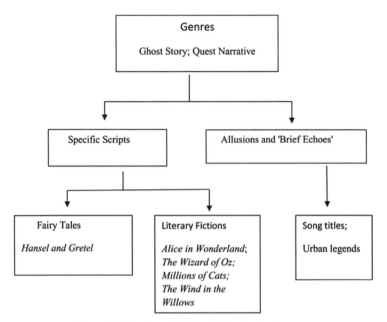

**Figure 2. Structure of Adaptation in *the Yggyssey***

Both *Little Odessa* and *the Yggyssey* are carefully structured according to the linear pattern of the quest narrative, and both refer to the oldest representation of travel and quest in the history of Western literature. In an interview, Van Olmen explains the connection with Homer's Odyssey in the following manner:

> I was reading James Joyce's *Ulysses*. A wonderful book! And it inspired me. The name of the heroine, little Odessa, has got everything to do with that. The main theme – Odysseus on his way home and to his family – was the point of departure. That's where I started. In my book a girl, little Odessa, searches for her parents and goes through a lot of adventures before she finally 'arrives home'. (Van Olmen 2009; interview by Annemie Leysen)[12]

By referring openly to the *Odyssey* in their title, both Pinkwater and Van Olmen show an awareness of the long literary tradition within which their adaptation is inscribed. At the same time they distance their texts from this particular pre-text by playfully altering the title. Van Olmen interrogates the stereotypical gender roles in quest narratives by creating a female protagonist who bears the name of a Greek hero; she even lends her name to the title of the book. Pinkwater's *the Yggyssey* (the 'odyssey' of a girl named Iggy, short for Yggdrasil, the name of the tree that connects all the worlds of Old Norse cosmography) has a looser relationship with Homer's *Odyssey*, and its very title points to a blurring of Greek and Old Norse sources (the two major mythologies drawn upon for adaptations in Western children's literature). On the other hand, its quest script entails a journey to an underworld and encounters with people often reminiscent of such *Odyssey* characters as Circe (Wanda the witch). It is apt, however, to blend such characters with characters from structurally similar scripts and schemas: the 'hoopies' (Pinkwater 2009: 162-65), for example, are a blend of the Lotus Eaters and a 1960s hippy community. By thus placing their texts within the Western literary tradition, both authors foreground an awareness that their retelling is part of a larger process of adaptation which crosses borders of language and culture. During this process the word 'odyssey' has come to refer not only to a specific pre-text, but also to the entire genre of quest narratives, covering the whole range from adventurous voyage to intellectual or spiritual searching. These examples demonstrate that genre itself guides interpretation. A reference in the title to the *Odyssey* functions as a cue to direct readers to the genres of the quest narrative and Greek mythology, which work as a frame for constructing meaning. For the 'knowing reader' it creates a horizon of expectation against which the text can be measured. The title is one of the 'textual cues', or, as John Frow terms them, 'metacommunications, aspects of the text which somehow stand out as being also, reflexively, about the text and how to use it' (2006: 115).

## Blending Scripts from Different Genres

Self-reflexive contemporary retellings, such as *the Yggyssey* and *Little Odessa*, engage playfully with the knowledge and expectations of readers by blending scripts from fact, fiction and literary genre. In *the Yggyssey*, for example, Pinkwater deals with the quest narrative script by blending it with the popular ghost story script. A similar principle is at work in *Little Odessa* where the epic tradition coexists with the fantasy genre and where a female child replaces the traditional male hero. Moreover, the linear structure of both novels is combined with a hypertextual structure whereby readers are prompted to move around and among texts. Thus, although some genres are more heavily culturally and ideologically charged than others, they can 'in turn be dealt with consciously and playfully' (Stephens 2009: 102). Greek mythology is an example of such ideologically sensitive material. In *Retelling Stories, Framing Cultures*, Stephens and McCallum point out how Greek mythology has been treated very cautiously and conservatively in retellings for children. As an important reason they state that

> adults whose retellings reproduce stories from classical mythology [...] are still apt to assert [...] that classical myths (among other functions) embody 'timeless and universal' significances and are an indispensible part of Western cultural heritage, that they are metaphorical expressions of spiritual insights, and that they address archetypal aspects of the human psyche[.] (Stephens & McCallum 1998: 10)

The way in which Pinkwater and, more elaborately, Van Olmen deal with classical mythology shows that the features of contemporary adaptation also pertain to retellings grounded in mythological pre-texts.

Pinkwater's 'Nazis and cowboys' joke about a conceptual blending so apparently outrageous as to become mishmash had already taken textual form in the graphic novel *Cowboys and Aliens* (2006), which, as befits a multimodal text, was produced by a team of thirteen people. The title of the novel is inherently comic in its preposterous proposition to blend such vastly disparate adventure genres as the Western and Science Fiction extraterrestrial invasion. Comedy is swept away, however, by a five-page Prologue in which each page is split into two columns, and further subdivided into four or six parallel panels. The left-hand column offers a summary account of the westward movement of the American frontier and its accompanying displacement and genocide of 'native populations', while the right-hand column depicts the 'same' story as a sci-fi narrative. Text boxes, which tell only the American story, are positioned to span both columns, so that the story told is identified as a script common to all wars of conquest and colonisation wherever and whenever they occur in time or space. Indeed, the novel opens by declaring itself an assault on the myth of 'manifest destiny', or the belief that 'a higher power' justifies the subjugation of one people by another. In declaring its underpinning theme so overtly at the outset, the novel evokes social critique of the US government's strategies of justification for the 'war on terror' and its conduct in terms of the tradition of Manifest Destiny (Wickham 2002; Youngberg 2005), and hence readers are prompted to extend the script beyond the visible parallel narratives. What have seemed to be extremely incompatible genres – cowboy stories and stories of alien invasion – have become both visually and cognitively blended in the novel's Prologue by means of its overt representation of visual parallels and mirror images, and the underlying script has been adapted to express a strong political statement as its 'third story'.

**Figure 3. Rosenberg et al.** *Cowboys and Aliens*, **2006**

A further important effect of the blurring or disruption of generic boundaries, as evidenced in *Cowboys and Aliens*, is to interrogate the ways in which genre itself can play a determining role in the production of meaning. Each of the two genres conjoined in *Cowboys and Aliens* brings with it its own metanarratives and history, but the homologies in form emphasise that the underlying scripts are discordant, so that 'manifest destiny' becomes rewritten as a script whose core elements are imperialism, colonialism and genocide. The startling conjunction in this work might prompt a recognition that conceptual blending can also occur with other, apparently more concordant forms, as with Pinkwater's blending of Greek and Old Norse heroic narratives in *the Yggyssey*. What will readers make of this blending? To a great extent, it loosens the possible relationships of text to presumed pre-texts, and enables the mishmash effect of importing a plethora of stories and scripts. The modern setting of *the Yggyssey* further contributes to this loosening of connection back to pre-text. A similar effect can be seen in Simon Van der Geest and Jan Jutte's *Dissus*, in which the setting in a contemporary Netherlands (a world of bicycles, plain landscapes, windmills, and so on) enables a wide range of contemporary reference. Moreover, *Dissus* is a free verse novel in contemporary Dutch, characterised by English influences which are common in today's colloquial Dutch youth language (for example, 'sneak ik je stiekem binnen' [I will secretly sneak you in] 84) and frequently reminiscent of rap music. The monsters the protagonist encounters on his quest to find his way home are based on characters from the Odyssey, but are altered to fit the new context (e.g. in rendering the 'Cattle of the Sun' episode from the *Odyssey* the text introduces a farmer named Zonnema, combining the Dutch word for sun ('zon') with the stereotypical suffix '–ma' for a person's last name; Skylla becomes a trench digger; Polyphemus is simply named *Eenoog* [One eye]). This setting in historical time is on the one hand enhanced by abundant importations from popular culture – comic book characters (Popeye, the Hulk, Donald Duck); games (Pictionary); movies ('It reminds me of films with shotguns, drugs and corpses' 96)[13] – and on the other hand subverted by the fantastic and unrealistic aspects of the story.

Modern adaptations of familiar scripts often use such apparently playful tactics to challenge meanings deemed to inhere within a script or identifiable pre-text. In a domain such as classical mythology, which is commonly assumed to be a form of cultural capital within the intangible heritage of Western societies (see Stephens & McCallum 1998: 10), the genre's high status might prompt contemporary adapters to challenge this status by exploiting contemporary, ludic evolutions in adaptation. Such retellings might, for example, assume an ideological stance which, from the outset, questions the teleologies underlying the familiar scripts, and do this by embedding the text within the multi-modal context within which their readers are situated and from which they will engage with the text.

## Constructions of Myth from Narrative Gaps

Retellings or adaptations of mythologies which require their audiences to engage in gap-filling – whether to supply apparently missing information, or to make connections between elements not explicitly connected in the text – offer further examples of very inventive engagements with the possibilities of hypertext. While they vary in how close they are to their sources, comparable strategies are evident in, for example, Neil Gaiman's *Odd and the Frost Giants* (2008), *Dissus*, and *Percy Jackson and the Lightning Thief*. All three novels employ a technique in adaptation that teases readers into going away to do some research; thus a story is hinted at, partly told, but always incomplete, even after several references to it. For example, in *Odd and the Frost Giants* the story of how Loki transformed himself into a mare is cited in brief allusions:

> Stay in [animal form] too long and you become what you pretend to be. When Loki was a horse —
> 'We don't talk about that,' said the fox [Loki in animal form]. (Gaiman 2008: 43)
> 'It must be hard to be an eagle. He could get lost in there. When I was a horse —'
> 'A mare, you mean,' said the bear with a grunt.
> The fox tossed its head and walked away. (ibid.: 55)

The references are leading up to a story retold in Snorri Sturluson's *Edda* about the giant builder who offered to build a wall around Asgard, the realm of the gods, within a single winter, and would have succeeded with the help of his stallion Svaðilfari if Loki had not transformed himself into a mare in oestrus and lured the stallion away. After running all night in the forest with the stallion, Loki subsequently gave birth to a foal. The story is alluded to again on page 77, but without connection to horses or Loki: 'One time one of [the frost giants] wanted the sun, the moon, and Lady Freya.' At this point, a reader cannot connect the references unless she knows the story, and thus the retelling offers two possibilities. First, a reader may have taken the earlier bait and gone searching. The full story can be found, after persistent reading, under the heading 'Loki, Svaðilfari, and Sleipnir' at http://en.wikipedia.org/wiki/Loki; or extended, imaginative retellings appear in Kevin Crossley-Holland's *The Penguin Book of Norse Myths: Gods of the Vikings* (1996) or Barbara Leonie Picard's *Tales of the Norse Gods* (2001). A reader who has done this will then have the pleasure of recognising the story and filling in the gaps (there is no mention of the foal, Odin's magical horse Sleipnir, in the story). Second, a reader may suspect that the hints are going somewhere, and decide to store them mentally until more is disclosed. The largest fragment of the story is told by a Frost Giant (Gaiman 2008: 89) as an analogy with and justification for his own actions. His account includes the story of the horses but does not mention Loki, although by now Odd 'was beginning to have his suspicions about who the mare had been' (ibid.). *Odd and the Frost Giants* is not a retelling of an already existing story, but a new story built up from a compendium of motifs familiar to a reader with a reasonable knowledge of Norse myths and of folktale more generally. Odd is a cinderlad, for example, a young boy who has lost his father, has a maimed leg caused by an accident when he tried to take his father's place, and is abused by his stepfather. He frees a bear whose paw is caught between a rock and a tree, and the bear turns out to be the god Thor, who has been transformed, along with Odin and Loki, into animal forms by the frost giant, who has stolen Thor's hammer and taken over Asgard. Odd thus takes on a quest to free Asgard from the giant, and he does this by peaceful means, grows in mental and physical stature, and his leg is mostly healed (he has a limp, but no pain).

Quest narrative also furnishes the script for *Dissus* (2010), an exceptional retelling of the *Odyssey*. As in *Little Odessa,* the connection with this particular pre-text is established by the name of the protagonist and the title of the book. Although *Dissus* maintains a closer relationship with the Odyssey than *Little Odessa,* the pre-text of the retelling is only mentioned on the book cover where a blurb from a newspaper review drops the name: 'A highly original and refreshing adaptation of the Odyssey'.[14] The book itself doesn't contain any open references to its pre-text, but the script of the Odyssey clearly underlies the structure of *Dissus*. Such treatment of the story as script enables a free adaptation of the pre-text whereby the numerous references to the Homeric epic are marked by a playful tension between sameness and difference. The division of the novel into two parts, for example, refers to the two thematic parts which can be distinguished in the Odyssey. 'Seriously lost'[15] could function as a humorous title for the first twelve books of the epic which mainly concentrate on Odysseus' search for home (Van der Geest 2010: 9). In the first part of *Dissus* we witness how a boy named Dissus gets lost together with his friends on his way home from the local swimming pool. What follows is an adventurous and dangerous quest during which the boys encounter monsters and other deathly perils. By the time Dissus arrives home, he, like Odysseus, is the only survivor. The title of the second half of *Dissus* is a Dutch proverb with a childish undertone literally meaning 'who gets up from his seat loses it' (ibid.: 63)[16] and wittily grasps the content of the second twelve books of the Odyssey where the hero's struggle to overcome the suitors and regain the rule over Ithaca is described. In Van der Geest's novel, Dissus, too, has to struggle to recover his place, as his parents have forgotten all about him ('as if their harddisk crashed/ and I was deleted' ibid.: 88)[17] and have replaced him with a dog. Dissus regains his place, but has altered and has achieved the subjective agency readers have observed him struggling to attain throughout the novel.

The opening scene of the novel neatly illustrates the playful and ambiguous relation it maintains with the *Odyssey*. Dissus is introduced in the swimming pool taking refuge in the toilet from a fight with 'de Grote Jongens' [the Big Boys] who bully him: 'The chlorine was making my eyes sting. Snot was running out of my nose and I didn't want anything else than to just, just go home' (ibid.: 5).[18]

The boy depicted here lacks all the qualities associated with the classical hero, such as bravery, self-assurance, sense of leadership and physical strength. The Big Boys call him 'een niemand' [a nobody] and 'een spriet' [a sprig] (ibid.: 4). However different both heroes might seem, though, Dissus' openly expressed longing for home unmistakably brings Odysseus to mind. Moreover, a closer reading reveals remarkable parallels between this scene and the opening scene of the *Odyssey*. In the latter, the narrator describes how Odysseus longs for his wife and return home while he is a prisoner on the island of the powerful nymph Calypso. Hence, while Dissus is stuck in the toilet of the swimming pool, Odysseus is imprisoned by an all-surrounding sea and Dissus' longing for the secure home with his parents mirrors Odysseus' longing to be with his wife and child. It is typical of Van der Geest's adaptation technique that he does not simply establish one-to-one relationships between the pre-text and his version of the story. The first chapter is entitled 'Oorlog' [War] (ibid.: 4) and the illustration shows the bullying and fighting 'Big Boys' as Trojan soldiers with characteristically shaped helmets. Hence, the scene refers to Odysseus' stay with Calypso as well as to the schema of the Trojan War which preceded Odysseus' adventures on his way home.

The further development of the story makes clear that the pre-text functions here in the first place as a site or script on which to model a contemporary coming of age story. The main focus of the story is the protagonist's search for identity. Dissus' daydream on the toilet, where his original longing to go home is displaced by a new wish, is the first indication of a gradually changing attitude:

> What I really want now, is that I were the hero, the hero of the story and that we get seriously lost and very far and free and full of danger, on the way some die and everybody cries except for me and that's when I say: Hey come on, walk along with me. (ibid.: 6)[19]

When the bus is carried away by a terrible storm, Dissus' dream comes true. The lost boys' first dangerous encounter is with a one-eyed farmer, Van der Geest's updated version of the Cyclops Polyphemus. Dissus avails himself of this opportunity to show the change in his personality. Just like Odysseus he is the only one who dares to introduce himself to the cannibal: 'They call me Nobody' (ibid.: 15).[20] In Odysseus' case these words simply mark his craft and bravery. In the mouth of Dissus, however, they painfully echo the Big Boys' taunt. This makes clear that Dissus at the same time attempts to overcome the frightening monsters and his own fears and weaknesses. Moreover, the fact that Dissus is given the name 'Nobody' symbolizes his loss of identity. A similar meaning can be attributed to the episode with the dog. The beast has not only taken his place at home and in his parents' heart, but has also taken his name: 'He has my name, my hut, my home – then who am I, and am I at home?' (69)[21] The dog can be interpreted as an embodiment of the deepest inner fears and conflicts of the maturing child. Dissus finally wins the battle with his monstrous Doppelgänger and hence gains subjectivity and an individual identity: 'So I walk on step by step alone, but never alone and with nobody to call me nobody or a sprig. I am called Dissus: that is my name, and you should know that' (ibid.: 119).[22] As such, *Dissus* is a blend of the script of the quest narrative and that of the coming of age novel. The story follows the pattern of the traditional quest story and is therefore divided into three stages: separation, initiation, return, and thus accords with the large number of children's books which structure the maturation process of a young protagonist around these stages, now in the form: home, departure from home/adventure, return home (see Nodelman 2003 [1992]: 199). By transposing the structure of the Odyssey into a contemporary context and by transforming the great hero into an ordinary boy, Van der Geest has exploited an already existing correspondence between the quest narrative and the 'circular journey' pattern. The result is an adaptation of a classical narrative which is at the same time a magic realist and modern coming of age story.

*Dissus*, however, breaks with the conventional ending of these traditions. Both the quest story and the 'circular journey' traditionally present home as a safe place to which the hero can return after his perilous adventures. For Dissus, the arrival home is far from reassuring, as he has been forgotten by his parents and even replaced. Even though he has gained in subjectivity and can take up his place at home, the certainty of domestic security and parental love is undermined by parental negligence. Hence the maturation process is presented as entailing loss: 'Since I am home, the air is a bit more empty' (Van der Geest 2010: 117).[23] Thus, Van der Geest simultaneously follows and challenges the scripts of the Odyssey and of the traditional coming of age novel. Dissus' parents are obviously not as loyal as Penelope and the outcome is not unequivocally positive and reassuring. By creating an ending which sharply contrasts with two strongly ideologically charged genre schemas onto which the novel is modeled, the teleology of the tradition is undermined. Hence, readers are not only prompted to search for the numerous incomplete references to the Odyssey, but also to question their relation to the pre-text. In such a manner *Dissus* challenges young readers to question authority, of adults as well as of tradition, and to take up an active role and a critical position.

Just like the text, the illustrations in *Dissus* are a blend of contemporary and traditional, mythical scripts and schemas. Jan Jutte combines references to classical myth and aspects of Greek vase painting with the simplicity of modern graphics. The use of colours is restricted to orange-terracotta and black and the style of drawing is characterized by a modern clear line in combination with the shadowy figures so typical of classical vase paintings. At first sight the characters and scenes are recognizable and activate schemas from everyday experience. Jutte's version of the Cyclops, for example, is a clichéd representation of a Dutch farmer, wearing peasant's clothing. The clogs and the checked hat, especially, are cues to activate the schema of a Dutch farmer. The reader, however, finds his expectations frustrated by several elements strange to this schema, the most obvious of which are, of course, the presence of only one eye in the middle of the farmer's forehead and his size, which mark him as a mythological giant rather than a farmer. Moreover, the presence of geometrical figures, taken from Greek vase painting, on the sleeves of his shirt, at the bottom of his pants and to mark his knees, reinforce the alienating effect, especially in contrast with Dissus, who looks like a very normal boy wearing standard shorts and trainers.

**Figure 4. 'Eenoog' in: Simon Van der Geest, Jan Jutte. 2010. *Dissus*, 14-15**

The depiction of the episode with the sirens is another compelling example of the principle of conceptual blending as the illustration has a clear isomorphic relation with a well-known Greek vase painting. Not only is the Siren almost a copy of the Siren depicted on that particular vase, the composition is also analogous to that of the vase painting. The main difference is that the boat with its row of oarsmen has been replaced by a row of boys on bicycles with chewing gum in their ears. The rendering of the boys as silhouettes and the seemingly carved-in details again bring to mind the characteristics of vase painting. Readers puzzled by the strange elements disrupting this everyday script are likely to search the internet. Googling 'Greek vase Odysseus sirens' – or even simply 'sirens' – will easily lead them to the famous red-figured vase painting on which the illustration is modelled.

Figure 5. 'Sirenen' in: Simon Van der Geest, Jan Jutte. 2010. *Dissus*, 36-37

Figure 6. *Odysseus and the Sirens*, eponymous vase of the Siren Painter, ca. 480-470 BC
(British Museum)

The innovative kinds of adaptation evident in *Odd and the Frost Giants* and *Dissus* appear in a different form again in Riordan's *Percy Jackson and the Lightning Thief*. This book (the first volume of a series) is a little like a compendium of myths organised around a quest narrative. It is thus more closely structured than earlier collections (but not nearly as complex as Ovid's *Metamorphoses*). Percy (actual name Perseus), who at the beginning of the book discovers he is a demi-god (son of Poseidon), is given a quest to find Zeus' archetypal thunderbolt and prevent a cataclysmic war between Zeus, Poseidon and Hades which would destroy the world. His companions are Annabeth (daughter of

Athena, and hence Percy's hereditary foe) and Grover, a satyr. Although, like Percy himself, these characters are modern additions to the Perseus script, between them they possess two of the magic objects enjoyed by the original Perseus: a hat that bestows invisibility and shoes that enable the wearer to fly.

Throughout the book, information is constantly withheld from Percy, and the quest for knowledge and understanding is imparted to readers, who attempt to fill in the blanks. As with *Odd and the Frost Giants*, fragments of story are transmitted, and there is no guarantee that any more will be forthcoming. Many brief episodes are complete in themselves, but often turn out to be like classical mythology itself – lacking in detail, incomplete, and contradictory. Readers thus have the option of looking at other resources to fill in the blanks as they go, or hoping that more information will be added later. An excellent example to work with is the Medusa episode (Chapter 11), which we referred to earlier. In the episode, 'We Visit the Garden Gnome Emporium', in which the trio encounter Medusa, Percy has to kill her again, but there are some hints that Medusa is herself a victim of divine whim, since she is resolved to turn Annabeth to stone and then crush her to dust: 'Annabeth's mother, the cursed Athena, turned me from a beautiful woman into this' (Riordan 2010: 180). Earlier, Annabeth had explained that she and Percy couldn't be friends because, '[o]ne time my mom caught Poseidon with his girlfriend in Athena's temple, which is *hugely* disrespectful' (ibid.: 157; emphasis in original), but no overt connection is made with the Medusa story. The two fragments are brought together after Medusa has been slain, when Annabeth explains:

> 'Don't you remember? Medusa was Poseidon's girlfriend. They decided to meet in my mother's temple. That's why Athena turned her into a monster. Medusa and her two sisters who had helped her get into the temple, they became the three gorgons. That's why Medusa wanted to slice me up, but she wanted to preserve you as a nice statue. She's still sweet on your dad. You probably reminded her of him[.]' (ibid.: 185)

The attraction of the Medusa story is that nowhere in classical sources is it told in a comprehensive way, and never from Medusa's point of view. Insofar, then, as there is a *Medusa-script* that is more than an adjunct to the story of Perseus, the script has evolved as its retellers, perceiving both injustice in Medusa's treatment and a potential for rich symbolism in the motifs attached to her (Judson: 137; McGann: 7), have devised numerous interpretations of her story which, at least potentially, underlie Chapter 11 of *Percy Jackson*. The always implicit script and the core *Medusa-schema* have thus acquired variables that shift their significance. In Els Pelgrom's adaptation (*Donder en Bliksem* [Thunder and Lightning], 2007), for example, the script is varied by bringing it into conformity with the numerous examples of the *deity-rapes-maiden-script*, which commonly includes metamorphosis to an inferior form. In declaring that Medusa was raped by Poseidon, Pelgrom thus reinscribes her as a victim.

Our examination of a variety of texts in Dutch and English indicates that contemporary forms of adaptation which involve conceptual blending, mishmash and multimodal text processing are emerging in the children's literature of both languages, and we surmise that the study of the literature of other languages will yield similar results. As we remarked earlier, the process of adaptation is about identity and modelling possible life-worlds, and in our 'online era', a time of rapid growth of information and textual forms, young people are active consumers of images, signs and commodities through which such life-worlds are modelled, and they require texts of a kind which adapt the cultures of the past to engage with the diffuse nature of contemporary textuality and information flows. In their web browsing, young people mostly prefer trial and error searching, which means they work in a random swirl of information. This swirl is reproduced in some contemporary adaptations, where it is both a source of entertainment and a challenge to negotiate a critical path through the excess of information available. The web adds a crucial resource to writerly assumptions that an audience has some degree of familiarity with particular pre-texts, with a story category to which the particular example conforms, or with the underlying metanarrative. It seems further typical of contemporary adaptation that textuality is shaped by playful discourse which, in turn, audiences must negotiate as possible meanings emerge from a text's negotiations with its adapted pre-texts and intertexts. The accessibility of information also gives way to looser forms of adaptation of pre-texts in genres which are strongly ideologically charged and which, until quite recently, were treated cautiously and conservatively in both English and Dutch children's literature. On the one hand these practices indicate a continuous interest in traditional narratives; on the other hand, the playful nature of these adaptations challenges readers to question the role of traditional narratives in contemporary society. The principle of *mishmash* as a semiotic mode herein functions to delight audiences by its disruptions of their assumptions about 'well-made' stories and about how meanings are made.

# Bibliography

## *Primary Sources*

Crossley-Holland, K. 1996. *The Penguin Book of Norse Myths: Gods of the Vikings.* Harmondsworth: Penguin.

Dros, I. 2000 [1988]. *De Reizen van de Slimme Man.* Amsterdam & Antwerpen: Querido.

Dros, I., L. Salway (trans.). 1992. *The Journeys of the Clever Man.* Stroud: Turton & Chambers.

Gaiman, N. 2008. *Odd and the Frost Giants.* London: Bloomsbury.

Pelgrom, E. & T. Tjong-Khing (ill.). 2006. *Donder en Bliksem.* Tielt: Lannoo.

Picard, B. L. 2001. *Tales of the Norse Gods.* Oxford: Oxford University Press.

Pinkwater, D. 2009. *The Yggyssey.* Boston: Houghton Mifflin Books.

Pinkwater, D. 2010. *The Adventures of a Cat-Whiskered Girl.* Boston: Houghton Mifflin Books.

Riordan, R. 2010 [2005]. *Percy Jackson and the Lightning Thief.* New York: Penguin Group.

Rosenberg, S. M., F. Van Lente, A. Foley, D. Calero & L. Lima. 2011 [2006]. *Cowboys and Aliens.* New York: HarperCollins Publishers.

Van der Geest, S. & J. Jutte (ill.). 2010. *Dissus.* Amsterdam & Antwerpen: Querido.

Van Olmen, P. 2009. *De Kleine Odessa. Het Levende Boek.* Houten: Van Goor.

## Secondary Sources

Buchan, M. 2001. 'Food for Thought: Achilles and the Cyclops', in: K. Guest (ed.), *Eating Their Words: Cannibalism and the Boundaries of Cultural Identity*. Albany: SUNY Press, 11-33.

Carrington, V. 2003. '"I'm in a bad mood. Let's go shopping": Interactive dolls, consumer culture and a "glocalized" model of literacy', in: *Journal of Early Childhood Literacy* 3: 83-98.

DiMarco, D. 2011. 'Going Wendigo: The Emergence of the Iconic Monster in Margaret Atwood's *Oryx and Crake* and Antonia Bird's *Ravenous*', in: *College Literature* 38.4: 134-155.

Fauconnier, G. & M. Turner. 2002. *The Way We Think: Conceptual Blending and the Mind's Hidden Complexities*. New York: Basic Books.

Frow, J. 2006. *Genre, The New Critical Idiom*. New York & London: Routledge.

Herman, D. 2002. *Story Logic:Problems and Possibilities of Narrative*. Lincoln and London: University of Nebraska Press.

Hutcheon, L. 2006. *A Theory of Adaptation*. New York & London: Routledge.

Judson, B. 2001. 'The Politics of Medusa: Shelley's Physiognomy of Revolution', in: *ELH* 68.1: 135-154.

Lankshear, C., & M. Knobel. 2003. 'New technologies in early childhood literacy research: A review of research', in: *Journal of Early Childhood Literacy* 3.1: 59-82.

Landow, G. P. 2006. *Hypertext 3.0: Critical Theory and New Media in an Era of Globalization. [3rd ed], Parallax: Re-Visions of Culture and Society*. Baltimore (Md.): Johns Hopkins University Press.

Levitt, L. 2010. 'Death on Display: Reifying Stardom through Hollywood's Dark Tourism', in: *The Velvet Light Trap* 65: 62-70.

McGann, J. 1972. 'The Beauty of the Medusa: A Study in Romantic Literary Iconology', in: *Studies in Romanticism* 11.1: 3-25.

Nodelman, P. 1985. 'Expectations: Titles, Stories, Pictures', in: *Children's Literature Association Quarterly* 10.1: 9-13.

Nodelman, P. & M. Reimer. 2003 [1992]. *The Pleasures of Children's Literature*. Boston: Allyn and Bacon.

Stephens, J. & R. McCallum. 1998. *Retelling Stories, Framing Culture: Traditional Story and Metanarratives in Children's Literature*. New York & London: Garland Publishing, Inc.

Stephens, J. 2009. 'Retelling Stories across Time and Cultures', in: M.O. Grenby & A. Immel (eds), *The Cambridge Companion to Children's Literature*. Cambridge: Cambridge University Press, 91-107.

Toscano, M. M. 2009. 'Homer Meets the Coen Brothers: Memory as Artistic Pastiche in *O Brother, Where Art Thou?*', in: *Film & History: An Interdisciplinary Journal of Film and Television Studies* 39.2: 49-62.

Turner, M. 2003. 'Double-scope Stories', in: D. Herman (ed), *Narrative Theory and the Cognitive Sciences*. Stanford: Center for the Study of Language and Information, 117-142.

Van Olmen, P. 2009. 'Interview with Annemie Leysen', in: *De Morgen* 25 November 2009: 41. <http://www.dekleineodessa.com /?page_id=88> Accessed 13 July 2012.

Wickham, J.A. 'September 11 and America's War on Terrorism. A New Manifest Destiny?', in: *The American Indian Quarterly* 26.1: 116-144.

Youngberg, Q. 'Morphology of Manifest Destiny: The Justified Violence of John O'Sullivan, Hank Morgan, and George W. Bush', in: *Canadian Review of American Studies* 35.3: 315-333.

# Notes

1.  Meneer Frank had me verteld over de reis van de slimme man van zijn eiland terug naar zijn eiland dat was ook zijn eigen reis van Amsterdam terug naar Amsterdam. De verhalen liepen door elkaar heen. De grot van de reus met het ene oog was een kelder zonder kaarsen. De vijanden waren buiten en de deur zat dicht. Het was oorlog en het oog van de vijand zag alles. (2003 [1988]: 106-107)

2.  Mark Buchan asserts that 'the blinding of the man-eating Cyclops' is the best-known episode from the Odyssey (2001: 13). This familiarity also applies in retellings for children, so that here, and in the examples from Van Olmen's *Little Odessa* and Simon Van der Geest and Jan Jutte's *Dissus* mentioned below, it can be assumed that the script is readily accessible to readers.

3.  We zitten met z'n drieën bij elkaar, misschien lijkt onze kamer hier wel op onze kamer in Amsterdam, dezelfde lamp, dezelfde planten, de radio staat aan, mijn moeder zingt gedachteloos mee terwijl ze roert in haar beker. (2003 [1988]: 130)

4.  The development of the Wiki marks another watershed moment in the mid-1990s. By enabling an internet community to work online collaboratively, and hence to edit one another's web pages, the Wiki transforms text into malleable, shared material. Ward Cunningham, deviser of the Wiki program, derived its name from the Hawai'ian word wiki 'quick' in 1994. The first site appeared on the Internet in 1995.

5.  'Wie is dat?' fluisterde ze tegen het meisje naast haar. [...]
    'Ben je nieuw of zo? Dat is Dostojevski! Een van de grootste schrijvers aller tijden. Ken je hem echt niet? Hij schrijft heel dikke boeken vol menselijke drama's. Maar je kunt beter geen ruzie met hem zoeken. Hij is heel opvliegend. Iedereen is bang voor hem [...] Die opgedirkte kerel naast hem, met die groene anjer in zijn revers, is Oscar Wilde. En die daar met die grote walrussnor, zie je hem, die achteroverleunt en op zijn buik trommelt? Dat is Flaubert. Die magere ernaast met die flaporen en gitzwarte ogen is Kafka. Dat is pas een eigenaardige kerel, die vindt altijd regeltjes uit die niemand begrijpt'
    All translations are by John Stephens and Sylvie Geerts, except for the excerpts from *De reizen van de slimme man*, whose English counterparts were taken from the 1992 translation by L. Salway (Dros 1992).

6.  Reproduced in Wikipedia from 'Memorias de un loco, de Gustave Flaubert', in: *la República Cultural.es* <http://www.larepublicacultural.es/local/cache-vignettes/L282xH350/876-a08ba.jpg> Accessed 10 August 2011. The image is in the public domain.

7.  See <http://www.dekleineodessa.com/?page_id=136> Accessed 13 July 2012.

8.  De mannen vonden een paal en scherpten er een punt aan en maakten die hard in het vuur. Waarom hadden ze die zin doorstreept? Wat waren die mannen van plan geweest met die paal? Waarom mochten ze hem niet meer gebruiken? [...] Ze zat in een grot tussen ruige mannen die naar zweet en goedkope wijn roken, en in het vuur staarden. De grot was ruim en hoog. Ze hoorde schapen. Door de opening van de grot kon ze het behaarde onderbeen van een reus zien. De cycloop. Hij zat op een rots, te midden van een kudde schapen. [...] 'Wat! Omdat jij in een andere wereld een proef moet afleggen, riskeren wij hier ons hachje? Wie denk jij wel dat je bent? Red jij ons dan maar!'

9.  *De mensen zijn meester van hun eigen verhaal en niemand zal dat ooit veranderen.*

10. Thus in his notes on the soundtrack of the Coen Brothers' film, *O Brother, Where Art Thou?*, Robert K. Oermann describes the music as a 'joyous mishmash of periods and styles' (cited in Toscano 2009: 59).

11. Such a mishmash has been around for a while – sword-and-sorcery fantasy has been a notable mishmash of periods and cultures. An excellent contemporary example is Alexis Fajardo's *Kid Beowulf and the Song of Roland*: the meeting of characters from the oldest English epic (8-9th century), the oldest French (12th century), and Victor Hugo's novel *The Hunchback of Notre-Dame* (1831) makes the meeting of Nazis and Cowboys look commonplace.

12. 'Het zit zo: ik was *Ulysses* van James Joyce aan het lezen. Een schitterend boek! En het inspireerde me. De naam van de heldin, de kleine Odessa, heeft daar trouwens alles mee te maken. Het basisgegeven – Odysseus op weg naar huis en zijn familie – was het uitgangspunt. Daar ben ik mee begonnen. In mijn boek maakt een meisje, de kleine Odessa, op haar zoektocht naar haar ouders heel wat avonturen mee voor ze eindelijk "thuiskomt".'

13. Ik moet denken aan films met shotguns, drugs en lijken

14. Een hoogst originele en verfrissende bewerking van de Odyssee

15. Zwaar verdwaald

16. Opgestaan is plaats vergaan

17. alsof hun harddisk is gecrasht/en ik ben gewist

18. Mijn ogen prikten van het chloor / Snot liep mijn neus uit / en ik wilde / niets anders / dan gewoon / gewoon / naar huis

19. Wat ik nu echt wil, / Dat ik de held was, / de held van het verhaal en dat we vet verdwalen en heel ver en vrij / en vol gevaar, onderweg sneuvelen er een paar en iedereen huilen / behalve ik / en ik, ik zeg dan: / Hé kom op. / Loop maar mee met mij.

20. Ze noemen mij Niemand

21. Hij heeft mijn naam, mijn hut, mijn thuis / wie ben ik dan, / en ben ik thuis?

22. Zo loop ik verder / pas voor pas / Alleen, maar nooit alleen / en niemand die me niemand noemt / of een spriet / Dissus heet ik / da's mijn naam / Zou je moeten weten

23. Sinds ik thuis ben / is de lucht / een stukje leger

# Adapting the Pleasures of Dramatic Irony in Comics

## Joe Sutliff Sanders

In those long, dark years, now almost lost to memory, when I was a graduate student, I spent one evening watching a film I had always heard about but never made time to watch: Akira Kurosawa's *Ran*. I had recently reread – and loved – *King Lear*, and this seemed an obvious time to watch the film. After all, *Ran* is widely held to be the masterpiece of Kurosawa's later years, an adaptation of *Lear* that Kurosawa was already practicing for when he made the daunting *Kagemusha*; *Ran* is also the return to Shakespeare for which critics and fans longed since a much younger Kurosawa revised *Macbeth* in 1957's *Throne of Blood*. It's the kind of film one has to see, and I would never be better situated to enjoy it fully than after having reread *Lear*.

I settled in, comfortable both because of my third-hand couch – I *was* in graduate school – and because the opening scenes of the film reminded me that although to the characters this story was new, to me it was familiar. I quickly realised that the main character, Hidetora, was the film's version of Lear and that although Hidetora had sons instead of daughters, both fathers had the same number of offspring – and the same problems. The elder sons, like Lear's elder daughters, protested their hyperbolic love of their father, whereas the youngest son followed in the tradition of the truthful Cordelia. Hidetora-Lear behaved as he should (badly), the court jester behaved as he should (oddly), Lord Tango played the role of Kent, and so on. I knew this story, and although I felt sympathy for the very human characters, I also felt that comfortable superiority that comes when watching a story unfold that one has heard many times over, if in slightly different forms. I was in on the joke: the director and I were playing a prank together on the characters, clucking our tongues from behind a second-story window as the tragedy – new to them, familiar to us – unfolded below.

Just over an hour into the movie, the director pushed me out of that window. I still recall the sense of shock I felt when the film took a path dramatically different from that which its source text followed, the path I had assumed the entire film would follow. After Hidetora divides up his kingdom, just as I expected, and excommunicates the one truthful child, just as I predicted, after his greedy sons pull apart the infrastructure of his remaining power, just as I knew they would, and after this stand-in for Lear begins his famous fall into madness, the eldest son, Taro, is shot dead. The moment is stunning – not least of all for Taro – in particular because Taro, who until now has so clearly been Kurosawa's Goneril, supposedly should not have died in the film until the moment Goneril dies in the play, namely in the final act. Indeed, he should not have died until more than halfway through *the final scene* of the final act. Without Goneril, the narrative that appeared to be a retelling of *Lear* would lack a major source of its momentum: lacking a Goneril to squabble with Regan, a Goneril to sound the theme of sexual impropriety with Edmund, a second child to compete for the inheritance of the kingdom, what story was left to tell?

I sat on that cheap couch, stunned, playing the scene over and over, trying to figure out what had gone wrong. The film had promised me – through its reputation, the advertising copy on the back of the box, the opening scene, and the very premise of the tale – that I could use my knowledge of *Lear* to predict the movements of the film. But in the moment of Taro's death, that promise was broken. In that moment, I slipped from a comfortable, privileged viewer to one more person as shocked by Taro's death as were any of the fictional characters. I wasn't in on the joke: I was its victim.

In this article, I want to talk about the second time I experienced that feeling, and I want to explore the fundamental role of adaptation in the production of such a stunning moment. My broader point is that although adaptation scholarship has largely ignored comics – the medium in which I experienced this sensation for the second time – comics are an obvious place to look for adaptation, indeed to look for adaptation that relies on a kind of participation that is fundamentally similar to the kind of participation on which *Ran* also relies. To illustrate that point, I will focus on only one instance of adaptation in comics, but in unearthing this moment of shock from that one instance, I will explain why it is that comics deserve more attention in adaptation studies and how it is that comics lend themselves to exactly this sort of reading.

My central example begins with a classic of children's literature, namely Osamu Tezuka's *Tetsuwan Atom* – better known abroad as *Astro Boy* – and ends with Naoki Urasawa's multi-volume series *Pluto*, which is an adaptation of Tezuka's most famous story from *Tetsuwan Atom*. The core of my analysis comes from my realisation that adaptations such as *Ran* and *Pluto* count on their audience's knowledge of the source text to flatter and then surprise their readers. The aspect of adaptation of which I write is one that seems taken for granted in a great deal of adaptation scholarship, but it has remained curiously unexplored, even in scholarship that seems to sense that such potential is there. What I hope to show is that dramatic irony, an element common in adaptations, typically offers its audience a privileged position, but in rare and memorable adaptations such as this adaptation of *Tetsuwan Atom*, it can make and then rescind that offer, leaving the audience just as bewildered as the characters – indeed, perhaps more so.

If my broad claim is that comics are an ideal place to look for this rare and eloquent aesthetic use of adaptation, that claim is grounded in three more specific claims. First, I hope to demonstrate that scholarship on adaptation has not paid enough attention to comics, and I assume that lack of attention comes in part from a lack of conviction that scholarship knows how to talk about comics. Second, I want to show that scholarship on adaptation has not paid enough attention to dramatic irony, a formalist term that has long been out of fashion in literary scholarship but that is ideal for explaining how serial fiction – such as comics – adapts earlier stories for an audience ready to recognise the adaptation. Third, I intend to explain how scholarship on dramatic irony has not paid enough attention to this rare but striking use of such irony.

## Comics and Adaptation

Comic books and the characters they have launched provide obvious objects of study for adaptation theory. *Tetsuwan Atom* alone has thrived on adaptation, enjoying a rich publication history in comics, cartoons, and film from 1951 to 2009.[1] Other comic book properties have similarly profited from decades of adaptation across media form: indeed, it is one of the major contentions of Will Brooker's book-length study of Batman that it is *because* of adaptation that the character has proved so profitable to his corporate handlers. But comic books are not simply the source of characters that can be revised as they cross genre and media boundaries. Rather, comics themselves compulsively revisit earlier comics, offering pleasure for their readers along the way. At times, such pleasure is offered by comics that return characters only 'true' fans will recognise – for example in Neil Gaiman's resurrection of Prez, a character who had been written out of continuity, as the subject for *Sandman* #55 (1993). At other times, adaptations of familiar characters touch off heated – which is to say pleasurable – debates, even over topics, such as 2010's debut of lengthened trousers for Wonder Woman, that might otherwise seem trivial. Indeed, it might be the case that comic books have *more* instances of adaptation than any other late modern form.

But for all that, scholarship on adaptation has not paid much attention to comics. Two recent articles address adaptation of a specific comic book to a specific film, but in these instances the emphasis is on what the film has done, a far cry from a study of adaptation within comics themselves.[2] The most notable exception is *A Theory of Adaptation* (2006), Linda Hutcheon's cornerstone work on adaptation, which brings up comics more than half a dozen times. But even in this best example of how adaptation theory can address comics, comics appear as examples that are supplemental, even ancillary to her larger points, as when she mentions Yvonne Navarro's novelisation of the film *Hellboy*, which borrowed from the earlier comic book series of the same name (Hutcheon 2006: 8; she echoes this argument in a point about *League of Extraordinary Gentlemen* on page 39), and when Hutcheon names two comics whose adaptation as film seems natural because 'telling is not the same as showing' (ibid.: 43). And perhaps the most obvious examples of adaptation and comics – the decades of material provided by *Classics Illustrated* – appear in Hutcheon's study only to set up a reading of a *television* series that adapts Shakespearean plays (ibid.: 117). Thus, even in the best case venue, comics somehow manage to avoid sustained notice in adaptation studies, despite the form's consistent use of adaptation.

## Comics, Collectors, and Dramatic Irony

The comics collectors' market prompted another use for adaptation, and here we begin to draw closer to the link between the strategy of adaptation at work in Kurosawa's *Ran* and the medium of comics. Before the collectors' market, comic books in most countries were purely ephemeral objects, sold alongside disposable texts such as newspapers because comic books were, like newspapers, to be read and thrown away. Conceived of as a form that would not last, comics had to present stories that relied on nothing more permanent than character recognition. Although the writers of, for example, a popular superhero title could expect readers of one issue to recognise the series' major heroes and villains, they could not expect readers to know what had happened in the immediately previous issue, which might have been thrown away in the process of tidying a child's room or discarded by the newsvendor when new comics arrived. All that changed with the collectors' market and, eventually, specialty shops. Between collectors and the shops they frequented, a rich library of back issues and reliable distribution of new issues emerged. With such a knowledgeable consumer base, comics began to sustain story arcs over multiple issues and allude to previous stories more often, in short, to provide the network of recognisable stories that allows a frequent tool of adaptation: dramatic irony.

Dramatic irony was a favorite tool of methods that are now badly out of fashion in international literary criticism. It was a frequent tool of the method of close reading that has come to be identified in America with scholarship of the first half of the twentieth century and, in Europe, with what Roland Barthes dismissively characterises as an appeal to 'the reassuring alibi of the 'concrete'' (1974: 12). As such, it is a term that today requires definition. Peter Goldie's 'Dramatic Irony, Narrative, and the External Perspective' – an essay, tellingly, about ethics, not about literature – is one of the few recent mobilisations of the term for analysis. His definition cites the best-known examples of dramatic irony:

> In drama, we the audience sometimes know something that one of the characters in the drama does not know. In Sophocles' *Oedipus Rex*, we know that Oedipus killed his father at the crossroads, but Oedipus believes that he killed a stranger. In the *Odyssey*, we know that Odysseus has returned home to Ithaca, but Penelope, at least initially, does not know this. In *King Lear*, we know that blinded Gloucester, who wants to die, is wrong when he thinks that he is on the edge of the cliffs of Dover [...]. (Goldie 2007: 72)

The Belgian scholar Germaine Dempster, too, writing not of drama but of Chaucer, highlights the 'strong contrast' between what a character knows and what the story tells its audience (1959 [1932]: 7). The 'irony' in 'dramatic irony' comes from the disjuncture between what audiences know and what characters know, just as I knew that Hidetora's elder children would flatter him and the youngest would speak a plain truth for which he would be disowned.

Importantly, though, there is more to dramatic irony than simply the disconnect between what characters know and what their audience knows: in dramatic irony, that disconnect provides the audience with a sense of superiority. Such a sense is presumed in both Goldie's and Dempster's definitions, but the pleasure inherent in such superiority is stated more explicitly in C. Hugh Holman and William Harmon's *Handbook to Literature*.[3] Their entry on 'dramatic irony' confirms that although the best-known examples are from the stage, the terms may fairly be applied to 'nondramatic narrative', and the authors go on to write that '*dramatic irony* is responsible for much of the interest in fiction and drama because the reader or spectator enjoys being in on the secret' (Holman & Harmon 1992: 151; emphasis in original). The authors link this definition to an example 'in which a character uses words that mean one thing to the speaker and another to those better acquainted with the real situation' (ibid.: 480).[4] These examples articulate an important source of the pleasure that dramatic irony offers readers: the audience not only 'enjoys being in on the secret', but the audience's knowledge is assumed to be 'the real situation', the truthful situation, and the audience's 'better acquaint[ance]' is a truer, more valid acquaintance (ibid.). Therefore, not only do scholars – correctly, to my mind – assume that audiences enjoy their understanding, but they also specify that the enjoyment comes about because of the superiority of the audience's understanding to that of the characters. Who wouldn't enjoy such a position? It is a smug, self-congratulatory joy, to be sure, but it is joy nonetheless. When, indeed, could such a position offer anything other than a comfortable pleasure?

Obviously, one time that such a position might yield something other than comfort is when that superior position is dramatically revoked. This is the case in the moment of Taro's death, as the audience – me, in this case – loses its elevated perspective and falls out that second-story window. But film is perhaps a surprising place to find such an experience: *Ran* is most effective for someone who has recently read or seen *Lear*, and that seems a strange thing to expect of any modern audience, whether Japanese theater-goers, attendees at international film festivals, or graduate students watching the video at home on comfortable couches.

Comics, however, are an ideal place to look for such an experience, especially in an era in which the collectors' market, specialty shops, and trade compilations (often called 'graphic novels') are an everyday reality. Because comics love to retell stories told in earlier comics and because comics have come to anticipate an audience knowledgeable about earlier iterations of retold stories, comics are not only ideal places to look for adaptation, they are ideal places to look for adaptation that depends on dramatic irony.

## Recognising 'The Greatest Robot on Earth'

Naoki Urasawa's *Pluto*, a text that positions itself as a revision of Osamu Tezuka's *Tetsuwan Atom*, is a strong example of the uses to which comics can put dramatic irony. *Pluto* is not simply a borrowing of characters from *Tetsuwan Atom*, but a revision of a specific story – 'The Greatest Robot on Earth' – that Urasawa had every reason to think would be immediately familiar to his original audience at the turn of the current century. The little robot whom the world outside Japan would come to call 'Astro Boy' first appeared in Japan in 1951. By January 1965, when he finished serialising the 'Greatest Robot on Earth', Tezuka had reached dizzying heights of popularity in his home country, largely on the back of the manga series *Tetsuwan Atom* and, beginning in 1963, the animated series of the same name. 'The Greatest Robot on Earth' was an immediate and lasting success, a classic by any definition, appearing in multiple animated adaptations, prompting one fan website to speculate that 'this is *the* most popular of our little hero's adventures' ('Greatest Robot'; emphasis in original).

In *Tetsuwan Atom*, Atom is the protagonist, a powerful but caring robot boy who lives in a human family and repeatedly saves the human world from disaster. In the two-part story

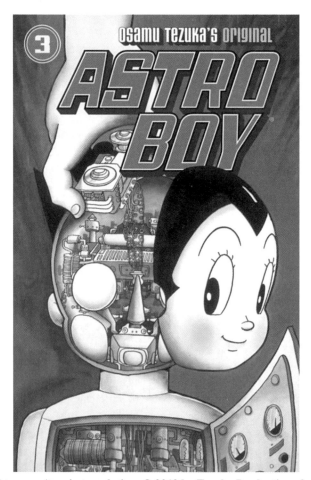

**Figure 1. *Tetsuwan Atom* in translation; © 2012 by Tezuka Productions for all Tezuka images; English edition © by Dark Horse for all Tezuka images**

'Greatest Robot on Earth', Tezuka also introduces the villainous robot Pluto, who is the extraordinarily powerful puppet of the spoiled Sultan Chochi-Chochi Abba. The sultan's mission for Pluto is clear: he must destroy the other seven most powerful robots on the planet so that Pluto will be the undisputed strongest of all the robots, bringing glory to the sultan. Pluto immediately begins working his way across the planet, making short work of all the robots he meets. He develops an affection for Atom's little sister, Uran, and shows brief moments of mercy to Atom himself, but by the final act of the story, Pluto has destroyed six of his rival robots and is preparing for a deadly battle with Atom. When a nearby volcano comes to life, Atom breaks off the fight to plug the volcano while Pluto asserts that he won't waste his energy on anything other than fighting. Finally, Pluto has a change of heart, and the friendship he forges with Atom during their rescue efforts enables him to overcome his programming and refuse to duel with Atom. Unfortunately, *another* great robot has been built, and *this* robot destroys Pluto. The story ends with a transparent homage to the liberal humanism that has drawn Tezuka consistent praise for

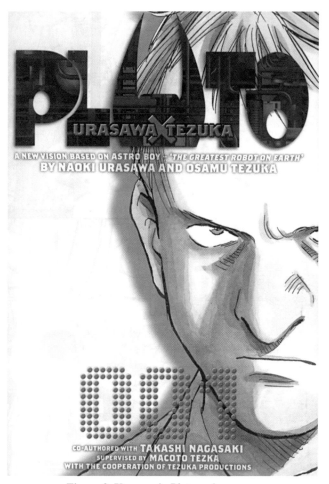

Figure 2. Urasawa's *Pluto*, volume one

decades, here in two of the forms most common to Tezuka's work: a call for international fraternity – the seven great robots are from different nations – and a pronouncement of the ethical poverty of defining greatness strictly according to physical might. Its two heroes are the tragic hero Pluto, who turned too late to the side of good, and Atom, the perpetually youthful face of the series' optimism.

Naoki Urasawa's adaptation of 'The Greatest Robot on Earth' clearly anticipates that its readers will recognise the source text. That adaptation – importantly, named after the heroic *villain* rather than after the optimistic hero – structures its dramatic beats according to revelations that are melodramatic to a reader who has never read the original story, but, in keeping with what others have said about dramatic irony, those same revelations invite more profound pleasures from readers who recognise the characters and mysteries at play. The earliest example of such a dramatic beat comes with the title logo for the series, which takes the name of Tezuka's villain and hints at the trademark horns Pluto wields (see Figure 2). A mere four pages into the first volume, a dramatic, full-page image (also

**Figure 3. The heroic Atom**

known as a 'splash page') that launches the first chapter gives a glimpse of Pluto's face without explanation – whereas the first page of Tezuka's story opens with a full-body view of the robot and the sultan pronouncing his name (see Figure 4). The way each story handles the first appearance of the villain gives a strong indication of the level of familiarity each story anticipates from its audience: for Tezuka, a complete view of the robot along with the use of the robot's name in dialog indicates a sense that the character is new to the audience; for Urasawa, the abstract, obstructed view of only the most recognisable part of Pluto indicates the later story's belief that the audience will fill in the missing pieces of the villain's identity based on the knowledge of previous iterations that they bring to *Pluto*.

The villainous robot is not the only character Urasawa reveals with a sensitivity to the reader's familiarity. For example, the viewpoint character for most of volume one announces that he is 'made of a very special alloy' (Urasawa 2008 [2004]: 72.8), an echo of the phrase the same character uses twice in 'The Greatest Robot on Earth' (Tezuka 2002 [1964-5]: 53.7 and 56.3).[5] The fourth chapter of Urasawa's story also gives its splash page to the first revelation of a familiar character, this time North No. 2, and the powerful splash page at the end of chapter seven – not coincidentally, the splash page at the end of the first bound volume – is given to none other than Atom himself. For the reader of *Pluto* unfamiliar with *Tetsuwan Atom*, particularly unfamiliar with 'The Greatest Robot on Earth', these full-page reveals are likely to be oddly anticlimactic: references to the special alloy will mean nothing, and the dramatic emphasis given to the reveal of Atom at the cliffhanger ending of the first volume will indicate that he is important, but not why. But this dramatic misfire is a sign that the story was designed for someone familiar with the earlier comic. And considering the extraordinary saturation this particular story has achieved in Japanese culture, it is not hard at all to imagine how, to revise phrases from existing scholarship on dramatic irony, the spectator's superior acquaintance with the story in which the characters find themselves could offer the knowledgeable reader a distinctly comfortable pleasure in these moments. Urasawa's *Pluto*, an adaptation of

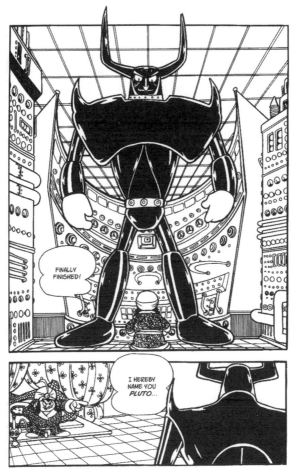

**Figure 4. Tezuka introduces Pluto**

Tezuka's children's classic, plays to an audience that is knowledgeable about the earlier story. Urasawa's adaptation offers such a reader pleasures that are conventional for dramatic irony: it comforts, even flatters the reader who recognises these characters and anticipates the narrative in which these characters find themselves.

But Urasawa, like Kurosawa, offers this initial comfort only to revoke it in a moment that is dramatic for both the characters and the suddenly non-privileged readers. Unlike Kurosawa, Urasawa foreshadows his departure from the earlier text. In Tezuka's version of the story, Pluto's violence is incidental, the result of his simple programming, deplorable but hardly ghastly. When he destroys Mont Blanc, for example, he flexes his robot muscles and moves on to his next victim (see Figure 6). But in Urasawa's adaptation, Mont Blanc's destruction takes place off-panel, and apart from the glimpse of Pluto in the story's opening pages, the new version does not show the villain at work. Instead, much later, Gesicht, the detective investigating Mont Blanc's destruction, shares an image from the battlefield: the image of Mont Blanc's decapitated head, with tree limbs

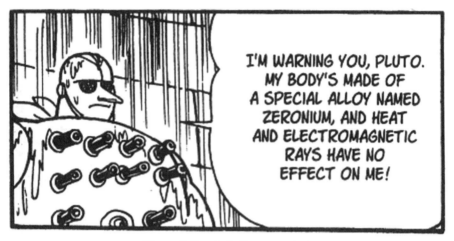

**Figure 5. Tezuka's German robot**

shoved into the ground to give the impression of horns. The contrast between the earlier text's – forgive the expression – cartoonish villain and this text's villain, who seems to take a sick glee in his victory, is a significant departure. That departure is played up a few pages later, as the detective visits Professor Reinhardt, one of the countless human beings who loved Mont Blanc. Reinhardt tells the detective that 'Witnesses say a huge tornado touched down before the fire started… I know there's also speculation that it was all just a *natural disaster*… That was *no accident*' (Urasawa 2008 [2004]: 41.4, 5, and 7; emphasis in original). But in the space between those last two sentences, Urasawa inserts a disturbing panel. This panel reprises the earlier image of Mont Blanc's mutilated remains, but it does more than re-present that image: the image is grainy with enlargement, indicating the traumatic, poorly understood nature of the recollection, and Urasawa leaves the frame off the panel, robbing this panel of the stability and psychological closure present in the other moments represented on the page.

But the most stunning moment of departure from the version of this story with which Urasawa's original audience would have been so comfortably familiar comes several scenes later. It is here that Urasawa, much like Kurosawa before him, dramatically rewrites the rules of the story. After Gesicht has recovered the memory chip of a police robot destroyed near the scene of one of Pluto's murders, he delivers the chip to the police robot's widow. The widow plays her husband's final memories over and discovers that the reason her husband was slain was that he was distracted momentarily. What distracted him was the villain leaving the scene of the murder Gesicht has been investigating. But the villain is not the great horned robot glimpsed in the opening pages of the series, the comically monstrous robot familiar from Tezuka's version of the tale. It is, the widow announces to the stunned Detective Gesicht, a human being (ibid.: 62).

There are various reasons to believe that this moment is supposed to be at least as surprising for the reader as it is for the detective. First, and perhaps most obviously, the figure whom the widow insists must be human is leaping an impossible distance for a

**Figure 6. Tezuka's cartoonish villain**

human being: a gap between two high-rise buildings. From any reading position, it is surprising that a character would insist that a figure making such a leap is human. And Urasawa's use of the tools of storytelling in comics further supports such a reaction. Importantly, the page on which this revelation is made is the final page of the chapter, producing the equivalent of a cliffhanger in the original, serial printing of the story. Also, the page makes use of various storytelling conventions of comics to emphasise the dramatic, startling tone of the moment. The composition of the page, for example, is out of balance, with a left-hand panel (ibid.: 62.3) extending farther both horizontally and vertically than the column of panels matching it on the right-hand side (ibid.: 62.1-2). The final panel, in which the widow announces that the figure is human, has an internally unbalanced composition (although the shape of the panel is regular, the use of lights and darks within the image skews its balance) as well as dramatic lighting (the television screen, evidently the only source of light in the room, throws ominous shadows) and a remarkably increased panel size, devoting half the page to the panel in which this revelation is made (ibid.: 62.4). But none of this reading requires 'acquaintance with the real situation' (Holman & Harmon 1992: 480), only a passing familiarity with the codes of storytelling in comics; at the level of both plot (someone identified as human is doing something human beings cannot do) and aesthetics (composition, lighting, layout), this moment is dramatic in its own right.

At a second level of reading, though, one informed by Tezuka's earlier version of the story rather than by Urasawa's visual artistry, the surprise is heightened *in spite* of the rules Urasawa's story has established. First, it is important to understand that within the logic of Urasawa's story, the announcement that the jumper is human is in fact *not* a surprise. As Gesicht points out, the building from which the figure is leaping is the building in which the murder took place, and he immediately infers that this fantastic figure is the murderer. But if it is impossible – as we know from our experience of human beings and the distance between skyscrapers – for a human being to make such a leap, it is equally impossible – as we know from how this fictive world has educated us about itself – that the murderer is a robot. After all, the chapter opens with a sequence during which the story establishes – through Gesicht's testimony – that robots in this world cannot kill humans (Urasawa 2008 [2004]: 23.8). Further, Gesicht also discovers that the first victim is a human (ibid.: 13.6). Thus, it makes sense – despite the figure's impossible leap – that the chief suspect in the case would be human. The announcement that the suspect is human therefore, to a reader who is aware only of the rules of reality within the world of the story, actually works *against* the surprise that this page otherwise works to enforce: the idea that the murderer is human does nothing but confirm what the story has already implied.

The idea that the suspect is human is, however, *more* startling if the reader is familiar with 'The Greatest Robot on Earth', in which the only murderer is a robot. A reader who recognises Tezuka's story behind Urasawa's story can be relied upon to have two reactions in a predictable order. First, that reader can be relied upon to assume, despite what the logic of the world has already stated, that the murderer is a robot. In this reaction, the reader is using the superior knowledge that comforts an audience, the dramatic irony that places a reader with previous knowledge in a privileged position. The second reaction is one of surprise, in that this previous knowledge is suddenly invalidated. Importantly, the aesthetic element privileged in this moment of storytelling is one that relies heavily on adaptation, specifically, on the reader's reading of the new text through the memory of the old text. The logic contained within *Pluto* itself insists that *of course* the murderer is human: this very chapter has already insisted that robots in this world are programmed not to kill humans. But the surprise the page hopes to deliver – and the visual aesthetic of the page makes it difficult to assume that any other emotion is the chief goal of the page – would be short-circuited if the logic of the current story were to take precedence. This page is *more* surprising because the reader is anticipating a villain cut from the cloth fabricated by 'The Greatest Robot on Earth'.

There are two more important points to be drawn here. The first is purely related to Urasawa's text and this rare – for media other than comics, anyway – use of dramatic irony within it. By flattering the reader's knowledge, knowledge that offers pleasure through its smug superiority over the knowledge of the characters within the story, Urasawa sets the reader up for a startling realisation that not only invalidates the former sense of superiority, but attempts to trap the reader in the same experience of dislocation and bewilderment that the characters feel. In short, to make a point that speaks only to the artistic use of dramatic irony in the text, this moment so similar to the death of Taro in *Ran* has the potential to grant the reader a feeling of confusion and dread that the viewpoint character is experiencing. This use of dramatic irony bears fruit for the story by magnifying a sense of mystery in a story that is, after all, a mystery.

But I want to close by drawing a larger point, one more relevant to the study of adaptation than to the study of Urasawa. This revision of dramatic irony in *Ran* and *Pluto*, a revision that is more likely in comics than in other media, has implications for the way we talk about adaptation. Previous scholarship on adaptation has frequently come close to pinpointing the role of dramatic irony in adaptation, notably in Hutcheon's championing of Michael Alexander's term 'palimpsestuousness' to describe texts 'haunted at all times by their adapted texts' (Hutcheon 2006: 6). But even Hutcheon never quite names dramatic irony, affirming at one point that 'there is a difference between what characters and therefore what we *see* and what they might actually *know*' (ibid.: 55; emphasis in original). But rather than exploring what that discrepancy might mean, she immediately turns to the question of how an adaptation may tweak narrative perspective to communicate a text's opinion on the absurdity of war (in the adaptation of Gustav Hasford's *The Short-Timers* into the film *Full Metal Jacket*; ibid.: 55) or give the audience a giggle over an ironic allusion (in a throwaway line in Peter David's 2002 novelisation of the film *Spider-Man*; ibid.: 126). Clearly dramatic irony has more potential than this, so in part I am merely calling for better attention to 'dramatic irony', a term that I think will be of significant use to us.

Even more importantly, I want to point out that the revision of dramatic irony so obvious in both *Ran* and *Pluto* expands significantly on the *pleasures* that can be found in adaptation. Hutcheon writes compellingly of the experience of 'immersion' across adaptations, by which she means how, for example, a video game might require different kinds of audience participation than would a play (2006: 22). The term 'immersion' is suggestively relevant to my experience of watching *Ran* shortly after reading *Lear*. But her real interest is in how media newer than print (and comics) may allow for participatory 'immersion', so she does not pursue the joy inherent in such deep engagement. Julie Sanders speaks more pointedly about the pleasures of adaptation, and it is here that I see the clearest potential for this expanded understanding of dramatic irony. Sanders emphasises that, 'as readers and critics, we also need to recognise that adaptation and appropriation are fundamental to the practice, and, indeed, to the enjoyment, of literature' (2006: 1). Elsewhere, she argues that

> part of the sheer pleasure of the reading experience must be the tension between the familiar and the new, and the recognition both of similarity and difference [...]. The pleasure exists, and persists, then, in the act of reading in, around and on (and on). (ibid.: 14)

Sanders makes a compelling argument throughout her study for the pleasure that comes from watching an adaptation confront the outdated ideology of canonical texts, and to some extent that approach explains the pleasures of *Pluto*, whose subtitle includes the phrase 'Urasawa X Tezuka' (see Figure 2), as though the authors were featured on the title card of a boxing match. But *Pluto*'s tone is perhaps too affectionate toward *Tetsuwan Atom* to be conceived of as antagonistic toward its predecessor. Rather, the pleasures of adaptation in Urasawa's text come from the – comforting, empowering, superior – recognition of similarities between *Pluto* and *Tetsuwan Atom as well as* the – startling, disempowering, bewildering – differences between the two texts. Rather than disappointment in a failure of fidelity, *Pluto* invites its audience to feel as intentional and aesthetically relevant a departure from the original that privileges and then dethrones an audience 'better acquainted' with the source text (Holman & Harmon, 1992: 480).

This kind of pleasure is inherent in any aspect of dramatic irony, and as such, it is a pleasure to which adaptation theory should attend. However, dramatic irony is especially likely in comics, a medium that adaptation theory has largely ignored. Because comics regularly revisit their older stories, comics are an excellent place to explore adaptation. The pleasures afforded by the process of flattering and then contradicting an audience's knowledge of earlier versions of the text provide a key insight into the process of adaptation upon which comics often rely. And the uncommon use of dramatic irony that comics practice so commonly provides an exciting new angle on adaptation.

## Bibliography

Barthes, R. 1974. *S/Z*. Trans. Richard Miller. New York: Hill and Wang.

Brooker, W. 2001. *Batman Unmasked: Analyzing a Cultural Icon*. New York: Continuum.

Dempster, G. 1959 [1932]. *Dramatic Irony in Chaucer*. New York: The Humanities Press.

Gaiman, N. 1993. 'The Golden Boy', in: *Sandman* 55.

Goldie, P. 2007. 'Dramatic Irony, Narrative, and the External Perspective', in: Hutto, D. (ed.), *Narrative and Understanding Persons*. Cambridge: Cambridge University Press, 69-84.

'Greatest Robot', in: *Tezuka in English*: <http://tezukainenglish.com/?q=node/329> Accessed 1 May 2011.

Holman, C.H. & W. Harmon. 1992. *A Handbook of Literature*. New York: MacMillan.

Hutcheon, L. 2006. *A Theory of Adaptation*. New York: Routledge.

*Ran*. 2005 [1985]. dir. Kurosawa, A. Nippon Herald Films.

Miller, F. 1986. *Dark Knight Returns*. New York: DC Comics.

Moore, A. 1987. *Watchmen*. New York: DC Comics.

Sanders, J. 2006. *Adaptation and Appropriation*. London: Routledge.

Silveira, M. 2011. '"This Is Sparta!": The Reinvention of the Epic in Zack Snyder's *300*', in: Burgoyne, R. (ed.), *The Epic Film in World Culture*. New York: Routledge, 19-38.

Tezuka, O. 2002 [1964-1965]. *Astro Boy, Volume Three*. Trans. F. L. Schodt. Milwaukie, OR: Dark Horse Comics.

Urasawa, N. 2008 [2004]. *Pluto, Volume One*. Co-authored with T. Nagasaki. Trans. J. Cook & F. L. Schodt. San Francisco: Viz Media.

Wood, D. 2010. '"The Times They Are A-Changin": The Passage of Time as an Agent of Change in Zack Snyder's Adaptation of *Watchmen*', in: *Colloquy: Text, Theory, Critique* 20: 104-120.

## Notes

1.  See for example, following Atom's first appearance in 1951, a comic book series launched in 1952, an animated series in 1963, another animated series in 1980, a third series in 2003, and a film that opened in 2009.

2.  See Monica Silveira's '"This Is Sparta!": The Reinvention of the Epic in Zack Snyder's *300*' and Daniel Wood's '"The Times They Are A-Changin": The Passage of Time as an Agent of Change in Zack Snyder's Film Adaptation of *Watchmen*.'

3.  C. Hugh Holman & W. Harmon, 'Dramatic Irony,' *A Handbook to Literature*. 6th ed.

4.  C. Hugh Holman & W. Harmon, 'Tragic Irony,' *A Handbook to Literature*. 6th ed.

5.  The English versions of *Tetsuwan Atom* and *Pluto* I am using were both translated by Frederik L. Schodt; although Schodt was one of two translators for the adaptation, it is likely that this coincidence of phrase was at least approved by him.

# Enchanted Conversations

## The Reverse Adaptation of Fairy Tales in Online Culture

### John Patrick Pazdziora

Andrew Lang, in his classic late-Victorian fairy tale 'Prince Prigio' (1895), tells the story of a fairyland king and a rationalist queen. The queen determines that their son, Prigio, should grow up undeceived by silly tales of fairies and wonders and magic; she makes sure he has a good, sensible education (Lang 1895: 5-9). Prigio, however, is the great-grandson of Cinderella, and at his christening receives dozens of magical gifts from the fairies: seven-league boots, a wishing cap, the purse of Fortunatus, and so on. The queen sees only old boots, a battered felt cap, and a worn-out purse, and hides the magical gifts away in the lumber-room (ibid.: 9). J. R. R. Tolkien alluded to this tale when he compared fairy tale anthologies for children to 'lumber-rooms', repositories of magical treasures denied their magic (2008 [1947]: 50). He suggests that:

> the association between children and fairy-stories is an accident of domestic history. Fairy-stories have in the modern lettered world been relegated to the 'nursery', as shabby or old-fashioned furniture is relegated to the play-room, primarily because adults do not want it, and do not mind if it is misused[.] (ibid.)

Through shifting fashions, children inadvertently became the inheritors of a folkloric tradition 'far older (and perhaps wiser) than the society that discarded it' (ibid.).

In an attempt to study or rewrite the fairy tale as a literary genre, the reality of this shift is unavoidable; most writers first encountered these tales as children. Jack Zipes observes that 'children are continually exposed to fairy tales through reading, viewing, and listening. They are encouraged to sort out their lives through fairy tales', whether for good or ill (1997: 10). Although these tales were in most cases originally conceived for adults, they were adapted to become 'more appropriate for children' (ibid.: 5-6). They became, in essence, an entire canon of children's literature: the lumber-room became sacrosanct (Zipes 2006: 1-2).

The rise of online culture has offered a new platform for popular retellings of fairy tales, as web-based fairy tale journals and magazines have emerged over the last decade. This article will examine three of these online journals – *Scheherezade's Bequest*, *Enchanted Conversation*, and *New Fairy Tales* – each of which illustrates a somewhat differing approach to the adapting and retelling of children's fairy tales. My interest is both critical and professional; each of these journals has published some of my own short stories. Through this study, I am attempting to bring the perspective of a literary critic to the work my creative colleagues and I have undertaken. Fairy tales are endlessly fascinating, inviting continual variations and retellings; this may derive in part from their origins in the oral folk tradition. This study will first suggest a way in which the process of retelling fairy tales may be understood, and then explore each online journal as typifying a different approach to retelling: the fairy tale as a subgenre of speculative fiction, the fairy tale as a cultural artefact, and the fairy tale as an ongoing creative tradition. These stories, which have for good or ill become primarily children's tales in Western culture, have been transformed and adapted to suit the needs and desires of adult writers and readers; in other words, they are regaining the function of a type of literary folklore, a process I choose to call 'reverse adaptation', as the adult writers seem to return to fairy tale narratives in an attempt to explain or vindicate their interactions with a no longer childlike world.

## Reverse Adaptation and Dual Existence

Diane Purkiss has discussed in some detail the transmutation of fairies and fairy tales from their folkloric function into children's literature. Victorian and Edwardian constructs of the cute and cheery child, she writes, allow parents to indulge 'in paroxysms of soppy joy every time they venture into the nursery' (Purkiss 2000: 255-256). The literature emerging from these constructs

> allows adult narcissism to flower. Adults can enjoy imagining that they too were once just as attractive as the fictional children prancing before them, while luxuriating self-pityingly in regret for the loss of the innocence fictionally grafted on to the young. (ibid.: 256)

According to Purkiss, the relegation of the fairy tale to the literary lumber-room serves a cathartic purpose for the adults who snubbed them as children's literature. This may offer a reason for the change in fashion Tolkien postulated, as parents sought to vindicate and replay their own upbringing and childhood fantasies. Once in the lumber-room, however, the fairy tales serve as models for children as well, reinforcing constructs of childhood and adulthood that bring the narcissism of nostalgia to the fore. The adaptations, or diminutions, of a fairy tale into a pedagogical children's story have become the primary sources of a new folklore. When children who have been raised on these tales grow into the privileged position of the adult, they are left unsure how to re-appropriate the fairy tale tradition with its soppy surface and darker folkloric moorings. An adult writer, then, who chooses to adapt a fairy tale does not usually come at it through the folkloric or literary original, but through the narcissistic lens of childhood adaptations.

The ever-rising wave of fairy tale retellings for grown-ups might be suitably defined as 'reverse adaptation', the adaptation of tales adapted for children back into tales for adults. These stories began, of course, as tales for grown-ups, but it is not the grown-up tales that are being retold. The tales have passed through the lumber-rooms of children's anthologies; for good or ill, they can be considered as continuations of and reversions from this repertoire of children's literature.[1] To explore how reverse adaptation works, I suggest that there seem to be two intrinsic dimensions of the tale: the 'linguistic' and the 'mythic'. I derive this notion partly from C. S. Lewis' theory of story. In his essay 'On Stories' (1940), Lewis draws a distinction between the technicalities of telling a story – narrative style, character delineation, structure, and so on, what I am calling the linguistic dimension – and 'the Story itself, the series of imagined events', which, he insists, is where the potency of a story actually resides (1982 [1940]: 3). He elaborates this idea much further in *An Experiment in Criticism* (1961), where he describes Story as 'extra-literary', capable of possessing 'a value independent of its embodiment in any literary work' (1992 [1961]: 41).[2] He calls this extra-literary story 'myth' (ibid.: 42). A myth, he says,

> depends hardly at all on such usual narrative attractions as suspense or surprise. Even at a first hearing it is felt to be inevitable. And the first hearing is chiefly valuable in introducing us to a permanent object of contemplation – more like a thing than a narration – which works upon us by its peculiar flavour or quality, rather as a smell or a chord does. (ibid.: 43)

The myth, according to Lewis, is an 'experience [...] not only grave but awe-inspiring. We feel it to be numinous' (ibid.: 45). Such myths are 'contemplated but not believed, dissociated from ritual, held up before the fully waking and logical mind' (ibid.); they are works of power and beauty.

I wish to suggest that any folkloric story – perhaps, more correctly, any story told to and loved by children, thus becoming a type of folklore (see Zipes 1997: 11-12) – contains a 'mythic' dimension: a pattern of events that affects the reader profoundly, not as a linguistic, verbal experience, but as an object of contemplation like a dream before a waking mind. This is true no matter how soppy and bowdlerised a particular literary embodiment, or 'linguistic' version, of a story might be. Each story, possessed of both 'linguistic' and 'mythic' dimensions, can be said to have a 'dual existence'. There are the words of the story, which the reader experiences directly, and there is the Story itself, the contemplative object which the words reveal to us. When a writer chooses to retell a fairy tale, there is a version or versions of the tale already present in their mind. The urge to retell seems to arise at least partly from dissatisfaction with the linguistic versions already present; the writer senses a disharmony between the mythic centre and the linguistic exterior, and seeks to reconcile them. Alternatively, the retelling may arise from a dislike of the mythic centre, and an attempt to re-imagine it with a new linguistic setting. Regardless of the motive, the fairy tale as an idea in the mind of the writer and the fairy tale as it is executed on the page remain to a certain extent distinct; there is the recognisable tale or tale type, and then there is the telling of it. This is what is meant by 'dual existence'. In other words, the 'mythic' dimension is the artefact found in the lumber-room; the 'linguistic' dimension is how an individual writer has put this artefact to use. Two distinct 'linguistic' stories could thus be argued to possess a single 'mythic' centre.[3] The reverse adaptations rise from these mythic centres; in particular, they confront the mythic versions of the tales through linguistic versions that are intended for children. The dissatisfaction with a tale can thus extend to dissatisfaction with constructs of childhood and the socialising implications in the tales. It could be argued, then, that rewriting fairy tales involves rewriting childhood; the liminal spaces of the tale seem inevitably to involve the metamorphoses between childhood and adulthood, the world as given in children's stories and the world as received in adult experience. To begin understanding the dynamics of that interrelation, this study turns to the online journals.

## *Scheherezade's Bequest*: Fairy Tale as Subgenre

*Scheherezade's Bequest* began online in 2005 as an imprint of the larger website *Cabinet des Fées*, under the editorial direction of Erzebet YellowBoy Carr. Its aim is to reflect a wide diversity in tales, both in the sources and the retellings ('About CdF'). Many of the writers featured are already established in genre fantasy and speculative fiction;[4] in order of publishing, the fantasies and science fiction come first, and reverse adaptation comes later. In *Scheherezade's Bequest*, fairy tales appear to function as a subgenre of speculative fiction. The retellings are primarily deconstructions, many of them feminist.[5] Characters are re-gendered, re-oriented, and eroticised;[6] plots are re-shaped, re-arranged, and even obliterated.[7] The happy ending – what Tolkien called the '[c]onsolation' of fairy tales, 'the sudden joyous turn' (2008 [1940]: 75) – is certainly questioned, and frequently absent.[8]

Patricia Russo's story 'Afternoon Tale', for instance, challenges and subverts the importance of the hero in children's literature. A little girl asks her aunt to tell her a story.

> What kind of story, I asked. A story about heroes, she said. You mean, like the boy who killed the bear who had three heads, or the girl who returned the moon to the sky? No, no, my niece said. Not made-up stories. A for-true story. So, I asked, like about doctors or firefighters or folks who jump into rivers to save people who don't know how to swim? No, no, no, she said, looking at me in the way that four-year-olds do when they can't believe how dense you are being. A story with you and my daddy in it. (Russo 2010)

Her aunt demurs. 'Well, I said, I can't honestly say I ever knew any heroes personally. […] But I can tell you a story about a person who set an example. Will that do?' (ibid.) The child agrees, but remains 'sceptical' (ibid.). So the aunt tells her a story about an old woman named Lulka, who 'never spoke to anybody, and never smiled'; she wasn't 'mean', the aunt explains, just 'indifferent':

> Like… suppose you were playing outside her house, and you fell down and hurt yourself. She wouldn't care, you see. She wouldn't push you and make you fall, but she wouldn't come out to make sure you were all right if you did. […] I told you this wasn't a story about a hero. (ibid.)

The village where Lulka lives is a liminal space after the style of fairy tale villages: 'In Brimeden, at the turn of every season, a little bit of magic dropped by' (ibid.). This magic takes the form of ordinary household implements; they are highly coveted and said to bring blessings – health, long life, flight, wishes – to those who possess them. One afternoon, Lulka finds a bit of magic on the ground, and stands looking at it. A crowd gathers, urging her to pick it up and claim its blessing. Instead: 'She said, firmly, "It's not mine." […] Lulka looked at the piece of magic for another minute or two, then walked around it and continued down the street toward her house' (ibid.). Telling this story to the child, the aunt declares that Lulka 'did the right thing', and that 'magic isn't the most important thing in the world. Never let anybody tell you it is' (ibid.).

The example that Lulka sets appears to be that of maintaining personal dignity, accepting oneself without pining for change or magical transformation. Russo suggests that the example of a woman proud to be who she is, rather than of a hero who pursues or undergoes metamorphosis, should be offered to children. The rejection of magic and the miraculous should be the encoded message of fairy tales; only such a tale can be considered 'for-true'. The project of the fairy tale, the creation of wonder through the encounter of the other and the magical, is rejected; magic is presented as no different and no better than normal household implements. Lulka's actions demonstrate that magic adheres to the same rules for property and ownership as material objects; one can be content without accumulating either. Both magical and material possessions are, in that sense, irrelevant to a healthy construct of the self. So, the aunt explains, after seeing Lulka's example she herself leaves the village for the city, where there is no magic but there is opportunity for self-realisation. In a story narrated to a child, fairy tales are rejected. Tales of wonder are shown to be of didactic value to children, but 'heroes' are beyond experience – not 'for-true', and thus not worth imagining.

Dismantling the fairy tale seems to be part of the point – a revolt against the stories of childhood as incompatible with the real or desired world of adulthood. This appears starkly in Mike Allen's short story 'Then a millstone came along…'. The story begins: 'So all the stories were true' (Allen 2005). Nathan, a quiet, suburban professional, has come home to discover in his foyer a legendary millstone enchanted to crush evildoers. When it doesn't crush him, he fears for his family. 'None of them were home at the moment. He had time to stop the fairy tale from coming true' (ibid.). This becomes his quest: to stop a 'true' tale from coming true. Nathan, as it happens, is saved by an unexpected visit from his mother-in-law, but this concept of the disrupted fairy tale seems to inform the retellings in *Scheherezade's Bequest*. The story is in some sense 'true', but it must somehow be stopped. Reverse adaptation serves here as a simultaneous embrace and rejection. The stories from childhood can be kept, but onlyif they can be metamorphosed into more acceptable tales for grown-ups.

It is informative to compare these stories with a more hopeful tale. 'The Souk of Dreams' by Keyan Bowes is a romance about a gay couple who rediscover their faith in love and human goodness (Bowes 2010b). However, the setting of the tale – a fantasy market in the desert – is described as a sci-fi convention with real extraterrestrials. Any moorings to the mythic versions of fairy tale have been cast off. Hope is discovered in reinventing according to a new medium – speculative fiction. Reverse adaptations serve here primarily to rebuke and tear down the alleged deceptions of childhood.

The question arises – and it seems helpful for understanding *Scheherezade's Bequest* – why tell reverse adaptations at all? The answer emerges in Amanda Downum's story

'Brambles'. A soldier finds a fairy, or wood-wife, caught in a cruel trap: 'Dusk tarnishes the light when I find the faerie woman, caught in brambles at the edge of the forest' (Downum 2006b). The setting is the classic tableau of liminal encounter – a mortal man meeting the perilous fairy woman on the borders of the woods (Purkiss 2000: 65-76). The fairy is beautiful but vampiric: 'Sharp-toothed beneath her glamorie, ruthless as the forest. Cold and treacherous. Fae' (Downum 2006b). And she is in pain. The threat of nightfall and danger mars the beauty of the fairy tale; the dusk tarnishing the sunset seems to serve as a metonymy for the ominous uses and ideas of fairy tales. Downum is under no bowdlerised illusion about the sweetness and innocence of these creatures or tales; the fairy is predatory and evil. The soldier considers killing her – 'One more little beauty snuffed' – and thinks perhaps she deserves it (ibid.). But instead, he chooses empathy with the fairy; as a soldier, he has killed as many if not more people than she has: 'Death hangs over my shoulders, a pall I have yet to shed' (ibid.). He recognises her as a co-sufferer and co-victim of the world's brutality; the fantastic and enchanted, like the modern and cynical, suffer from the same malaise and confront the same horror. So he cuts her free from the brambles and lets her go. Watching her flee into the forest, he reflects: 'Her next kill is on my hands, like so many others. But at least one beautiful thing is left unbroken' (ibid.). Despite his cynical knowledge of the dangers and treachery of the fairy, the soldier chooses empathy with the other and the preservation of wonder. If the fairy is read as metonymic of the fairy tale, then these tales are worth retelling because in their mythic centre is beauty; their cruelty and harshness merely serves to remind us of our own. They are worth exploring and adapting so that, despite the horror of the world, 'at least one beautiful thing is left unbroken' (ibid.).

## *Enchanted Conversation*: Fairy Tale as Cultural Artefact

*Enchanted Conversation*, edited by Kate Wolford, is a different sort of publication from *Scheherezade's Bequest*. It has served primarily to promote unknown and unpublished writers, hobbyists and beginners rather than career professionals. The literary quality of the stories has usually not been as refined as in *Scheherezade's Bequest*, but the fairy tales are more likely to be retold on their own terms. The tales are treated less as a literary subgenre than as cultural artefacts to be preserved and remembered. Each issue takes a single tale as its theme. Thus the various linguistic versions share, or have the potential to share, a single mythic version. The retellings intersect at different points of the tale, ideally creating a prismatic effect or dialectic, but occasionally simple redundancy. There is, for instance, a limited number of times the villain of a piece can tell his or her side of the story before that storytelling technique loses its lustre.

The retellings are often whimsical.[9] But, again, the idea of heroes and happy endings is challenged, even despaired of.[10] The happy ending formula learned as children is not seen as compatible with a grown-up way of looking at the world. So Cathy C. Hall, in her poem 'The Problem with Fairy Tales', writes:

> Once upon a time, long, long ago,
> You fed the fairy tales to a

Wispy-haired, apple-cheeked girl,

Wide-eyed and wide open. [...]

What are you supposed to do,

Now that she's grown up, up, up and can't find

A single beanstalk, or an employed Prince,

Much less a soul-waking kiss?

(C.C. Hall 2010: lines 1-4; 9-12)

The stories, Hall insists, are divorced from reality; the promise of fairy tales has been nullified and betrayed. The girl who grew up delighting in the sweetness of the tales cannot escape from a mundane, uninspiring world, and finds no meaning or self-authentication in romantic relationships. Hall first postulates the distance between the idealised state of childhood and the reality of adult life. The tales were told '[o]nce upon a time, long, long ago'; childhood itself has become remote – a fairy tale, a fantasy, an incredible fiction. This seems to align with Purkiss' suggestion that adult narcissism and self-absorption create a fictitious, enchanted childhood that is in fact divorced from real childhood and damaging to the children (2000: 256). The receptive little girl, accepting the constructs of both childhood and fairy tale, is 'apple-cheeked' like many a fairy tale heroine, but 'wispy-haired' like an older stepsister or crone (C.C. Hall 2010: line 4); she cannot attain the standard set in the fairy tale constructs of childhood which she receives, 'wide-eyed and wide open', hungry for wonder and sexual maturation. The phallic suggestion of the single – that is, eligible – beanstalk anticipates the lack of 'a soul-waking kiss' as the now grown-up girl cannot find romantic or sexual fulfilment; the image of the missing beanstalk may also suggest the emasculation of her childhood fantasies. Certainly, neither physical nor psychological maturation have proved satisfactory. The missing beanstalk also entails the lack of adventure and escape; there is no magic transformation, no land of giants above, only the starving hardship of the ground below; the child cannot any longer hope to escape into an adult world. 'What are you supposed to do?' she demands. The child has fulfilled the fairy tale, growing like the beanstalk, but failed to reach any enchanted world, or even any pleasure in the ordinary world. The problem with fairy tales, Hall suggests, is that they are lies. They are irresponsible storytelling. These cultural artefacts deserve to be lost in the lumber-room – all felt hats and old boots.

Even if happily ever after is not true, does that mean the tales themselves are not true, or should not be told? Most of the stories in *Enchanted Conversation* are not so bleak.[11] There is a purpose, they argue, even in telling not 'for-real' tales; quaint or not, these artefacts retain their beauty. And here they seem to have struck something essential to the mythic dimension of the fairy tale. This is seen most clearly in Claire Massey's poem, 'The Sleeping Beauty: a showman's tale'. The poem is a free verse dramatic monologue; the narrator is a showman displaying a clockwork model of the enchanted princess, which he swears is the real girl. 'You've heard the story,/now come and see a real/princess' (Massey 2010b: 17). She is a fake, and he runs a sideshow, huckstering deceits as truths.

The fairy tale has become a flea circus. But something other than the model's figure draws the crowds; something enchants even the cynical heart of the showman:

> I pack her in rags,
> load her in and out of the cart,
> oil and wind the clockwork parts
> where her heart should be
> and sometimes
> as the movement winds down
>
> I swear I see her eyelids flutter.
> (ibid.: lines 31-37)

A clockwork heart beats where a real heart should; a mechanised, deceptive world has replaced the natural, credulous promise of childhood. And yet the magic, the enchantment, is not quite gone. Even the shrewd and worldly-wise showman believes his own tales. It is a poignant image of the potential of fairy tale. A reverse adaptation, like any literary fairy tale, is inevitably a construct, and in that sense artificial. The cultural artefacts and memories which *Enchanted Conversation* re-appropriates are kept like the clockwork princess, in the boxes and rags of anthologies and scholarship. Critics and re-tellers alike take them apart to keep them relevant, a pseudo-reality which reminds adults of the images they once possessed but which no one needs to believe. And yet they engender belief and wonder in spite of this. In the liminal moment between sleeping and waking, dreaming and reality, movement and winding down, these lifeless things from the lumber-room flutter suddenly in the hand. The hope of the fairy tale, Massey suggests, is that the spell of loss and forgetfulness will someday break, and beauty will be restored to the world.

## *New Fairy Tales*: Fairy Tale as Creative Tradition

It is this restoration of beauty that informs, in part, the third publication, *New Fairy Tales*. Unlike *Scheherezade's Bequest* or *Enchanted Conversation*, *New Fairy Tales* does not publish retellings of old tales, but new tales told in the old way. The mythic versions of these tales are discrete, not directly derivative or interrelated. Also, *New Fairy Tales* commissions original artwork for the stories, so that the mythic dimensions are from first printing already interpreted with visual art; in fact, the illustrations are often more evocative of the mythic dimension than the stories are. Thus in the inaugural issue, the editor, Claire Massey, says: 'We don't believe the fairy tale canon is complete or that we should only retell old stories. We believe that there are many new fairy tales out there waiting to be written and read and loved' (2008b: 2). *New Fairy Tales* represents the writing of a new folklore; the fairy tale stands apart as a continuing creative tradition. As Massey explains:

> Fairy tale bequeaths us a language rich in motifs which I believe we should feel free to plunder. Fairy tales have always belonged to the tellers, their

listeners and readers; they belong to us all. And rather than stuffing them away in a cupboard we should play with the form, experiment with its language, make it our own, tell the stories that mean something to us, the stories that dance at the edge of our dreams… (Massey 2009: 3)

Here the process of reverse adaptation does not consist of taking a mythic version, distorting or changing it, and draping a different linguistic version around it. Rather, it is an adaptation of a form, the memory not of a particular story but the state of wonder certain stories created, and an attempt to recreate that wonder in a new story. Themes of wonder and rediscovery run throughout the journal,[12] as do transformation and metamorphosis.[13] These, indeed, seem to be the primary motifs of the journal. The force of the new tales is not an adult rejecting or sentimentalising childhood, but rather a childlike rediscovery and continuance of wonder during the metamorphic process of maturation.

In Frederick Hilary's 'The Giant's Last Feast', for instance, a giant emerges from long isolation in search of a child to eat (2010: 22). Hilary's image of the giant's 'dark old house surrounded by a high wall' invokes memories of Oscar Wilde's 'The Selfish Giant' (ibid.). Whereas in 'The Selfish Giant' the children are constantly climbing the wall to enjoy the beautiful garden, in 'The Giant's Last Feast' the garden is derelict and choked with crab grass; the children are gone, and do not come anymore, despite the giant's hunger (ibid.). So the giant decides to risk 'the pikes and pitchforks of villagers [and] even death' in order to 'chew on the bones of a child one last time' (ibid.). But he meets no danger. In fact he doesn't meet anyone, until he finds another giant who appears to be gnawing on a small child. They begin to discuss the savoury pleasures of eating children:

> 'It's all there, in the taste of the meat. A child's joyful springing through summer meadows. His first tears for a lost pet. His frolics in the little river, splashing amongst the minnows. The bedtime stories that make his eyes mist over and go to sleep.'

> 'Don't tell any more,' said the giant. 'I can't take it. I've tasted all those things myself. I've eaten the wild abandon of play. I've swallowed fledgling dreams. I've munched and chewed on school holidays filled with adventures and carefree wanderings. I've tasted meat that is wholly local, that has known only the grass of one happy spot, and never been beyond the farthest-sighted hills; the meat of a child who thinks his father a giant like ourselves, and his mother the kindest being on earth.' (ibid.: 23)

The other giant flies into a rage; he is not, in fact, eating a child but a 'rancid-looking turnip'. He demands:

> 'Don't you try to imagine everything tastes like child meat? Though it never does. I thought you knew. I thought you were just playing along. But what you said just then – all that stuff about play and youthful dreams and the rest – it was just too much! It made me sorry for everything.' (ibid.: 22-23)

There are no children left. Giants only eat turnips now, and dream of the good old days when succulent children and livestock roamed the hills.

So the giant goes on wandering, craving the taste of 'sweet dreams and innocent tears', until at last he discovers a child – the *last* child' – playing by the river (ibid.: 25; emphasis in original). Yet when he tries to seize him to devour him, the child manages to overpower him and throw him under the water. The giant emerges, bewildered and afraid of the innocent-seeming child in front of him. The child understands his hunger. I will let you eat me, the child tells him, if you 'let me swallow you up, and spit you out whole' (ibid.: 25-26). The giant is so hungry he agrees, and the child does, devouring him with 'a searing pain, a pain that flooded his whole body […] as if great talons had ripped through his flesh, or fire engulfed him' (ibid.: 26). Then the giant discovers that he is no longer a giant: he has become a child.

**Figure 1. Laura-Kate Chapman, illustration for 'The Giant's Last Feast', 2010. Watercolour, pencil, crayon, felt tip, and collage. © Laura-Kate Chapman. Reproduced by kind permission from the artist**

The child – for he was giant no more – looked down upon his small hands and at his bare feet. In his reflection in the river he saw his blue eyes and soft golden hair like lamb's wool, and laughed. He spun his gaze around. He saw summer meadows, looked towards the farthestsighted hills and felt all kindness radiating from the earth. There was only this one bright, happy spot, and the land of giants was no more. He had been one once, but would never go back that way. (ibid.: 26)

The giants appear to be jaded and narcissistic adults; childhood and the dreams of childhood are to be destroyed, taken advantage of, scorned as weak or used to preen adult sensibilities and grown-up interpretation of the world. They twist the narratives of childhood to match their own desires, fantasising idealised and idyllic childhoods not for the sake of the children living them, but to heighten their own destructive appetites. This devouring glorification of childhood has eradicated the very children it longs for. But when the giant submits to a child and the narratives of childhood – when he is willing to enter into a story rather than crush it for being smaller than his grown-up world – he discovers a wonder and a beauty that turns him into a child again. In other words, by re-entering into the tradition of storytelling, enjoying the tales like a child rather than looming as critic over them, he lets the stories shape the world and infuse it with hope. In Laura-Kate Chapman's striking illustration of this tale (see figure 1), the child stands by the river, looking out across it and playing in the water; the giant, however, towers above, fists clenched, grimacing in rage. Yet he, too, is tethered to the river with an umbilical-like connection. There is something foetal and helpless about this blustering and pompous giant-adult; he, like the child, draws life from the river despite his unwillingness or inability to acknowledge it. The river sustains him even despite his contempt for it, and his devouring sentimentalism and nostalgia. By allowing the child to subsume him back into the greater narrative, he becomes a part of the story he seeks to occlude. The child narrates to the giant-adult a view of the world not marked by narcissism and nostalgia, but by curiosity and hope. Thus the giant himself undergoes a sort of reverse adaptation, returning to a state of wonder that he did not know he needed.

Marina Warner has called metamorphosis 'a defining dynamic' of fairy tales (2002: 18). The surprise of transformation, she says, creates a fictional world the reader delights to inhabit. 'Moreover,' she writes, 'some kinds of metamorphosis play a crucial part in anagnorisis, or recognition, the reversal fundamental to narrative form, and so govern narrative satisfaction […] Stories of this kind promise us change, too' (ibid.: 19). It is this promise which seems to typify not only 'The Giant's Last Feast' but *New Fairy Tales* as a whole. The continual process of metamorphosis and variation that is the fairy tale tradition, the continual reinvention of folklore, engages the *New Fairy Tales* in a riot of tale telling. The transformations stories engage the reader vicariously in the hope and prospect of their own transformation. Transmuting from child to adult to child, the tellers and readers of this tradition are enabled to hear fairy tales as if for the first time; these are tales which have not been told before, and the reader is invited to savour new changes, new transformations, and the promise that they bring.

If there is a theme running through *New Fairy Tales*, it is that story has power to change the world, and especially that fairy tales can give wonder and hope and meaning even in a troubled and broken world. Strikingly, in these tales the sense of disenchantment – anger against heroes and happy endings – is nearly absent. The new tales can still be subversive, and still challenge stereotypes from the traditional fairy tales, but they do not discard the notion of a fairy tale itself. 'The Ice Candle', by A.K. Benedict, tells the tale of a little boy, Mark, who is trying to understand his grandmother's approaching death. He wants to find a way to make her better. Escaping from the sick-chamber of his home into the forest, he meets the Ice Gardener – the identity of this figure in 'white overalls, white wellies, and a long white coat' is never quite explained – who tells him he's lucky (Benedict 2009a: 12).

> 'I don't feel very lucky.' Mark looked back up at Grandma's window. The curtains were drawn and the house blanked him. 'My Grandma is really sick. And there's nothing I can do.'
>
> 'There's always something you can do,' the Ice Gardener said, looking up into the sky. (ibid.)

By turning Mark's gaze away from the death-chamber to the sky, the Ice Gardener reorients him from despair to hope; he shows the boy how to look at dying within the greater context of life as a contiguous whole. And he gives Mark a quest. Mark is to make a lantern for the Ice Candle from snowballs gathered at three places that frighten him. The tale moves swiftly from place to place as Mark's love for his grandmother helps him overcome his fears, and he brings the Ice Candle in its snowball lantern back to his grandmother. But she does not get better.

Enraged at this seeming betrayal, Mark returns to the Ice Gardener. The Ice Gardener has lied, Mark claims, and has given him nothing to help his grandmother. But the Ice Gardner tells him, 'You can help her by telling her your story [...]' (ibid.: 15). So Mark does: '"I've got a story for you," he said, "Like the ones you told me"' (ibid.). He doesn't prevent his grandmother's death, but by living and telling a story, he helps her die peacefully and content in the knowledge of his love. He returns the gift of story and wonder she had given him. The reverse adaptation is itself reversed, as a child discovers new stories to tell grown-ups, to help them make sense of the world. The child, not the adult, becomes the narrator and tale-teller; his story is one of fear and danger, confronting death and loss, rather than soppy stories of innocence and unmitigated happy endings. The child narrative and the child's adaptations of old narratives illuminate the transformative promise of the fairy tale. Even though the world does not function according to happy endings, that is no reason not to tell fairy tales. That, in fact, may be the very reason to tell them.

## Conclusion

This analysis has highlighted three kinds of fairy tale reverse adaptation: as a subgenre of speculative fiction, as the rediscovery of a cultural artefact, and as an ongoing creative tradition. Each of these methods has its own pitfalls.With the first, the worry is in deconstructing the tale until nothing is left; one has only the distant echoes of fairy tale with a genre piece, and nothing more. The mythic centre is lost. The second method risks redundancy: the simple repetition of tales already told, asking of tales questions already asked, resulting in a possessive enclosing of the mythic centre in retellings that may ultimately lead readers away from the original tale. The third method risks wandering too far, turning fairy tales back into a literary pastime for adults, or replacing the great mythic centres of childhood folklore with tales of lesser strength. But of all the pitfalls, this last may also be the one of least concern.

It seems fitting to end at the beginning. Prince Prigio is too 'extremely wise, and learned, and scientific' to 'believe in fairies, [and] in fairy gifts' (Lang 1895: 34). Until, unwitting and unexpected, he falls madly in love with an ambassador's daughter. Lang writes:

> Now, at this very moment – when the prince, all of a sudden, was as deep in love as if he had been the stupidest officer in the room – an extraordinary thing happened! Something seemed to give a whirr! in his brain, and in one instant *he knew all about it!* He believed in fairies and fairy gifts, and understood that his cap was the cap of darkness, and his shoes the seven league boots, and his purse the purse of Fortunatus! He had read about those things in historical books: but now he believed in them. (ibid.: 37; emphasis in original)

The old tales are meaningless to Prigio until he has an experience that gives them meaning. Having loved once, he can understand forever. This, indeed, may be the mystique of the fairy tale – why we, as grown-ups, return to the stories of our childhood, in anger or weariness or hope, to listen and to tell them again. The tales transform us from jaded and narcissistic giants back into delighted and curious children. The world can be a place of wonder, despite our pain. The lumber-room becomes enchanted again.

## Bibliography

'About CdF,' in: *Cabinet des Feés: a journal of fairy tales*:
    <http://www.cabinetdesfees.com/about-cdf/>
    Accessed 18 January 2011.

Allen, M. 'Then a millstone came along...' 2005, in: *Scheherezade's Bequest* 2:
    <http://www.cabinetdesfees.com/2005/then-a-millstone-came-along/>
    Accessed 16 January 2011.

Ambrogio, O.M. 2010. 'The Handless Maiden (Revisited)', in: *Scheherezade's Bequest* 10:
    <http://www.cabinetdesfees.com/2010/the-handless-maiden-revisited/>
    Accessed 11 May 2011.

Anderson, V.K. 2010. 'The Not-So-Little Mermaid', in: *Enchanted Conversation* 1.3:
    <http://www.enchantedconversation.org/2010/06/not-so-little-mermaid-by-valerie-koines.html>
    Accessed 12 May 2011.

Anthony, S. 2010. 'Manley and the Missing Link', in: *Enchanted Conversation* 1.2:
    <http://www.enchantedconversation.org/2009/04/more-than-once-manley-saw-bigfoot.html>
    Accessed 11 May 2011.

Arkenberg, M. 2010. 'A Servant's Tale', in: *Enchanted Conversation* 1.2:
    <http://www.enchantedconversation.org/2010/04/servants-tale-by-megan-arkenberg.html>
    Accessed 11 May 2011.

Beckford, A. 2010. 'Sleeping Beauty Unplugged', in: *Enchanted Conversation* 1.1:
    <http://www.enchantedconversation.org/2009/11/sleeping-beauty-unplugged-by-avil.html>
    Accessed 11 May 2011.

Benedict, A.K. 2009a. 'The Ice Candle', in: *New Fairy Tales* 4: 11-15.
<http://www.newfairytales.co.uk/pages/issuefour.pdf>
Accessed 18 January 2011.

Benedict, A. K. 2009b. 'The Zoetrope', in: *New Fairy Tales* 2: 6-8.
<http://www.newfairytales.co.uk/pages/issuetwo.pdf>
Accessed 23 May 2011.

Berger, M. 2010. 'The Magic Kiss', in: *Enchanted Conversation* 1.2:
<http://www.enchantedconversation.org/2009/04/magic-kiss-by-mike-berger.html>
Accessed 11 May 2011.

Bobet, L. 2006. 'Coffee Date', in: *Scheherezade's Bequest* 4:
<http://www.cabinetdesfees.com/2006/coffee-date/>
Accessed 18 January 2011.

Bowes, K. 2010a. 'Nor Yet Feed the Swine', in: *Scheherezade's Bequest* 9:
<http://www.cabinetdesfees.com/2010/nor-yet-feed-the-swine/>
Accessed 11 May 2011.

Bowes, K. 2010b. 'The Souk of Dreams', in: *Scheherezade's Bequest* 11:
<http://www.cabinetdesfees.com/2010/the-souk-of-dreams-by-keyan-bowes/>
Accessed 16 January 2011.

Brannon, D.J. 2008. 'My Small Army of Souls', in: *Scheherezade's Bequest* 6:
<http://www.cabinetdesfees.com/2008/my-small-army-of-souls/>
Accessed 11 May 2011.

Brays, C. 2010. 'The Ice Baby', in: *New Fairy Tales* 6: 4-8.
<http://www.newfairytales.co.uk/pages/issuesix.pdf>
Accessed 23 May 2011.

Bucklew, J. 2010. 'Two Sides to Every Story', in: *Enchanted Conversation* 1.4:
<http://www.enchantedconversation.org/2010/11/two-sides-to-every-story-by-janet.html>

Burke, A. 2010a. 'The Guardian', in: *Enchanted Conversation* 1.1:
£<http://www.enchantedconversation.org/2009/12/guardian-by-aisling-burke-even-clocks.html>
Accessed 11 May 2011.

Butterworth-McDermott, C. 2005. 'Hansel', in: *Scheherezade's Bequest* 2:
<http://www.cabinetdesfees.com/2005/hansel/>
Accessed 11 May 2011.

Campbell, J. 1993 [1949]. *The Hero With a Thousand Faces*. London: Fontana Press.

Campisi, S. 2010. 'The Glass Girl Looks Back', in: *New Fairy Tales* 5: 37-39.
<http://www.newfairytales.co.uk/pages/issuefive.pdf>
Accessed 23 May 2011.

Clark, J.T. 2008. 'Wellspring', in: *Scheherezade's Bequest* 6:
<http://www.cabinetdesfees.com/2008/wellspring/>
Accessed 11 May 2011.

Colona, S.E. 2010. 'Lies the Fairest', in: *Scheherezade's Bequest* 9:
<http://www.cabinetdesfees.com/2010/lies-the-fairest/>
Accessed 11 May 2011.

Corrigan, P. 2009. 'La Chureca', in: *New Fairy Tales* 4: 23-28.
<http://www.newfairytales.co.uk/pages/issuefour.pdf>
Accessed 23 May 2011.

Cosma, F. 2009. 'Dream Peddlers', in: *New Fairy Tales* 3: 6-7.
<http://www.newfairytales.co.uk/pages/issuethree.pdf>
Accessed 23 May 2011.

Cowens, D. 2010. 'Beauty and the Old Maid', in: *Enchanted Conversation* 1.2:
<http://www.enchantedconversation.org/2009/04/beauty-and-old-maid-by-debbie-cowens.html>
Accessed 17 January 2011.

Crinnon, E. 2008. 'The Mountain Ringer', in: *New Fairy Tales* 1: 5-7.
<http://www.newfairytales.co.uk/pages/issueone.pdf>
Accessed 23 May 2011.

D'Arcy, J. 2009. 'Jorab the Selfish', in: *New Fairy Tales* 2: 12-14.
<http://www.newfairytales.co.uk/pages/issuetwo.pdf>
Accessed 23 May 2011.

Davis, A.C. 2010. 'Duck', in: *Enchanted Conversation* 1.4:
<http://www.enchantedconversation.org/2010/12/contest-winner-duck-by-amanda-c-davis.html>
Accessed 12 May 2011.

Davis, B.R. 2010. 'A Modern Tale of Today's Young Bell', in: *Enchanted Conversation* 1.2:
<http://www.enchantedconversation.org/2009/04/modern-tale-of-todays-young-bell-by.html>
Accessed 11 May 2011.

Day, R.W. 2008 'Diamonds', in: *Scheherezade's Bequest* 4:
<http://www.cabinetdesfees.com/2008/diamonds/>
Accessed 11 May 2011.

Downum, A. 2006a. 'Gingerbread and Time', in: *Scheherezade's Bequest* 3:
<http://www.cabinetdesfees.com/2006/gingerbread-and-time/>
Accessed 11 May 2011.

Downum, A. 2006b. 'Brambles', in: *Scheherezade's Bequest* 4:
<http://www.cabinetdesfees.com/2006/brambles/>
Accessed 16 January 2011.

Duffy, M. 2010a. 'Fairy in Stilettos', in: *Enchanted Conversation* 1.1:
<http://www.enchantedconversation.org/2009/11/fairy-in-stilettos-by-maria-duffy-now.html>
Accessed 11 May 2011.

Duffy, M. 2010b. 'The Rogue Rose', in: *Enchanted Conversation* 1.2:
<http://www.enchantedconversation.org/2009/04/rogue-rose-by-maria-duffy.html>
Accessed 11 May 2011.

Eade, O. 2009. 'The Goblin King and the Pig', in: *New Fairy Tales* 2: 23-26.
<http://www.newfairytales.co.uk/pages/issuetwo.pdf>
Accessed 23 May 2011.

Eliav, E. 2010. 'The Lost Mermaid', in: *Enchanted Conversation* 1.3:
<http://www.enchantedconversation.org/2010/06/lost-mermaid-by-eva-eliav.html>
Accessed 12 May 2011.

Forrest, F. 2010. 'The River of the Fire of Life', in: *New Fairy Tales* 6: 36-42.
<http://www.newfairytales.co.uk/pages/issuesix.pdf>
Accessed 23 May 2011.

Gabbitas, J. 2008. 'Moth and the Jade Rabbit', in: *New Fairy Tales* 1: 12-14.
   <http://www.newfairytales.co.uk/pages/issueone.pdf>
   Accessed 23 May 2011.

Gage, J. 2010. 'Talia, Risen', in: *Scheherezade's Bequest* 9:
   <http://www.cabinetdesfees.com/2010/talia-risen/>
   Accessed 11 May 2011.

Gardner, L.C.A. 2010. 'Waking Beauty', in: *Scheherezade's Bequest* 9:
   <http://www.cabinetdesfees.com/2010/waking-beauty/>
   Accessed 11 May 2011.

Garrison, L. 2010. 'The Young Bride's Dream', in: *Enchanted Conversation* 1.3:
   <http://www.enchantedconversation.org/2010/06/young-brides-dream-by-laura-garrison.html>
   Accessed 12 May 2011.

Hagey, C. 2010. 'Nettie's Tale', in *New Fairy Tales* 6: 9-13.
   <http://www.newfairytales.co.uk/pages/issuesix.pdf>
   Accessed 23 May 2011.

Hall, C.C. 2010. 'The Problem with Fairy Tales', in: *Enchanted Conversation* 1.1:
   <http://www.enchantedconversation.org/2009/11/problem-with-fairy-tales-by-cathy-c.html>
   Accessed 17 January 2011.

Hall, L. 2010. 'Sugar Coated Dreams', in: *Enchanted Conversation* 1.4:
   <http://www.enchantedconversation.org/2010/11/sugar-coated-dreams-by-loralie-hall.html>
   Accessed 12 May 2011.

Hall, N. 2010a. 'Beastly', in: *Enchanted Conversation* 1.2:
   <http://www.enchantedconversation.org/2009/04/beastly-by-nikki-hall.html>
   Accessed 12 May 2011.

Hall, N. 2010b. 'The Sea Witch', in: *Enchanted Conversation* 1.3:
   <http://www.enchantedconversation.org/2009/06/sea-witch-by-nikki-hall.html>
   Accessed 12 May 2011.

Hardy, E. 2009. 'A Birthday Wish', in *New Fairy Tales* 4: 19.
   <http://www.newfairytales.co.uk/pages/issuefour.pdf>
   Accessed 23 May 2011.

Helper, J. 2005. 'Bloodlines and Survival', in *Scheherezade's Bequest* 1:
   <http://www.cabinetdesfees.com/2005/bloodlines-and-survival/>
   Accessed 16 September 2011.

Hilary, F. 2010. 'The Giant's Last Feast', in: *New Fairy Tales* 6: 22-37.
   <http://www.newfairytales.co.uk/pages/issuesix.pdf>
   Accessed 18 January 2011.

Hoffman, E. 2008. 'The Fall of Fairy Castle', in: *Scheherezade's Bequest* 6:
   <http://www.cabinetdesfees.com/2008/the-fall-of-fairy-castle/>
   Accessed 12 May 2011.

Hopkinson, E. 2009. 'Silver Hands', in: *Scheherezade's Bequest* 7:
   <http://www.cabinetdesfees.com/2009/silver-hands/>
   Accessed 18 January 2011.

Howard-Hobson, J. 2010. 'After', in: *Enchanted Conversation* 1.3:
   <http://www.enchantedconversation.org/2010/06/after-by-juleigh-howard-hobson.html>
   Accessed 12 May 2011.

Hunter-Frederick, A. 2010. 'Their Daughter Rose', in: *Enchanted Conversation* 1.2:
    <http://www.enchantedconversation.org/2009/04/their-daughter-rose-by-allison-hunter.html>
    Accessed 11 May 2011.

Hutcheson, T. 2010. 'Bonita and the Hacienda', in: *Enchanted Conversation* 1.2:
    <http://www.enchantedconversation.org/2010/04/bonita-and-hacienda-by-thea-hutcheson.html>
    Accessed 12 May 2011.

Jeffrey, D. 2009. 'The Terrible Troll', in *New Fairy Tales* 2: 19-20.
    <http://www.newfairytales.co.uk/pages/issuetwo.pdf>
    Accessed 23 May 2011.

Jones, P. 2010. 'A Girl's Liberation', in *Enchanted Conversation* 1.4:
    <http://www.enchantedconversation.org/2010/11/girls-liberation-by-paula-jones.html>
    Accessed 17 January 2011.

Jones, V. 2010. 'Water Sprite', in *New Fairy Tales* 6: 28-32.
    <http://www.newfairytales.co.uk/pages/issuesix.pdf>
    Accessed 23 May 2011.

Keller, R. 2010. 'Borealis and the Thing-Finder', in *New Fairy Tales* 5: 19-24.
    <http://www.newfairytales.co.uk/pages/issuefive.pdf>
    Accessed 23 May 2011.

Lang, A. 1895. *My Own Fairy Book.* Bristol: Arrowsmith.

Labbé, M. 2010. 'Her Heart Would Surely Break in Two', in: *Scheherezade's Bequest* 9:
    <http://www.cabinetdesfees.com/2010/her-heart-would-surely-break/>
    Accessed 11 May 2011.

Laity, K.A. 2008. 'The Princess and the Pig', in *New Fairy Tales* 1: 18-19.
    <http://www.newfairytales.co.uk/pages/issueone.pdf>
    Accessed 23 May 2011.

Leen, G. 2010a. 'Broken', in: *Enchanted Conversation* 1.4:
    <http://www.enchantedconversation.org/2010/11/broken-by-gerri-leen.html>
    Accessed 12 May 2011.

Leen, G. 2010b. 'Like Flies on a Wall', in: *Enchanted Conversation* 1.2:
    <http://www.enchantedconversation.org/2009/04/like-flies-on-wall-by-gerri-lean.html>
    Accessed 11 May 2011.

Lewis, C.S. 1992 [1961]. *An Experiment in Criticism.* Cambridge: Cambridge University Press.

Lewis, C.S. 1982 [1940]. 'On Stories', in: W. Hooper (ed.), *On Stories, and other essays on literature.* New York: Harcourt, 3-20.

Lim, R. 2010. 'Chinese Rapunzel', in: *Scheherezade's Bequest* 10:
    <http://www.cabinetdesfees.com/2010/chinese-rapunzel/>
    Accessed 11 May 2011.

Littlewood, A.J. 2009. 'Yellow John', in *New Fairy Tales* 3: 14-17.
    <http://www.newfairytales.co.uk/pages/issuethree.pdf>
    Accessed 23 May 2011.

Loory, B. 2010. 'The Woman, the Vase, and the Flowers', in: *Enchanted Conversation* 1.2:
    <http://www.enchantedconversation.org/2009/04/woman-vase-and-flowers-by-ben-loory.html>
    Accessed 18 January 2011.

Lovett, K. 2010. 'Prince of Dreams', in: *Enchanted Conversation* 1.2:
    <http://www.enchantedconversation.org/2009/04/prince-of-dreams-by-katie-lovett.html>
    Accessed 11 May 2011.

MacFarlane, A.D. 2010. 'Snow White at the Automat', in: *Scheherezade's Bequest* 10:
    <http://www.cabinetdesfees.com/2010/snow-white-at-the-automat/>
    Accessed 11 May 2011.

Malcolm-Clarke, D. 2006. 'The Sending', in: *Scheherezade's Bequest* 3.
    <http://www.cabinetdesfees.com/2006/the-sending/>
    Accessed 18 January 2011.

Marlowe, A. 2010a. 'Happily Ever After', in: *Enchanted Conversation* 1.1:
    <http://www.enchantedconversation.org/2009/12/happily-ever-after-by-amanda-marlowe.html>
    Accessed 11 May 2011.

Marlowe, A. 2010b. 'Expectations', in: *Enchanted Conversation* 1.2:
    <http://www.enchantedconversation.org/2009/04/expectations-by-amanda-marlowe.html>
    Accessed 11 May 2011.

Massey, C. 2008a. 'Letter from the Editor', in: *New Fairy Tales* 1: 2.
    <http://www.newfairytales.co.uk/pages/issueone.pdf>
    Accessed 23 May 2011.

Massey, C. 2008b. 'The Silent Kingdom', in *New Fairy Tales* 1: 20-21.
    <http://www.newfairytales.co.uk/pages/issueone.pdf>
    Accessed 23 May 2011.

Massey, C. 2009. 'Letter from the Editor', in: *New Fairy Tales* 2: 3.
    <http://www.newfairytales.co.uk/pages/issuetwo.pdf>
    Accessed 18 January 2011.

Massey, C. 2010a. 'The Blackpool Mermaid', in *Enchanted Conversation* 1.3:
    <http://www.enchantedconversation.org/2010/06/blackpool-mermaid-by-claire-massey.html>
    Accessed 12 May 2011.

Massey, C. 2010b. 'The Sleeping Beauty: a showman's tale', in: *Enchanted Conversation* 1.1:
    <http://www.enchantedconversation.org/2009/12/sleeping-beauty-by-claire-massey.html>
    Accessed 17 January 2011.

Masurel, P. 2009. 'The Story-blind Princess', in *New Fairy Tales* 2: 15-18.
    <http://www.newfairytales.co.uk/pages/issuetwo.pdf>
    Accessed 23 May 2011.

Matthews, E. 2010. 'The Lady Wore a Shawl', in *New Fairy Tales* 5: 14-17.
    <http://www.newfairytales.co.uk/pages/issuefive.pdf>
    Accessed 23 May 2011.

McGuire, C. 2010. 'Knives Then Foam', in: *Enchanted Conversation* 1.3:
    <http://www.enchantedconversation.org/2010/06/knives-then-foam-by-cathy-mcguire.html>
    Accessed 12 May 2011.

Merrill, T. 2010a. 'Ophelia's Remembrance', in: *Enchanted Conversation* 1.3:
    <http://www.enchantedconversation.org/2009/06/water-lilies-for-remembrance-by-tahlia.html>
    Accessed 12 May 2011.

Merrill, T. 2010b. 'Sugarcoated', in: *Enchanted Conversation* 1.4:
<http://www.enchantedconversation.org/2010/11/sugarcoated-by-tahlia-merrill.html>
Accessed 12 May 2011.

Mohlere, V.M. 2005. 'Demeter and Persephone: 1969', in: *Scheherezade's Bequest* 1:
<http://www.cabinetdesfees.com/2005/demeter-persephone-1969/>
Accessed 11 May 2011.

Morgan, D.R. 2010. 'Phoenix Song', in: *New Fairy Tales* 6: 14-16.
<http://www.newfairytales.co.uk/pages/issuesix.pdf>
Accessed 23 May 2011.

Ness, M. 2009. 'Remembering Fur', in: *Scheherezade's Bequest* 7:
<http://www.cabinetdesfees.com/2009/remembering-fur/>
Accessed 11 May 2011.

Novitzky, A. 2008. 'Three Sisters', in: *New Fairy Tales* 1: 15-17.
<http://www.newfairytales.co.uk/pages/issueone.pdf>
Accessed 23 May 2011.

Nutick, M. 2005. 'Scorned', in: *Scheherezade's Bequest* 1:
<http://www.cabinetdesfees.com/2005/scorned/>
Accessed 11 May 2011.

Oehlers, A. 2010. 'Dear Little Emmie', in: *New Fairy Tales* 5: 25-31.
<http://www.newfairytales.co.uk/pages/issuefive.pdf>
Accessed 23 May 2011.

Ormonde, R. 2010. 'Wondertale', in: *New Fairy Tales* 5: 40.
<http://www.newfairytales.co.uk/pages/issuefive.pdf>
Accessed 23 May 2011.

Pack, J. 2009. 'The Snow Bride', in: *New Fairy Tales* 4: 20-22.
<http://www.newfairytales.co.uk/pages/issuefour.pdf>
Accessed 23 May 2011.

Paxon, C. 2009. 'The Parrot Prince', in: *New Fairy Tales* 3: 10-11.
<http://www.newfairytales.co.uk/pages/issuethree.pdf>
Accessed 23 May 2011.

Pazdziora, E. 2010. 'The White Bird', in: *Enchanted Conversation* 1.4:
<http://www.enchantedconversation.org/2010/11/white-bird-by-eric-pazdziora.html>
Accessed 12 May 2011.

Pazdziora, J.P. 2010. 'Ragabone', in: *New Fairy Tales* 5: 7-13.
<http://www.newfairytales.co.uk/pages/issuefive.pdf>
Accessed 23 May 2011.

Phillips-Sears, C. 2005. 'Riding Hood', in: *Scheherezade's Bequest* 2:
<http://www.cabinetdesfees.com/2005/riding-hood/>
Accessed 11 May 2011.

Purkiss, D. 2000. *Troublesome Things: A History of Fairies and Fairy Stories*. London: Allen Lane.

Quattrone, D. 2005a. 'In Defense of a Queen', in: *Scheherezade's Bequest* 1:
<http://www.cabinetdesfees.com/2005/in-defense-of-a-queen/>
Accessed 11 May 2011.

Quattrone, D. 2005b. 'Mother, Maiden, Crone: Fireside Views', in: *Scheherezade's Bequest* 2:
<http://www.cabinetdesfees.com/2005/maiden-mother-crone-fireside-views/>
Accessed 11 May 2011.

Quattrone, D. 2006a. 'Frog Prince?', in: *Scheherezade's Bequest* 3:
<http://www.cabinetdesfees.com/2006/frog-prince/>
Accessed 11 May 2011.

Quattrone, D. 2006b. 'Wolf, Musing', in: *Scheherezade's Bequest* 4:
<http://www.cabinetdesfees.com/2006/wolf-musing/>
Accessed 11 May 2011.

Quattrone, D. 2008. 'Wicked', in: *Scheherezade's Bequest* 5:
<http://www.cabinetdesfees.com/2008/wicked/>
Accessed 11 May 2011.

Runolfson, J.C. 2006. 'Swan Daughter', in: *Scheherezade's Bequest* 3:
<http://www.cabinetdesfees.com/2006/swan-daughter/>
Accessed 11 May 2011.

Russo, P. 2006. 'Cinder Road', in: *Scheherezade's Bequest* 4:
<http://www.cabinetdesfees.com/2006/cinder-road/>
Accessed 11 May 2011.

Russo, P. 2008. 'Dear, Dear', in: *Scheherezade's Bequest* 5:
<http://www.cabinetdesfees.com/2008/dear-dear/>
Accessed 11 May 2011.

Russo, P. 2010. 'Afternoon Tale', in: *Scheherezade's Bequest* 10:
<http://www.cabinetdesfees.com/2010/afternoon-tale/>
Accessed 16 January 2011.

sarah, l. 2008. 'Cloudberries', in *New Fairy Tales* 1: 11.
<http://www.newfairytales.co.uk/pages/issueone.pdf>
Accessed 23 May 2011.

Seidel, A. 2010. 'The Other Road', in: *Scheherezade's Bequest* 10:
<http://www.cabinetdesfees.com/2010/the-other-road/>
Accessed 11 May 2011.

Sexton, J. 2010. 'Things That Cannot Be Eaten', in *Enchanted Conversation* 1.4:
<http://www.enchantedconversation.org/2010/11/things-that-cannot-be-eaten-by-jazz.html>
Accessed 12 May 2011.

Stahl, K. 2010. 'Just in Case', in: *Enchanted Conversation* 1.1:
<http://www.enchantedconversation.org/2009/02/contest-winner-spindle-power.html>
Accessed 11 May 2011.

Taafe, S. 2008. 'Bonny Fisher Boy', in: *Scheherezade's Bequest* 5:
<http://www.cabinetdesfees.com/2008/bonny-fisher-boy/>
Accessed 11 May 2011.

Teintze, B. 2010a. 'Finding Beauty', in: *Enchanted Conversation* 1.2:
<http://www.enchantedconversation.org/2010/04/finding-beauty-by-breanna-teintze.html>
Accessed 12 May 2011.

Teintze, B. 2010b. 'The Fisherman's Tale', in: *Enchanted Conversation* 1.3:
<http://www.enchantedconversation.org/search/label/Breanna%20Teintze>
Accessed 12 May 2011.

Thayer, L. 2010. 'The Girl in the Tower', in: *Scheherezade's Bequest* 11:
<http://www.cabinetdesfees.com/2010/the-girl-in-the-tower-by-laurie-thayer/>
Accessed 12 May 2011.

Tolkien, J.R.R. 2008 [1947]. *Tolkien On Fairy-stories: Expanded Edition, with Commentary and Notes.* V. Flieger & D.A. Anderson (eds), London: HarperCollins.

Tomlinson, M. 2010. 'Der Kindraube', in *New Fairy Tales* 5: 41-47.
<http://www.newfairytales.co.uk/pages/issuefive.pdf>
Accessed 23 May 2011.

Tracy, E. 2010. 'Little Hans', in: *Enchanted Conversation* 1.4:
<http://www.enchantedconversation.org/2010/11/little-hans-by-erika-tracy.html>
Accessed 12 May 2011.

Truslow, T. 2009. 'The Siren's Child', in *New Fairy Tales* 2: 23-25.
<http://www.newfairytales.co.uk/pages/issuetwo.pdf>
Accessed 23 May 2011.

Tulli, J. 2010. 'Lamentation for a Little Mermaid', in: *Enchanted Conversation* 1.3:
<http://www.enchantedconversation.org/2009/06/dumb-foundling-it-was-you-who-saved-my.html>
Accessed 12 May 2011.

Valente, C.M. 2005. 'The Maiden Tree', in: *Scheherezade's Bequest* 1:
<http://www.cabinetdesfees.com/2005/the-maiden-tree/>
Accessed 11 May 2011.

Valentine, G. 2008. 'Count', in: *Scheherezade's Bequest* 6:
<http://www.cabinetdesfees.com/2008/count/>
Accessed 11 May 2011.

Valentino, S. 2010a. 'Cooking Children! With Witch Wanda', in: *Enchanted Conversation* 1.4:
<http://www.enchantedconversation.org/2010/11/cooking-children-with-witch-wanda-by.html>
Accessed 12 May 2011.

Valentino, S. 2010b. 'The Diary of Beauty's Sister', in *Enchanted Conversation* 1.2:
<http://www.enchantedconversation.org/2009/04/diary-of-beautys-sister-by-samuel.html>
Accessed 11 May 2011.

Valentino, S. 2010c. 'The Twelfth Fairy Confesses', in: *Enchanted Conversation* 1.1:
<http://www.enchantedconversation.org/2009/12/by-samuel-valentino-everyone-blames.html>
Accessed 11 May 2011.

Vanderhooft, J. 2005. 'The Story of the River and Ophelia', in: *Scheherezade's Bequest* 2:
<http://www.cabinetdesfees.com/2005/the-story-of-the-river-and-ophelia/>
Accessed 11 May 2011.

Vanderhooft, J. 2006a. 'Dame Ragnelle Takes a Husband', in: *Scheherezade's Bequest* 3:
<http://www.cabinetdesfees.com/2006/dame-ragnelle-takes-a-husband/>
Accessed 11 May 2011.

Vanderhooft, J. 2006b. 'How a Tree Transforms to Wood', in: *Scheherezade's Bequest* 4:
<http://www.cabinetdesfees.com/2006/how-a-tree-transforms-to-wood/>
Accessed 11 May 2011.

Vanderhooft, J. 2008. 'Eurydice's Lament', in: *Scheherezade's Bequest* 5:
<http://www.cabinetdesfees.com/2008/eurydices-lament/>
Accessed 11 May 2011.

Vann, D. 2010. 'His Soul Inspiration', in: *Enchanted Conversation* 1.3:
<http://www.enchantedconversation.org/2010/06/his-soul-inspiration-by-dorlana-vann.html>
Accessed 12 May 2011.

Vemuri, A. 2010. 'To Dance on Swords', in: *Enchanted Conversation* 1.3:
<http://www.enchantedconversation.org/2010/06/to-dance-on-swords-by-ashley-

vemuri.html>
Accessed 12 May 2011.

Wade, L.A. 2008. 'The Tower', in *New Fairy Tales* 1: 8-10.
<http://www.newfairytales.co.uk/pages/issueone.pdf>
Accessed 23 May 2011.

Walker, D. 2010a. 'Eyes as Blue as Conflowers', in: *Enchanted Conversation* 1.3:
<http://www.enchantedconversation.org/2010/06/eyes-as-blue-as-cornflowers-by-deborah.html>
Accessed 12 May 2011.

Walker, D. 2010b. 'The First Queen's Maid', in: *Enchanted Conversation* 1.1:
<http://www.enchantedconversation.org/2009/11/first-queens-maid-by-deborah-walker.html>
Accessed 17 January 2011.

Ward, S. 2009. 'A Lighter Load', in *New Fairy Tales* 2: 21-22.
<http://www.newfairytales.co.uk/pages/issuetwo.pdf>
Accessed 23 May 2011.

Warner, M. 2002. *Fantastic Metamorphoses, Other Worlds*. Oxford: Oxford University Press.

Willits, Jr., M. 2010. 'I Am a Beast', in: *Enchanted Conversation* 1.2:
<http://www.enchantedconversation.org/2009/04/i-am-beast-by-martin-willitts-jr.html>
Accessed 11 May 2011.

Wilson, A. 2009. 'Harp', in: *Scheherezade's Bequest* 8:
<http://www.cabinetdesfees.com/2009/harp/>
Accessed 18 January 2011.

Wilson, J. 2009. 'Bears', in *New Fairy Tales* 4: 5-10.
<http://www.newfairytales.co.uk/pages/issuefour.pdf>
Accessed 23 May 2011.

Wissink, L. 2010. 'Waking Belinda', in *Enchanted Conversation* 1.1:
<http://www.enchantedconversation.org/2009/11/high-in-mountains-of-central.html>
Accessed 11 May 2011.

Woodruff, A. 2010. 'Roses on Snow', in: *Enchanted Conversation* 1.2:
<http://www.enchantedconversation.org/2009/04/roses-on-snow-by-arial-woodruff.html>
Accessed 11 May 2011.

Woods, A. 2010. 'Dollface', in *New Fairy Tales* 6: 17-20.
<http://www.newfairytales.co.uk/pages/issuesix.pdf>
Accessed 23 May 2011.

Woodward, G. 2008. 'The Sorrows of Elaine', in: *Scheherezade's Bequest* 5:
<http://www.cabinetdesfees.com/2008/the-sorrows-of-elaine/>
Accessed 11 May 2011.

Woolf-Hoyle, V. 2009. 'The Mock Mother', in *New Fairy Tales* 3: 8-9.
<http://www.newfairytales.co.uk/pages/issuethree.pdf>
Accessed 23 May 2011.

Young, R. 2010. 'Home to the Sea', in: *Enchanted Conversation* 1.3:
<http://www.enchantedconversation.org/2009/06/home-to-sea.html>
Accessed 16 September 2011.

Zimmerman, T. 2008. 'Rereading A Midsummer's Night Dream', in: *Scheherezade's Bequest* 5:
<http://www.cabinetdesfees.com/2008/rereading-a-midsummer-nights-dream/>
Accessed 12 May 2011.

Zipes, J. 1997. *Happily Ever After: Fairy Tales, Children, and the Culture Industry.* London: Routledge.

Zipes, J. 2006. *Why Fairy Tales Stick: The Evolution and Relevance of a Genre.* London: Routledge.

# Notes

1.  I am indebted to Julie Sanders for suggesting the concept of 'repertoire' as being more fluid and open to reinterpretation than 'canon', and also for our conversations relating the repertoire of jazz standards to the repertoire of standard fairy tales. The term and the ideas behind it are, I believe, immensely helpful to the study of fairy tales, and fairy tale retellings in particular, but a more thorough discussion of this topic is beyond the scope of the present study.

2.  This appears at some level to anticipate theories of narratology, particularly in regards the Hjelmslevian distinction of subject and form; however, it is doubtful whether Lewis would have considered himself a narratologist, and his theories contain several unique features that set them apart from formalism and narratology in general. While the comparison may well be worth pursuing, it is necessarily beyond the scope of the present study.

3.  Not, however, in Joseph Campbell's popular theory of the monomyth, as the tales themselves remain separate. There is no mistaking "Puss in Boots" for "Rumplestiltskin"; the so-called 'mythic' dimensions are distinct, even if the 'monomythic' structures might arguably be the same. Cf. Campbell 1993 [1949]: 245-251.

4.  Notably: Bobet 2006; Hopkinson 2009; Malcolm-Clarke 2006; Wilson 2009; et al.

5.  Ambrogio 2010; Bobet 2006; Bowes 2010a; Clark 2008; Colona 2010; Day 2008; Labbé 2010; Lim 2010; MacFarlane 2010; Mohlere 2005; Quattrone 2005b; Runolfson 2006; Vanderhooft 2006a. Cf Downum 2006a; Quattrone 2008; Russo 2008; Seidel 2010; Taafe 2008; Vanderhooft 2006b; et al.

6.  Butterworth-McDermott 2005; Brannon 2008; Downum 2006a; Gage 2010; Helper 2005; Ness 2009; Nutick 2005; Russo 2008; Valente 2005; Zimmerman 2008. Cf. Phillips-Sears 2005; Quattrone 2006b; Woodward 2008; et al.

7.  MacFarlane 2010; Quattrone 2005a; 2006a; Russo 2006; Taafe 2008; Vanderhooft 2005; 2008.

8.  Butterworth-McDermott 2005; Gardner 2010; Ness 2009; Nutick 2005; Quattrone 2006a; Russo 2008; Valente 2005; Valentine 2008; Vanderhooft 2005; 2008; Wilson 2009; Woodward 2008. Cf. Day 2008, Hoffman 2008; Thayer 2010; Zimmerman 2008.

9.  Beckford 2010; A.C. Davis 2010; B.R. Davis 2010; Duffy 2010a; 2010b; Leen 2010b; Loory 2010; Merrill 2010b; Valentino 2010a; 2010b; Woodruff 2010. Cf. Anthony 2010; Eliav 2010; Hutcheson 2010; Hunter-Frederick 2010; Stahl 2010; Walker 2010a; Wissink 2010.

10.  Arkenberg 2010; Berger 2010; Bucklew 2010: Cowens 2010; L. Hall 2010; Howard-Hobson 2010; P. Jones 2010; Leen 2010a; Marlowe 2010a; 2010b; McGuire 2010; Merrill 2010a; Sexton 2010; Tulli 2010; Vann 2010; Vemuri 2010; Walker 2010b. Cf. Anderson 2010;

Burke 2010 a; Garrison 2010; C.C. Hall 2010; N. Hall 2010a; 2010b; Valentino 2010c; Willits, Jr. 2010.

11.  Noteworthy examples include: Lovett 2010; Massey 2010b; E. Pazdziora 2010; Teintze 2010a; 2010b; Tracy 2010; Young 2010. Cf. Massey 2010a; et al.

12.  Brays 2010; Campisi 2010; Cosma 2009; Crinnon 2008; Hagey 2010; V. Jones 2010; Keller 2010; Masurel 2009; Morgan 2010; Ormonde 2010; J.P. Pazdziora 2010; sarah 2008 [Per the byline; see comment in bibliography]. Cf. Forrest 2010; Laity 2008; Novitzky 2008; Tomlinson 2010; Ward 2009.

13.  Benedict 2009b; Brays 2010; Eade 2009; Gabbitas 2008; Hagey 2010; Littlewood 2009; Massey 2008b; Oehlers 2010; Paxon 2009; J.P. Pazdziora 2010; Wade 2008; Woods 2010. Cf. Corrigan 2009; D'Arcy 2009; Hardy 2009; Jeffrey 2009; Matthews 2010; Novitzky 2008; Pack 2009; Truslow 2009; J. Wilson 2009; Woolf-Hoyle 2009.